MODERN
MEXICO

LATIN AMERICAN PERSPECTIVES Readers

Published in cooperation with *Latin American Perspectives*

Managing Editor: RONALD H. CHILCOTE
University of California, Riverside

Collective of Coordinating Editors

William Bollinger, *Interamerican Center for the Study of History & Culture, Los Angeles*
Donald Bray, *California State University, Los Angeles*
Marjorie Bray, *California State University, Los Angeles*
Trevor A. Campbell, *California State University, Los Angeles*
Frances B. Chilcote, *Laguna Beach, California*
Norma Chinchilla, *California State University, Long Beach*
Robert Dash, *University of California, Riverside*
Nora Hamilton, *University of Southern California*
Timothy F. Harding, *California State University, Los Angeles*
Richard Harris, *San Jose State*
Michael Kearney, *University of California, Riverside*
Daniel Manny Lund, *Universidad Autonoma Metropolitana, Iztapalapa*
Lois Oppenheim, *Whittier College*

Latin American Perspectives Readers are focused collections of articles on current topics of interest in Latin American Studies drawn from the popular and widely used journal **Latin American Perspectives**. Material is selected so as to provide a current introduction and analysis on timely issues concerning the countries, institutions and trends of the region. Each reader is designed for learning and teaching, whether in the academic classroom, a study group in the community, or organizations working on Latin America. These readers will be of interest for classes throughout the social sciences, history, literature, and other disciplines.

Volumes in this series:

Nora Hamilton and Timothy F. Harding, **Modern Mexico**

MODERN MEXICO

State, Economy, and Social Conflict

Edited by
Nora Hamilton
Timothy F. Harding

LATIN AMERICAN PERSPECTIVES Readers, Volume 1
Published in cooperation with *Latin American Perspectives*

SAGE PUBLICATIONS
The Publishers of Professional Social Science
Beverly Hills   Newbury Park   London   New Delhi

For information address:

SAGE Publications, Inc.
275 South Beverly Drive
Beverly Hills, California 90212

SAGE Publications Inc.  SAGE Publications Ltd.
2111 West Hillcrest Drive   28 Banner Street
Newbury Park   London EC1Y 8QE
California 91320   England

SAGE PUBLICATIONS India Pvt. Ltd.
M-32 Market
Greater Kailash I
New Delhi 110 048 India

Printed in the United States of America

Library of Congress Cataloging-in-Publication Data

Main entry under title:

Modern Mexico—state, economy, and social conflict.

(Sage readers from Latin American perspectives ; v. 1)
"Published in cooperation with Latin American
perspectives."
Includes bibliographies.
1. Mexico—Economic conditions—Addresses, essays,
lectures. 2. Mexico—Politics and government—Addresses,
essays, lectures. 3. Labor and laboring
classes—Mexico. 4. Mexico—Rural conditions.
I. Hamilton, Nora, 1935-   . II. Harding, Timothy F.
III. Latin American perspectives. IV. Series.
HC135.M68 1985   330.972′0834   85-22055
ISBN 0-8039-2552-2 (pbk.)

FIRST PRINTING

CONTENTS

Introduction
  NORA HAMILTON and TIMOTHY F. HARDING   7

Part I. The Mexican State

1. The Mexican State, 1915-1973:
   A Historical Interpretation
   JUAN FELIPE LEAL   21

2. Women, Class, and Education in Mexico:
   1880-1928
   MARY K. VAUGHAN   43

3. Mexico: The Limits of State Autonomy
   NORA HAMILTON   67

Part II. The Mexican Economy

4. Mexico's Albatross: The U.S. Economy
   DAVID BARKIN   106

5. Social Conflict and Inflation in Mexico
   DAVID BARKIN and GUSTAVO ESTEVA   128

6. State-Class Alliances and Conflicts: Issues
   and Actors in the Mexican Economic Crisis
   NORA HAMILTON   148

**Part III. The Working Class and
           Popular Mobilization**

7. The Mexican Labor Movement: 1917-1975
   RAÚL TREJO DELARBRE   177

8. The Mexican Economic Debacle and
   the Labor Movement: A New Era or
   More of the Same?
   BARRY CARR   205

9. Immiseration, Not Marginalization:
   The Case of Mexico
   JAMES D. COCKCROFT   233

Part IV. Rural Sector, Agrarian Reform, and Peasantry

10. Collective Agriculture and Capitalism in Mexico: A Way Out or a Dead End?
    RODOLFO STAVENHAGEN   262

11. Capitalism and the Peasantry in Mexico
    ROGER BARTRA   286

12. The Class Basis of Patron-Client Relations
    FRANCES ROTHSTEIN   300

Introduction

by
Nora Hamilton and Timothy F. Harding*

Mexico's position as one of the largest and most developed of the Latin American countries, its unique history as the first Latin American country to experience a major revolution during this century, its proximity to the United States and its long dependence on the U.S. economy, its increasingly significant international role (currently manifested in the impact of its international debt crisis and in its leadership in efforts to seek a negotiated solution to the conflicts in Central America)—all underline the importance of Mexico both in its own right and in the Latin American context. In the ten-year period between 1975 and 1985, *Latin American Perspectives* has published 38 articles on Mexico, including two special issues, both of which have sold out. The editors of *Latin American Perspectives* have therefore decided to publish a collection that brings together several of these articles.[1]

The authors, who include Mexican social scientists as well as U.S. and European specialists, apply new data or analysis of existing data to an examination of substantive issues important to Mexico, often with broad implications for other Latin American countries. In so doing they have taken up some of the major theoretical debates of the period: the role of the state in late-developing or dependent capitalist societies; the relationship between economic dependence and underdevelopment; the role of women as household workers in the daily and generational replacement of labor power for capitalist production; capitalist accumulation as a source of relative surplus labor and immiseration; and the implications of proletarianization and "repeasantization" (or the "refunctionalization of the peasant economy") for the agrarian structure.

These articles share a critical orientation, and most are informed by a Marxist perspective. They are critical in evaluating any social structure as problematic that tolerates or reinforces inequality, based on a relationship of domination and subordination between different sectors of its population. They are Marxist to the extent that they locate the roots of this inequality in the structure of production and in the class relations implicit

*Nora Hamilton is Associate Professor of Political Science at the University of Southern California. Timothy F. Harding is Professor of History at California State University at Los Angeles. Both are Coordinating Editors of *Latin American Perspectives.*

in this structure, and focus on structural contradictions and class conflict as the source of change within a given society and of transition from one social structure to another.

Marxists and others have long been fascinated by what some have called the "paradox" of the Mexican Revolution (1910-1917), which effected far-reaching structural change but was eventually succeeded by new forms of domination and subordination. Part of this paradox is the role of the state, which is discussed in the articles in the first section. In his chapter on the Mexican state, Juan Felipe Leal provides a historical overview of the process of state formation and consolidation following the Mexican Revolution, tracing the struggles among the various factors of the revolutionary armies and the efforts of the dominant faction in turn to establish its hegemony over the groups and classes of Mexican society. In the process, and with the subsequent development of capitalism in Mexico, the ideology and role of the state itself undergo substantial modifications.

Several of the issues raised by Leal are discussed in subsequent articles. Writing in 1975, Leal raises the question of whether Mexico's long-term political stability, facilitated by the sustained economic growth of the postwar period, can endure in a period of economic crisis and stagnation—one of several issues addressed by Nora Hamilton and Barry Carr, both writing in what appears to be a period of sustained crisis and stagnation. Carr is concerned specifically with the continued viability of the state's incorporation of the union bureaucracy that Leal describes in terms of its historical origins and transition. Leal discusses the economic role of the state in the development of capitalism; subsequently Roger Bartra and Gustavo Esteva discuss the state's role in responding to the economic demands of various sectors and classes.

Chapter 3 is concerned with identifying those forces expanding or contracting the possibilities of state autonomy in the context of a class system within a situation of dependency. Hamilton's focus is on the Cárdenas administration (1934-1940), a period when state autonomy in relation to dominant social classes and foreign capital appears to have been most advanced, and the role of the state most closely approximated the goals of the Mexican Revolution (articulated in the constitution of 1917) of ensuring social justice and national sovereignty. In discussing the articulation of the state with different classes and sectors (the peasantry, labor, the Mexican private sector, and foreign capital), Hamilton identifies contradictions that limited state autonomy even during the Cárdenas period and ultimately led to a divergence of the state's role from the defense of revolutionary goals as conceptualized by the Cárdenas administration to a defense of dominant class interests.

In her chapter on women, class, and education in Mexico, Mary K. Vaughan focuses on the role of the state in the ideological reinforcement of a system of production and class system. Specifically, she examines the role of the state educational system in reinforcing the role of women in "the daily and general replacement of labor for production" during the prerevolutionary Porfiriato (1880-1910) and during the revolutionary and immediate postrevolutionary periods (1910-1928). In both periods education assigned women—especially poor women—a specific and subordinate role in reproducing the family, both for sustaining the present working class and for preparing future generations of workers within the framework of capitalism. Vaughan points out that the effective absorption of an ideology depends on both material and ideological factors— including the material conditions of the targeted sector and the effectiveness of competing ideologies.

Although the articles on the Mexican state tend to focus on the period of its formation and consolidation, the subsequent section on the Mexican economy is concerned chiefly with Mexico's economic process in the period following 1940, including the period of accelerated economic growth from 1940 to 1970, and particularly the period of the past three presidential terms (*sexenios*): that of Luís Echeverría Alvarez (1970-1976), José López Portillo (1976-1982), and the current administration of Miguel de la Madrid Hurtado (1982-1988). These three sexenios have witnessed dramatic changes in Mexico's economic fortunes—from stagnation under Echeverría to an economic boom stimulated by the development of Mexico's petroleum resources in the context of escalating oil prices under López Portillo, followed by a growing crisis brought on by the drop in oil prices and other factors, including Mexico's growing debt, leading to the situation of recession and stagnation that currently confronts Miguel de la Madrid.

But even in the period of accelerated economic growth from 1940-1970, when Mexico's growth rate averaged 6 percent a year, a large number of people were left out of the "Mexican miracle." James Cockcroft, in Chapter 9, sees the expulsion of ever larger numbers of workers from the productive process as an integral part of accelerated capitalist growth in a Third World economy. As stated by David Barkin in his chapter on the impact of the U.S. economy, "Mexico is a country of poor people living in the midst of an elite becoming rich at their expense." Barkin chronicles the structural problems underlying the Mexican economic miracle, including sharp and increasing income inequalities; the concentration of agricultural, industrial, and financial resources in the hands of a small number of foreign and national owners; regional economic disparities;

growing balance of payments deficits; and foreign indebtedness. He traces many of these problems to the development strategy of Mexico's postwar industrialization characterized by heavy inflows of foreign investment and loans, which has resulted in the progressive denationalization of Mexican industry and U.S. domination of the Mexican economy. In the context of a capitalist organization of production, this domination has contributed to many of Mexico's long-term structural problems.

In their chapter on social conflict and inflation in Mexico, David Barkin and Gustavo Esteva dispute the view that inflation is purely a monetary phenomenon and argue that it is a political and social phenomenon. They contend that the issue in inflation is not simply monetary expansion, because it is necessary to seek the cause of monetary expansion, which can be found in social conditions. Thus inflation is a reflection and expression of the conflict among diverse forces and groups that make up society and the increase in government spending is an effort to respond to the economic demands of these groups. Barkin and Esteva trace the relationship among Mexico's development model, the changing demands and pressures of different groups, and the government response from the early postwar period through the Echeverría administration.

The contradictions underlying Mexico's economic growth model became evident in 1982, when international and internal factors converged to produce a major economic crisis, manifested in a resurgence of inflation, massive speculation, capital flight, and a threat of default on Mexico's foreign debt. In the last chapter in Part II, Hamilton examines the impact of the economic crisis on the role of the state and on Mexico's internationalist development model, focusing on the 1982 nationalization of private banking and the debt negotiations. Although in the past economic crisis has led to an increase in state autonomy and a restructuring of society, the prognosis for the current economic situation seems to be a reinforcement of Mexico's present tendency toward a tighter integration among the state, private domestic capital, and foreign capital.

Part III deals with the working class and popular mobilization, and helps to answer the question of why the Mexican Left has been relatively ineffective in building a movement to challenge the Mexican bourgeois state, despite the background of revolutionary struggle involving popular masses and the impressive revolutionary culture developed between 1920 and 1940. The authors examine the role of the state, analyzed in Part I, in containing the demands of working people who are increasingly denied a fair share of the products of the economy, a theme treated from a different perspective by Barkin and Esteva. Through control of unions and other organizations of the economy, the state tries to orient these demands in ways that do not threaten the stability of the system. They also show how the workers continue to struggle to break free from these controls.

Raúl Trejo Delarbre's study traces the Mexican organized labor movement from the consolidation of state control by the revolutionary bourgeois state under Carranza and Obregón until the mid-1970s. Carr's study examines the labor movement in the 1970s, focusing on the upsurge of independent unionism, and discusses the contradictory character of that movement. Then he focuses on the impact of the 1980s economic crisis on organized labor and why the crisis did not result in growth of the independent labor sector. Carr analyzes why the rapid decline in workers' real income did not set off a wave of uncontainable radicalization among workers and why the workers' challenge to a policy of cuts in real wages seemed relatively weak. He points to the importance of nonwage benefits to workers in unions allied with the government party, which the workers were understandably afraid to give up despite the decline in wages.

James Cockcroft's article on the nonunionized poorest workers sheds new light on the growing sector of semiemployed and unemployed section of workers whose ranks have mushroomed as a result of the fiscal policies adopted in the face of Mexico's credit crises of the 1980s. Cockcroft critiques the characterization of this massive population as "marginal," arguing that their terrible poverty is central to the process of capital accumulation in countries such as Mexico. He shows how the poor communities have developed grass-roots organizations that tie together the demands of poor communities, migrants from rural areas, and peasant organizations, along with some labor unions. They concentrate on struggles against high food prices, demands for housing and social services, struggles against electoral fraud, land seizures, higher wages for unorganized workers, and so on. And if traditional labor union members have not precipitated a confrontation with state policies, as Carr points out, residents of poorer sectors have taken the lead. Carr notes that the Mexican Left, part of which unified in the Partido Socialista Unificado de Mexico (PSUM) in 1981-1982 (*Latin American Perspectives*, 1982) tended to see the class struggle too narrowly in terms of a proletarian struggle led by industrial workers. He argues that the decline of the Mexican industrial economy under the impact of the fiscal crisis of the 1980s weakened the strategic position and militancy of this sector and required a strategy based more broadly on the human needs of women, the unemployed, government employees, and the like. This explains the strategic importance of the new mass organizations. Increasingly the parties on the Left, so far unable to develop a strong organized base in the labor movement, and trying to take advantage of the electoral reforms that allow them greater political participation, looked to these mass grass-roots organizations to lead the way to revolutionary change. Although the left-wing parties have ties to several of these mass groupings, the movements have refrained from being defined by only one party, and have been suspicious of partisan control, partly because this could target them for greater repression. However, Cockcroft also points out how the government works constantly to destroy such movements through a sophisticated combination of cooptation or repression, just as it had done in the organized labor and peasant movements.

The final section of this anthology analyzes the recent developments of and problems in Mexico's agrarian sector. In Mexico, land distribution and agrarian reform, although needed for capitalist development, came about primarily because of peasant pressures. However, the character of the reform benefited capitalist accumulation on the one hand and political manipulation of the peasantry by the bourgeois state on the other. This is demonstrated in Rodolfo Stavenhagen's study, which shows how the agrarian reform of the Cárdenas period gave way to pressure to convert peasant collective or cooperative *ejidos* to provide profit accumulation for the private sector.

Roger Bartra analyzes the failure of the agrarian program of the Echeverría administration (1970-1976), which Stavenhagen critiqued in midcourse. He calls the Echeverría strategy "technocratic populism," a policy designed to create an alliance between monopoly capital and the agrarian middle bourgeoisie, and a challenge to the "old populism," used to control peasant communities through political manipulation of peasant organizations, credit, and so forth. Bartra argues that this explains the emphasis on collectivization of ejidos and land distribution during the early 1970s. The counterattack by the northern large agrarian owners at the end of Echeverría's presidency led the government to attempt to punish this group with even more land expropriations, but the "technocratic populism," which never achieved its objectives in terms of overcoming the agricultural crisis, was abandoned by the incoming López Portillo administration (1976-1982).

Partly as a result of foreign capital investments in commercial export production, capitalist relations of production in Mexican agriculture have been accelerated.[2] As commercial export crops have expanded, domestic food production has fallen in relation to the needs of the local population. The government policy of holding down food prices has increased the flood of rural workers into urban centers, as income for food producers dropped. "Half of the tortillas consumed in Mexico are now made with imported corn" (Calzada, 1980: 3; cited in Harris and Barkin, 1982: 5).

To resolve this crisis, the López Portillo administration (1976-1982) established the Sistema Alimentario Mexicano (SAM), which constituted a kind of reversal of the agrarian policies of the Echeverría administration, which had been to increase food production by supporting more land distribution, promoting collectivization of ejidos, and funneling more capital to the medium landholders (middle bourgeoisie). The SAM of López Portillo proposed to reduce the number of small holdings to increase productivity. This would force more peasants into urban employment. The SAM's key law, the Ley de Fomento Agrário (Law for Agrarian Development), allows the "association" of ejidos and collectives with private landholders or agribusiness to permit the introduction of large amounts of technology and capital. This opens the ejidos, which had been protected by law from being rented or sold, to unhindered capitalist exploitation. One result could be a further decline in domestic food production and an increase in export crops; another is sure to be the elimination of the safety valve the ejidos provide in keeping large numbers of peasants off the job market in a situation of explosively high unemployment (Harris, 1982: 5-7).

Marxists have argued over the questions of why peasant producers with small holdings (such as the noncollective ejidos) have survived despite capitalist growth (Harris, 1978: 3). Bartra represents one side of the ongoing polemic about Mexico's agrarian structure and the development of programs to deal with agrarian problems. Bartra argues that peasant production represents a precapitalist "simple mercantile" mode of production that is "articulated" with the encompassing capitalist mode of production (Harris, 1978: 3). He describes the dual character of the peasant as both petty-bourgeois capitalist (independent producer) and worker. He is a worker in that he is exploited both by the market (which underpays the peasant for time spent in producing) and by the state (which finances and controls the production of much of the peasantry) (Bartra, 1975: 15). Peasants are further proletarianized by their need to supplement their earnings with salaried labor. He argues that "the rural masses have today an essentially proletarian, and not peasant, character. . . . Little by little, behind every land invasion, every march, every demonstration and every protest, an authentically proletarian struggle is appearing which directs its blows against the bourgeoisie and its political representatives" (Bartra, 1974: 20: translation Harris, 1978).

Bartra also offers an analysis of how the poverty of the Mexican peasantry is linked to capital accumulation, just as Cockcroft shows the link between the urban poor and capitalist growth. Bartra argues that the peasantry are exploited by low market prices paid by the bourgeoisie, so that part of their labor is not paid for. This labor is then appropriated and results in surplus value appropriated by urban bourgeois capital (Bartra, 1974; see Margulis, 1978, for a differing view). But keeping peasants poor through such mechanisms, as well as denying them adequate land resources, also reduces the cost of labor of peasants who are forced to seek work in capitalist agriculture or urban (not necessarily industrial) employment. The self-sufficiency of the peasantry makes them a very low-cost "producer of labor for the rest of society" (Harris, 1978; Margulis, 1978).

Taking the opposite viewpoint, Gustavo Esteva (1978) argues that the most important characteristic of the rural population is their resistance to depeasantization and proletarianization and their collective efforts to remain tied to the land. He sees land invasions as part of the strengthening of peasant class consciousness resulting in the formation of organizations of struggle such as those described by Cockcroft in this volume.

Luisa Paré (1977) points out that peasants are depeasantized (separated from dependence on land for subsistence) without being proletarianized (converted into wage earners) because the situation of vast unemployment in Mexico does not allow them to be absorbed into the wage-labor force. The Bartra study published here is partly a reply to those who criticized his 1974 study. Many Marxists disagree with both Bartra's and Esteva's opposite positions as oversimplifications (see Harris, 1978: 21-24).

These different analyses lead to different strategies. Bartra represents an important position in the Partido Socialista Unificado de Mexico on the party's strategy in the rural sector. He sees a proletarianized rural working class joining with the urban working class; Esteva (1978) wants the working class to support the struggles of the peasants to develop as peasants with more resources (land, capital, technology).

In her study of the class basis of patron-client relations, Frances Rothstein argues against the predominant view of patron-client relations as removed from, or mutually exclusive of, class relations. Studying a rural community in Central Mexico, she sees the pervasive patron-client relations in Mexico as a way of selectively limiting the distribution of the benefits of dependent capitalist development. She analyzes how the clientelistic dispensing of favors and protection is integrated into the economic system dominated by foreign capital. She also shows how political control at the local level intersects with union leadership and employment opportunities, and that access to the relative privilege of an industrial job operates at the town level, even when finding that job requires the worker to migrate to a larger community. This case study of a town in Puebla shows how the working population, which is neither peasant nor urban labor, is integrated into the political system in such a way as to increase the stability of the state.

As Rothstein points out, three-fourths of the Mexican labor force is not covered by social security benefits, and, for those covered, real access to benefits may depend upon loyal support of a union leader who is simultaneously an elected or appointed official and member of the ruling PRI party. This supports Carr's view on the durability of officially controlled unions. At the same time, the group she studies is developing organizations of struggle in several regions (as Cockcroft points out in his study in Part III) that act as an alternative to patron-client methods of securing benefits.

This discussion suggests the scope of the issues treated by *Latin American Perspectives* authors writing on Mexico; a further indication is found in the list that follows this introduction, showing *LAP* articles not included in this anthology. A number of areas of inquiry remain. How does the increasing interpenetration of the U.S. and Mexican economies, including the exportation of industrial production from the United States to Mexico (for example, auto plants and *maquiladoras*) and the importation of Mexican unemployed workers to the United States shape the development of production decisions and politics on both sides of the border? What forms of struggle lie ahead to reshape Mexican society in the interests of the vast majority of its people? *Latin American Perspectives* will continue to encourage analysis of such problems.

At the same time, the recurrence of certain basic themes—the state and its relations to social groups and classes, the causes and implications of the economic crisis, agrarian reform and the transformation of the peasantry—in each of the chapters included here attests to their relevance for an understanding of Mexico. This volume should thus meet the needs of readers who are concerned about a broad range of topics and are also interested in an intensive exploration of critical issues and debates.

NOTES

1. With the exception of Chapter 8, by Barry Carr, all studies in this volume were published previously in *Latin American Perspectives*.

2. The following analysis borrows extensively from Harris (1978) and Harris and Barkin (1982).

REFERENCES

Bartra, Roger
1974 *Estructura agraria y clases sociales en México*. Mexico City: Ediciones Era.
1975 "Sobre la articulación de modos de producción en América Latina." *Historia y Sociedad* 5 (Spring): 5-19.
Calzada, Julio César
1980 "Cada vez menos alimentos básicos." *Razones* 7 (April 20): 22-26
Esteva, Gustavo
1978 "¿Y si los campesinos existen?" *Comercio Exterior* 28 (June): 699-732.
Harris, Richard
1978 "Marxism and the Agrarian Question in Latin America." *Latin American Perspectives* 5 (Fall): 2-26.
Harris, Richard and David Barkin
1982 "The Political Economy of Mexico in the Eighties." *Latin American Perspectives* IX (Winter): 2-19.
Latin American Perspectives
1982 "Proposal for a New Revolutionary Party of the Left." 9 (Winter): 112-116.
Margulis, Mario
1978 "Acerca del valor en la estructura agraria." *Cuadernos Agrarios* 1 (May): 3-23.
Paré, Luisa
1977 *El proletariado agrícola en México*. Mexico City: Siglo XXI.

ARTICLES ON MEXICO IN
LATIN AMERICAN PERSPECTIVES
NOT APPEARING IN THIS ANTHOLOGY:

Bartra, Roger
1975 "Peasants and political power in Mexico: a theoretical approach." 2 (Summer): 125-145.

Bennholdt-Thomsen
1980 "Toward a class analysis of agrarian sectors: Mexico." 7 (Fall): 100-114.

Bluestein, William
1982 "The class relations of the hacienda village in prerevolutionary Morelos." 9 (Summer): 12-28.

Cook, Scott
1984 "Rural industry, social differentiation and the contradictions of provincial Mexican capitalism." 11 (Fall).

Crespi, Roberto Simon
1979 "José Revueltas (1914-1976): a political biography." 6 (Summer): 93-113.

de la Peña, Sergio
1982 "Proletarian power and state monopoly capitalism in Mexico." 9 (Winter): 20-35.

Edelman, Marc
1980 "Agricultural modernization in smallholding areas of Mexico: a case study in the Sierra Norte de Puebla." 7 (Fall): 29-49.

Folbre, Nancy
1977 "Population growth and capitalist development in Zongólica, Veracruz." 4 (Fall): 41-55.

Fox, Jonathan
1985 "Agrarian reform and populist politics: a discussion of Stephen Sanderson's *Agrarian Populism in the Mexican State.*" 12 (Summer): 29-41.

Fuentes, M. Luisa
1982 "Mexico's changing political reality: an analysis of the eighties." 9 (Winter): 102-105.

González Casanova, Pablo
1982 "Mexico: the most probable course of development." 9 (Winter): 78-88.

Hamilton, Nora
1982 "The state and the national bourgeoisie in post-revolutionary Mexico: 1920-1949." 9 (Fall): 31-54.

Harris, Richard L.
1982 "A critique of North American leftist analyses of Mexico." 9 (Winter): 106-110.

Horn, James J.
1983 "The Mexican Revolution and health care or the health of the Mexican Revolution." 10 (Fall): 24-39.

Joseph, Gilbert
1979 "Mexico's popular revolution: mobilization and myth in Yucatan: 1910-1940." 6 (Summer): 46-65.

Monsiváis, Carlos
1975 "Clasismo y novela en México." 2 (Summer): 164-179.
1978 "Notas sobre cultura popular en México." 5 (Winter): 98-118.

Niblo, Steve
1975 "Progress and the standard of living in contemporary Mexico." 2 (Summer): 109-124.
Niblo, Steve
1983 "British propaganda in Mexico during the Second World War: the development of cultural imperialism." 10 (Fall): 114-126.
Olson, Wayne
1985 "Crisis and social change in Mexico's political economy." 12 (Summer): 7-25.
Paoli Bolio, Francisco Jose
1982 "Petroleum and political change in Mexico." 9 (Winter): 65-77.
Síndico, Domenico E.
1980 "Modernization in nineteenth century sugar haciendas: the case of Morelos (From formal to real subsumption of labor to capital)." 7 (Fall): 83-99.
Singelmann, Peter
1978 "Rural collectivization and dependent capitalism: the Mexican collective ejido." 5 (Summer): 38-61.
Singelmann, Peter
1982 "Land without liberty: continuities of peripheral capitalist development and peasant exploitation among the cane growers of Morelos, Mexico." 9 (Summer): 29-45.
Stavenhagen, Rodolfo
1978 "Capitalism and the peasantry in Mexico." 9 (Summer): 27-37.
Tenenbaum, Barbara H.
1975 "Straightening out some of the *Lumpen* in the development." 2 (Summer): 3-16.
Towner, Margaret
1977 "Monopoly capitalism and women's work during the Porfiriato." 4 (Winter/ Spring): 90-105.
Vaughan, Mary Kay
1975 "Education and class in the Mexican Revolution." 2 (Summer): 17-33.
Villanueva, Margaret A.
1985 "From Calpixqui to Corregidor: appropriation of women's cotton textile production in early colonial Mexico." 12 (Winter): 17-40.

PART I

THE MEXICAN STATE

1

The Mexican State, 1915-1973
A Historical Interpretation
by
Juan Felipe Leal*

From the outset, the Mexican Revolution has been viewed as a two-pronged movement, as defined by two plans and two slogans resulting from the insurrection: "Effective Suffrage—No Reelection" (San Luis Plan) and "Land and Freedom" (Ayala Plan).[1]

The first group of revolutionaries struggled for political reform and advocated the "return to '57." That was, the abandonment of positivism and the presidential dictatorship; a return to liberalism and to constitutional government, with the consequent supremacy of legislative power; respect for the sovereignty of each state; restitution of freedom to municipal governments; observance of individual guarantees, and free elections. Those demands were basically of interest, within the oligarchical organization of the country, to specific regional factions of the Mexican bourgeoisie, which had been excluded from power, or which participated in some minor way in the formulation of policy that the dictator and intellectuals established from the Capital. Nevertheless, it would be erroneous to consider this movement of political renovation as the direct and exclusive plan of those factions of the bourgeoisie that sought political readjustment. In truth, this movement was generated, organized, and directed by a provincial *intelligentsia*, which, though reflecting the existing disagreement of the oligarchy with regard to the distribution of power among the dominant classes, factions, and groups, soon assumed a life of its own. This movement fed on the political crisis that existed during the final years of the Diaz regime, as well as on its own strength, and, because of this, experienced a change or new direction in its political struggle. In effect, although it continued to carry the stamp of its origin, in practice it followed methods of action and organization that proved incompatible with the more limited ones of the oligarchy then prevailing. It was in this manner, much the same way that a newly founded political party gains in national prestige through the establishment of local organi-

*Juan Felipe Leal is a Professor in the Facultad de Ciencias Políticas y Sociales at the Universidad Nacional Autónoma de México (Mexico City).

zations, that it generated a national political force that immediately diminished the power of local and regional authorities of the dictatorship, and that of Diaz himself. The electoral campaign of the opposition undermined to an even greater extent the bases of legitimacy of the regime and brought to light an enormous variety of conflicts, that, until then, had been kept concealed, thanks to the isolated nature of the regime. As a consequence, a powerful movement of the masses, expressly anti-oligarchical, gradually emerged that caused the original demands for political reform to acquire new meaning: they ceased to be the arguments of the dominant factions and groups, and became the political weapon of an alliance of the oppressed classes and groups in its struggle against the dictatorship.

The second movement constituted a reaction by the peasantry—principally from the states of Morelos, Puebla, Tlaxcala, Mexico, and the southern part of the Federal District—to the spread of capitalism in rural areas and to the manner and speed with which it was growing. It was an attempt to reorganize the mass of peasant farmers, a group that had become alienated and further impoverished by the vertiginous irruption of capitalism in specified agricultural zones in Mexico. This movement originated in towns engaged in a desperate battle against the expansion and growth of large estates (*latifundia*), and was led by ranchers, small businessmen, country schoolteachers, and others from the middle strata of the population. Supported by landless, but free, farmers and by indentured servants on the large estates, the movement rapidly spread far and wide.

Both movements concentrated their efforts in a revolution against a common enemy: the dictatorship of Porfirio Diaz and the pro-Diaz faction of the Mexican bourgeoisie. As a result, the political-military cycle of the Mexican Revolution was initiated, which lasted the better part of a decade, encompassing demands and movements during this period that were not present at the beginning.

DESTRUCTION OF THE
LIBERAL OLIGARCHICAL STATE AND
ESTABLISHMENT OF A NEW STATE

After four years of civil war, the popular armies defeated and lay ruin to the professional army, thereby sweeping aside the last vestiges of the liberal oligarchical state. However, after the defeat of the common enemy, a confrontation between the contradictory forces of the Revolution ensued, and precisely their diversity of origin and purpose led them once again to the battlefield. Thus, the popular insurrection, in fact, created a political vacuum: the old bloc in power lost its capacity to govern, while the struggle among different popular armies was beset by the difficulty—over a long period of time—of having to achieve a definite and undisputed triumph of one over the others.

Certainly, the destruction of the state, in 1914, resulted in the loss by the classes and class factions in power of their apparatus for domination. With no army, no police force, no "*rurales*," no political bosses, no ministers or judges, with no legitimacy whatsoever, the dominant classes of the Díaz regime were rendered incapable to govern or to designate representatives to a nonexistent state. The Díaz bourgeoisie, therefore, lost its political power. The mass of peasant farmers, undoubtedly the principal force of the revolution, showed itself, time and again, to be incapable of "forming a government." The industrial proletariat, small in number, widely dispersed geographically, and extremely heterogeneous in composition and political consciousness, likewise proved incompetent to establish itself as an independent organization, capable of assuming the leadership of the revolution. To fill the void the radical sectors of the petty bourgeoisie, urban and rural, stepped in and imposed their particular views (Shulgovsky, 1967: 6-7). Nevertheless, this petty-bourgeois leadership, transformed by the revolution itself and by the context that it propitiated into a bureaucracy—military and political—appeared at that time as the only force capable of structuring a new state. In this manner, the political vacuum brought on by the destruction of the liberal oligarchical state was filled by a coalition of forces, precarious and contradictory because of its multiclass structure, but under the relatively firm leadership of a political-military bureaucracy, whose plan of action pointed toward the implementation of reforms within the framework of capitalism, and not outside of it. As a result, the Revolution established itself as a great social upheaval, capable of carrying out important changes in existing relationships, institutions, and structures, but never suggesting or implying the dominance of the proletariat over the bourgeoisie (Villa, 1972: 32). More precisely, the change was consistent with the establishment of a new form of capitalistic state, with the reorganization of the bloc in power, under the hegemony of the bureaucracy that emerged from the Revolution, and with the redefinition of the existing relationships between the bloc in power and the mass of the oppressed classes.

BUREAUCRACY AND THE STATE

Over and over again, the question has been raised as to whether the social force that triumphed in the civil war constituted a social class, a class faction, or a specific social category; in other words, a bureaucracy. In truth, it has been characteristic of the majority of these discussions to attempt to reduce the group in question to the individual origin of some of its most outstanding members: a static procedure, filled with defects, that has only succeeded in evading the primary problem.

In my judgment, it was a bureaucracy that assumed power at the conclusion of the war, for the following reasons: the bourgeoisie lost their power and authority to lead the nation at a time when the working class had not yet acquired the capability to replace it. The popular armies, under petty-bourgeois leadership, lacked sufficient strength to annihilate those led by the peasantry (Gilly, 1971: 115-171); neither were they in a position to eliminate the proletarian insurgency effectively. Thus a situation existed in which the forces fighting among themselves were so evenly matched—a catastrophic balance, to be sure—that to continue the struggle would have led only to mutual destruction, thereby opening the door to foreign military intervention. This situation led the popular armies under the petty-bourgeois to adopt the demands of the industrial proletariat, in an effort to break the stalemate, persuade these forces to come over to their side, and wipe out the armies of their adversaries. By proceeding in this way, however, the leaders were no longer the same: although victorious in the war, they found themselves bound to ideologies that, in the beginning, were foreign to them, but that, henceforth, were to become their own and constitute their principal base of political support. And, in fact, some have seen this compromise as purely ideological or, rather, rhetorical. In reality, an in-depth analysis proves it to be an effective compromise, indeed, such was the weakness of its developing political power.

The high command of the victorious armies found themselves in a new political situation, which impelled them to increase and intensify their relative autonomy vis-à-vis all social classes—the dominating as well as the dominated—and which gradually transformed them into a bureaucracy. Actually, the possibility of structuring a new state depended, within the context of a catastrophic balance such as the one we have been discussing, on the existence of a social force capable of rising above—at times in appearance and at others, in reality—class conflict; for only in this way would it be able to carry out the functions of conciliation and arbitration that the situation demanded. This arbitral power, to function effectively, tended to represent society as a whole, which was only possible so long as it conserved a high degree of autonomy vis-à-vis each particular social class. Consequently, the arbitrative force could not be reduced to that of a mere representative of the immediate interests of one social class or class faction, which would have eventually crystallized into a specific social category—a bureaucracy.

It is clear, nonetheless, that the foregoing did not exclude individuals and groups, members of the bureaucracy, from rising to top management positions in business, industry, and agriculture by means of wealth accumulated while working for the government. On the contrary, groups with managerial talent systematically flowed from the government bureaucracy into the private sector; but the bureaucracy continued to thrive and replenish itself in spite of these defections.

POLITICAL-MILITARY UNITY

By the year 1916, the political panorama of the country was characterized by the victory of the popular armies commanded by Carranza and Obregón, on the one hand, and by the nonexistence of a national state, on the other. Consequently, the popular armies constituted the only organized force upon which it was feasible to base an attempt at reconstructing the state. One thing, however, should be made clear: no matter how important the social composition of an army may be—especially when dealing with a popular army—its nature and direction were determined by its commanders, its political-military leadership. In this case, the behavior of the high command revealed an outlook of the general population and an exceptional autonomy with regard to social classes; characteristics not normally associated with the petty bourgeoisie but with a bureaucracy that was established prior to the existence of the state; all of which conferred upon it a specific content.

In effect, in the absence of a state there was no conventional bureaucracy or professional army. There existed a centralized power, at once political and military, that proposed the establishment of a state. What existed was an original unity of politics and militarism, contradictory and dynamic, that operated within the bureaucracy, not outside. For the same reason, the high command of the popular armies was an enforcer of military and a political power and, as such, was made up neither of soldiers nor of civilians, but of both at the same time.

Yet, as the foundations for the new state were being established, a division of labor took place within the ruling bureaucracy, in response to the mounting complexity of governmental machinery. Gradually a civil branch and a military branch emerged within the political bureaucracy, more and more clearly differentiated and institutionalized, but unified at the top by a presidential figure who embodied the political-military unity of the bureaucracy.

This unity was, as has already been pointed out, contradictory; but, it was an internal contradiction the manifestations of which should not be interpreted as struggles between perfectly distinct spheres of the political system, as American historians are wont to do (see Liewen, 1968). These historians pose a false dilemma, consisting of a purported fight between the advocates of "militarism" and their opponents, in which "militarism" would be synonymous with dictatorship and the opposing view, democracy. Notwithstanding the ideological character of this dichotomy, it should be pointed out that this theory overlooks the ultimate unitarian nature of the ruling bureaucracy.

In reality, what happened was that, as the state was being established, a series of institutions emerged—such as a regular, professional army with precise and well-delimited duties—that lacked the degree of freedom that the previous popular armies enjoyed. As such, the armed forces were no longer the cornerstone of political power, and the position of dominance tended to shift from the military branch to the civil branch of the state organization. This gave rise, as would be expected, to serious disputes between groups within the political bureaucracy who were associated with one branch or the other in this system. This rather quiet bureaucratic battle was kept in check—to a certain extent—by the leader or president, in whom both branches were united.

Nevertheless, the transfer of predominance from the military branch to the civil branch represented an authentic "death-defying leap on horseback," in which the rider was the "Leader," the "Supreme Commander," "Mr. President." The danger in this step was illustrated by the military revolts of 1923, 1927, and 1929. But the true magnitude of danger it represented for the embryonic state and for the bureaucracy was determined by the strength of the economic vestiges of the old order: the landowners and foreign companies who lived under the threat of important reforms, which they always managed to postpone. The latter fed the fires of clerical belligerence and allied themselves with certain revolutionary leaders who, in disagreement with the proposed professionalization of the army, dissociated themselves from the bureaucracy in order to defend—at the same time—personal interests and those of the landowners and foreign companies (Tobler, 1971: 46-77). The principal question, thus, rested on the conservation of the situation of catastrophic balance—

mutatis mutandi—by which the establishment and consolidation of the state proceeded exceedingly slowly and erratically. Meanwhile, the institution of a professional army became even more urgent, as the revolutionary leadership continued to be both the cause and effect of political instability, thereby constituting an obstacle to the consolidation of the new order.

In an attempt to gain the highest degree of cohesion possible, in 1929 the political bureaucracy founded the National Revolutionary Party (PNR). This organism pursued several objectives at the same time. In the first place, it sought to bring together, at the national level, "the vast majority of the revolutionary elements dispersed throughout the country and to properly discipline the tendencies of the small regional organisms which hindered the progress of the Revolution" (Portes Gil, 1954: 211). In this way, they sought to give a national coherence to the different groups of the political bureaucracy—in every branch—and to strengthen the center position of this bureaucracy at the expense of regionalism and localism, which had been in command. This stand not only implied reinforcement of the Center position, but that of the president of Mexico as well, all of which reinforced the relative autonomy of the political bureaucracy vis-à-vis regional and local interests, which had been eroded by the phenomenon of revolutionary leaderhip. In the second place, it endeavored to guarantee the military high command their positions within the political bureaucracy, provided they would accept the political rules of the game inherent in the PNR. In this manner, an institutional framework was established—a ground for compromise—for the peaceful transfer of power from one president to another, and an operative mechanism for the gradual transfer of superiority from the military branch to the civil branch of the political bureaucracy. In the third place, they wished to create a social basis of support for the political bureaucracy and the state, through the institution of a state organization—with electoral objectives in mind—that would encompass all public employees and unite a multiplicity of local, regional, and national electoral organisms (Manjarrez, 1930).

It follows from this that the PNR was not strictly an organism of the masses, as the Party of the Mexican Revolution (PRM) was during the Cárdenas era. In effect, the PNR was, above all else, an institution whose raison d'être was that of integrating and giving cohesion to the political bureaucracy itself, and to contribute to its unity, without which it would have lost its capacity to govern.

Even so, the compromise the PNR reflected was not definitive; so much so that when—during the regime of Lázaro Cárdenas—the effective transfer of superiority from the military branch to the civil branch of the political bureaucracy took place, it was due to the process of structural reforms, the mobilization and the political induction of urban and rural laborers into state organizations, and the militarization of these social forces, as the only guarantee possible for the execution and maintenance of these reforms.

To be sure, those economic and social reforms were opposed not only by interests directly affected by them. The military branch of the political bureaucracy also resisted them, for it saw quite clearly that, as new, organized forces were added to the state organization, the army necessarily suffered in importance.

One thing, nevertheless, bears repeating: the military high command was not excluded from the political bureaucracy, although it most assuredly recognized that it had diminished in importance within the political bureaucracy as well as in its relationship to the whole of the state organization. In sum, the political-military unity of the ruling bureaucracy displayed—in spite of its internal alterations—a line of continuity that endures to the present time. The existence of this unity contains several implications; for example, a relative facility of the system of dominance to militarize and demilitarize itself, since it does not require the complete modification of the political system.

THE BUREAUCRATIC HEGEMONY

As we have previously noted, the situation of catastrophic balance that provoked the revolution of 1910 made possible the hegemony of a specific social category, and not of a social class or class faction. However, this hegemony of the bureaucracy, arising from the revolution, was not an automatic result of the situation in question; to a great extent it was also the product of the political action of the very same bureaucracy. As seen from this perspective, the bureaucracy, indeed, worked at establishing its hegemony. To succeed, it needed consciousness and organization.

The political-military bureaucracy acquired consciousness of the place it occupied in society and of its own interests through direct, practical means—a pragmatic program of trial and error. The organization that finally took shape was equally the result of empirical experience. The bureaucracy left the elaboration and formal presentation of this knowledge to its lawyers and journalists, who attempted to establish its basis on the most diverse economic, social, and political doctrines: the patrimonial tradition of the Spanish crown, classical liberalism, pamphletary socialism. But, it was more difficult to establish a hegemony than to justify it, and it was the former task that most concerned the bureaucracy that assumed power.

In effect, during the process of constituting its hegemony, the ruling bureaucracy faced serious crises that placed its very existence in danger. Such was the case of the confrontation between "moderates" and "Jacobins" in the constituent Congress of 1916-1917; of the presidential succession of 1920 and the insurrection of Agua Prieta; of the de la Huerta revolt in 1923; of the political crisis of 1928; of the 1935 dispute between Calles and Cárdenas; and of the entire Cárdenas period, from which a firmly hegemonic political bureaucracy and a completely consolidated state finally emerged. From then on, the problem facing the political bureaucracy consisted of conserving the hegemony obtained. More will be said about this point later in this study.

THE STATE AND THE SOCIAL PACT

After seven years of civil war, with imperialistic maneuverings mixed in, the victorious Carranza-Obregón coalition organized, through the Constitution of 1917, a new capitalistic model, which was the formal expression of the social pact that the conditions created by the revolution imposed. Nonetheless, it should be understood that this accord was not a result of the popular insurrection alone, but of its systematic destruction as well.

Concerning its political nature, the state born of this scheme of contradictory interests has three characteristics that stand out above all others: a representative democracy, a presidential dictatorship, and corporatism.

Certainly, the Mexican state is composed of a peculiar combination of these three elements, all differing in importance, especially when observed over a period of time. It is no mere coincidence that the Constitution of 1917 grants equal sanction and legality to these three aspects of the political organization of Mexico. Let us take a look:

On the one hand, the text of the Constitution was inspired by liberalism, and, for this reason, it establishes the equality of all men before the law along with a series of individual guarantees; it affirms the sovereignty of the people, who exercise it through their elected representatives; it establishes a separation of powers—executive, legislative, judicial—and it conceives the country as a republic divided into states, which are free and sovereign with regard to their internal affairs, but united through a federal pact.

On the other hand, in accordance with the Document of Querétaro, the president of Mexico has the right to introduce laws and issue decrees, and thereby is established as another legislative power. But that is not all. The president also has the power to appoint and remove judicial authorities. In short, the executive power is such that it absorbs and is complementary to the powers of the other two branches of government. In addition, the sovereignty of the states is found to be extremely limited by the Federation and subject to the discretionary powers of the president. The result is the establishment of a constitutional dictatorship of the presidential variety (Calderón, 1972: 79-133).

Finally, but equally as important, Articles 27 and 123 of the Constitution grant the president of the Republic virtually full authority to legislate matters concerning property and labor, making him the "Supreme Arbiter" of the country (Clark, 1934: 3-260). And it is precisely these arbitrative functions (Goodspeed, 1954) that give rise to an entire corporate structure.

Thus, for example, the labor law, which has its origin in Article 123, recognizes the existence of the basic classes of a capitalistic society—as well as their antagonism—and proposes an institutional method for regulating the class struggle. The conciliation of these opposing interests is left to the state, which—through the Courts of Conciliation and Arbitration—is obliged "to secure the balance of the diverse factors of production, bringing into harmony the labor laws with those of capital" (see Constitución Política; Ley Federal, 1931; Nueva Ley Federal, 1969).

In this way, conceiving of the state as a power apparently independent of the social classes, the door is opened to the integration of a variety of tripartite bodies, in charge of class conciliation: Labor Relations Boards, National Commission on Minimum Wages, National Commission for the Participation of Workers in Company Profits, Technical Council of the Mexican Institute of Social Security, National Council on the Development of Human Resources for Industry, National Institute of the Fund for Workers Housing, National Tripartite Commission, and so forth. These bodies are corporative, because they integrate the social classes—through specific areas of economic activity and in a vertical manner—into the state organization. In other words, the social classes receive their recognition and organization, directly and expressly from the state.

The preceding does not mean that Mexican corporatism is fascist in nature. Fascism begins by denying class struggle and integrates, indiscriminately, labor and management into the same union. On the contrary, Mexican corporatism does recognize the fact of class struggle and incorporates workers and capitalists into separate unions, who then participate in tripartite bodies, with the state in the role of an "independent third party." It is clear, however, that the Mexican state is in no way a completely independent party, because its initial function is to "obtain a balance among the factors of production"; that is, guarantee the operation of the system, which is, obviously, capitalistic. Thus, its primary objective is to produce and reproduce the dominance of capital, checking its excesses and seeking class conciliation, "national unity," and "progress" or "economic development" for the country. All of this, naturally, at the expense of the wage earner.

Nothing better defines the capitalistic nature of the Mexican state than its own labor legislation. Certainly, the guarantee of equal rights to labor and management—rights of association and suspension of activities—neglects to mention the inequality of the parties, a fact that translates into a benefit for the capitalists. Moreover, because these rights are elaborated in detail in the labor legislation, this body of law becomes a formidable instrument of political control in the hands of the state. As a result, the unions have a very precise function within the new society, which consists of fighting for the interests of its members in order to obtain a "balance" among the factors of production, if this "balance" should be upset. In short, official unionism displays—from its inception—a reformist nature, previously delimited by law. The unions do not exist to fight for the historical emancipation of the proletariat, but to check the excesses of capital. Therefore, any conflict involving workers' claims must be recognized and arbitrated by the state, and must proceed through the legal channels that the prevailing authority has imposed; otherwise, they run the risk of their fight being considered illegal and a criminal offense.

But in addition to the legal control that the state exercises over the unions, we become increasingly aware of a direct political control as well. In effect, as the unions became absorbed into large labor organizations that, in turn, became a part of the party of the state, these same unions are transformed into organizations of public order. With this, the chain of command—state-party-union—was established, and conditions were laid down for the crystallization, within the union organizations, of a union bureaucracy, representing the state within the labor movement (Padgett, 1966).

This union bureaucracy constitutes a specific structure inside the political bureaucracy; a relatively autonomous sphere within the state organization; a type of network that covers the entire sector of unionized workers. The union bureaucrats, commonly known by the nickname "*líderes charros*" (labor officials who sell out to management), band together in highly homogeneous cliques, revolving around personal loyalties and expectations; but, clearly conscious of their common interests, of their position within the structure of command in Mexico, of their usefulness in the accumulation of capital. The union bureaucrat is, thus, deprived of what might be called a "micro-ideology," that is manifested in the fact that a very minor official of a small union understands that all his mobility—political and economic—is tied to that of an intermediate official, and so on, until reaching the level of an authentic hierarch, such as Fidel Velásquez. Consequently, this entire organization of control, which includes gangsterism, manipulation of elections—union and territorial—expulsion of workers who are troublemakers, participation in the Courts of Conciliation and Arbitration, its presence on the National Commission on Minimum Wages, on the Tripartite, and so forth, shows itself to be highly personified.

The working masses were grouped into political organizations that were foreign to their interests and at the service—in the final analysis—of their class enemies. This submission was greatly facilitated because both the labor officials and the workers lacked an ideology of their own, and took up the ideological stand of the Mexican Revolution, which is, after all, bourgeois.

In sum, the Constitution of 1917, which outlines the essential features of the new state, is clear testimony to the contradictions that the political-military bureaucracy—its creator—had to deal with. So, if in some parts of the Constitution we observe the classic precepts of liberalism, in others they are denied. In the same way, the equal rights of all citizens are recognized, as is class antagonism. And it is precisely to prevent this irreconcilable antagonism from destroying society in a senseless war that the intervention of an "impartial arbiter" is proposed, a power apparently rising above the fundamental classes of society that is in charge of regulating the dispute. This "arbiter" is the state, and, in the beginning, more than the state—that has not been consolidated: the ruling political-military bureaucracy.

THE STATE AND THE ECONOMY:
THE ECONOMY AND POLITICS

This situation seems to be, in reality, a mere variation on the processes of change characteristic of late-developing capitalism: Japan, Germany, Italy, Spain. In all of these cases, a peculiar relationship exists between the state and the economy, and between the economy and politics, that constitutes one of its distinctive features. The function the state fulfills in those countries that passed through a phase of free enterprise and in which the concentration of capital was a slow process is distinct from the one it acquires in countries where capitalism develops under conditions imposed by an imperialistic system (Cordera, n.d.: 18-28). This whole matter poses specific problems and theoretical difficulties that cannot be overlooked.

In effect, fascism in Italy, nazism in Germany, Japanese totalitarianism, and, to a lesser extent, Spanish falangism and Portuguese statism embody the answer that the countries of late-developing capitalism give to the crisis of transition from liberal to monopolistic capitalism. The classic capitalism of England, France, the United States, and other countries, likewise, responds to the new situation, though in a different manner and, in particular, as a result of the world crisis of 1929. The result is, nevertheless, similar: a new method of state intervention in the economy, recognition and integration into the system of so-called interest groups, such as unions; increasing deterioration of classial liberalism and of the parliamentary forms of territorial representation and, in short, a diverse corporatization of the state and society.

As we have seen, the Mexican state is no exception to the rule, although it definitely displays certain peculiarities that are, basically, a result of the Revolution of 1910, and it is precisely this event that precipitates the transformation. Thus, the state that is born of the revolution is already a "reformed" capitalistic state, "more advanced" than certain countries of late-developing capitalism and "ahead" in certain respects of the capitalistic powers mentioned in the previous paragraph. Because of its status as a dependent national state during the era of imperialism, the Mexican state takes on a nationalistic attitude, and, with the subrogation of the rights of the Spanish crown—Article 27 of the Constitution—it becomes a source of proprietary rights and limits the prerogatives of the imperialistic enclaves within the Mexican economy (González Navarro, 1970: 8). At the same time, because of the fact that it was born within the context of the structural weakness of the basic social classes, the "new order" establishes the supremacy of the state over society and its disputes, not only in a general manner—which is true of any capitalistic state—but in a specific manner as well. From now on, the state assumes authority to grant recognition to and participate directly in the organization of the classes and class factions, advising them of the institutional boundaries within which disputes are permitted, with the stipulation that they are always subject to state arbitration. This final point guarantees the hegemony of the ruling bureaucracy. Finally, the state assumes the role of master, public administrator, and principal agent in the management of the economy (Ianni, 1974a).

CORPORATISM THEN (AND NOW)

The corporative nature of the Mexican State, already present in the Constitution of 1917, has gradually unfolded in proportion to the degree of development reached by the productive forces and by the basic classes of capitalistic society: the bourgeoisie and the proletariat.

Generally speaking, the contemporary Mexican state has gone through two clearly distinct stages. In stage one, the bureaucracy in power, after defeating, containing, and integrating the agrarian masses, succeeded also in organizing labor and management, thereby subordinating them to the state. By the end of this stage—which lasted from 1915 to 1940—the "revolutionary regimes" had carried out large-scale agrarian reforms; nationalized vital enterprises that had been under imperialistic control; remodeled the economic, social, and political structure of the country; created new institutions; consolidated the state, whereby it obtained a wide, social base of support; and gained general acceptance of the illusion that they represented, equally, the interests of "the different social sectors." The thesis of "national unity" flourished in a society the social classes of which were organized directly by the state into mass organizations like the CNC, CTM, and so forth (Alcázar, 1970). In stage two, which begins around 1940, each succeeding government has witnessed a growing deterioration of its social base of support; as a result, the governments have resorted—more and more frequently—to direct repression as a means of stifling criticism from peasants, workers, the middle strata of the population, and, ultimately, from small and medium capitalists.

It should be pointed out that, of those two stages, the first dealt with the reorganization of society and the state, and showed very modest economic growth; the second has developed, conserving the same political organization, and has experienced, essentially, an accelerated growth in the economy. However, it would be naive to suppose that the political organization has remained unchanged through this entire process, especially if we take into account the degree of development attained by capitalism in Mexico, as well as the class structure it has generated.

In fact, at present, we cannot speak of an incipient development of either the Mexican bourgeoisie or the proletariat; as a result, the political bureaucracy must, out of necessity, perform a distinct role from that which it carried out during the 1920s, for example. In addition, we can state quite categorically that the new situation repeatedly raises questions as to the hegemony of the political bureaucracy.

To put it another way, if corporatism "then" corresponded to a predominantly agrarian society, in which the bureaucracy derived its power not only from the structural weakness of the bourgeoisie and the proletariat, but also from its "agrarian pact" with the peasantry, corporatism "now" corresponds to a society the center of gravity of which has shifted from the country to the city; consequently, the political bureaucracy is able to maintain its hegemony only to the extent that it is capable of bringing about a "labor pact"—at a new level and qualitatively distinct from the "agrarian"—that will permit it to reestablish its social base of support, if only partially. In light of these facts, the union bureaucracy tends to occupy an increasingly important—and, at the same time, strategic—position in the new political situation.

All considerations indicate that a readjustment of the political organization can no longer be delayed, and that the presumed changes will take place within the organization itself and not involve its complete transformation. It is from this perspective that the creation of the National Tripartite Commission, for example, should be seen (Presidencia de la República, 1971: 69-131). This is a supraparliamentary body, legally authorized to discuss and, in fact, decide issues that supposedly belong to the legislative branch. The novelty does not lie in the fact that the "houses of representatives" are condemned to lead a ritualistic and symbolic life (González Casanova, 1965: 21-58), but, fundamentally, in that the "mechanisms for consultation" that the president of Mexico has traditionally made use of are now established institutionally—in a new manner, at a new level. In short, before the integration of the National Tripartite Commission, the president "consulted" with the diverse "sectors" and even the different components of each sector in an isolated and private manner. Out of these consultations and negotiations came decrees, proposed law, or state policy to which the Legislature gave its rubber stamp of approval. Now, things have changed. In the first place, the consultations that were formerly held in secret are now semipublic, with the intention of giving them an air of legitimacy and of obtaining more stable and lasting compromises. In the second place, all of this takes place at an institutional level, involving a kind of permanent congress of bankers, industrialists, merchants, public officials, and union bureaucrats, where the most diverse matters are discussed; in essence, it is a group on the fringes of "national representation," constituting a parallel system of decision making. In the third place, the direct, though limited, nature of the confrontations causes the degree of presidential arbitration to increase. There is no doubt that the National Tripartite Commission—and, to a lesser extent, the state and local commissions—is a state organization that, due to the nature of its integration, guarantees that the "sectors" be present in all of their heterogeneity, giving rise to an extensive political game, evidently intended for the benefit of the "Supreme Arbiter," who is none other than the president of the country and who, naturally, presides over the National Tripartite Commission.

THE ENIGMA OF POLITICAL STABILITY

The majority of political studies on Mexico agree that, from the beginning of the Second World War to the middle of the past decade, the country experienced relative political stability and sustained economic growth. The recognition of this fact, however, has propitiated a static view of the phenomenon to the extent that many analysts have come to consider this political stability as an inherent attribute of the Mexican political system, under any conditions. To be sure, evidence is lacking regarding the efficiency of the same political system in times of crisis and prolonged economic stagnation. Neither has this possibility been examined from an analytical point of view, and the enigma remains to be solved.

MONOPOLISTIC CAPITAL AND THE STATE

All the governments "emanating from the revolution" have followed a policy tending to favor capital, particularly of the domestic variety, and even this within the limits established by the state. The state, as we have already seen, became a public entrepreneur and key element in the orientation of the economic process almost from the beginning. The state as economic administrator, a concept already to be found in the Constitution of 1917, becomes a full-fledged reality during the Cárdenas administration and, more particularly, with the initiation of the industrialization process directed by the state since the Second World War (Shaffer, 1954). Today, there are close to 500 enterprises, some completely public and others in majority or minority partnership with the state, that employ more than a half million people (Barros Velero, 1972; Torres Maya, 1973).

Such a policy has sought to consolidate the large, public, monopolistic enterprises and private enterprise in general. This economic policy has been carried out through the implementation of a variety of measures: nationalization of natural resources and of certain foreign monopolies; introduction of protective measures regarding domestic production; tax exemptions for enterprises registered as Mexican that import capital goods; exercise of control over the volume and rate of incoming and outgoing foreign capital; creation of government institutions to stimulate and direct private investment; formation of state enterprises or ones of mixed capital; sale of goods and services produced by the state below their cost of production; realization of public capital investments in infrastructure works; low taxes for enterprises; determination of minimum and maximum prices; establishment of guaranteed prices for certain agricultural and cattle products; fixing of minimum wages; offer of fiscal, monetary, and technological incentives to management, and so forth.

This policy did not prevent the rise of sectors of monopolistic capital—domestic and foreign—outside of the traditional enclaves and the so-called public sector of the economy. As a result, a dozen domestic financial groups gradually developed, which by the 1960s were already negotiating with the president directly and, thus, bypassing the "consulting organizations" that the state had instituted for the management sector, such as CONCAMIN, CONCANACO, and CANACINTRA. A similar situation would take place with some 250 transnational enterprises that, from 1940 to the present, became more and more involved in the industry of transformation (Hernandez and Trejo Delarbre, 1974: 17-39).

As a consequence, the increasing complexity of Mexican capitalism led to the strengthening of financial capital, which has seen its capacity to intervene in political matters increase to the level commensurate with its own position: that of the most important faction of the bourgeoisie. It has diminished the autonomy of the ruling bureaucracy and, particularly, of the president of the country, who have faced mounting difficulties in representing the interests of the whole of the bourgeoisie, without favoring any particular faction of it (Stavenhagen, 1973). The integration and complementariness between the bureaucratic organization and financial capital has provoked, as would be expected, dissatisfaction among the small and medium capitalists.

But the implications of these facts are, indeed, much greater. A panoramic view of the whole of Mexican industry reveals to us two of its most important characteristics: an evident concentration, on the one hand, and the persistence of innumerable small and medium installations, on the other. Such is the case that, according to the 1965 Industrial Census, there were 2,100 plants with more than 100 workers, representing 1.7 percent of all existing enterprises. These industries, however, involved 75 percent of the capital invested in this area, accounted for 70 percent of the value of production, and employed 53 percent of all industrial workers. Moreover, there were only 300 industries employing more than 500 people, which corresponded to .2 percent of the total of industrial establishments, involving 36 percent of the invested capital, accounting for 34 percent of the value of production, and employing 25 percent of industrial personnel.

At the same time, the crafts industry, small and medium, was of great significance in 1965, not so much for its economic impact as for its capacity to absorb the labor force. In addition, this sector of the industry has constituted one of the traditional bases of social support for the state party and for the political organization in general. The situation of the crafts industry, small and medium, is illustrated in Table 1.1.

Within this framework, the transition to a new stage in the industrialization process, the necessity of increasing the export of manufactured goods, and greater technological requirements tend to accentuate the bonds of subordination of Mexican capitalism to U.S. imperialism. In effect, the enormous and indiscriminate affluence of foreign capital has had repercussions on the domestic policy of the country, reinforcing the superiority of a large capital, capable of allying itself with foreign monopolies and of enlarging its sphere of action. Consequently, small and medium entrepreneurs, incapable of handling the competition, are eliminated from the market, thereby accelerating the monopolistic concentration of capital and gravely affecting the capacity of industry to absorb the growing labor force.

IMPERIALISM AND THE STATE

At this point, it is necessary to make reference, however brief, to the existing relationship between the national dependent state and imperialism.

As noted above, toward 1940 it appeared that the Mexican state—after remodeling the economic, social, and political structure and redefining its relationship with the imperialistic order—had established the basis for capitalistic development, with considerable autonomy vis-à-vis the imperialistic system. Nevertheless, by the end of the Second World War it was evident that the new standards for the international reproduction of

TABLE 1.1
Situation for the Crafts Industry

	Number of Personnel	Establishments (No.)	(%)	Value of Production (%)	Capital Invested (%)	% Employed
Crafts	no paid personnel	69,600	(51)	1.1	.5	7.5
	1-5 persons	44,700	(33)	2.8	1.3	8.7
Small	6-25 persons	13,900	(10)	7.6	6.4	11.4
Medium	26-100 persons	5,400	(4)	18.4	17.1	19.1
Subtotal		133,600	(98)	29.9	25.3	46.7

SOURCE: Calculated on the basis of data provided in the 1965 Industrial Census, SIC, Mexico.
NOTE: Percentages are calculated on the basis of the corresponding total of the industrial sector.

capital were capable of influencing, at an ever-increasing rate, the state organization of dependent countries, no matter how nationalistic they were. This absorption did not happen overnight, nor did it manifest itself directly. However, already by the 1950s it was quite evident that the active participation of the subordinate national state in the economy, far from constituting an obstacle for imperialistic domination, represented the *conditio sine qua non* of foreign investment (Ianni, 1973: 1105-1114).

The absorption of the dependent national state by the new "techniques" of imperialism was accomplished through the creation of multilateral organizations and agencies, established by conventions, agreements, or conferences of chiefs of state. As symbols of the new configuration of international capital and, at the same time, as an expression of U.S. hegemony over the capitalistic states, two multilateral financial organizations were created in 1944: the International Monetary Fund (IMF) and the International Bank for Reconstruction and Development (IBRD), also known as the World Bank.

These multilateral organizations, along with others we shall see later, expressed the restructuring of the relationship between the capitalistic states and were primarily concerned with the reconstruction of the economic systems affected by the war in order to put a stop to the expansion of "communist totalitarianism": all of this under the hegemony of the United States and within the scope of the cold war.

In Latin America, the United States sponsored the formation of the Organization of American States (OAS), the InterAmerican Development Bank (IDB), the Latin American Free Trade Association (LAFTA), and dozens of other multilateral organizations. It is through these agencies, as intermediary, that the United States, as hegemonic nation, maintains and protects its interests; and it is through these agencies, as intermediary, that the interests and projects of the transnational enterprises are carried out, which are the primary sources of the production and the export of capital from Latin America to the United States (Ianni, 1974b: 119-157).

As a result, the present imperialistic structures and relationship confer new characteristics on the Mexican state, which has come to be an important link in the global operation of imperialism. And, under certain conditions—depending on the correlation of forces between social classes at the domestic level—the state organization becomes a mere appendage of the international structure that rules over the operation of the transnational corporations.

THE MEXICAN STATE AS
A REPRESSIVE DEPENDENCY

The Mexican state is, after all, a dependent capitalistic state. Its primary mission consists of promoting the capitalistic development of the country under conditions imposed by the imperialistic system. It shares many of the characteristics of the "states of exception," even though this may be a permanent, not circumstantial, situation. From the preceding, it derives a corporative and authoritarian structure; a centralized and discretionary organization of "de facto" powers, guaranteed by the political constitution itself; a political and ideological subjugation of the working masses, with almost unlimited repressive possibilities; and a bourgeoisie—splintered into numerous factions—that has not been able to reach political hegemony nor govern through its direct representatives. This bourgeoisie formulates and carries out its interests by means of a political bureaucracy, charged with making the state institution run, with confronting the masses, and with constantly readjusting the capitalistic development of Mexico to the demands of the imperialistic powers.

NOTE

1. Concerning this point, the most radical precursor movement of the Mexican Revolution, that represented by the Mexican Liberal Party, is omitted, since, at the outset of the Revolution, the Magonist movement was already fading, disorganized, and isolated. For these reasons, its influence on the course of events is ideological rather than an authentic social force.

REFERENCES

Alcázar, Marco Antonio
     1970 *Las organizaciones patronales en México*. Mexico: El Colegio de México.
Barros Valero, Javier
     1972 *Las empresas públicas, el caso de México*. Mexico: UNAM, FCPS, Tesis de Licenciatura.
Calderón, José María
     1972 *Génesis del presidencialismo en México*. Mexico: Editorial "El Caballito."
Clark, Marjorie Ruth
     1934 *Organized Labour in Mexico*. Chapel Hill: University of North Carolina Press.
Cordera, Rolando
     n.d. *Estado y desarrollo en el capitalismo tardío y subordinado. Síntesis de un caso pionero: México: 1920-1970*. Mexico: ENE, UNAM.
Gilly, Adolfo
     1971 *La revolucíon interrumpida*. Mexico: Ediciones "El Caballito."
Gobierno Federal de México
     Constitución Política de los Estados Unidos Mexicanos (Art. 123).
     1931 *Ley Federal del Trabajo* (August 28).
     1969 *Nueva Ley Federal de Trabajo* (December 2).
González Casanova, Pablo
     1965 *La democracia en México*. Mexico: Editorial ERA.
González Navarro, Moisés
     1965 *México: El capitalismo nacionalista*. Mexico: B. Costa Amic (ed.).
Goodspeed, Stephen S.
     1954 "El papel del jefe del ejecutivo en México." *Problemas agrícolas e industriales de México*, Mexico.
Hernández, Salvador and Raul Trejo Delarbre
     1974 "Transnacionales y dependencia en México (1940-1970)." Mexico: UNAM, FCPS, Centro de Estudios Latinoamericanos.
Ianni, Octavio
     1973 "Estado nacional y organizaciones multilaterales." *Comercio Exterior* 23 (November): 1105-1114.
     1974a "Clase dominante y clase gobernante." *La Cultura en México* (February 20).
     1974b *Sociología del imperialismo*. Mexico: SEP-SETENTAS, no. 125.
Liewen, Edwin
     1967 *Mexican Militarism. The Political Rise and Fall of the Revolutionary Army: 1910-1940*. Albuquerque: University of New Mexico Press.

Manjarrez, Froylán C.
1930 *La jornada institucional: (1) La crisis política y (2) La crisis de la violencia.* Mexico: Editorial "Diario Oficial."

Padgett, L. Vincent
1966 *The Mexican Political System.* Boston: Houghton Mifflin.

Portes Gil, Emilio
1954 *Quince años de política mexicana.* Mexico: Editorial Botas.

Presidencia de la República
1971 El gobierno mexicano. (August).

Schaffer, Gordon
1954 "La administración pública mexicana." *Problemas Agrícolas e Industriales de México.* Mexico City.

Shulgovsky, Anatol
1967 "El caudillismo revolucionario." *Historia y Sociedad* (Spring): 6-7.

Tobler, H. W.
1971 "Las paradojas del ejército revolucionario." *Historia Mexicana* (July/September): 46-77.

Torres Maya, Patricia
1973 "Lista completa de los organismos y empresas estatales." *Revista de Revistas* (December 5).

Villa, Manuel
1972 "Discusión de algunas categorías para el análisis de la revolución mexicana." *Revista Mexicana de Ciencia Política* (October/December).

2

Women, Class, and Education in Mexico
1880-1928

by
*Mary K. Vaughan**

One of the major characteristics of capitalist society is the primary role of women as household workers in the daily and generational replacement of labor power for production.[1] In precapitalist societies, women participate in production within the family unit, which produces for its own subsistence and for others (the state, landlords, and so forth). The historical advance of capital accumulation and market production deprives the family of its productive role. Peasant and artisan families, expropriated of their means of subsistence and production, are forced to sell their labor power in the market and are increasingly forced to substitute goods purchased in the market for those that are homemade. In the early period of industrialization, members of peasant and artisan families—men, women, and children—are thrown into market production. Subjected to exceedingly low wages, long hours, and unhealthy working conditions, the family is threatened with disintegration, and, in effect, the capitalist class is engaged in a self-defeating process of preventing the daily and generational replacement of labor power, which has been a historical function of family life. This early crisis is overcome to a large extent by removing women from production and thereby preserving the family structure of the working class. Woman's primary economic role becomes the reproduction of labor power through household work, although she continues to act as part of the reserve army of labor occasionally and/or marginally employed. The extent to which women can spend most of their time in the home depends upon the level of capital accumulation in a particular society. For instance, in the United States for some time in the twentieth century, it was economically possible for

*Mary K. Vaughan is Associate Professor of History and Latin American Studies at the University of Illinois—Chicago. She is the author of *The State, Education and Social Class in Mexico, 1880-1930* (Northern Illinois University Press, 1982), also published in Spanish by the Secretaria de Educacion Publica and Fondo de Cultura Economica, Mexico. She is currently working on questions of the politics and practice of socialist education in Mexico in the 1930s.

working-class women to remain most of the time in the home: Since 1960, with rising inflation eroding the wages of male workers and with increased technification of production and the growing importance of its marketing and servicing aspects, women have once again entered the labor force in large numbers.[2] In contrast, in a society such as Mexico, where the process of capital accumulation was late and subordinate to the capital accumulation process in advanced countries, it was not materially possible to remove women in large numbers from the labor force, although it was possible to keep them in marginal, low-paying, and backward sectors of the economy.

One question that arises from the thesis of woman's primary role as a reproducer of labor power is how this process occurs, that is, how women are removed from factory production, how the family is restored and restructured to play not only a specific economic role in the replacement of labor power but also *an ideological role* in the reproduction of the social relations of production, that is in the legitimization of the subordination of labor to capital. Although not intending to underestimate either the extent to which changes in the role of women and the family result from economic changes or the extent to which women's alleged political conservatism is a reflection of their backward and isolated mode of production in the household, this paper focuses upon political events and forces that intend to or in effect bring about such changes. The factors most obvious in preserving family life are shorter working hours, higher wages, and limitations on the labor of women and children. These are concessions won by workers in the course of class struggle and accepted by farsighted employers and state bureaucrats as a means of maintaining social order and increasing production. The Mexican case, where the effort to remove women from production was not entirely successful but was nonetheless very real, would indicate the important role played by political forces not only in trying to save the family but in attempting to restructure it so as to permit a rapid and uninterrupted accumulation of capital. Whereas workers in the Mexican Revolution (1910-1917) struggled and achieved labor legislation facilitating somewhat the maintenance of family cohesion, and although the male-dominated trade union movement probably wished to strengthen woman's primary role in the home, petty-bourgeois reformers, bureaucrats of the state, sought to restructure the working-class family as a unit stabilizing a society wracked by class conflict. They consciously saw the family as a unit that, if correctly organized, could sustain itself on a minimum income while reproducing a healthy but pliable labor force, imbued with the values of work, discipline, and subordination to authority. Further, they consciously saw a strengthening of the private family unit as an alternative to the otherwise public life of the working class, which, in their opinion, generated immorality, lack of discipline, and political consciousness and action.

Restructuring family life also involved its subordination to capital and to the state. In the period after 1876 and especially through the Mexican Revolution, the state expanded to absorb many functions of the family. Its growing role in the socialization of children, the provision of health protection, and other services took place simultaneously with the economy's usurpation of the family's productive function and subjection of the same to market relations of production and consumption.[3] What is suggested in this period of Mexican history is an attempt on the part of the expanding state apparatus to subordinate the family and to reduce and define its social role as one compatible with the process of private capital accumulation. This effort involved breaking the existing and potential class consciousness of women and reaffirming and strengthening their traditional subordinate role to men, within the family, within production, and within the society as a whole. This paper focuses primarily on one aspect of this process, the expansion of public schooling, and secondarily on the extension of other social services by the state.

Finally, this paper is not an exhaustive treatment of Mexican women as participants in class struggle, although it makes observations about the Mexican women's movement at a particular point in historical time. Essentially, it is argued here that during the Mexican Revolution, educated petty-bourgeois women "reformers" employed by the state sought to develop and strengthen the subordinate role of working-class women in the home and in production in reaction against the mobilization of peasants and workers in the Mexican Revolution. Their implemented ideology in the field of education and other social services was a manifestation of the level of class struggle in the Mexican Revolution. Second, the failure of the workers' movement to generate an effective women's movement to counteract that of bourgeois feminism[4] lay in the youth, size, composition, and ideological immaturity of the Mexican working class, which likewise determined its inability to dominate the Mexican Revolution.

THE STATE, EDUCATION, AND
WOMEN IN THE PORFIRIATO (1876-1910)

In 1867, after a half-century of anarchy and foreign invasion, Mexican liberals, whose victory over the Church resulted in the secularization of clerical property and its increasing utilization for large-scale agricultural production, were able to lay the foundations of a modern state for purposes of capitalist growth. Dictator Porfirio Díaz, military chieftain who ruled Mexico between 1876 and 1910, elaborated a state structure for growth that won the loyalties of regional oligarchic groups, but not without sacrificing the liberal vision of independent capitalist development. The penetration of foreign capital resulted in its fusion with and/or subordination of Mexican precapitalist oligarchies and capitalist groups in such a way as to inhibit the potential for long-range viable growth. The result was a particularly violent process of primitive accumulation through the expropriation of peasants' lands and incipient industrialization in light consumer goods production that generated widespread misery. Although the Porfirian state proved in the end too fragile to sustain economic growth, it nonetheless provided institutions and apparatuses that would be refined and extended through the Mexican Revolution. One of these was a public school system, which, although deficient in extension and penetration (70 percent of the Mexican population was still illiterate in 1910), was nonetheless highly explicit in its intent to create an efficient and pliable modern labor force to meet the needs of private capital accumulation.[5] Wrote Justo Sierra, the architect of Mexico's public school system:[6]

> *Here there is not a class on the move except the bourgeoisie. . . . It absorbs all the active elements of inferior groups. . . . With the individual entrepreneur creating wealth and work, the Indian held back by his community, the lazy campesino, and the impoverished dreamer will disappear [Córdova, 1973: 75].*

While the entrepreneur would create "national conditions of work," the school would form proper values and habits (punctuality, obedience to authority, love of work, and patriotism) in the labor force.

Women were included in the educational projection of the Porfiriato, for in a general effort to substitute "scientific" values for superstitious ones, to eradicate "traditional" attitudes toward work thought to be bound to the Church, and to eliminate the pilfering of wages at Church fiestas also associated with drunkenness, the mind set of women, who were seen as bearers of traditional Catholicism, had to be secularized. In a very real sense, the state through public education was engaged in a process of transferring loyalty from the Church to the nation-state and its economic base. It incorporated many of the values taught by the Church (restraint, submission, obedience, and modesty) into a new ideology compatible with the needs and values of a bourgeois elite that emphasized work, discipline, savings, and national loyalty. The bourgeoisie called for an economic and secular organization of family life. The education of women was intended to strengthen their primary role in the home as replacers of labor power and transmitters of values. In elementary schools, they learned home economics while boys learned manual arts.

Certain vocational training was opened to women of the petty-bourgeois and artisan sectors in areas that were extensions of their role in the home. Schoolteaching, which was an unprestigious and poorly remunerated job in this period, was opened to women. A number of industrial and commercial schools offered training in clerical work and extensions of household industries such as sewing, cooking, hatmaking, interior decorating, and artificial flower making. Although these schools were designed to provide some training that could supplement the role of woman in home and marriage, they were as much concerned with increasing the efficiency and moral organization of the household. As Justo Sierra told the students of the Escuela Miguel Lerdo de Tejeda, the family was the cornerstone of the stability of the nation:

> *In all Mexican schools we are forming men and women for the home; this is our supreme goal. Doing it, we believe firmly that we are performing a service beyond comparison with any in the benefit of the Republic. . . . The educated woman will be truly one for the home; she will be the companion and the collaborator of man in the formation of the family. That is what we want and that is what you are being so firmly morally prepared for. . . . You are called to form souls, to sustain the soul of your husband; for this reason, we educate you. Niña querida, do not turn feminist in our midst. . . . No, you and ourselves are mutually complementary; we form a single personality called to continue the perpetual creation of the Patria [Sierra, 1948: 329].*

Some ambiguity wracked the expansion of women's education, for Sierra confused it with feminism, which he regarded as a threat to family structure. He essentially wished women to confine their activities to the home:

> *While they win the bread, you take charge of the order, tranquility, and well-being of the home and above all contribute with your own superior bread to the formation of souls; this is the supreme task. . . . Let the man struggle with political questions and write the laws; you struggle the good struggle, that of the sentiments and form souls, which is better than forming laws [Sierra, 1948: 329].*

Thus Sierra expressed cognizance of the essential role of woman not only in the home as a refurbisher of male labor power, but also as a bearer of values and ideology compatible with social stability, that is, she "formed souls." When he stated that women were immensely superior to men "in moral life, in the world of feelings and sacrifice" (Sierra, 1948:

329), he reflected not only a traditional Catholic approach to women but most likely an emerging Victorian ideology of family life emanating primarily from British social thought in which Sierra was immersed. Although the notions of saving, self-control, and work had been basic to the bourgeois family in its early years of development and had involved husband, wife, and children in a productive process in which home and workshop or office were usually one, the development of the factory system in the late eighteenth and early nineteenth centuries in Europe had effected a separation between home and work in which the productive function of women and children was lost. Although the material basis for patriarchy (management of the productive unit) ceased to exist, the patriarchal bourgeois family, in addition to its role of reproducing the dominant class and guaranteeing its inheritance, continued to perform ideological functions that Victorian writers began to articulate and to mystify. In its authoritarian structure, which inhibited the freedom and development of women and children, the family[7] nurtured values (that is, discipline and obedience) necessary to the reproduction of social order. The family came also to be regarded as the only refuge of love and security in an increasingly brutal and competitive world—an extension of and refuge for the individualized male. Portraying women as the fount of purity, goodness, and love, Victorian writers apologized for the lack of these values in the male world while extolling the male world as the epitome of reason and progress.[8] As W.E.H. Leckey wrote in his *History of European Morals:*

> Morally the general superiority of women over men is, I think, unquestionable. . . . Men excel in energy, self-reliance, perseverance, and magnanimity: women in humility, gentleness, modesty, and endurance [quoted in Figes, 1971: 114].

Moral superiority of woman was thus linked with her association with submissive and emotional values, her withdrawal from the public world and lack of understanding of it, and her role in uncritically reproducing it. In its authoritarian structure and associated values, the family was increasingly regarded as the center and archetype of the bourgeois state (Figes, 1971: 105-106, 110).

The notion of restructuring working-class family life to conform with this bourgeois model was only partially articulated in the Porfiriato. Reacting with moral indignation and alarm to the disintegration and proletarianization of artisan and peasant migrant families (increased subjection to the "depraved" atmosphere of the factory, the rise in prostitution, and the growing number of begging and unattended children), educators suggested night schools and work schools where workers of both sexes and all ages could learn habits of civilized behavior and industrial skills. The primary focus for the working class, however, remained the primary school, where the attempt to usurp the family's socializing function was more blatant for these children than it was for those of other social classes. The school taught manners; it intended to initiate good taste; and utilizing models of efficiently organized and amply comfortable white, "middle-class" homes, it urged children to transform the moral and material deficiencies of their homes. The food they ate, the clothes they wore, the houses they lived in—all came in for moral reprobation in an effort to strengthen the family's function as the generator of a healthy and disciplined labor force (Secretaría de Instrucción Pública y Bellas Artes, 1912: 485). In an era when casual unions and prostitution were material necessities for many women and when sex education and birth control were taboo in the dominant society, the school insisted that only civilly registered marriages formed moral unions. This thrust was more a reaction to changing social conditions than it was a coherent plan for restructuring family life. In fact, the school system was unable to extend itself effectively to large numbers of working people.

Simultaneously, the Mexican trade union movement began to raise cries of alarm and protest at the factory system's assault on family life. Until 1906, this movement was largely dominated by artisans to whom family life had conformed to the incipient bourgeois model inclusive of emphasis upon values of savings, work, and patriarchy.[9] The expulsion of wives and daughters from the home and into the factory disrupted family structure just as increased industrialization undercut the productive function of the family unit. The fact that women in the textile, clothing, and tobacco industries endured not only excessively long hours of work and abysmally low wages but sexual exploitation at the hands of male employers and managers deeply angered the male-dominated workers' movement. They called for increased educational opportunities for women at once to assist in moralizing them, secularizing their values, and upgrading their skills. Essentially, the union movement suggested that women should be in the home, the patriarchal structure of which the artisans wished to preserve. At this juncture then, there was a compatibility between the ideology of bourgeois educators and the ideology of male artisans in relation to the role of women in society, although the workers' movement sought to mitigate exploitation by a class whose interests the educators represented. This contradiction became clearer around 1906 when the unionization of industrial workers in railroads, mining, and textiles brought forward a new militancy and a more profound sense of class consciousness. In this movement, singular women played leadership roles reflecting their politicization through the workplace.

THE MEXICAN REVOLUTION: LIMITS OF FEMINISM

The immediate cause of the Mexican Revolution was the inability of the Porfirian political system to respond to the reformist demands of oligarchic groups increasingly excluded from the Díaz political equation and in many cases negatively affected by the economic crisis, which beginning in 1905 challenged the viability of the Porfirian model of dependent capitalist development. The underlying cause of the Revolution was inherent in the capitalist model: the violence basic to the process of primitive capital accumulation through land expropriation and the resultant misery it created both in the countryside and the city, to which the state refused to respond except at the level of repression. Correspondingly, the increasing monopolization of wealth in the hands of a few (native and foreign) not only alienated sectors of the elite, but also the petty bourgeoisie[10] of rural and urban property owners, businessmen and farmers, urban professionals and bureaucrats—those whose possibilities for mobility were limited by the increasingly closed nature of the regime. Although precipitated by alienated oligarchic groups in their political challenge to Díaz between 1904 and 1910, the Mexican Revolution was an explosion of diverse and fragmented discontent on the part of peasants, workers, and the petty bourgeoisie.

The Mexican Revolution was bourgeois not in its class base, but in its trajectory. Neither the working class (small, recently organized, and ideologically young) nor the peasantry (dispersed, divided, and generally parochial in its demand for land) could definitively capture hegemony that passed instead to leadership within the Constitutional Army. This leadership was of petty-bourgeois origin, and despite a diversity of ideological viewpoints, it operated consistently within a capitalist framework. The possibility of anything other than a bourgeois revolution ended in 1915 when, in order to defeat the peasant forces of Pancho Villa and Emiliano Zapata, the Constitutional Army allied itself with the organized workers' movement in Mexico City and thus established tentative hegemony over both workers and peasants. Although after 1915 worker and peasant mobilization grew in ideological sophistication and organizational capacity to create a situation of continuing class conflict, class struggle developed within a scenario in which petty-bourgeois leadership attempted to dominate (especially in its capacity as a political-bureaucracy) and to elaborate a new state structure, which would at once carry out limited social reform while providing a greater regulation of capital for purposes of more rapid and more nationally oriented accumulation and growth.[11] The extension of the new state implied an attempt to usurp family functions (health, education, protection) and to define a more specific economic and ideological role for the family. Petty bourgeois educators—many of them women—articulated a fairly clear notion of the stabilizing and depoliticizing effects to be won from the development of a patriarchal-bourgeois family model within the working class. At the purely ideological level, the Mexican state's efforts in this area were probably assisted by the absence of strong countervailing forces in the feminist and working-class movements.

Events in the Yucatan between 1915 and 1924 illustrate both the possibilities and limitations of feminism in the Mexican Revolution. General Salvador Alvarado, a member of the Constitutional Army and governor of the state from 1915 to 1918, was a vigorous reformer within a capitalist framework. His belief in individual freedom and competition led him not only to abolish debt peonage on *haciendas*, but to champion the liberation of women from religious, male, and economic servitude. He abolished prostitution and legislated contracts for female domestic servants—one of the most exploited sectors of women's labor. He advocated women's rights to divorce, political participation, and education, inclusive of increased vocational training and admission to the professions.

In his labor reforms, which were incorporated into the Mexican Constitution of 1917, he laid a skeletal base for the survival of family life: the right of workers to organize and bargain, minimum wages and maximum hours, limits and protection of women's and child labor, maternity leaves, and rest periods for nursing mothers. Alvarado envisioned a paternalistic welfare state that would protect a controlled trade union movement and arbitrate conflicts between labor and capital, while at the same time guaranteeing capital the climate it needed for expansion. Aware of the need to subordinate labor to capital, he called for workers' restraint:

> *I am firmly convinced that if we cannot achieve an equilibrium between capital and labor, industry and production will not be possible . . . with the immediate consequence of desolation and ruin. Because of this, I have always advised workers to moderation, savings, and self-control [Córdova, 1973: 210].*

In developing his idea of the disciplined worker, Alvarado suggested the importance of the working-class family as the primary focus of emotional life and a consuming unit in the expanding market economy. Placing his hopes in his children's education as a path to mobility, the worker would implicitly forestall his own demands upon the system. Seeking to convince workers of the advantages to be gained from an education, Alvarado described an educated, well-paid worker capable of sustaining a "free and happy home":

> *Once he begins to enjoy something of the happiness he deserves and obtains a more equitable part of the wealth to which his labor has contributed, he will feel that life is something more than eating tortillas . . . sleeping in a frayed hammock, dressing in . . . coarse cloth, and languishing ignorant of hope and the good. Spurred by the new stimulus, he will increase his needs. He will become civilized and feeling needs . . . , he will desire better clothes, better shoes, better food; he will have commodities he never knew. . . . Raising his moral level, he will concentrate on his duty to the family. Anxious to educate his children, to feel noble pride in seeing them enjoy even more fully the benefits of life [Mediz Bolio, 1968: 17].*

Alvarado's approach to women was class-based. In 1915, he called upon *gente decente* (middle- and upper-strata women) to participate in Mexico's first feminist conference. In suggesting educational and political means for their advancement, he encountered real conservatism. With the exception of a radical minority, these women were reluctant to struggle for political rights, arguing that Mexican women—especially the poor—were unprepared to vote. They further clung to the sanctity of woman's domestic, subordinate role (El Primer Congreso Feminista de Yucatán, 1916: 98-109). This attitude, which was widespread among educated women, acted not only as a brake on the spread of feminist consciousness to the working class, it contributed to the transfer of the bourgeois family model to the poor. In the midst of social upheaval, the majority of these women opted to civilize poor women rather than to liberate them. As in Mexico City, proper Yucatecan ladies undertook a charitable crusade among poor women, lecturing them on domestic economy, hygiene, anti-alcoholism, and morality (Mediz Bolío, 1968: 21-23).

A militant minority of petty-bourgeois women in the Yucatán moved into the Partido Socialista del Sureste (PSS), a quasi-socialist mass movement of urban and rural workers and peasants.[12] Operating on the principle that "the liberation of the worker is the task of the worker himself," the PSS surged to the fore in Yucatecan politics after Alvarado's departure in 1918 under the leadership of Felipe Carrillo Puerto, who was governor of the state from 1922 until his assassination in 1924 by right-wing elements of the Constitutional Army. Engaged in a near civil war with the *henequen* owners and their allies, the PSS, organized into Ligas de Resistencia, not only carried out labor actions on plantations, *ejidos*, and in the cities, it developed an elaborate structure of "mutual conservation and defense" deeply rooted in people's lives. The Ligas penetrated into rural communities where, made up of local residents, they were responsible for land distribution, production, consumption, marketing, health, schooling, and political struggle. Based upon sentiments of workers' democracy and self-actuation, the PSS used education to awaken class consciousness and militancy.

Within this context, the PSS made several advances in relation to women's rights. Not only was schooling coeducational with its defanaticizing role focused to a large extent on women, the PSS involved the direct participation of men and women in both production and political struggle. The party recognized the special oppression of women. As Miguel Ruz said at a PSS congress:

> *Men have suffered the tyranny of capital and the laws but women have not only suffered the tyranny of capital and the law but the tyranny of husband and parents and many times children. Previous governments have not given importance to the rights of women as human beings. In these hours which are so firmly ending prejudices, it is a human duty to allow women to participate in the cause of their revindication [Partido Socialista del Sureste, 1919: 60-61].*

In what appears to have been confluence between radical petty-bourgeois women and working-class and peasant women, autonomous feminist leagues formed around issues such as political rights and equality. They struggled to ameliorate working conditions, including those of market vendors, and in their campaigns around health, they put forward the necessity of birth control (Rico, 1922: 26; Rascón, 1975: 159).

However, the reluctance on the part of male PSS leadership to fully accept women's equality revealed a general lack of feminist consciousness in even the most progressive sectors of the Mexican revolutionary struggle. In 1921, when women demanded voice and vote in the PSS congress, the presiding committee was unconvinced that they were sufficiently anti-clerical to exercise their rights (*Historia Obrera*, 1975: 48). There is some suggestion that an exaggerated sense of anti-clericalism was one of several ideological weaknesses in the Mexican workers' movement that not only inhibited workers from seeing the overall political potential of women but also that of *campesinos*, and often led to compromises with governments that did not objectively represent the interests of the working class (see Basurto, 1975: 167-168, 280). Following its alliance with the Constitutional forces against the organized peasantry in 1915, the Mexican Labor movement fragmented. Its strong organization was the class-collaborationist Confederación Regional de Obreras Mexicanos (CROM), which derived its strength from the support it received from the state; this strength it used to weaken more radical, independent workers' organizations. The outstanding women militants of the Mexican Revolution functioned within its most radical sectors that never enjoyed official support: the PSS, the Zapatista movement, the anarchist Confederación General de Trabajo (CGT), and the Communist Party. Many of these women formed the nucleus of a working-women's movement that emerged in the 1930s but was not strong enough to counterbalance those women allied with the emerging state.[13] The weakness of working-class feminism in the Mexican Revolution corresponded both to the weakness of the Mexican workers' movement within the overall context of the revolution and its limited feminist consciousness.

THE STATE, WOMEN,
AND THE FAMILY (1915-1928)

Although the Mexican revolutionary state did not begin to take shape until 1917, a general approach to education was earlier laid out by petty-bourgeois revolutionaries for whom a vast extension of public schooling was to serve as an instrument of social control and integration and as a means of training an increasingly differentiated and hierarchically structured labor force for advancing industry. Unlike their Porfirian counterparts, revolutionary educators focused on poor women in their response to the general social upheaval of the day. In 1915, Felix F. Palavicini, acting official in charge of education under Venustiano Carranza (head of the Constitutional Army), was especially fearful of the socialization un-schooled mothers would give to their children:

Children abandoned to the immorality of the gutter, the filth of the factories, and the temptation of vice will be the men who form our society of tomorrow, citizens and a people sovereign by law . . . .

From the pallid lips of wives and mothers will come the first phrases of children emerging in a seething oration of hate. They will grow with incongruent impulses, without discipline or orientation. . . . While the disciples of Max Stirner and Nietzsche await the triumph of a superman, a

> stronger force can emerge from the union of proletarians who organize,
> form unions, and join hands as a single strong body sustaining the torch
> which illuminates consciences and the hatchet which breaks their chains.
> If this force surprises us as enemies rather than as allies, we will be the
> losers [Palavicini, 1910: 12-15].

In his concern, Palavicini was assisted by a core of educated women who had emerged from or worked within Porfirian women's schools. In 1915, they reached out to open technical education to poor women as a means of upgrading their skills, curbing prostitution, and reforming family structure. Such education was to

> aid [la mujer pobre] by theoretical-practical training to save her from the
> dangers into which she stumbles and habilitate her to duly fulfill her social
> duties as well as her duties as a woman of the home [Secretaría de Instruc-
> ción Pública y Bellas Artes, 1914: 126].

Many *gente decente* women participated in the Universidad Popular, Mexico's first university extension program created in 1912 to pacify and incorporate the capital's workers, then in a state of growing consciousness and agitation. Wrote Laura Mendez de Cuenca, a leading educator and participant in the Universidad Popular:

> If we ignore woman leaving her in . . . ignorance we would establish in
> **the Mexican home a regrettable disequilibrium tending to multiply marital**
> disasters so unfortunately abundant in our society. If someone is in need of
> education it is the woman. Her mission is to raise and care for the family;
> she is the exquisite engraver of society. The man sustains the home
> materially—he represents the physical force of the home . . . but the
> woman, wife and mother, nourishes the soul of her children and strength-
> ens that of her husband with wise teachings and prudent advice [Universi-
> dad Popular Mexicana, 1916: 188-189].

The instruction of women in household duties and efficiency, hygiene, and childcare, had its counterpart in general lectures to men and women on the importance of averting strikes, practicing savings, and respecting law and work. The disciplined working-class home could presumably sustain itself on a minimum income. The purpose of the Universidad Popular was to divert the public life of the working class from streets, taverns, and politics, and to orient it in defined directions, that is, lectures on culture and social organization and the formation of choirs and sports teams. Part of this scheme involved an effort to refocus working-class life on the family as the primary unit of association and emotional attachment. This thrust deepened in the 1920s with the Secretaría de Educación Pública's organization of workers' cultural centers and night schools.

In the 1920s a larger number of schools opened to women for training in clerical work, home economics, and domestic-related industries such as sewing, soap, and artificial flower making, cooking, toy and shoe-making. These, as well as night centers for working women, were designed more explicitly to remove women from factory production— preparing them for household work while providing them with a trade they could practice independently at home such as sewing, embroidery, or candy-making (Secretaría de Educación Pública, 1922: 238; 1923: 81, 109-112; 1923-24: 111-117, 133-36, 300-302; 1927c: 69-62). This morally motivated trend suggested an attempt to strengthen woman's primary role in the home as a replacer of labor power while marginalizing her participation in the labor force. It in fact suggested a return to domestic piecework, one of the most exploitative forms of work in which women had been engaged. The trend was further strengthened by limiting skilled training for increasingly capital-intensive industry to men.

Women's vocational training reflected and reinforced a class-stratified society and woman's pervasive subordination within it. Different curricula were offered to middle-income women in homemaking and clerical work, to domestic servants in household industries, and to working-class women in household work and home industries for market sale. The product models and consumer values promoted by the schools reflected those of the bourgeoisie with the consequence that less affluent women would be encouraged to desire and to subordinate themselves to such models and values. Annual exhibits at women's schools included richly furnished homes replete with crystal flower bowls, tiffany lamps, fine linen, and fashions the press called "chic" (Secretaría de Educación Pública, 1923-24: 134, 296-312; 1925b: 136-137). Further, the industries open to women, whether in fashions, cooking, or beauty parlors, were almost entirely designed to please men and so tended to perpetuate the subordinate role of women in society. The type of work was often individual or confined to the small shop such as the beauty parlor or clothing store, and thus was not propitious to the development of political consciousness. Even if women worked in production, because the school emphasized their primary role in the home and defined for them an apolitical and submissive role, their potential for politicization through work might be limited.

More than simply returning women to the home, educators saw the need to restructure working-class family life. Woman educators were concerned with increasing the economic efficiency of the worker's home to perform the double function of sustaining labor on a minimum income and internalizing values such as subordination, discipline, and efficiency of time and space, which the worker needed in factory production. In lectures in schools and over the government radio station, home economics professors discussed the function of the housewife:

> *The head of the household has to be active; if she is lazy or indolent, there will never be enough time and her tasks will always be behind, the meal will not be served when it should, the clothes will not be ready, and she will look dirty and disheveled. Nearly always these things arise from laziness and disorder. . . . In the home the lack of order is failure since without order, it is impossible to develop faculties and to form good habits; if the child is made to wash his face one day and stops doing it for three or four, to ask him again on the fifth day—and if he does not do it again for eight days—means he will not acquire the habit of washing himself [Secretaría de Educación Pública, 1926: 162].*

The educators portrayed the wife as a worker who had to efficiently balance the factors of time, work, and money to facilitate a regular performance of tasks with appropriate rest periods to avoid exhaustion. Such budgeting was not only essential to the economical organization of the home, but to the inculcation of proper values among family members:

> *Good schedules in the home produce exactitude and punctuality. The child learns to fulfill each of his obligations at the appointed hour and when he comes to govern himself, will be punctual and exact in all his acts. . . .*
>
> *When the schedule of the home does not exist or is badly regulated, the whole family is hurt and it is impossible to form good habits [Secretaría de Educación Pública, 1926: 164].*

As a worker, the housewife had to maintain her health:

> *The head of the house needs, above all, to have good health to support the tremendous fatigue and exhaustion her work produces; if she is sick and delicate, she must give most of her time to care of her health; her talent and good qualities are cancelled in great part. Her character becomes bitter because of her sufferings and a good part of family income must be spent on medicine [Secretaría de Educación Pública, 1926: 162].*

To nourish working men and raise children, her home had to be healthy:

> *To live normally man needs solar light. In darkness, he gets sick, his muscles lose their vitality, his life is altered, his character modified and soon anemia sets in . . . the majority of microbes which breed contagious dis-*

eases . . . grow in darkness and produce weakened, depressed individuals, incapable of action [Secretaría de Educación Pública, 1926: 170].

To allow for "rest," "inspiration," and "tranquility," the home had to be well decorated, clean, and attractive (Secretaría de Educación Pública, 1926: 173).

To a degree, the notion of woman's work as time-oriented prepared her for her increasing role as a consumer of market-made household goods. The lecturers argued that the housewife should economize her efforts "since if machines become worn out from continual work, the delicate organism of woman is even more affected" (Secretaría de Educación Pública, 1926: 166). Her aids were refrigerators, sewing machines, and vacuum cleaners; as poor women could not afford these, they could purchase ammonia, borax, bicarbonate of soda, and other aids. Above all, lecturers insisted upon the importance of savings. Poor people could survive on a minimum income if they mended and dyed old clothes, bought vegetables only in season, and staples in quantity. Concluded the professor:

Ojalá, Señoras, amas de casa, that my poor suggestions are well-taken by some of you that they serve to alleviate the heavy task weighing on male heads of families who looking toward the future struggle to realize the great task of constructing the Patria by bettering the home [Secretaría de Educación Pública, 1925b: 228].

This approach led to a mystification both of household labor and of the family as the central focus of emotional and social life in place of class and community. Gabriela Mistral, the Chilean poetess who taught in the Escuela del Hogar Gabriela Mistral founded in 1922, wrote a book for Mexican women to "form mothers—the only reason for [women's] being on earth" (Mistral, 1923: 8), in which the notion of transferring a bourgeois family model to the working class reached its highest level of ideological statement. She reprinted from John Ruskin, ideologue of the Victorian family, a passage on the home as refuge from a public world of conflict and competition:

It is a place of peace: the refuge not only against all aggravation, but against all error, doubt, and division. In so far as it is not this, it is not a home; in so far as the anxieties of exterior life penetrate it, and the society of the inconscient soul, the anonymous and loveless soul of the external world is admitted by husband or wife, it ceases to be a home; it is only a part of the world you have left and where you have lit the fire [Mistral, 1923: 17].

The home became by implication a compensation for the pains and exploitation inflicted by the world of work. If it became the primary focus of love and emotion for the worker—and in essence an extension of his individualized consciousness—it could assist in divorcing him from politics; the solace and authoritarian structure of his home could offer compensation for the humiliation endured in work. This burden upon the family fell hard upon children but hardest upon women from whom it demanded submission and absorption of men's frustrations:

> *She ought to be patient, incorruptibly good, instinctive, infallibly wise— wise not for her own advantage, but through self-renunciation—wise not with the sin of insolent pride or absence of love, but with the impassioned nobility of modest sacrifice [Mistral, 1923: 19].*

The role of mother was to hide conflictive reality by constructing an order within the home that did not exist outside:

> *You establish a clear harmony between the chairs, the tables, the buffets . . . simple things . . . nothing disturbs this harmony as nothing disturbs the harmony of the universe [Mistral, 1923: 24].*

In addition to the wife's absorbing her husband's frustrations, wife and husband alike were obliged to suppress the conflicts of the adult world from children:

> *The disagreements, the discussion, the anger, all this world of inevitable contrarity, you must keep from the eyes of children . . . or you will force them to take sides which is equivalent to breaking the harmony of its affectivity [Mistral, 1923: 23].*

Underlying this romanticization was the legitimization of an authoritarian structure replicating a similar structure in the larger society and tending to repress questioning, creativity, critical thought, and conflict. From the woman this structure demanded submission, which Mistral mystified in a process of transferring Catholic values to the modern state:

> *In as many hours as has the day, you give*
> *although it be only a smile, a hand, a word of relief.*
> *In as many hours as has the day you seem like Him*
> *who is none but perpetual giving and diffusion.*
> *You should fall on your knees before the Father and say unto Him:*
> *Thank you because I can give, Father.*

Never will the shadow of impatience pass over me.
Truly it is worth more to give than to receive [Mistral, 1923: 203].

As the state attempted to define a specific role for the family, it simultaneously sought to absorb family functions such as socialization, health, protection, and other social services in such a way as to suggest an attempt to subordinate and limit the family as a source of authority, ideas, and independent thought and action. Thus in the extension of schools in the 1920s, the Secretaría de Educación Pública sought to organize parents to support the school but without giving them any say in what took place in the school (Secretaría de Educación Pública, 1925a: 24; 1928b: 292). Although in this period of Mexican history such a move may have stemmed specifically from the state's fear of the growing opposition of the Church to the revolution, this created disjuncture is typical of the expansion of public school systems. Further, the teacher was to instruct parents on the proper moral and economical home life for children (Secretaría de Educación Pública, 1925a: 25, 75; 1927a: 79, 81; 1927c: 282-283; 1928a; 12, 152, 157, 168, 202-203, 219, 260). In 1927, an effort was made to organize mothers' clubs by identifying their socializing role with patriotism. To be truly patriotic, however, the mother had to reform herself or "your children will lack this moral formation which will make them useful and vigorous citizens" (Secretaría de Educación Pública, 1927b: 180-181). The content of this reform involved instruction in childcare and household organization and narrowed political and social participation to the formation of choirs, drama clubs, savings associations, and cooperative sewing machine centers.

This effort to subordinate the family to the authority of the state and by implication to inflict or reinforce a sense of inferiority was apparent also in the extension of other social services. The beneficial school health service intruded upon the home to upgrade its hygiene. In 1925, a Protective Council for Children requested "patria potestad" over the "integral development" of childhood (Secretaría de Educación Pública, 1925a: 140). Seeking control over delinquent and unattended children and the right to place them in day-care centers and special homes, it bid also for the right to intervene in labor contracts negotiated between families and employers to see that the minor had a school certificate, a state medical certificate, and a safe job. The council proposed to introduce to the home the social worker who, equipped with a knowledge of hygiene, childcare, home economics, psychology, history, and civics, would provide "moral" education to the family to

channel people who need it in the direction of the good, alleviating hard-
ships, helping them to save themselves from frequent hostile situations with
others and their relatives by decorous and non-violent means; to stimulate
sentiments of dignity, love for others, and horror of vice, to persuade them
of the need to be less concerned with their personal benefit and more with
that of society. To develop in them the thought that the most humble work is
indispensable to life because it is a factor of progress, a cornerstone in the
enormous social fabric, and those who exercise it are as valuable to soci-
ety as those who dedicate themselves to activities considered higher [Se-
cretaría de Educación Pública, 1925b: 211-212].

This intervention was by implication an ideological act at once suggesting
the inferiority of the working-class home and the authority of the state and
its bourgeois representatives. While transmitting direct information
tending to legitimize a specific social order (instruction in history and
civics), to individualize the worker in his performance of a specific task
within a sanctified socioeconomic hierarchy, and to focus upon the family
as an extension of the atomized worker at the expense of the collective
experience of work and community, the social worker was to teach forms
of recreation that could be enjoyed in the home. In short, the extension of
social services by the state was not a neutral undertaking: it was ideologically loaded to mirror an existing class structure and to legitimize the
subordination of labor to capital, specifying at the same time an important but circumscribed role for the family in the reproduction of the social
relations of production.

CONCLUSION

In conclusion, the dissemination of ideology on the part of the state
does not guarantee its effective absorption by masses of people. Such absorption depends both upon material and ideological conditions. In a material sense, it depends upon the financial capability of the state to expand
its bureaucracies in such a way as to effectively disseminate ideology. It
depends also upon the material conditions of masses of people that effect
their ability to act within the ideology and to see its logic within their own
lives. For instance, at the material level, the public life of the poor could
not be privatized without drastic changes in economic structure: families
were interwoven in productive processes in rural villages, while in the
cities they were forced to interact with one another in crowded neighborhoods and tenements where their interaction was an important human

mechanism of survival and resistance. Ideological conditions are likewise important, that is, the strength and existence of ideological forces countering official messages. In this period of Mexican history, for example, the state lacked the political, economic, and labor power to accomplish the task it defined for itself, while the lives of people remained open to messages of the Church, union organizers, and rural activists as an outgrowth of the struggles provoked by the Mexican Revolution.

Between 1900 and 1940, the participation of women in Mexican industry declined from 76,542 to 34,041 (Keremitsis, 1976: 15). Although this change resulted from economic processes (the trend toward more capital-intensive industry), it also reflected political changes, that is, the organization of the trade union movement, the institution of laws limiting and protecting women's labor, and a variety of programs and policies on the part of the state including education, which especially at the vocational level limited skilled industrial jobs to men and sought to return women to the home, to domestic piecework, and to marginal sectors of the economy. Although the above qualifications as to the effective reception and internalization of ideology must always be considered (in much greater depth than this essay permits), it seems important to argue that in examining the increasingly important role of woman in the home as a replacer of labor power, one must take into account political forces and events, including ideological institutions such as education and other state social services, which, in this case, sought to legitimize woman's subordinate domestic role as necessary to the process of capital accumulation. Woman's role in the home as a reproducer of labor power is not simply economically functional; it has an ideological component; that is, her role in the family replicates a structure of authority and subordination that deepens with capitalism. Woman's political conservatism stems not only from the isolated nature of her household work, but also from ideological forces operating on her.

NOTES

1. This thesis is extremely well argued by Larguía and Dumoulin (1975).

2. For a discussion of recent participation of women in the U.S. labor force, see Braverman (1974: 377-409).

3. In no sense has this process in Mexico been as complete as it has been in the United States. The level of capital accumulation limits both the state's capacity to absorb these functions effectively and the economy's total usurpation of the family's productive function (for instance in Mexico today many rural families, although they function within a capitalist economy, carry out productive functions as a unit).

4. By *feminism* I understand a political movement and/or ideology that recognizes the special oppression of women in society. Bourgeois feminism stems from the bourgeoisie and petty bourgeoisie: it is designed to facilitate the greater participation of women in bourgeois society. It implicitly and explicitly legitimizes the subordination of labor to capital. Socialist feminism understands the special oppression of women within the context of an analysis of capitalism and seeks to overcome it through a revolutionary movement led by the working class and aimed at eliminating the subordination of labor to capital. Because a socialist-feminist movement was only incipiently and partially developed through the Mexican Revolution, it is perhaps most accurate to refer to feminism as it emerged in the Mexican working-class movement as *working-class feminism*. Further research on the Partido Socialista del Sureste and especially on the women's movement of the 1930s is necessary before a final statement on ideological orientation is possible.

5. For a more detailed analysis of public schooling in this period within this framework, see Vaughan (1975).

6. As a congressman in the 1880s, Sierra sought approval of obligatory public instruction and the adoption of a well-defined, singular school program. He served on numerous commissions for the expansion of education and played a leading role in the first educational congresses in 1889 and 1890. In 1901, he took charge of the educational branch of the Secretaría de Justicia y Instrucción Pública y Bellas Artes.

7. For further analysis of the Victorian family, see Figes (1971), Henrik Ibsen, (1972: 179-188), John Stuart Mill (1972: 162-178), and Zaretsky (1973: 90-106).

8. Charles Darwin argued "scientifically" that men had greater intellectual powers of reasoning, imagination, and worldly management than had women, who, in addition to greater tenderness and less selfishness, had greater powers of intuition, perception, and perhaps imitation, which he identified as "characteristics of the lower races, and therefore of a past and lower state of civilization" (Figes, 1971: 111-112).

9. For an interesting and lengthy examination of the position of the nineteenth-century workers' movement on women and the family, see Centro de Estudios Históricos del Movimiento Obrero Mexicano (1975). For an analytical framework within which to read these documents, see Basurto (1975).

10. The term *petty bourgeoisie* is being used here to define a social category that came to play an extremely important role in the Mexican Revolution because of the particular historical point of capitalist development in Mexico, the destruction of the Porfirian state and temporary weakening of the bourgeoisie (foreign and national) in the Revolution, and the failure of peasants and/or workers to capture the Revolution. Strictly speaking, the petty bourgeoisie are small producers whose control over their means of production is being threatened by expanding capitalism. In the case of Mexico, it was not only these who participated in the Revolution, but also those small and medium-size capitalists who wanted to expand their properties, and an extremely important professional-bureaucratic category that had expanded as a result of economic and state growth in the late nineteenth century. I use the term petty bourgeoisie to include these different groups for lack of a more precise term. In relation to professionals and bureaucrats who made education and social service policy, the term is useful because their ideology was basically petty-bourgeois (a contradictory defense of small property, open competition, and private ownership) even if their relationship to production was not.

11. It seems important here to distinguish between the expansion of the state in the United States at the turn of the century and the expansion of the state in Mexico as a result of the revolution. In the United States, the state expanded with the transition from laissez-faire to monopoly capitalism: it assumed a greater role in the regulation of the anarchy inherent in capitalism, protection of the expansion of U.S. capital abroad, and in functions

of cooptation and social control (education, social services, welfare, regulatory labor laws, and so forth). In contrast, the Mexican state in the late nineteenth century had played a more direct role in capital accumulation than its U.S. counterpart of the same period. In the Mexican Revolution, the state vastly expanded its functions for purposes of facilitating and redirecting capital accumulation and for purposes of social control. The hope was that such a state apparatus could counter the domination of foreign capital through a renegotiation of the terms of foreign participation to effect an "equal partnership" between Mexican and foreign capital. This approach failed to appreciate the competitive edge accruing to the United States as it entered the era of monopoly capital and the very strength of the expanded U.S. state in promoting the interests of imperialism. A series of accommodations following the Mexican Revolution laid the foundations for a new set of imperialist relations between Mexico and the United States. However, it is important to note for purposes of this paper that state expansion in Mexico in the field of education and social services drew heavily from North American examples. In both countries, the state had to control the working class while increasing its productivity. In state education and social service programs, the Mexicans adopted North American techniques, programs, approaches, and even materials. Many of their implemented programs were inspired by direct visits and study in the United States, participation in North American and Pan-American Union conferences as well as League of Nations meetings.

12. The most complete study on the PSS to date is that of Francisco José Paoli Bolío (1976). See also Bustillos Carillo (1959: 207-247), Rico (1922: 7, 39, 117), and the Partido Socialista del Sureste (1919).

13. For further reading on these women, see *Historia Obrera* (1975: entire issue) and Rascón (1975).

REFERENCES

Basurto, Jorge
    1975 *El proletariado industrial en México, 1850-1930*. Mexico: Instituto de Investigaciones Sociales, UNAM.
Braverman, Harry
    1974 *Labor and Monopoly Capital: the Degradation of Work in the Twentieth Century*. New York: Monthly Review Press.
Bustillos Carrillo, Antonio
    1959 *Yucatán al servicio de la patria y la revolución*. Mexico: Casa Ramirez, Editores.
Centro de Estudios Históricos del Movimiento Obrero Mexicano
    1975 *La mujer y el movimiento obrero mexicano en el siglo XIX. Antología de la prensa obrera*. Mexico: CEHSMO.
Córdova, Arnaldo
    1973 *La ideología de la revolución mexicana. La formación del nuevo régimen*. Mexico: Ediciones Era.
Figes, Eva
    1971 *Patriarchal Attitudes*. New York: Fawcett World Library.
Historia Obrera (Mexico)
    1975 Number 5 (June).

Ibsen, Henrik
  1972 "The Doll's House," pp. 179-188 in M. Schneir (ed.) *Feminism: The Essential Historical Writings*. New York: Random House.
Keremitsis, Dawn
  1976 "Women workers in the Mexican Revolution, 1910-1940: advance or retreat?" (unpublished)
Larguía, Isabel and John Dumoulin
  1975 "Aspects of the condition of women's labor." *NACLA's Latin America and Empire Report* 9 (September): 4-13.
Mediz Bolío, Antonio
  1968 *Salvador Alvarado*. Mexico: Secretaría de Educación Pública.
Mill, John Stuart
  1972 "The subjection of women," pp. 162-178 in M. Schneir (ed.) *Feminism: The Essential Historical Writings*. New York: Random House.
Mistral, Gabriela
  1923 *Lecturas para mujeres*. Mexico: Secretaría de Educación Pública.
Palavicini, Felix F.
  1910 *Problemas de la educación*. Valencia: F. Sempere y Compañia, Editores.
Paoli Bolío, Francisco José
  1976 "El partido socialista del sureste y la revolución mexicana." Mexico. (unpublished)
Partido Socialista del Sureste
  1918 *Tierra y libertad. Bases que discutieron y aprobaron el primer congreso obrero socialista celebrado en la ciudad de Motul, estado de Yucatán, para todas las ligas de resistencia del Partido Socialista de Yucatán*. Mérida: Talleres Tipográficos del Gobierno del Estado.
Primer Congreso Feminista
  1916 *El primer congreso feminista de Yucatán, convocado por el C. gobernador y comandante militar del estado, Gral. Don Salvador Alvarado*. Mérida: Talleres Tipográficos del "Ateneo Peninsular."
Rico, Juan
  1922 *La huelga de junior*. Mérida.
Rascón, Maria Antonieta
  1975 "La mujer y la lucha social," pp. 139-174 in Elena Urrutía, *Imagen y realidad de la mujer*. Mexico: SepSetentas.
Schneir, Miriam (ed.)
  1972 *Feminism: The Essential Historical Writings*. New York: Random House.
Secretaría de Educación Pública
  1922 *Boletín*, 1, 3 (January).
  1923 *Boletín*, 1, 4.
  1923-1924 *Boletín*. 1, 5 and 6.
  1925a *Boletín*. 4, 8 (November, 1925).
  1925b *Boletín*. 4, 9 and 10 (November-December).
  1926 *Boletín*. 5, 6 (June).
  1927a *Boletín*. 6, 3 (March).
  1927b *Boletín*. 6, 4 (April).
  1927c *Boletín*. 6, 6 (June).
  1928a *Boletín*. 7, 1 (January).
  1928b *Boletín*. 7, 4 (April).

Secretaría de Instruccíon Pública y Bellas Artes
    1912 *Congreso nacional de educación primaria. Antecedentes, actas, debates y reso-
    luciones*, Vol. 1. Mexico: Secretaría de Instrucción Pública y Bellas Artes.
    1914 *Boletín de Educación* 1 (September).
Sierra, Justo
    1948 *Obras completas, La educación nacional*, Vol. 7. Mexico: UNAM.
Universidad Popular Mexicana
    1916 *Boletín de la Universidad Popular Mexican*, Vol. 2. Mexico: Universidad Popu-
    lar Mexicana.
Vaughan, Mary Kay
    1975 "Education and class in the Mexican Revolution." *Latin American Perspectives* 2
    (Summer): 17-33.
Zaretsky, Eli
    1973 "Capitalism, the family and personal life: part one." *Socialist Revolution* 4 (Sum-
    mer): 90-106.

3

Mexico
The Limits of State Autonomy

by
*Nora Hamilton**

The predominant role of the state in advanced capitalist societies as well as so-called Third World countries has been widely discussed in Marxist literature (Miliband, 1969; Murray, 1971; O'Connor, 1973; Warren, 1972; Quijano, 1972; Ianni, 1974; Pompermayer and Smith, 1973; see also the journal *Kapitalistate*, and the Winter 1974 issue of *Politics and Society*). There is considerable disagreement among these studies with respect to such questions as the social basis of the state, the distinction between class power and state power, the mechanisms of class-state interaction, and the relative autonomy of the state (particularly in postcolonial societies) and its consequent role in shaping the social formation that emerges. Rather than discussing these differences, which have been analyzed and debated elsewhere (for example, Miliband, 1969, 1973; Poulantzas, 1969; Wolfe, 1974; Sardei-Biermann et al., 1973; Alavi, 1972; Girling, 1973), the following article proposes to draw upon them in an attempt to construct a generalized model of the state in advanced capitalist and dependent societies. This model will in turn serve as a basis for examining the interpretations of the state that emerged from the Mexican Revolution of 1910-1917 and particularly the conceptualization of the autonomous state that appeared to guide the program of the Cárdenas government (1934-1940).

An examination of the state in Mexico must take into account the apparent paradox of the Mexican Revolution and of Mexico's subsequent development. As stated by Roger Hanson in no major Latin American country has the government done more for the new industrial, commercial, and agricultural elite, nor less for the lowest 25 percent of society—despite Mexico's being the only Latin American country to undergo a

---

*Nora Hamilton is Associate Professor at the University of Southern California. This article was written during the process of a research project on the Mexican state that was subsequently published as *The Limits of State Autonomy: Post-Revolutionary Mexico* (Princeton University Press) and in Spanish as *Mexico: Los límites de la autonomia del Estado* (Ediciones Era).

profound social revolution during the first half of this century (1971: 87-88). An important element of this revolution was a conceptualization of the state as an autonomous entity that would utilize its power on behalf of the downtrodden groups and classes of Mexico—a conceptualization that was to some extent realized in the administration of Lázaro Cárdenas during the 1930s. It is a tentative proposition of this study that the contradictions inherent in this conceptualization of the state, and in its attempted realization within the context of a dependent, incipiently capitalist system, explain at least in part the divergence of the present system from that contemplated in the ideology of the revolution and the program of the Cárdenas administration.

SOME PROPOSITIONS REGARDING THE STATE IN CAPITALIST AND UNDERDEVELOPED SOCIETIES

According to Marx and Engels, the state first developed in Asiatic society with the original function of safeguarding common interests; with the development of classes it becomes an instrument for maintaining a system of production beneficial to a few and subjugating subordinate classes or groups, while ostensibly mediating the conflict between dominant and subordinate classes (Moore, 1957: 17-20). The social bases of the state constitute those groups, classes, or sectors that benefit from this production system and therefore from its preservation and rationalization. In general terms, then, within class societies, the state may be defined as an institution for the preservation and rationalization of a given socioeconomic order, particularly the system of production and the class relations it embodies.

Although the state may be defined as an instrument for the (direct or indirect) domination of a given class, its form and functions will vary not only in accordance with the development of the system of production but also according to the ability of different classes and groups to manifest their interests in unified action (Moore, 1957: 26ff.; Villa, 1972: 424-425; Wolfe, 1974: 139). Although this ability will accrue disproportionately to the dominant class, subordinate groups may also organize sufficiently to demand state attention to their needs—always within the context of the dominant system (Villa, 1972: 425; Miliband, 1969).

The question of the articulation of class-state relationships constitutes one of the most important debates in contemporary studies of the capitalist state. Basically, the dilemma seems to be to what extent can one affirm the distinction between state power and class power (which, among other things, enables the state to function in the interests of the capitalist class as a whole rather than specific class interests) without also affirming the neutrality of the state (as an instrument capable of being utilized by any social class) (Sardei-Biermann et al., 1973: 60-62)? In general, theories may be divided into those that emphasize the direct influence of the dominant class, including the recruitment of class members into positions of state power, campaign financing, and the like (Domhoff, 1970; Miliband, 1969), and those implying limited sovereignty of the state, foreclosing the possibility of anti-capitalist policy (Poulantzas, 1969: 73-74; Sardei-Biermann et al., 1973: 60-62).

The definition above includes elements of both types of theories, with the identity of the state within a given system of production—and the economic power of the dominant class—constituting a major constraint preventing state neutrality. A minimum function of the capitalist state, for example, is the protection of private property. Should the state under a given form fail to preserve the existing order of private ownership of the means of production, the dominant class will utilize its economic (or political) power to "reorient" the state (for example, through new elections), or change its form (for example, through a military coup)—as has occurred in Chile. The power of the dominant class thus constitutes a major constraint limiting the state to options within a given system of production. Within this constraint the form and the functions of the state will vary—as noted above—according to the degree and type of influence of the dominant class, pressures brought to bear by subordinate classes and groups, and developments within the system of production.

In order to study the state empirically within a given society, it is necessary to identify concretely the institutional apparatus of the state and those who directly control it. Of the various institutions identified by Miliband as constituting the state system, the government (consisting of individuals or groups directly controlling the state apparatus), the civil bureaucracy (administration)—including ministries, public corporations, and central banks—the military, and subcentral government are most relevant for a study of Mexico (Miliband, 1969: chap. 3).

It is also essential to recognize the historical dimension—the fact that the institutions of the state apparatus have been shaped by past experience and are therefore separable from, and to a greater or lesser extent resistant to, the incumbents in positions of authority (the government). Inasmuch as the state encompasses both the government and the bureaucracy, it will almost inevitably be characterized by contradictions, however consistent the actions of a given regime or administration may be. These contradictions will of course be accentuated when the government is innovative.

Within capitalist societies, the state operates to ensure conditions of capitalist production (that is, characterized by private ownership of the means of production and the appropriation of surplus on the basis of exploitation of wage labor) and, increasingly, the management of contradictions arising from capitalist production.[1] The establishment and maintenance of conditions of capitalist production include protection of private property and the provision of inputs (land, labor, capital) either directly (for example, through land concessions or manpower training programs) or indirectly (for example, through abolition of restrictions on the movement of people and commodities).

Contradictions arising from capitalist production derive from the basic contradiction of capitalism: the growth of the productive forces on the one hand and the restrictions of production relations—which results in restrictions on product realization (markets) on the other. Economically, these contradictions are manifested in overproduction (of commodities and/or capital), supply bottlenecks, unemployment, anarchic competition, and so forth. Politically they are manifested in class conflict and conflict within and between sectors of the capitalist class.

These contradictions constitute the basis for historical change within the capitalist system and ultimately for a change from capitalism to a different system of production. Management of these contradictions, by the capitalist class or by the state, prevents or postpones this transition. As a result, change occurs, but this change takes place within the context of the capitalist system (Weinstein, 1968: intro. [on the cooptation of pressures for change in the United States by business elites], chap. 2 [on the specific example of workmen's compensation]).

Within advanced capitalist societies, management of contradictions arising directly from production includes the provision of investment outlets and markets (for example, through military spending), planning (wage and price controls, indicative planning to control supply bottlenecks and limit unemployment), and regulation of trusts (Warren, 1972; Kolko, 1963).

The contradiction between the growth of production and restricted realization of production is also an element in imperialism—capitalist expansion beyond national boundaries to secure inputs (raw materials, labor), markets, investment outlets, and competition among national capitals (Bukharin, 1973: 104). The role of the state in the management of external relations includes aggressive support of national capital in foreign expansion (including colonial conquests, economic and military aid to foreign states, diplomatic pressures, and capitalist wars), and defense of domestic capital (through import quotas and tariffs) (Murray, 1971: 85-92).

The management of contradictions at the political level involves the management of class conflict so as to ensure the necessary order and stability for capitalist production (Kolko, 1963: 3). This has usually involved some form of institutionalizing class conflict through labor legislation, arbitration of labor disputes, and the direct or indirect incorporation of working-class parties and organizations within the existing political framework. Management of class conflict may also take the form of coopting reforms of radical movements that can be accommodated within the existing system (welfare policies, social security, medical care, and the like). Finally, there are various forms of socialization (to establish the legitimacy of the existing system) and social control (when legitimacy breaks down), ranging from the elaboration of ideology and its propagation through the educational system, media, and so on, to coercion—strike breaking and police repression, for example (Miliband, 1969: chaps. 7, 8; Dahrendorf, 1959: 64-67; Weinstein, 1968). The legitimacy of the state is also reinforced by its success in institutionalizing class conflict and in its reform efforts. Again, the national state may be involved in securing order and stability for domestic capital on an international scale through diplomacy, aid, military intervention, or indirect intervention, for example, economic and military support of sympathetic regimes (MacEwan: 1972).

In a relatively less developed society (one in which the productive forces are at a lower or precapitalist stage of development), the state itself may perform the role of capitalist in capital accumulation—a role that is often necessitated in late-developing countries due to the increased economic and technical requirements of twentieth-century capitalism in comparison with the nineteenth century. In such a case, the position of the state in relation to the various classes may be strengthened (in that the owning classes are more directly dependent upon state inputs), and the state may have a role in shaping the social formation that emerges. In the absence of direct control of the means of production, however, power over the state passes to the economically dominant class.

This situation is often complicated to the extent that the less developed society is incorporated into the world system in a manner in which its economic independence is eroded—that is, the productive system and its development are subjected to a greater or lesser degree to the needs of foreign capital. This situation of dependency is obviously the opposite side of imperialism and varies both in terms of type of relationship with foreign capital (trade dependence, direct foreign investment, capital dependence, technological dependence) and in terms of the structure of the dependent economy (colony, enclave economy, dependent capitalism). It generally involves some form of collaboration with classes or groups in the dependent society who benefit from this relationship—a *comprador* class, or in dependent capitalist societies an important segment of the domestic bourgeoisie. In this latter case, the major relationship of exploitation is that by the foreign and domestic bourgeoisie of the workers (Bodenheimer, 1970; Cardoso, 1972: 87-91; Quijano, 1972: 5). To the extent that a distortion of the productive structure and its development occurs as a result of dependency, societies are sometimes defined as underdeveloped—*underdevelopment* here construed as a process accompanying the development of the advanced capitalist countries (Baran, 1957).

An analysis of the relations of production and class structure of underdeveloped societies must include foreign capital in its individual and collective manifestations—the latter often being the foreign state. However, with the integration of foreign and domestic capital in dependent capitalist societies, the state in the dependent society may perform the function of preserving and rationalizing the existing system in the interests of foreign as well as domestic capital (Murray, 1971: 98). It may also attempt to regulate foreign capital; its ability to do this will generally depend to some extent on the strength and cohesion of domestic classes (usually the national bourgeoisie, but also labor in some cases) and the extent of their integration with foreign capital.

The state must also attempt to rationalize the contradictions arising from dependent capitalism. In societies in which multinational corporations control important sectors of the manufacturing industry, for example, the "premature" imposition of advanced capitalist forms may mean that sectors of the economy become monopolized and/or dominated by capital-intensive technology prior to the effective incorporation of the majority of the population into the labor or consumer markets (Sunkel, 1971: 39-41). Thus the basic contradiction between production and realization is aggravated. To the extent that institutions for state management of class conflict are tied to production relations (trade unions, social security, labor parties, and the like), large sectors of the population are excluded from both the benefits and control mechanisms of these institutions.

INTERPRETATIONS OF THE STATE WITHIN THE MEXICAN REVOLUTION

In Mexico, the conceptualization of the revolutionary state derives from elements of Mexico's prerevolutionary history as well as the struggles of the revolution itself. The authoritarian state of Porfirio Díaz was imposed in contradiction to the weak government postulated in the liberal constitution of 1857 (Córdova, 1973: 15-16). The interventionalist state proposed by Francisco Mújica and other radical delegates to the 1917 constitutional convention to some extent opposed the decentralized political structure advocated by Madero and by most of the liberal precursors of the revolution (although perhaps implicit in their reforms advocated in the 1906 program of the Liberal party). At the same time, state intervention on behalf of the underprivileged contradicted the Porfirian notion of intervention on behalf of national and foreign property owners who needed security to carry out their functions of developing the wealth of the nation (Córdova, 1973: 16-17, 26-27).

Most of these elements were to some extent manifested in the debates of the constitutional convention of 1916-1917. Venustiano Carranza, head of the constitutional forces, advocated the ideal of the state not compromised with any sector of society, and a strong executive (limiting the attributes of the legislature, expanding those of the executive in proposing laws and legislating by decree; and providing for direct presidential elections; Córdova, 1973: 26-28). The radical delegates, consisting chiefly of young generals led by Francisco Mujica and influenced by the Plan of Ayala of the Zapata forces, held that the state could not permit the exploitation of the underprivileged, which would occur if the economy operated without intervention. Greater state power would be necessary to carry out measures such as the agrarian reform, including power over property. At the same time, they envisaged a tutelary role for the state, which would be responsible for educating citizens to loyalty to nation rather than to the Church and would direct them in building the nation (Wilkie, 1967: 51; Córdova, 1973: 26-27).

The 1917 constitution, while enumerating individual freedoms, stating that national sovereignty resides essentially in the people, and providing for division of powers, also implicitly guarantees the authority of the state, and specifically the federal government, as the embodiment of the national interest, exercising sovereignty over the national territory and responsibility for the education of its citizens. It accepts the regime of property and capitalist production relations, but enables the state to impose restrictions on property, carry out an extensive agrarian reform, and revise monopolistic concessions to individuals and companies. It also provides for the implementation of an extensive labor reform, including the eight-hour day, minimum wage, and right to organize and to strike. Under Article 27, the state is explicitly authorized to take measures to divide up large landed estates and to distribute the lands to individuals and population centers. It further provides that population centers lacking communal lands shall be guaranteed land grants by the federal government. Inasmuch as over 80 percent of the active population was rural, and at the time of the revolution an estimated 97 percent of the rural population was landless, the implications of this article for radical structural change are apparent.

Anti-monopoly provisions, the establishment of national sovereignty over subsoil rights, as well as Article 123, outlining labor rights, can be seen as directed against foreign interests that exercised hegemony or near hegemony in key economic sectors. In short, the role of the state as envisaged in the constitution is revolutionary and anti-imperialist, but not anticapitalist; its function may be understood as the elimination of feudal and precapitalist production forms as well as foreign domination over natural resources as a means of implicitly establishing the necessary conditions for national capitalist production. In view of the limited development of capitalist productive forces, such a function would imply a creative role for the state in shaping the new social formation. At the same time it would assume that the state retains sufficient autonomy within the new social formation to intervene on behalf of the weaker class or underprivileged groups. Thus the state may be considered both interventionist, in terms of its relation to the economy as a whole, and authoritarian and paternalistic, in terms of its relations with labor and the peasants. The authoritarian nature of the state is reinforced by its tutelary role in eradicating the influence of the Church and taking over its function in the education of citizens—that is, forming the national consciousness. The state is in fact the embodiment of the nation in carrying out its functions, as is evident in the stipulations regarding property.

In the actual conduct of postrevolutionary governments, two general interpretations of the state emerged. Both assumed an authoritarian state, autonomous with respect to class interests, with a strong executive and an interventionist role in the economy; both asserted its representation of national sovereignty in relation to foreign interests. But within the first interpretation, the state is above class interests and its role is one of conciliation, in which class antagonisms are overcome in the higher interest of the nation. The second recognizes the existence of class conflict and explicitly advocates the exercise of state power on behalf of the weaker class. In the first case, while postulating an ideology of nationalism and cooperation in national development, the state implicitly sides with the capitalist class. In the second case, the state becomes caught up in the contradictions between its advocacy of the interests of subordinate groups and its function of protecting a system of capitalist production.

With some simplification, the first interpretation may be said to characterize the immediately postrevolutionary governments of Mexico. During this period there was increasing centralization of power in the federal government, and particularly the executive, through the elimination or cooptation of local *caciques* (political bosses), the professionalization of the army, and the institutionalization of mass participation under state control—a process that culminated in the establishment of a single government party, the Partido Nacional Revolucionario (PNR) in 1929 (González Casanova, 1970: 33-35; Meyer, 1972: 120-122). In many respects, economic measures of this period can be seen as a continuation and rationalization of the system that existed in the prerevolutionary regime of Porfirio Díaz. Banking reform laws passed in the mid-1920s reconstituted the system of Díaz and his finance minister Limantour with the addition of a central bank having the sole right to issue notes. Other economic activities—the building of infrastructure, especially roads, the promotion of industry, and the establishment of an agrarian credit bank also had precedents in the prerevolutionary government.

The government of Calles (1924-1928) constituted the most radical interlude during this period; an extensive land distribution program was initiated, and Calles challenged American interests by passing enabling legislation for Article 27, the Petroleum Law, and the Alien Land Law (Smith, 1973: 231). However, extensive pressure from U.S. oil and banking interests, as well as the State Department, resulted in modifications in implementation policies that in effect maintained existing dependency relations (Smith, 1973: 258-259). The trend toward reform and nationalism was reversed; the leadership of the major labor confederation was coopted into the government and ceased to represent the interests of the working class, land distribution came to a virtual standstill, and foreign capital was again welcomed in Mexico (Brandenberg, 1964: 75). In fact, according to Córdova, a salient characteristic of this period (during which Mexico benefited from the economic boom of the 1920s) was the opportunity provided—and taken—for revolutionaries to turn themselves into capitalists. Old classes—industrialists, businessmen, landowners— were largely left intact and given dynamism by new capitalists drawn from the ranks of the middle-class revolutionaries (Córdova, 1972: 30). Calles himself promoted and benefited from this situation, and through his control of succeeding presidents ensured its continuation.

THE CARDENAS YEARS AND
THE AUTONOMOUS STATE:
CONCEPTUALIZATION

In the 1930s, the absence of serious reform and the effects of the world depression on the Mexican economy were factors in the growth of agrarian and labor unrest, which in turn were instrumental in bringing the radical sector of the government party to state control (Labastida, 1972: 108). This shift was manifested in the approval of the first six-year plan of government in the national party convention of 1934 and the nomination and consequent election of Lázaro Cárdenas, who as governor of the state of Michoacán had carried out extensive agrarian reform in that state. Basing its power on the peasants and the working class, the Cárdenas government broke the control exercised by Calles and his clique over the party and government and enacted a series of reforms designed to restructure Mexican society (Meyer, 1972: 123-124).

Cárdenas and other government leaders explicitly recognized the class conflict inherent in the capitalist system, and projected the transformation of the system into a workers' democracy, in which workers would control the means of production, as an ultimate goal of the Mexican Revolution (Wilkie, 1967: 72ff.). This was long-term goal, however, and although the state would actively promote its realization (for example, through the institution of socialist education and the establishment of cooperative systems of production), in the meantime it acted to promote the welfare of the workers within the capitalist system.

This second conceptualization of the autonomous state—nationalist and anti-imperialist, operating within the constraints of the capitalist system, recognizing the class conflict inherent in such a system and intervening on behalf of dominated groups—is evidenced in various speeches of Cárdenas as candidate and as president. The role of the state in promoting national economic development and thereby liberating the people from the exploitation of foreign capital is suggested in Cárdenas' preelection speech of June 20, 1934:

> It is indispensable to carry out the principles of the six-year plan, which signify the formation of a national economy directed and regulated by the State which frees Mexico from the character of a colonial economy . . . where the essential incentive of capitalism is none other than the obtention of primary materials with cheap labor [Cárdenas, 1972: 244].

In a radio broadcast (March 14, 1936) in response to a statement issued by associations of Mexican bankers, industrialists, and businessmen complaining of government policies with respect to business and capital-labor relations, the right of the state to intervene in economic production is asserted:

> An abstention, an owners' boycott, whatever be its magnitude, would demand the intervention of the state, by perfectly legal means, to prevent eco-

nomic life from being disturbed. And the most that could occur would be
that determined branches leave the orbit of private interests to be converted
into social services [Cárdenas, 1972: 245].

In the same speech, he clearly enunciates the doctrine of state intervention in class conflict on behalf of labor:

The modern concept of the function of the state, and the nature itself of
labor legislation . . . require that cases of doubt be resolved in the inter-
ests of the weaker party to give equal treatment to two unequal parts is not
to impart justice or to work with equity. Labor legislation, as is known, has
in all countries a tutelar character with respect to the workers, because it
tends to strengthen their weakness in confrontation with the power of the
owning class, in order to approach as closely as possible solutions of effec-
tive justice [Cárdenas, 1972: 75].

And in a speech to the Patronal Center of Monterrey, a major nucleus
of right-wing opposition to the Cárdenas government and the working-
class struggle, Cárdenas outlined fourteen points of the president's labor
policy, concluding that those businessmen who grow tired of the social
struggle can deliver their industries to the workers or to the state (Cárdenas, 1972: 190-191).

The speeches of Cárdenas often imply an authoritarian or paternalistic
role for the state in relation to the working class. This paternalism is even
more evident in government speeches to peasants, who constituted the
beneficiaries of the government agrarian reform program. Nevertheless,
Cárdenas persistently urged the organization of peasants and workers to
defend their own interests and to pressure the government to act on their
behalf:

The organization of the worker, as that of the peasant, is indispensable for
the country to comply with its laws. It is not enough, as I have already said
on a different occasion, to depend on the good will of the public function-
aries nor the mandates contained in the legislation which guides us. It is
necessary that a superior force, which cannot be other than the organized
workers, contend to overcome the resistance which unfortunately opposes
the economic betterment of our people [Cárdenas, 1972: 116-117].

The Cárdenas administration represented the most serious effort during the postrevolutionary period to articulate and realize the goals of the
Mexican Revolution. Nevertheless, this orientation was quickly reversed
in the conservative regimes that followed Cárdenas, during which the
state was oriented to the defense of business interests, including those of
foreign capital, and the suppression of the weaker classes. This apparent

reversal even began during the Cárdenas administration, the last three years of which were characterized by the general slowing down of reform and an emphasis on consolidating existing gains.

It is here suggested that this apparent shift in policy was due not to any personal failing or manipulation on the part of Cárdenas, but to the contradictions inherent in this conceptualization of the state as well as its attempted implementation within the context of Mexico's past history and existing structure. The shift to a more conservative position may be seen to follow logically, if not inevitably, from the consequences of a state orientation to the defense of subordinate class interests against those of dominant classes and groups while leaving the system of domination intact.

THE CARDENAS YEARS AND
THE AUTONOMOUS STATE:
IMPLEMENTATION

To understand the importance of the reforms of the Cárdenas years, it is necessary to understand the context in which they were implemented. During the 1930s, Mexico was characterized by class struggles emanating from the exploitation of labor by foreign and domestic capital as well as by a feudal oligarchy that maintained its control over much of the rural population. Foreign capital continued to be dominant in petroleum, mining, railroads, and utilities. Under the Cárdenas administration, payment of the public debt, including the payments of U.S. claims against Mexico resulting from the revolution, constituted 10 percent to 15 percent of the government budget (Wilkie, 1967: 110ff.). Mexico's imports from the United States constituted about 65 percent of its total imports; exports to the United States ranged from 50 percent to 75 percent (González Casanova, 1965).

The struggle of the peasants and working class was met with various forms of repression, which increased in reaction to reforms of the Cárdenas government. Hired mercenaries or "white guards" paid by landowners and oil companies murdered and terrorized peasants and laborers. In the state of Veracruz alone, an estimated 2,000 persons were killed during the first eighteen months of the Cárdenas administration as a result of armed conflicts between white guards and peasants. Rural schoolteachers, who often doubled as community activists and organizers and constituted the vanguard of the anti-clerical, socialist education movement, were particular targets of terrorism by religious fanatics and hacienda retainers. In mid-1938, the Union of Educational Workers reported that an average of three murders a month was the toll among rural teachers (*Mexican Labor News*, July 28, 1938). Company unions in such employer strongholds as Monterrey divided the labor movement, while in some instances state governors promoted labor organizations to break up existing unions (Weyl and Weyl, 1939: 238-239). The textile region of Puebla was the scene of frequent outbursts of violence between unions. In addition, there were threats of armed revolt by *caudillos* such as Saturnino Cedillo, a former supporter of Cárdenas, who had received moral if not financial support from the foreign oil companies to overthrow the Cárdenas government (Cronon, 1960: 212). Fascist organizations such as the "gold shirts," believed to be supported by Calles and business interests, also played a disruptive role against unions and peasant organizations (Ashby, 1963: 29). Major daily newspapers, such as *Excelsior* and *Universal* in the capital, kept up a constant barrage of criticism against initiatives of the Cárdenas regime. Exhortations of Cárdenas and other government leaders to peasants and workers to "defend the *ejido* and the rural school," to end interunion rivalry and form united organizations to defend their interests, and to mobilize against the enemies of the revolution were not idle phrases.

The Cárdenas government therefore acted within the constraints of a system characterized by economic dependence, exploitation, and class struggle. Nevertheless, it succeeded in transforming the state into an agent of the Mexican Revolution—carrying out an extensive agrarian reform, promoting the organization and unification of peasants and workers, nationalizing the foreign-controlled oil interests, and enlarging the role of the state in economic development. In the process, the working class and the peasants became increasingly dependent upon the state, while the options of the state itself became increasingly constricted to those acceptable to the owning classes.

THE STATE AND STRUCTURAL CHANGE: THE AGRARIAN REFORM

The agrarian reform carried out by the Cárdenas government went far to restructure the rural system of production in Mexico. In the years preceding the election of Cárdenas in 1934, some 8.7 million hectares of land had been distributed to approximately 778,000 peasants. Although this had been sufficient to cause uncertainty among landowners and to lead to production cutbacks, the bulk of the peasants remained landless and the *latifundia* structure remained basically intact. Land distribution was oriented to small holdings, with the ejidos (village communal holdings) seen as an intermediate step to individual farms. Dissatisfaction with the limited agrarian reform had led to the mobilization of groups of peasants, who had constituted the bulk of the revolutionary armies. Agrarian leagues and federations had been formed in several states, and in the 1933 convention of the government party (PNR), at which Lázaro Cárdenas was selected as presidential candidate, peasant leaders introduced measures to accelerate the agrarian reform (Huizer, 1972: 77).

It is clear that Cárdenas himself considered the structural reform of rural production—involving 75 percent to 80 percent of the active population of the country—as a primary goal of his administration. During the Cárdenas administration more peasants received land than under all previous administrations (810,000), and over twice as much land was distributed (17.9 million hectares) (Chevalier, 1967: 168). The Cárdenas government is generally credited with having effectively destroyed the latifundia system, although at the end of his administration half the latifundia were intact and half of the peasant population remained landless, and Cárdenas himself recognized that much remained to be done (Raby, 1972: 46; Cárdenas, 1972: 81).

In contrast to previous administrations that had emphasized the small landholding, with the ejido to be divided into individual plots, the Cárdenas government emphasized the ejido and its collective operation, inasmuch as only large-scale productive units would be sufficiently efficient and economical to maintain and increase production for internal and external markets (Cárdenas, 1972: 130-131; Chevalier, 1967: 163ff.). It was also recognized that land distribution was useless if the beneficiaries lacked credit for the necessary means to work the land. In 1935 the Banco Nacional de Crédito Ejidal was established and heavily subsidized by the government to provide credit for the ejidos; the Banco Nacional de Crédito Agrario, which had previously provided credit for both ejidatarios and small landowners, would concentrate exclusively on the latter.

The structure of the ejidal bank was indicative of state paternalism toward the peasants. One of the premises of the establishment of a special bank for the ejidos was that the ejidos had special credit problems, not only because ejidal land could not be sold (and therefore mortgaged), but also because the ejidatarios, as former peons of the large estates, were poorer, less educated, and less productive than the small landowners. The Ejidal Bank was responsible for organizing local credit societies; providing credit; organizing production and the sale of harvests; buying and reselling seeds, fertilizers, and agricultural implements; and representing the members before federal and local authorities. Agents and inspectors were appointed to oversee the functioning of the ejidos (Moore, 1963: 148-149).

Whether or not such a supervisory role was necessary during the early stages of the ejidal credit societies (and whether government functionaries were equipped to perform such a role), the long-term implication of the ejidal credit structure was to institutionalize the dependence of the peasants of the ejido upon state functionaries who may or may not act in their interests. Even during the Cárdenas administration there were complaints of corruption due to bank officials keeping profits from the sale of harvests instead of turning them over to the ejidatarios (Michaels, 1970: 61). In 1937, executive officials of the ejidal bank issued fifty prosecutions against its employees (often local politicians) for financial irregularities (Weyl and Weyl, 1939: 225-226, who add, however, that by and large the bank officials were honest and competent).

In order to demonstrate the efficiency of the collective system of production, Cárdenas gave particular emphasis to new collective ejidos oriented to commercial production—notably the cotton-producing Laguna valley in the states of Sonora and Coahuila in the north, and the henequen region of the Yucatán. Agrarian credit was concentrated on these two projects, and Cárdenas paid extensive visits to these areas, attempting to mobilize not only the peasants themselves but also the working-class population as a whole around these endeavors, which epitomized the goals of the revolution (Michaels, 1970: 61-63; *Mexican Labor News*, August 11, 1937). This emphasis on commercial ejidos was understandable, but it meant less credit for the smaller, generally poorer ejidos of the central and southern states. Thus although the ejidos of the states of Guanajuato, Querétaro, Jalisco, Michoacán, and Guerrero constituted 26 percent of the ejidatarios, they received only 11 percent of the credit provided by the ejidal bank in 1941 (González Navarro, 1963: 158-159).

In summary, the agrarian reform was to have far-reaching consequences in eliminating the latifundia as the predominant structure of the countryside. It also represented an attempt to introduce cooperative forms of production that would be socially progressive and economically viable. At the same time, however, perhaps inevitably, the peasants became increasingly dependent upon the state for land and credit.

THE STATE AND THE ORGANIZATION OF LABOR

As noted above, the interpretation of the state relationship to the working class indicated in the speeches of Cárdenas is ambiguous: on the one hand suggesting the dependence of the working class on the government and the paternalistic role of the state and on the other emphasizing the importance of working-class and peasant organizations that could effectively defend their interests and pressure the government to act on their behalf. If the actual initiatives of the government seem to correspond more to the first conceptualization than to the second, it is also true that this followed to some extent the traditions of paternalistic relations within Mexican society and within the labor movement itself (Ashby, 1963: 10; Basurto, 1972: 57).

During the prerevolutionary regime of Porfirio Díaz, strikes and other attempts of workers to protest conditions of exploitation were crushed. Working-class organizations supported revolutionary leaders in return for protection through government legislation. Article 123 of the constitution established a partnership between the state and organized labor in which the former predominated (Ashby, 1963: 12). This was reinforced by the stipulations of the 1931 labor law, which provided that conflicts between labor and management be submitted to government boards of conciliation and arbitration, in which management, labor, and the government had equal representation, with government therefore casting the decisive vote.

Following the revolution, the labor movement was characteristically either split among various factions and confederations or united on the basis of a highly centralized structure with member unions and federations dependent upon the leadership. The first national labor confederation, the Confederación Regional de Obreros Mexicanos (CROM), formed in 1918, established the precedent of collaboration of organized labor with the state. By the late 1920s, its association with the Calles regime had become a mechanism for coopting the leadership rather than defending the interests of the members, and the opportunism and corruption of the leadership led several unions and labor leaders to break away and form new organizations. Among the most important was the Confederación General de Obreros y Campesinos de México (CGOCM), formed by Vicente Lombardo Toledano, with an explicit orientation to revolutionary struggle against the capitalist order as well as immediate economic goals (Ashby, 1963: 13-18; Basurto, 1972: 49-51). Lombardo Toledano also insisted that the CGOCM maintain its independence in relation to the state.

When Cárdenas became president at the end of 1934, the labor movement was in a general state of disorganization, with three labor confederations and a number of independent unions vying for power (Michaels, 1970: 65). During the first months of the Cárdenas government, there were a series of strikes—many of them against foreign-owned corporations—and, for the first time, many of them began to be decided in favor of labor by government arbitration boards. Plutarco Elías Calles, who had dominated Mexican politics (including presidents) for over a de-

cade, expected Cárdenas to take action against the strikes, which he himself condemned as risking the economic well-being of the country.
Cárdenas responded by defending the right of the workers to obtain better
conditions within the economic possibilities of the capitalist system, and
stated the resolve of the federal executive "to fulfill the program of the
revolution and to carry out the dictates of the six-year plan without regard
for the alarm expressed by representatives of the capitalist class" (Ashby,
1963: 24-27). The confrontation between Calles and Cárdenas, resulting
in the definitive break of Cárdenas with the Calles clique, can thus be
seen as a confrontation between two conceptualizations of the state in its
relation to capital and labor.

Unions of the CGOCM as well as independent unions formed the
Comité Nacional de Defensa Proletaria; this in turn constituted the basis
for the formation of the Confederación de Trabajadores Mexicanos
(CTM) in 1936, which quickly became the major labor confederation in
Mexico. As secretary general of the new confederation, Lombardo Toledano continued to insist upon the independence of the labor movement in
relation to the government, although the Comité Nacional de Defense
Proletaria supported Cárdenas in his conflict with Calles and the CTM
collaborated with the government on specific issues.

At the same time, support of the Cárdenas government for the working
class continued to be manifested in decisions of the government boards of
conciliation and arbitration in favor of labor. In some instances workers
were encouraged to take over plants when owners claimed they were unable to meet wage requirements. In 1936, the government passed legislation requiring that workers be paid for the seventh day of the week (an
obligatory day of rest), automatically increasing their weekly wage by
approximately 17 percent. This form of support was problematic, however, not only in its tendency to reinforce labor dependence upon the government but also because employers reacted by raising prices, thus
virtually wiping out wage gains (*Mexican Labor News*, February 24,
1937; April 7, 1937; November 10, 1938). Wage gains were also partially obliterated by retail price increases resulting from a decline in food
production on expropriated lands undergoing a process of reorganization
and on estates of landlords fearing expropriation (Weyl and Weyl, 1939:
185-187). A related problem—despite the ideological stance of Lombardo Toledano—was the frequent concentration of organizational energies upon immediate wage and related demands rather than structural
changes benefiting the working class as a whole.

The Cárdenas government experimented with the establishment of
worker control or management in several areas—particularly in industries processing agricultural products, such as the sugar cooperative at

Morelos, and in the growing state-owned sector. The results of these attempts to introduce semisocialist forms of production within a nascent capitalist system were mixed, but, in any event, their influence on the dominant structure of labor-capital relations was minimal.

In view of attacks from company unions and fascist organizations, as well as interunion conflict, Cárdenas persistently urged the working class to organize and unite. The chief beneficiary of increased working-class organization was the CTM, which included both national industrywide unions and state federations incorporating unions within a given state. Although the CTM maintained its independence of the government and the government party (prior to the formation of the Partido Revolucionario Mexicano) its own structure implied a strong degree of dependence of the members upon the leadership. Permanent authority was vested in a seven-member national executive committee; at the first national congress of the CTM in February 1938, the national committee, which had completed its two-year term, was unanimously voted to serve an additional three years (*Mexican Labor News*, February 24, 1938).

There were isolated protests against the control exercised by the national committee (and Secretary General Lombardo Toledano) over the confederation, but these were not sufficient to break its hegemony. In March 1937, the unions of the state of Puebla accused Lombardo Toledano of imposing his selection for congressional candidates on the state federation. The fourth national council of the CTM resulted in a split as the Communist party withdrew its delegates, followed by the railroad workers and electricians of the federal district, although the CP and railroad members subsequently returned. Lombardo Toledano was accused of imposing bureaucratic, personalist control over the CTM. With the CTM approval of the conservative Avila Camacho as presidential candidate in February 1939, dissident CTM unions issued a manifesto calling for a repudiation of CTM leadership and accused it of having imposed the candidacy of Avila Camacho behind the backs of the workers and the unions. The CTM responded that the so-called unions did not exist. The Federation of Workers of Michoacán also voted to repudiate the national leadership of the CTM (*Mexican Labor News*, March 31, 1937; May 5, 1937; March 30, 1939).

The CTM national committee in fact expressly discouraged debate among the member organizations of CTM regarding the relative merits of the candidates prior to the CTM nominating convention (*Mexican Labor News*, January 29, 1939). This admonishment—as well as the final support for the less controversial Avila Camacho against the radical candidate, Francisco Mújica—can be partly explained by Lombardo Toledano's belief in the need for united labor support behind a candidate who would also unite the divergent groups of the government party, in view of the threat of reaction in the form of a military coup or the selection of a reactionary candidate by groups outside of the party who would undo the reforms of the Cárdenas era (Michaels, 1971: 14). Nevertheless, it is perhaps symptomatic of the failure to include member unions and the rank and file in study and discussion of major issues affecting them and the country.

When Cárdenas became president, the situation in the countryside was more chaotic than that among the labor movement. At least half a dozen organizations existed that claimed affiliation of agrarian leagues and other groups in various states (González Navarro, 1963: 123). As noted above, ejidatarios and other peasants were targets of armed attacks by white guards hired by the landlords. Early in his administration, Cárdenas armed the peasants: "I will give the peasants the mauser, with which they made the revolution, in order to defend it" (Cárdenas, 1972: 114). By 1940, the peasant militia consisted of 60,000 armed peasants organized into 70 battalions and 75 cavalry regiments (Huizer, 1972: 79).

Unlike the CTM, the national confederation of peasants, while taking advantage of existing organizations, was directly organized by the state. Cárdenas designated the PNR, under the leadership of former president Portes Gil, to call a national constituent assembly and to organize peasant federations in states where they did not yet exist. According to Portes Gil, the state conventions were characterized by complete freedom of expression to the extent that various governors, military chiefs, and members of the presidential cabinet were criticized on several occasions (González Navarro, 1963: 140-142). Nevertheless, the organization of a national peasant organization by the PNR was opposed by certain groups on the left, among them independent agrarian federations and Lombardo Toledano. The opposition of the latter was due not only to his desire to unite the peasants with the organized workers in the CTM, but also to the connection of the PNR, and particularly its leader, Portes Gil, with the Calles clique. Most observers agree that the formation of a separate confederation by the government party (rather than including the peasants in the CTM) was at least partly motivated by Cárdenas's desire to prevent Lombardo Toledano from gaining control of peasants as well as labor (Weyl and Weyl, 1939: 188-190; Ashby, 1963: 80). Although Cárdenas has been blamed for thus separating the peasant and industrial labor movements, it is difficult to see how their unification would have made a difference, particularly given that both were incorporated in the Partido Revolucionario Mexicano (PRM), established in 1938, with Lombardo Toledano's acquiescence.

When Cárdenas proposed the formation of the PRM, Lombardo Toledano felt that this would effectively eliminate the influence of elements of the Calles group, which still retained influence within the PNR. He also approved its structure of functional democracy, which would incorporate the organized workers, peasants, army, and the so-called popular sector (composed of organized groups, such as government workers and small landowners, excluded from the other three sectors) (Basurto, 1972: 52; *Mexican Labor News*, January 13, 1938; April 7, 1938).

The party's declaration of principles stated that its most fundamental task was to prepare for a workers' democracy as a step toward socialism (Weyl and Weyl, 1939: 347) and in general its radical orientation was reflected by its first president, Luis Rodríguez, who had been a personal secretary to Cárdenas. Rodríguez was forced to resign, however, as a result of pressures from more conservative groups within the party. Although his successor, Gen. Heriberto Jara, had been a delegate to the constitutional congress of Querétaro, where he had argued for the inclusion of labor rights within the 1917 constitution, the resignation of Rodríguez was perhaps an indication of the power of groups other than the constituent organizations. A number of army officers, state governors, senators, and government officials had found politics a means of personal enrichment, and were interested in stemming the radical thrust of government politics (Michaels, 1970: 52). It was reported, for example, that a pact supporting Avila Camacho as PRM candidate had been signed by all but three state governors in the middle of 1938—some six or seven months before he was nominated at the CTM and CNC conventions—an action presumably prompted by fear of the candidacy of the radical Francisco Mujica, believed to be favored by Cárdenas (Raby, 1972: 54).

By this time, Cárdenas himself was seeking to widen his base of support, which required an appeal to less radical sectors of the population. The inclusion of the popular sector, as well as the military, in the PRM, was intended to "moderate" the more radical influence of the peasant and labor organizations (although initially Cárdenas had wished to exclude a fourth sector on the grounds that the party should be one of the vanguard of the revolution) (González Navarro, 1963: 144-145, 157-158).

The ostensible purpose of the organization and unification of peasants and working class was to strengthen their ability to defend their own interests and to pressure the government to act on their behalf. But it is questionable whether the structure of the relevant organizations—particularly the CTM, the CNC, and the party itself—enabled the rank-and-file membership to participate in the determination of goals and policies. Control from above facilitated a process whereby these organizations became instruments of state control over the membership rather than the reverse.

THE STATE AND PRIVATE CAPITAL

Although the Cárdenas government went further than any administration before or since in strengthening the position of the Mexican state with respect to foreign and national capital, it clearly continued to operate within the context of capitalist production relations and economic dependence. Moreover, Cárdenas felt that Mexico, as a capital-poor country, needed foreign capital. Although the government generally sided with labor in its conflict with foreign companies, and Cárdenas himself was unrelenting in his criticism of U.S. mining and petroleum companies in Mexico, he frequently asserted to U.S. Ambassador Josephus Daniels and other American emissaries that the right type of foreign investment—particularly in manufacturing—would be assured of protection (U.S. Department of State, 1936: 718).

The creation and expansion of state development banks and of legislation strengthening central bank control over the private banking sector constitute major elements of continuity between the Cárdenas administration and those preceding and following it. These initiatives, during the Cárdenas and previous and subsequent administrations, assumed a significant state role in orienting the economy and promoting economic development, and a private enterprise system in which the state role would complement, rather than supplant, that of private capital. In this respect, they also have parallels with state policy in other Latin American countries, such as Argentina, Brazil, and Chile, where the effects of the depression on economies highly dependent on foreign trade led to state intervention to encourage import substitution industrialization (Ianni, 1974: 129-130; Pompermeyer and Smith, 1973: 105). The continuity of financial policy of the Cárdenas government with those that preceded and followed may be partly due to the continuity of personnel in key financial positions. Montes de Oca, president of the Banco de México, had previously served as general comptroller and finance minister in the cabinets of presidents Portes Gil and Ortiz Rubio. The secretary of finance under Cárdenas, Eduardo Suárez, was to retain this position under the conservative government of Avila Camacho, where he would have a key role in formulating government industrialization policies.

During the 1930s all but one of the five major development banks that were to constitute a major mechanism for government economic intervention were created. (The National Agrarian Credit Bank had been established in 1926.) Two were established prior to the Cárdenas administration: the National Urban Mortgage and Public Works Bank, in 1933, and in 1934, Nacional Financiera (which was to expand into one of the largest and most prominent government banks in Latin America, but had only a limited financial role during the Cárdenas administration). The ejidal bank (discussed above) was established in 1935, and the Banco Nacional de Comercio Exterior in 1937. The latter was established at the instigation of the Banco de México, which was concerned about maintaining Mexico's balance of payments and foreign exchange; its basic function was the promotion of exports through providing credit facilities for producers engaged in production for export and managing the distribution and sale of certain export products. It also regulated food prices (Moore, 1963: 153-158). Its goals coincided, to some extent, with those of the agrarian reform program, which included the demonstration of the productive efficiency of the new ejidal and new collective forms of production. In addition, the National Workers' Bank of Industrial Promotion was created in 1937 to provide credit to organized producers lacking access to private credit (Moore, 1963: 160-165). As in the case of the ejidal bank, the workers' bank was enabled to exercise a considerable amount of control over its beneficiaries, having authority to remove officials of cooperatives at will, and to appoint accountants and bookkeepers (Weyl and Weyl, 1939: 263). But the resources allocated to the workers' bank were insufficient to meet the credit needs of the cooperatives, and in 1941 it was liquidated (Moore, 1963: 164).

That the two major government banks created during the Cárdenas administration were oriented to agricultural production (there were also special banks for specific products such as the National Union of Sugar Producers established in 1937) constitutes a major departure in the Cárdenas government from those that preceded and followed. The emphasis upon agrarian reform and the encouragement of agricultural production is also reflected in the structure of federal government expenditures during the Cárdenas years. For the first time, social and economic expenditures were greater than administrative expenditures, in part because for the first time military expenditures constituted less than 20 percent of the budget. Expenditures for agricultural credit (federal allocations to the agricultural credit bank and the ejidal bank) constituted 7.2 percent of the budget in 1935 and 9.15 percent in 1936, substantially more than in preceding years (Wilkie, 1967: 33, 102-103, 139).

With respect to sources of government revenue, the Cárdenas government seems to have utilized traditional tax sources, with little change, with the exception of an excess profits tax instituted in 1939. The major innovation was increased dependence upon loans from the central bank, which in the years 1937 and 1938 exceeded by far the allocations permitted by law (Moore, 1963: 101-104; Shelton, 1964: 143-145). This recourse to deficit financing, as well as wage increases granted to labor by government controlled arbitration boards, was blamed for the growing inflation that characterized the second half of Cárdenas's administration. With the exception of increased expenditures for agricultural credit, and the growing dependence upon central bank loans to finance government deficits, the fiscal policy of the Cárdenas government did not depart radically from that of previous administrations.

Although the Cárdenas government sought to encourage foreign investment in manufacturing and to channel private domestic financing into agricultural and industrial production, it does not appear to have had a developed industrial policy. Mosk (1950: 57) suggests that Cárdenas was interested chiefly in rural industry organized along cooperative lines, with industry tied to agriculture and the processing of agricultural products. However, Cárdenas's public works program, as well as the redistribution of income through agrarian reform and support of wage increases, directly and indirectly stimulated industry, resulting in an estimated 25 percent increase in manufacturing output between 1933 and 1938 (based on expanded utilization of existing capacity rather than industrial expansion) (Mosk, 1950: 59). Despite the inflationary effects of deficit financing to support the agricultural credit and public works program, Mosk feels that the benefits to the economy were greater than the damage resulting from inflation. Other pro-industry measures included the institution of tariffs in 1937 and 1938, which had the effect of extending protection to Mexican industry, and a decree of 1939 that for the first time made tax exemptions—heretofore limited to small firms—available to new firms of all sizes. Although these measures had little effect during the Cárdenas years, when private capital was on the defensive, they marked the beginning of extensive government subsidization and protection of industry that was to characterize succeeding administrations (Mosk, 1950: 63-64).

Direct government control over key economic sectors was also expanded under Cárdenas. Expropriated sugar mills, railroads, and finally the oil industry came under the jurisdiction of semigovernment corporations, often incorporating some form of worker control or self-management. Nationalization of certain industries often had the double function of eliminating foreign domination and extending state control over key economic sectors. Private interests saw the growth of the state sector as a threat, and were particularly chagrined by the introduction of worker management to these enterprises. In the long run, however, state sector enterprises have been operated in the interests of the private sector, in many cases providing subsidized inputs and services for industries.

The initiatives of the government in the creation of specialized credit agencies, in strengthening the role of the central bank in channeling private credit, and in extending state control in certain economic sectors were unquestionably innovative. However, they were innovative within the context of a general expansion of the economic role of the state, which was also occurring in other Latin American countries as well as the United States, and was to a large extent based on the application of Keynesian policies to the depression-ridden economies of the 1930s (Anderson, 1963: 119-120). At the same time, they established conditions for subsequent industrial growth under the pro-business governments that succeeded Cárdenas.

THE OIL EXPROPRIATION

In radically redefining the relationship among capital, labor, and the state, the government's expropriation of the British and U.S. oil interests in March 1938 is of central importance. On the one hand, it carries the conception of the state—as the embodiment of the national interest in relation to foreign capital and an entity above classes that intervenes actively in class conflict to protect the interests of the weaker class—as far as it was to go. On the other hand, it reveals the contradictions inherent in such a conception and its attempted application in a country such as Mexico.

The government's expropriation of the oil interests was the culmination of a lengthy labor conflict that began in November 1936, when the Union of Petroleum Workers, the result of a merger of 21 independent oil workers' unions, presented an industrywide contract to fifteen oil companies. After a 120-day negotiation period that failed to provide agreement, the oil workers went on strike on May 28, 1937, shutting down the industry. Fearing disastrous effects on the economy, however, the union ended the strike and instituted proceedings before the Federal Board of Conciliation and Arbitration. The Board's commission of experts undertook an extensive study of the oil industry, involving an audit of the companies' books, to determine whether they could afford to meet the demands of the unions. In August, the commission of experts issued its report recommending substantial wage increases as well as other benefits, justified on the basis of enormous industry profits and the manipulation of prices as a mechanism to transfer profits and evade Mexican taxation. After considering the recommendations of the committee and the objections of the companies, the Board gave its decision in December, basically following the recommendations of the experts, and the companies appealed the decision to the Supreme Court. On March 1, the Supreme Court handed down its decision upholding that of the Federal Board. The companies refused to abide by this decision and on March 18, Cárdenas announced their expropriation (Weyl and Weyl, 1939: 291-297; Cronon, 1960: 185).

The expropriation was significant for several reasons. First and most obviously, it asserted Mexican sovereignty in confrontation with powerful foreign corporations—among them Royal Dutch Shell (British owned) and Standard Oil of New Jersey—and terminated a particularly obnoxious form of foreign exploitation of Mexican resources and labor. The oil companies had been vociferous in their denunciations of Article 27 from the time of the promulgation of the constitution in 1917, and had on various occasions refused to comply with legislation respecting the exploitation of subsoil rights (Smith, 1972: 99). As pointed out by the committee of experts of the Board of Conciliation and Arbitration, the oil companies had consistently sold oil abroad to their subsidiaries at prices below the world level while charging prices above the prevailing world price for refined products. For some time, the oil companies had limited production in the Mexican oil fields, shifting production to their properties in Venezuela (Weyl and Weyl, 1939: 291-292). Finally, studies by the U.S. Department of the Interior and U.S. experts in the course of negotiations over compensation found that the oil companies had consistently overvalued their oil properties and exaggerated the amount of investment in reports to the State Department as well as to the Mexican government (Cronon, 1960: 261, 269-270). In short, the oil companies epitomized the worst evils of foreign exploitation of natural resources, and for a brief, euphoric moment all of Mexico was behind Cárdenas (Michaels, 1970: 55-56).

Second, the oil controversy was the most dramatic instance of a conflict between capital and labor in which the state intervened on behalf of labor. Although the decision of the arbitration board did not uphold all of labor's demands, it sided with labor in challenging the claims of the oil companies that they could not meet the wage increase requirements. Moreover, it appeared to vindicate the efforts of Cárdenas and Lombardo Toledano to organize and unify the working class, as it was the merger of independent oil workers' unions, supported by Cárdenas, which had enabled them to confront the industry as a whole.

Finally, while eliminating foreign control over the oil industry, the inclusion of this key industry within the parastatal sector at the same time strengthened the government's position with respect to foreign capital. In

1935, the government had established Petróleos de México (Pemex), a semiofficial company authorized to produce and market petroleum; in 1937 Pemex was reorganized and given powers to regulate domestic and export markets in the national interest (Weyl and Weyl, 1939: 291). The newly expropriated properties were turned over to Pemex; as in other government-owned industries they were worker-managed.

The petroleum expropriation resulted in severe accentuation of the strains on the Mexican economy caused by the failure of private enterprise to invest, the absence of capital with which to carry out reforms, and inflation. Capital outflows were accelerated, and the commitment of the Mexican government to pay compensation for the expropriated oil fields led to a retrenchment in those programs in which capital was required (Cronon, 1960: 227). In view of the insufficient availability of credit for the new ejidatarios, for example, the land distribution program was cut back (Michaels, 1970: 65-65). The oil companies immediately instituted an oil boycott, refusing to move Mexican oil on their tankers; instituted legal tie-ups of Mexico's oil shipments abroad; and persuaded U.S. manufacturers to refuse Mexico's prepaid cash orders for equipment needed to operate the oil industry (Meyer, 1972: 126; Weyl and Weyl, 1939: 304-306; Cronon, 1960: 208). The U.S. State Department cut back its purchases of Mexican silver (against the will of Treasury Secretary Henry Morgenthau, who recognized the repercussions on U.S.-owned silver mines in Mexico) and discouraged Export-Import Bank loans to Mexican industries. One ironic consequence of the initial refusal of the United States to permit oil imports or accept payment in oil was the necessity of the Mexican government to trade with Japan and Germany—despite its ideological opposition to fascism—to the consternation of Washington officials, who feared a shift from Mexican dependence upon U.S.-manufactured imports to a preference for those of Germany. Finally, the reorganization of the oil industry under the state-owned petroleum company placed the state in the ambiguous position of the capitalist as exploiter of wage labor, as became evident when the oil workers made demands for higher wages that the state was unable to meet.

The state's need for capital, and its dependence upon private sources, national and foreign, for that capital, led to a general deceleration of the Cárdenas reform program. The outbreak of war in Europe, and the Mexican government's support for the U.S. war effort, were also factors in discontinuing the attacks on U.S. capital in the interests of hemispheric solidarity against the threat of fascism. Ironically, during the last years of his administration, Cárdenas himself was urging the workers to think in terms of class collaboration rather than class conflict, and to work in the national interest (Michaels, 1970: 69). Thus the earlier conception of the state, which had characterized pre-Cárdenas administrations and was to become again ascendant in post-Cárdenas Mexico, was already implicit in the final years of the Cárdenas government.

THE CARDENAS YEARS AND
THE AUTONOMOUS STATE:
CONTRADICTIONS

The basic contradiction inherent in the conceptualization of the autonomous state operating within a system of capitalist production relations resides in the attempted segregation of political power from economic power. While the capitalist class is relatively weak, the state may be able to operate with relative autonomy; in the absence of direct state control over the means of production, however, state autonomy is transitional, and power over the state eventually passes to the economically dominant class.

Even in a country in which the system of production was relatively undefined, as in Mexico in the 1930s, the owning classes were sufficiently strong to threaten or sabotage many of the initiatives of the Cárdenas government. Their control of major newspapers gave them powerful leverage for promoting the legitimacy of pro-business, anti-government views. The ability of landowners and foreign and domestic companies to hire mercenaries, institute company unions, and support fascist organizations constituted a more direct means of sabotaging government reform. Labor legislation and rulings of government arbitration boards that increased workers' wages were countered by price increases on the part of employers.

To the extent that it refused to offer safeguards to private property—as indicated in the agrarian reform program and the expropriation of foreign oil interests—the government failed to fulfill one of its basic functions within a capitalist production system. The owning classes, foreign and domestic, retaliated with capital outflows, refusal to invest, and production cutbacks. In an underdeveloped country, the effects of the capital loss were particularly acute. Because the private sector was alienated by the government's reform programs, attempts by the government to channel funds away from speculation into productive channels and to encourage industry by tax concessions were ineffective.

A second implication of the segregation of economic and political power was the possibility of cooptation of political leadership. The ability to use political power to obtain economic concessions, and the rewards for protecting business interests, enabled army officers, state governors, and government officials at various levels to enrich themselves even during the Cárdenas regime (Michaels, 1970: 52). Having a vested interest in the system undoubtedly cooled their ardor to change it.

In addition to contradictions inherent in the conceptualization of state autonomy, there are contradictions within the state itself, inasmuch as this embodies not only the actual government and its program but also an existing institutional bureaucracy and its past history. The power of the executive to recall state governors, exercised by Cárdenas on several occasions, generally led to verbalized support for his government on the part of state and local officials, but there were instances of state support for business groups and company unions. At all levels of government, and within the government party, there existed continuity with the pro-business government of Calles and his followers, which renovation of key posts could not completely eradicate. To a lesser extent, these contradictions existed in new government institutions such as the ejidal bank, in which, given the control of officials at the local level over the ejidatarios, implementation of goals depended upon their competence and probity. It is also possible that the continuity of personnel at top levels of the Finance Ministry and the Banco de México with previous regimes (as well as their ties with the business sector) was a factor in the failure of the state to institute more stringent controls on capital.

Finally, in addition to contradictions within the conception of the autonomous state and within the state structure, there were those contradictions that arose in the course of implementing government programs, in which the ability of the state to operate autonomously confronted the implications of a system of production in which it did not control the means of production. This was most evident in the agrarian reform, when the state found itself unable to provide sufficient credit for the ejidatarios created by the land distribution program—the problem aggravated, of course, by the rapidity and extent of land distribution. Despite the rapid progress of the ejidal bank in organizing local ejidal societies, which numbered 5,152 and included 398,100 ejidatarios by 1940, these constituted only a fraction of the total number of ejidatarios, who by 1940 numbered 1,601,680. Furthermore, not all ejidal societies received bank support; those societies approved for credit numbered 3,473 with 239,407 members. Thus less than 15 percent of the ejidatarios received credit by 1940. The agrarian credit bank also benefited only a fraction of the small landowners (Moore, 1963: 142, 149-151).

One effect of the insufficiency of capital was to cut back reform efforts in view of the inability to finance them. In other cases, the state had recourse to private capital—including foreign capital. In Baja California, for example, the ejidal bank obtained loans from the subsidiary of Anderson Clayton, which purchased the cotton crop from ejidatarios as well as private owners. In subsequent years the ejidal bank was to receive substantial loans from the U.S. Export-Import Bank (via the Banco de Comercio Exterior).

One result of dependence upon private or foreign capital was the tendency to finance ejidal societies on the basis of their economic soundness and health rather than need. Criteria of economic efficiency were incorporated in the policy of the bank itself, as is evident in the following statement from its 1945 annual report:

> *Even when it does not pursue lucrative ends . . . the ejidal bank is and must be fundamentally a banking institution; thus, in performing the social and economic functions with which it has been entrusted it must take care that its operations not be carried out with losses, since only in this way can it have opened the doors of semi-official and private credit, and even that of the Federal Government, for the exclusive benefit of the ejidatarios who constitute our clientele.*
>
> *For these reasons, not only have we attempted to select those societies and members effectively solvent, but those which have made the greater commitment of sustaining the headquarters of the zone and the agencies which group them [cited in Moore, 1963: 220-221].*

This tendency of government credit institutions to emphasize economically sound ejidos (which could probably obtain credit elsewhere) may also have been a logical consequence of the emphasis of the Cárdenas government upon the large-scale, collective ejidos oriented to commercial production, such as the Laguna cooperative and henequén regions of Yucatán. Although this emphasis was explicable as a means of demonstrating the economic viability of collective enterprise, it may well have established a precedent for subsequent credit programs.

The attempt by officials of the Cárdenas government, party leaders, and labor leaders to establish a mechanism whereby the peasants and working class could effectively pressure the government to act in their interests through the organization of labor and peasant confederations and their incorporation into the new government party was thwarted by the top-down structure of these organizations, which concentrated organizational control in the hands of the leadership. With the cooptation of organizational leadership into the dominant system, these organizations have ceased to be instruments for achieving the welfare of their members and have instead become instruments for their domination and control.[2]

CONCLUSION:
THE LIMITS OF STATE AUTONOMY

The transformation from the autonomous state to one that functioned to maintain conditions for capitalist production was a rapid one. As has been noted, the process had already begun under the Cárdenas government. Under his successor, Avila Camacho, capital received the protection it wanted; reforms were slowed down and industrialization encouraged through tax concessions and tariff protection. Nacional Financiera was promoted to a full-fledged government development bank, and promoted investment in nearly every economic sector by means of loans, guarantees, or stock and bond purchases (Nacional Financiera, 1971: 18-20, 168-169; Shelton, 1961: 151; Blair, 1964: 213-214). Settlement of the oil compensation question and collaboration between the U.S. and Mexican governments on a wide range of projects during the war years aided the restoration of cordial relations between the two governments, and laid the basis for renewed American investments in Mexican industry. U.S. government officials—particularly the U.S. ambassador to Mexico, George Messersmith—as well as U.S. businessmen, saw Mexico as a promising postwar market for manufactured goods, especially heavy machinery, and for investment (Clash, 1972: 113-114, 122-123). U.S. investment in manufacturing in Mexico has tripled every decade since 1940 (National Chamber Foundation, n.d.: 67).

Under Miguel Alemán, president of Mexico between 1946 and 1952, capital formation was further encouraged, partly through regressive wage policies. Although prices increased 10 percent annually, wages were held down. When workers tried to protest these conditions, the army was used to repress strikes and dissident leaders were jailed (Hanson, 1971: 115).

By 1958, the state was no longer in a position to control industrial and commercial elites. When President López Mateos stated that he would govern "on the extreme left within the constitution," $250 million from the private sector was sent out of the country in a matter of days. The president quickly modified his position, which suggests that the process of transformation to the capitalist state could no longer be reversed (Hanson, 1971: 169).

Today, the role of the state in Mexico seems to be analogous to that of the state in advanced capitalist countries: the maintenance of conditions for capitalist production and management of contradictions—with the important distinction that in view of Mexico's dependence on foreign capital, the state is confronted with conditions and contradictions arising from dependent capitalist production. These conditions have been described in detail elsewhere (see González Casanova 1965; Aguilar y Carmona, 1967; Labastida, 1972; Villa, 1972; Martínez, 1972; Basurto, 1972; Barkin, 1971; Wionczek, 1970; Ceceña Gómez, 1963) and will be mentioned only briefly here. They include increased dependence upon imports—particularly machinery and other inputs for subsidiaries of multinational corporations, dependence of the public and private sectors on foreign loans, and the monopolization of certain industrial sectors by foreign capital or major industrial groups. Among the effects have been severe trade and payments imbalances resulting from profit repatriation, royalty payments, and service of loans; and certain distortions in industrial development. Thus production in many enterprises is based on capital-intensive technology and geared to high-income groups, with a consequent failure of industry to provide employment for a growing labor force or to include a significant proportion of the population in the commodities market (Labastida, 1972: 144; Wionczek, 1970: 457-458, 461-462; González Casanova, 1965: 42-43; Ceceña Gómez, 1963: 166; Ramos Garza, 1972: 212; Aguilar y Carmona, 1967).

The existence of oligopolistic control and in many cases capital-intensive technology in industry, as well as the mechanization of commercial agriculture, has been responsible for a growing process of marginalization, with significant proportions of the population unable to find employment in agriculture or in industry. As noted above, over half of the active rural population was landless by 1960; between 1950 and 1960 the average number of days worked by landless workers decreased from 190 days annually to 100 (Martínez, 1962: 11). Industry is able to absorb only approximately 10 percent of the new labor force of 500,000 annually; the remaining 450,000 workers are obliged to find work in the tertiary sector—often entailing employment in peripheral positions (Basurto, 1972: 65).

This process is reflected in the contrast between Mexico's impressive growth rates and its increasing income inequality. In 1963, half of the population received 15.5 percent of the income—down from 19 percent in 1950—while the top 10 percent continued to receive approximately 50 percent of the income. The income of the lowest fifth of the population did not increase in absolute terms between 1950 and 1963 (Barkin, 1971: 668).

Attempts by the state to lessen these contradictions have often led to new problems. The "Mexicanization" of industry (the requirement that enterprises be 51 percent owned by Mexicans) has to a large extent led to the further integration of foreign capital with the internationalized sector of the domestic bourgeoisie. Some analysts suggest that certain sectors of the state bureaucracy are fused with foreign interests and the internationalized bourgeoisie in a manner that facilitates economic stability (Labastida, 1972: 103, 117, 134).

Tariffs, import quotas, and tax concessions to protect and encourage domestic industry (particularly labor-intensive industry) have in many cases had the effect of maintaining inefficient, high-cost enterprises; they are also taken advantage of by multinational corporations (Nacional Financiera, 1971: 50-51; Wionczek, 1970: 454). Efforts to redistribute income and to lessen state dependence upon foreign loans through tax reforms frequently encounter the intransigence of domestic economic groups, whose economic control the state is apparently unable or unwilling to break (González Casanova, 1965: 139).

The instruments for the management of class conflict at the disposal of the state are formidable. Such organizations as the CNC and CTM, as well as the ejidal and agrarian banks and the PRI (Partido Revolucionario Institucional, successor to the PRM), constitute major mechanisms for cooptation and control. (See Anderson and Cockcroft, 1972: 230-240; and Fagen and Tuohy, 1972: 214-215, for descriptions of the cooptive processes of the PRI.) Left-wing movements or parties that attempt to challenge the hegemony of the PRI are coopted or repressed (Anderson and Cockcroft, 1972: 230-238). More direct methods of coercion by local landlords or political bosses are often tolerated by the federal government, which has also utilized the army to repress dissident groups that cannot be coopted; the massacre of demonstrators at the Plaza of Three Cultures on October 2, 1968, and the recent death of guerilla leader Lucio Cabañas and his followers after a five-month search by half of the Mexican army are two examples.

It is difficult to assess how long the Mexican state will be able to contain the political and economic contradictions arising from dependent capitalist development through the combined policies of economic rationalization, cooptation, and coercion, particularly in view of the growth of population sectors whose marginal situation places them outside of the benefits and control mechanisms of the state. It is clear, however, that those controlling the Mexican state today no longer have the option of effectively defending the interests of underprivileged groups against those of dominant groups and classes.

NOTES

1. The description of the functions of the state is based in part on Murray (1971: 197ff.), O'Connor (1973: 6-8, chap. 3), and Picciotti and Radice (1973: 63).

2. The most significant measure of the Cárdenas government was the agrarian reform. To the extent that it destroyed the semifeudal landowning system that had characterized Mexico (and continued to characterize most Latin American countries for another 25 years), it removed a major institutional obstacle to agricultural productivity. That the Cárdenas government had not intended its replacement by capitalist productive systems would seem to be obvious in view of the government's emphasis upon the establishment of ejidos and the institution of collective farming where possible. Nevertheless, the inadequacy of government credit (which led many small landowners and ejidatarios to sell or rent their land), the remnants of old forms of exploitation (through continued landowner control of credit, for example) and the institution of potential new ones (through the dependence of the ejidos upon the ejidal bank functionaries), and the ability of landowners to circumvent the law restricting the size of landholdings (for example, by distributing portions among relatives and friends) have led to the emergence of dual systems of agriculture in both the ejidal and private sectors, characterized by large-scale commercial units producing for the internal market on the one hand and minifundia oriented to subsistence production on the other. A second characteristic has been the growth in the number of landless workers—virtually half of the rural population by 1960—whose opportunities for employment in the increasingly mechanized commercial farms have been consistently reduced (Martínez, 1972: 5). At the same time, increased agricultural productivity has made Mexico potentially self-sufficient in food production and has permitted agricultural exports to support Mexico's industrialization program to a degree unparalleled in most Latin American countries (Hanson, 1971: 58-59; Del Campo, 1972: 115).

REFERENCES

Aguilar, M., Alonso and Fernando Carmona
    1967 *México: riqueza y miseria*. Mexico: Editorial Nuestro Tiempo, S.A.
Alavi, Hamza
    1972 "The state in post-colonial societies—Pakistan and Bangladesh." *New Left Review*, 74 (July/August).
Alcázar, Antonio
    1970 *Las agrupaciones patronales en México*. Mexico: Jornadas 66, Colegio de México.
Anderson, Bo and James D. Cockcroft
    1962 "Control and cooptation in Mexican politics," in James Cockcroft et al., *Dependence and Underdevelopment: Latin America's Political Economy*. Garden City, NY: Anchor.
Anderson, Charles
    1963 "Bankers as revolutionaries," in William P. Glade and Charles W. Anderson (eds.) *The Political Economy of Mexico*. Madison: University of Wisconsin Press.
Ashby, Joe C.
    1963 *Organized Labor and the Mexican Revolution Under Lázaro Cárdenas*. Chapel Hill: University of North Carolina Press.
Baran, Paul A.
    1957 *The Political Economy of Growth*. New York: Monthly Review Press.
Barkin, David
    1971 "La persistencia de la pobreza en México: un análisis económico estructural." *Comercio Exterior* 21 (August): 667-674.

Basurto, Jorge
1972 "Obstáculos al cambio en el movimiento obrero," in *Perfil de México en 1980*, Vol. 3. México: Siglo XXI.
Bennett, Robert L.
1965 *The Financial Sector and Economic Development: The Mexican Case*. Baltimore: Johns Hopkins University Press.
Blair, Calvin P.
1964 "Nacional Financiera: Entrepreneurship in a mixed economy," in Raymond Vernon (ed.) *Public Policy and Private Enterprise in Mexico*. Cambridge, MA: Harvard University Press.
Bodenheimer, Suzanne
1970 "Dependency and imperialism: The roots of Latin American underdevelopment." *Politics and Society* (May).
Brandenberg, Frank
1964 *The Making of Modern Mexico*. Englewood Cliffs, NJ: Prentice-Hall.
Bukharin, Nikolai
1973 *Imperialism and the World Economy*. New York: Monthly Review Press.
Cárdenas, Lázaro
1972 *Ideario político*. Mexico: Ediciones Era.
Cardoso, Fernando Henrique
1972 "Dependency and development in Latin America." *New Left Review* 74 (July/August).
Ceceña Gómez, José Luis
1963 *El capitalismo monopolista y la economía mexicana*. Mexico: Cuadernos Americanos.
Chevalier, Francois
1967 "The ejido and political stability in Mexico," in Claudio Velix (ed.) *The Politics of Conformity in Latin America*. London: Oxford University Press.
Clash, Thomas Wood
1972 "United States-Mexican relations, 1940-1946: a study of U.S. interests and politics." Ph.D. dissertation, State University of New York at Buffalo.
Constitution of Mexico, 1917 (as amended)
1972 Washington: General Secretariat, Organization of American States.
Córdova, Arnaldo
1972 *La formación del poder político en México*. Mexico: Ediciones Era.
1973 *La ideología de la revolución mexicana*. Mexico: Ediciones Era.
Cronon, E. David
1960 *Josephus Daniels in Mexico*. Madison: University of Wisconsin Press.
Dahrendorf, Ralf
1959 *Class and Class Conflict in Industrial Society*. Stanford, CA: Stanford University Press.
Del Campo, Julio Labastida Martín
1972 "Los grupos dominantes frente a las alternativas del cambio," in *Perfil de México en 1980*. Mexico: Siglo XXI.
Domhoff, G. William
1970 *The Higher Circles*. New York: Vintage.
Fagen, Richard R. and William S. Tuohy
1972 "Aspects of the Mexican political system." *Studies in Comparative International Development* 7 (Fall).
Girling, Sherry
1973 "The state in post-colonial societies—Pakistan and Bangladesh: comments on Hamza Alavi." *Kapitalistate* 2.

Glade, William P. and Charles W. Anderson (eds.)
1963 *The Political Economy of Mexico.* Madison: University of Wisconsin Press.
Gómez Palacio, Roberto Dávila
1955 "Concentración financiera privada de México." *Investigacíon Económica* (August).
González Casanova, Pablo
1970 *Democracy in Mexico.* New York: Oxford University Press.
González Navarro, Moisés
1963 *La Confederación Nácional Campesina (Un grupo de presión en la reforma agraria Mexicana).* Mexico: B. Costa-Amic-Editor.
Hanson, Roger
1971 *The Politics of Mexican Development.* Baltimore: Johns Hopkins University Press.
Hein, Wolfgang and Konrad Stenzel
1973 "The capitalist state and underdevelopment in Latin America: the case of Venezuela." *Kapitalistate* 2.
Huizer, Gerritt
1972 *The Revolutionary Potential of Peasants in Latin America.* Lexington, MA: D. C. Heath.
Ianni, Octavio
1974 *Sociología del imperialismo.* Mexico: Sep Setentas.
Johnson, Joel L.
1965 *Mexican National Agrarian Credit.* B.A. honors thesis, Wesleyan University.
Kapitalistate
1973 Introduction to Working Papers on the Kapitalistate, 1.
Kolko, Gabriel
1963 *The Triumph of Conservatism.* Chicago: Quadrangle.
Labastida Martin del Campo, Julio
1972 "Los grupos dominates frente a las alternativas del cambio," in *Perfil de Mexico en 1980.* Mexico: Siglo XXI.
MacEwan, Arthur
1972 "Capitalist expansion, ideology and intervention." *Review of Radical Political Economics* 4 (Spring): 36-58.
Martínez Ruiz, Jorge
1972 "Los campesinos Mexicanos: perspectivas en el proceso de marginalización," in *Perfil de México en 1980.* Mexico: Siglo XXI.
Mexican Labor News
1936-1940. Mexico: Workers' University of Mexico.
Meyer, Lorenzo
1972 "Cambio político y dependencia: México en el siglo XX." *Foro* 50 (October/December).
Michaels, Albert L.
1970 "The crisis of Cardenismo." *Journal of Latin American Studies* 2 (May): 51-79.
1971 The Mexican Election of 1940. Buffalo: State University of New York, Council on International Studies.
Miliband, Ralph
1969 *The State in Capitalist Society.* New York: Basic Books.
1973 "Poulantzas and the capitalist state." *New Left Review* 82 (November/December): 83-92.
Moore, O. Ernesto
1963 *Evolución de las instituciones financieras en México.* Mexico: Centro de Estudios Monetarios Latinoamericanos.

Moore, Stanley W.
1957 *The Critique of Capitalist Democracy: An Introduction to the Theory of the State in Marx, Engels, and Lenin*. New York: Paine Whitman.

Mosk, Sanford A.
1950 *Industrial Revolution in Mexico*. Berkeley: University of California Press.

Murray, Robin
1971 "The internationalization of capital and the nation state." *New Left Review* 67 (May/June): 84-100.

Nacional Financiera, S.A. y Comisión Económica para la América Latina
1971 *La política industrial en el desarrollo económico de México*. Mexico: NAFIN.

National Chamber Foundation and Council of the Americas
n.d. *Impact of Foreign Investment in Mexico*.

O'Connor, James
1973 *Fiscal Crisis of the State*. New York: St. Martin's.

Picciotti, Sol and Hugo Radice
1973 "Capital and state in the world economy." *Kapitalistate* 1.

Pompermayer, Malori J. and William C. Smith, Jr.
1973 "The state in dependent societies: preliminary notes," in Frank Bonilla and Robert Girling (eds.) *Structures of Dependency*. Stanford, CA: Stanford University Press.

Poulantzas, Nicol
1969 "The problem of the capitalist state." *New Left Review* 58 (November/December): 67-78.

Quijano, Aníbal
1972 "Imperialismo y capitalismo de estado." *Sociedad y Política* (Lima) 1 (July).

Raby, David L.
1972 "La contribución del cardenismo al desarrollo de México en la época actual." *Aportes* 26 (October).

Ramos Garza, Oscar
1971 *México antes la inversión extanjera: legislación, política y prácticas*. Mexico: Impresora Azteca.

Sardei-Biermann, Sabine, et al.
1973 "Class domination and the political system: a critical interpretation of recent contributions by Claus Offe." *Kapitalistate* 2.

Shelton, David H.
1964 "The banking system: money and the goal of growth," in Raymond Vernon (ed.) *Public Policy and Private Enterprise in Mexico*. Cambridge, MA: Harvard University Press.

Smith, Robert Freeman
1972 *The United States and Revolutionary Nationalism in Mexico, 1916-1932*. Chicago: University of Chicago Press.

Sunkel, Osvaldo
1971 "Desarrollo, subdesarrollo, dependencia, marginalización y desigualdades espaciales: hacia un enfoque totalizante." *Investigación Económica* 31 (January/March): 23-77.

U.S. Department of State
1933-1944 *Papers Relating to Foreign Relations of the United States* (volumes on the American republics). Washington, DC: Government Printing Office.

Villa, A. Manuel
1972 "Las bases del estado mexicano y su problemática actual," in *Perfil de México en 1980*, Vol. 3. Mexico: Siglo XXI.

Warren, Bill
   1972 "Capitalist planning and the state." *New Left Review* 72 (March/April): 3-29.
Weinstein, James
   1968 *The Corporate Ideal in the Liberal State: 1910-1918.* Boston: Beacon.
Weyl, Nathaniel and Sylvia
   1939 *The Reconquest of Mexico: The Years of Lázaro Cárdenas.* New York: Oxford
   University Press.
Wilkie, James
   1967 *The Mexican Revolution: Federal Expenditure and Social Change Since 1910.*
   Berkeley: University of California Press.
Wionczek, Miguel S.
   1970 "La inversión extranjera privada en México: problemas y perspectivas." *Investi-
   gación Económica* 30 (July/September).
Wolfe, Alan
   1974 "New directions in the Marxist theory of politics." *Politics and Society* 4
   (Winter).
Wright, Harry K.
   1971 *Foreign Enterprise in Mexico: Laws and Politics.* Chapel Hill: University of
   North Carolina Press.

PART II

THE MEXICAN ECONOMY

4

Mexico's Albatross
The U.S. Economy

by
*David Barkin**

Mexico is a faded success story. The "miracle" of past decades of growth has thrust the country into the grasp of the international capitalist system and created a panorama of misery and destitution behind a thin veneer of showcase industrialization and modernity. The present regime

> *has resolved to modify the strategy of our development in view of the evident bankruptcy of the growth structure that shaped the country during the past three decades. . . . We would no longer continue to travel the old beaten path that has led to the disproportionate concentration of income, growing unemployment, inflation and dependency. We chose to change the course when all signs pointed to an imminent social crisis of serious proportions [Zapata, 1972: 6].*

This evaluation by a senior member of the "inner family" of Mexican politicians is symptomatic of the desperate search now taking place for corrective policies that would reverse the explosive deterioration in the balance of payments, ensure continued high rates of economic growth, and channel some minimal volume of resources to the lower classes, who clearly pose a threat to the existing social order.

This paper outlines some of the features of the present socioeconomic panorama that resulted from unbridled capitalist development. It then examines the contribution that foreign economic penetration has made to Mexico's present problems. It is suggested that there is an intimate relationship between the present productive structure—and its pattern of control—and the social and economic problems the country is experiencing. This relationship emerges from the overpowering way in which U.S.

---

*David Barkin is Professor of Economics at the Universidad Autónoma Metropolitana and Research Director at the Centro de Ecodesarrollo. He was awarded the National Prize in Political Economy in 1978 for his book, *Inflación y Democracía* (with Gustavo Esteva), published by Siglo XXI Editores. His most recent books (with Blanca Suarez) are *El Fin del Principio: Las Semillas y la Seguridad Alimentaria* (1983) and *El Fin de la Autosuficiencia Alimentaria* (1985), both published by Editorial Oceano in conjunction with El Centro de Ecodesarrollo.

interests have molded the Mexican economic structure and, consequently, created the basis for the present social and economic unrest. An attack merely on the visible symptoms of malaise is not adequate. A permanent solution must recognize the integrity of productive and distributive structures and relate them to the dynamics of capitalist production; such a solution requires a transformation of the system as a whole.

THE DYNAMICS OF PAUPERIZATION

Mexico is a country of poor people living in the midst of an elite becoming rich at their expense. Wherever one turns, there is evidence of official policies and institutions that are heightening the differences among classes. Even the prosperity of the few, however, depends on the willingness of the U.S. government, tourists, and transnational corporations to guarantee the success of the development strategy that created the bankrupt growth structure mentioned above. The strategy now regularly requires more than $1 billion a year to compensate for the foreign trade deficit. Mexico's exports of agricultural and manufactured goods, however, cannot match the voracious growth of imports needed to satisfy the demands of its dependent bourgeoisie.

Some inkling of the tremendous differences in living standards among classes is evident in Table 4.1. The average monthly income of the richest 5 percent of the families in Mexico is now 36 times as great as that of the poorest 10 percent of Mexican families, whereas it was only (!) 30 times as great twenty years ago (compare column 12 with column 9). The richest tenth of the population consistently received about one-half of the total income while the poorest one-half of the population has received less than 20 percent of Mexico's total personal income. From the table we see, in fact, that the share of the top 10 percent has been rising over time while that of the bottom 50 percent has been falling. The situation was relatively better for the poor in 1940, although the available data do not permit us to confirm this statement statistically.[1]

The reasons for this continued concentration are made clear by an examination of the structure of the Mexican economy. In agriculture, the agrarian reform provided a stable institutional framework within which most beneficiaries (about 90 percent of the 2.8 million) received land that, however, did not produce enough income to support a family. At the same time, public agricultural development policy deliberately enriched a relatively small number of people who worked to develop a capital-intensive agriculture that could incorporate important advances in agricultural technology, the extension of irrigation, agricultural credit

TABLE 4.1
Distribution of Family Incomes in Mexico, 1950, 1958, 1963, 1969 (in percentages)

Deciles[a] (10% of families)	1950		1958		1963		1969		Average Monthly Income (1969 prices)			
	By Decile (1)	Cumulative (2)	By Decile (3)	Cumulative (4)	By Decile (5)	Cumulative (6)	By Decile (7)	Cumulative (8)	1950 (9)	1958 (10)	1963 (11)	1969 (12)
I	2.7	2.7	2.2	2.2	2.0	2.0	2.0	2.0	374	437	457	533
II	2.4	6.1	2.8	5.0	2.2	4.2	2.0	4.0	472	545	518	533
III	3.8	9.9	3.3	8.3	3.2	7.4	3.0	7.0	527	638	745	795
IV	4.4	14.3	3.9	12.2	3.7	11.1	3.5	10.5	610	745	865	927
V	4.8	19.1	4.5	16.7	4.6	15.7	4.5	15.0	665	880	1,069	1,193
VI	5.5	24.6	5.5	22.2	5.2	20.9	5.0	20.0	760	1,140	1,208	1,330
VII	7.0	31.6	6.3	28.5	6.6	27.5	7.0	27.0	968	1,220	1,528	1,860
VIII	8.6	40.2	8.6	37.1	9.9	37.4	9.0	36.0	1,190	1,660	2,308	2,390
IX	10.8	51.0	13.6	50.7	12.7	50.1	13.0	49.0	1,498	2,632	2,960	3,450
X	49.0	100.0	49.3	100.0	49.9	100.0	51.0	100.0	6,790	9,560	11,615	13,540
90-95%	8.8		10.7		11.6		15.0		2,450	4,124	5,395	7,960
95-100%	40.2		38.6		38.3		36.0		11,110	14,975	17,850	19,150
Total	100.0		100.0		100.0		100.0		1,385	1,935	2,328	2,651
Gini coefficient	0.50		0.53		0.55		0.58					

SOURCES: Navarrete (1970); 1969-1970 family income survey with adjustments.
a. Each decile represents 510,500 families for 1950; 640,510 for 1958; 732,960 for 1963 and 889,174 for 1969.
b. The last decile at the top of the scale of income has been divided into two parts of 5% each.

facilities, and price support programs. As a result, 3 percent of the farms (some 79,000 units out of a total of 2.5 million) produced 55 percent of all agricultural produce in 1960 and accounted for 80 percent of the increase in the value of production in the 1950s (Eckstein, 1968, and Table 4.2). There is every indication that the situation has deteriorated even further since then.

In industry the situation is little different. The 1965 industrial census enumerated almost 135,000 firms, but most of these were small, marginal operations with few resources. In fact, the 1,117 largest firms (0.82 percent of the total) accounted for 64.3 percent of total production and 66.3 percent of the invested capital reported that year; the concentration in Mexican manufacturing was exceedingly high but similar to U.S. levels (Cinta, 1972: Table 8; *Fortune*, May 1974).

Concentration does not, however, tell the whole story of Mexican industry. The industrial census also showed that it is precisely in the most dynamic industries where the least amount of labor is being used. In the same operations in which almost two-thirds of manufacturing output is produced, only about one-third (34 percent) of the industrial labor force is employed (Cinta, 1972). Thus the industries and enterprises with the highest rates of growth are precisely the ones that are aggravating the problem of insufficient employment growth. Of course, growing unemployment contributes to the continuing concentration of personal income in Mexico.

It is not coincidental that these same firms are also highly influenced, if not directly controlled, by foreign capital. Foreigners controlled more than one-quarter (26.7 percent) of the assets of the 938 largest manufacturing companies mentioned above, and this control was most selectively concentrated in the most dynamic capital-intensive industries of the country (see Tables 4.3 and 4.4) (Cinta, 1972: Table 10).

To match the pattern of concentration in agriculture and industry, the financial sector of the economy is also tightly controlled. Of a total of 74 independent organizations, 6 large commercial banks control more than four-fifths (83.4 percent) of all deposits. These banks further heighten income inequalities by "absorbing resources from the provinces without reinvesting a fair share in the most needy areas." Furthermore, these banks encourage the channeling of credit to the firms they control, reinforcing the "disequilibrating and concentrating" effect of the banking system on the national economy (*Comercio Exterior*, May 1971: 366-368, 390). It is difficult to document the tight interrelationships that are known to exist among the captains of industry, agriculture, and banking, but these ties, if not direct control by one group of operations in several sectors, exist and reinforce the pattern of cumulative concentration that is

TABLE 4.2
Proportional Distribution of Production and Resources, 1960

Type of Holding	Number of Plots	Value of Production	Value of Plots[a]	Cultivable Area	Value of Machinery	Irrigable Area	% of Farmers Receiving Credits	Contribution to Increase Production Between 1950 and 1960
Total	100.0	100.0	100.0	100.0	100.0	100.0	51.5	100.0
Infrasubsistence	50.3	4.2	6.7	13.6	1.3	–	20.5	–1
Subfamily	33.8	17.1	13.8	24.5	6.5	3.9	28.2	10
Family	12.6	24.4	22.6	19.2	17.0	27.0	58.1	11
Multifamily Medium	2.8	22.0	19.3	14.4	31.5	31.5	62.6	35
Multifamily Large	0.5	32.3	37.6	28.3	43.7	37.6	75.0	45

SOURCE: Centro de Investigaciones Agrarias (1973: Vol. I, 296; Vol. III, XIV-20, XI-144).

a. The value of the plot is composed of the value of the land, of fixed and semifixed capital, and of livestock. By *plot* is meant the ejidal plots (not the whole ejido) and the nonejidal plots.

b. Based on a regional sample survey and judged not to be representative of the nation as a whole.

TABLE 4.3
Mexico's 938 Largest Industrial Firms, 1965
(measured by total production)

Firms	Control of Total Production (%) of the 938	of the Country
Top 10	17.7	11.0
Top 100	49.4	30.6
Top 300	72.2	44.7
All	100.0	62.0

SOURCE: Based on information from the VIII Censo Industrial, 1965, and elaborated by Cinta (1970, 1972) as part of a larger study on the industrial entrepreneur and the economic development of Mexico in El Colegio de Mexico.

characteristic of the Mexican pattern of economic development. Table 4.5 shows the important role of banking in the major industrial corporations in Mexico.

Not surprisingly, the high concentration of ownership of the means of production has—inevitably—resulted in the worsening of regional disparities. Modern, commercial agriculture is concentrated in the northern part of the country (and in a few other irrigation districts) where public investments in irrigation are complemented by public and private agricultural credit programs and improved technology. In industry, the differences between the industrialized zones of the country (Valley of Mexico and Monterrey), the semi-industrial states of Coahuila, Chihuahua, Jalisco, Puebla, and Veracruz, and the rest of the country (classified as "subindustrial" by the government) have been growing steadily since 1940 (Nacional Financiera, 1971). As might be expected, banking further heightens regional differences by giving preferential treatment to industrial regions over agricultural regions.

The government also contributes to this geographic concentration, which results in regional differences, in spite of repeated declarations that one of its goals is to "mitigate and correct imbalances in regional development." Although the president declared, in 1970, that "this objective received special attention in the annual financing of investment programs," public investment was less widely dispersed in the 1964-1970 period than during the previous administration (Mexico, 1964, 1970). This lack of regional balance is also manifest in the wide disparities in educational opportunities available in each region; the poorer the area, the fewer the opportunities (Barkin, 1971, 1975). The same is true for almost every aspect of economic, social, and political life in which the government is involved. It goes without saying that these regional dispari-

TABLE 4.4
Distribution of 938 Largest Industrial Firms
by Composition of Capital, 1965

	Degree of Control of Total Production (%)			
Firms	Foreign	State	Private National	Total
Top 10	50.0	20.0	30.0	100.0
Top 20	55.0	15.0	30.0	100.0
Top 50	48.0	22.0	30.0	100.0
Top 100	47.0	13.0	40.0	100.0
Top 500	31.0	7.4	61.6	100.0
All	26.7	5.1	68.0	100.0

SOURCE: Based on information from the VIII Censo Industrial, 1965, and elaborated by Cinta (1970, 1972) as part of a larger study on the industrial entrepreneur and the economic development of Mexico in El Colegio de Mexico.

ties are only indirect indicators of the unequal distribution of income mentioned above.

It is not surprising, in light of this analysis, that the concentration of income is increasing with time as shown in Table 4.1 above. President Echeverría (1971) himself pointed out that "the unequal distribution of wealth in our country is, to a large degree, concomitant with an unequal distribution of productive activities and, above all, excessive concentration." It is remarkable that even before intensive industrialization began, the regional—and presumably to a large degree the personal—income distribution pattern of present-day Mexico had been indelibly engrained on the Mexican socioeconomic structure: "The regions which participated in the development which was initiated at the end of the past century are the same ones which now have a relatively high level of development, while those which were not integrated into the dynamics of the Porfirian economy still remain in the backwash, both economically and socially. . . . The economic and social chasm which separates the backward from the advanced regions has grown" even more profound in the ensuing years (Appendini and Murayama, 1972: 8).

Poverty and the striking contrast with the enclaves of affluence are the hallmarks of the Mexican environment. Economic concentration remains, and the strategy of "stabilizing development" played its role in further heightening problems of unemployment, urban decay, and rural isolation (Ortiz Mena, 1969; Barkin, 1974). The present administration bemoans the fact that "income in Mexico is still very small and inequitably distributed" but goes on to explain the cause for its preoccupation:

TABLE 4.5
The 50 Largest Companies in Mexico, 1970 (based on capitalization)

Company	Principal Shareholder	Capital (million pesos)
(1) Teleofonos de Mexico	government	3,070
(2) Banco Nac. Agropecuario	government	1,500
(3) Cia. Mex. de Luz y Fuerza	government	1,361
(4) Nacional Financiera	government	1,300
(5) CONASUPO	government	1,000
(6) Guanos Y Fertilizantes	government	1,000
(7) Banco Nal. de Credito Agr.	government	850
(8) Altos Hornos de Mexico	government	800
(9) Imp. de Papaloapan	government	750
(10) Cia Fundidora de Mty.	Banco Nacional de Mexico (BNM)	675
(11) Celanese Mexicana	BNM-Celanese	642
(12) Financiera Banamex	BNM	640
(13) Hojalata y Lamina	Garza Sada	580
(14) ANDSA	government	500
(15) Banco de Mexico	government	500
(16) Bco. Nal. de Obras y Ser Pub.	government	500
(17) Cerveceria Modelo	BNM (P. Diez)	500
(18) Soc. Mex. Cre. Industrial	government	500
(19) Banco Nacional de Mexico	BNM	475
(20) Cerveceria Cuauhtemoc	Garza-Laguera	440
(21) Fertilizantes Fosfatados	BNM-government-Panamerican Sulphur	440
(22) Tubos de Acero de Mex.	government-foreign*	406
(23) Asarco Mexicana	Am Smelting	400
(24) Banco de Comercio	Banco de Comercio	400
(25) Celulosa de Chihuahua	Banco Comercial Mexicano	400
(26) Cementos Tolteca	British Cement Mfgrs.	400
(27) HYLSA de Mexico	*	385
(28) Sears Roebuck	Sears	375
(29) Financiera Bancomer	Banco de Comercio	360
(30) Banco Nal. de Cre. Ejidal	government	350
(31) Cia Cigarrera la Moderna	Brown & Williamson	350
(32) Cerveceria Moctezuma	Banco Comercial Mexicano	330
(33) Cia Industrial de Atenuique	government	300
(34) Cia Mexicana del Cobre	government-foreign*	300
(35) Puerto de Liverpool	*	300
(36) Fabricas Automex	Chrysler	300
(37) Ford Motor Company	Ford	300
(38) Kodak Industrial	Kodak	300
(39) Volkswagen de Mexico	Volkswagen	300
(40) Anderson Clayton	Anderson Clayton	290
(41) Fierro Esponja	Hojalata Y Lamina-Garza Sada	290

TABLE 4.5 Continued

Company	Principal Shareholder	Capital (million pesos)
(42) Univex	foreign*	254
(43) Cementos Anahuac	BNM-J. Serrano	250
(44) Diesel Nacional	government	250
(45) Lever de Mexico	Unilever (UK)	250
(46) Cia Nestle	Nestle	240
(47) Cia Minera de Cananea	foreign*	240
(48) Valores Industriales	*	240
(49) Industrias Unidas	Ing. Alejo Peralta	235
(50) Cigarros El Aguila	British-American Tobacco	230

SOURCES: *Business Trends* (1971), Cecena (1970).
*Unspecified.

> *This [the low level and high concentration of income] has a negative impact on company profits, investment incentives, employment levels, and possibilities for technological improvement.*

Rhetoric notwithstanding, the state, the banking system, the private investment market, and the other institutions of capitalist control are thriving in spite of an inequitable income distribution; they have shaped the economic structure to provide rapidly rising incomes for a small proportion of the population while the masses are told to struggle and, most important, to wait.

> *Each citizen and each group should accept its responsibilities publicly. . . . We cannot destroy age-old evils with a single blow, nor win all battles in a single day, but we must fight them unceasingly [Echeverría, 1972].*

FOREIGN PENETRATION

(1) Direct Investment. Industrialization as it is known today is generally said to have begun in 1940 with the impetus from the Second World War. The institutional framework within which private enterprise developed stimulated private investment and encouraged foreign interests to show their "confidence" in Mexico by investing in the country. Economic policy has provided tax incentives for private industry, free remit-

tance of profits abroad, a cheap and well-disciplined labor force, and state stimulation of economic activity along with the public provision of an ample infrastructure.

The Second World War provided a very auspicious environment in which industrialization could thrive. Imports from the United States suddenly became scarce, and the demand for most traditional products increased markedly. Mexican industrialists responded with alacrity: textiles, cement, iron and steel, paper and pulp, and chemical production were all among the "war babies" that matured rapidly in the hothouse atmosphere of booming markets. These industrial undertakings were financed by a variety of methods in which U.S. direct investment combined with private Mexican capital and governmental financial support.

By the end of the war the country was ready for yet a new step forward in capitalist development: foreign producers began competing with domestic producers for existing markets in Mexico once the war-imposed scarcities in the United States ended. Protection was the order of the day, and it was further supplemented and enhanced by the mobilization of government power and wealth to stimulate private investment and ensure its profitability. After several years of adjustment and two devaluations, "foreign confidence" in Mexico's future was once again demonstrated by a massive inflow of foreign investment—more than $100 million a year for four years (1955-1958).

Mexican industrialists were wary of the growing preeminence of foreign producers. Although available data indicate that only one-sixth of the output of Mexican manufacturing enterprises was in U.S.-controlled enterprises in 1957, they clearly were strategically located in highly visible and competitive industries (Vernon, 1963: 113, n. 25); furthermore, many of those firms that were not directly controlled by foreigners operated with foreign licenses and technical assistance agreements that made the foreign influence seem even more all pervasive. As a result, greater insistence was placed on Mexicanization—joint ventures between Mexicans and foreigners—and on higher proportions of "domestic integration"—manufacturing with domestically produced components. Import quotas and other administrative regulations were combined with fiscal incentives to make it extremely attractive, and sometimes essential, to increase the domestic content of goods produced in Mexico; this element of the import-substituting industrialization policy reached its height in 1959 when the automobile industry was informed that it must raise its level of domestic integration to 60 percent by the mid-1960s. In general, however, these restrictions have not imposed insuperable barriers; now foreign investment, licenses, and technical assistance have become ever-increasing factors in the Mexican panorama.

Foreign investors have abandoned traditional areas of investment—agriculture and mining—to concentrate on modern manufacturing and service industries. Reinvestment of profits has complemented new direct foreign investment, and the national banking system has cooperated by providing relatively abundant and inexpensive credit to the foreign firms that asked for such financing. For those foreign interests willing to accommodate themselves to the growing nationalistic pressures for majority Mexican ownership, the increasing complexity of technology and the incapacity of the domestic elites to absorb available know-how or generate innovations ensured foreign control and design of domestic production.

The pace of foreign investment accelerated during the 1960s.

The total book value of private foreign investment increased from 1,080 million dollars in 1960 to approximately 2,300 millions in 1968; that is, it increased by more than 100 percent in less than ten years. During the sixties, practically all the new investments, reinvested earnings and financial resources freed by the disinvestment in traditional sectors (especially public services and mining) were channeled towards manufacturing and non-financial services, especially trade and tourism [Wionczek, 1974: 142].

Most of this investment was from the United States.

During recent years the process of foreign penetration has been accompanied by what is sometimes called a *progressive denationalization* of industry. In this way, large (principally North American) corporations achieve control of the most dynamic sectors of local industry through the direct purchase of already existing productive operations, thus minimizing even the limited benefits that new direct investment sometimes contributes to national development. Among the most notable fields in which this has occurred are the food industry, in which United Fruit, Heinz, General Foods, and Anderson Clayton are among the most visible foreign companies; consumer durables, chemicals, electronics, metallurgy; services such as department stores, hotels, and restaurants are also among the areas in which foreign interests have obtained control of local businesses.

Most of this investment—as might be expected—is undertaken by transnational corporations. According to a Harvard University survey of North American transnational corporations, Mexico is "privileged" to be the third (after the United Kingdom and Canada) most important host for the 187 U.S. corporations that account for the bulk of U.S. foreign direct investment in manufacturing; 162 of these companies and 412 subsidiaries operated in Mexico in 1967. Of the total number of subsidiaries, 225 were in the manufacturing sector; 143 were completely new firms, and 221 were either acquisitions or branches of other previously established businesses (Vaupel and Curhan, 1969). The growth of foreign investment by the transnational corporations amply confirms the picture of denationalization painted above.

Of the 162 firms canvassed in the study, approximately 80 percent were under full or majority control of the respective central offices of the transnational corporations in the United States of America. The concentration of subsidiaries by industry may be, in itself, a reflection of the nature of foreign penetration by this group; in descending order of importance, the fields were chemical-pharmaceutical and cosmetics, processed foods and drink, automobiles and related industries (including rubber, domestic appliances, and electrical and electronic equipment). All of these produce primarily consumer goods (durable and nondurable) and almost exclusively for the internal market, which creates other problems that will be referred to shortly.

These particular transnational corporations and investments do not, however, encompass the whole range of foreign investment and control in Mexico. On the basis of the 1965 industrial census, it is clear that foreign control is highly concentrated in the capital goods and basic intermediate goods industries rather than in the lighter industries and consumer goods sectors as was suggested by the earlier information. It is clear from this global evaluation that foreign control is located primarily in the most sensitive and crucial areas of the economy. Moreover, these are among the fastest growing enterprises in Mexico and, as a result, their participation in national output will continue to increase. In the study, there were 251 foreign firms among the 938 largest Mexican companies; of these, only 44 (18 percent) were in consumer goods production, and 49 were included among the 100 largest Mexican manufacturing enterprises (Tables 4.4 and 4.5).

Even this dramatic picture does not do full credit to the role of foreign capital in the Mexican economy and society. For example, Anderson Clayton's preeminent role in Mexican agriculture places it among the top 20 corporations when measured by reported capital; on the basis of earnings and sales it ranks even higher. Cotton is Mexico's leading export product and Anderson Clayton controls it through credit and marketing channels; it provides more credit for cotton than the National Ejidal Bank gives to all of Mexico's *ejidatarios*! The company also controls cotton production in the countries with which Mexico must compete: Brazil and the United States. Finally, Anderson Clayton periodically engages in cotton "dumping" to remind Mexico who is in control (Stavenhagen et al., 1968).

In recent years, Anderson Clayton has branched out into Mexican production of cattle feed, chocolates, planting seeds, edible oils, and insecticides. Other U.S. corporations have joined Anderson Clayton in effectively taking over Mexico's agribusiness, from production and sale of machinery and fertilizers to the processing and merchandising of agricultural goods; among the other better-known companies are John Deere, International Harvester, Celanese, Monsanto, Dupont, American Cyanamid, Corn Products, United Brands, and Ralston Purina (Cockcroft, 1974).

The story of direct foreign penetration of the Mexican economy is well enough documented to need no further elaboration at this point. Far from viewing this as a serious problem and thus requiring a basic rethinking of the role of foreign capital in Mexico, the present administration is instead going to great lengths to reassure the private business community, both domestic and foreign, that

> *attempts have been made—here and abroad—to give a distorted view of what is taking place in Mexico. The version offered is that of a government whose actions threaten the private sector and arbitrarily curb its expansion. This is false. . . . Foreign investment is necessary to a country not endowed with abundant capital but it would constitute an aggression against both our sovereignty and minimum economic rationality were we to adjust our laws to the needs or aspirations of foreign capital.*

The under-secretary of the presidency continued by reaffirming President Echeverría's inaugural statement on the matter.

> *Foreign investment should not displace Mexican capital but complement it through association when this is considered useful. Mexican capital, in any case, should direct such association with discernment, dignity and patriotism and use this capital to modernize its plants. Accordingly, we will accept, preferentially, investors from different countries who, under the guidance of Mexicans, wish to establish new industries and help promote the steady development of technology and the manufacture of articles for export to all markets, including their own [Zapata, 1972: 5-6].*

Although the rhetoric of the present Mexican administration has once again introduced the strong tones of nationalism characteristic of a previous epoch ("To the investor . . . who comes as a businessman and not as a colonizer"), the reality remains the same. The conditions may not be as generous as they have traditionally been (bankrupt firms will not automatically be bailed out by state action), but the functioning of the market will not be impaired and the concentration with foreign collaboration will continue unbridled.

(2) Balance of Payments Effects. The balance of payments fully reflects the crisis created by the Mexican development strategy. On the one
hand, there is a persistent and rising deficit on current account that the
government is attempting to keep within "manageable proportions."
There is, on the other, the rising tide of remittances by foreigners wanting
to realize some return on their loans and investments. Part and parcel of
the problem is the growing demand for imported consumer goods by the
elites and the seemingly unlimited wanderlust of the Mexican bourgeoisie. Together these elements led to a number of billion dollar-plus deficits
in the 1970s. They have thus occasioned intensive efforts at organizational and economic reform to limit foreign expenditures and increase
sales.

On current account, the Mexican import substitution program has
greatly reduced the purchase of consumer goods directly from foreign
producers. In its place, raw materials, intermediate goods, and capital
equipment imports have skyrocketed to provision the numerous factories
catering to the sumptuary demands of the oligarchy and affluent middle
class that may constitute as much as 30 percent of the entire population;
most of those imports come from the United States. The new economic
structure has created a very close association between the level of imports
and the growth rate of the economy; the room for maneuver is very limited. Past policies have led to an economic structure in which demands
are changing rapidly in response to consumption patterns of the rich; this
prevents the creation of high-volume production to cater to mass
demands—which are growing slowly because of the pattern of income
concentration—and, when combined with technological advances that
are being incorporated into production, set a limit on the possibility of
reducing imports as a share of gross domestic product (GDP) while
maintaining a "satisfactory" rate of economic growth (Navarrete, 1974).

Exports, too, show little promise of dramatic improvement in the coming years. In agriculture, the economy is faced with rising restrictions
from North American agricultural interests, which have manifested
themselves most recently in restrictions on tomatoes; quotas, "voluntary
restraints," and other administrative controls have effectively reduced the
possibility of the rapid growth of exports in the products that Mexico
could increase production of rapidly. Cotton, too, offers many marketing
problems in the current institutional framework. In industry many
foreign-controlled producers are not allowed to export local production
by their parent companies; such competition would upset the orderly division of the world the transnational corporations are attempting to establish. Other firms, however, are responding to export promotion
programs—including tax rebates and outright subsidies—and are in-

creasing manufactured exports; in spite of this, the current account deficit remains large.

Tourist expenditures and border transactions are usually expected to contribute to closing the gap between exports and imports. A slowdown in U.S. tourists visiting Mexico and an increase in travel abroad by affluent Mexicans in the 1970s reduced the potential contribution this might have made. Calls for greater restrictions on tourism by Mexican government officials (including the Foreign Trade Bank) and Antonio Ortiz Mena (a former secretary of the treasury) have gone unheeded, but the government has undertaken an intensive tourist development program. It is likely, though, that the high concentration of income and the inability to impose restrictions on Mexican spending abroad will continue to erode the gains made on the tourist account.

Traditionally, Mexico has relied on direct investment and foreign borrowing to fill this gap. As a result, a substantial proportion of all export earnings are now needed to pay for past foreign debt obligations and the repatriation of profits and other income for foreign investors. During the 1960s direct investment amounted to $1,600 million, but almost one-half of this foreign investment is not from new resources being brought into the country but rather from the direct reinvestment of earnings (Table 4.6); in spite of this high volume of reinvestment, repatriation of profits is greater than the net inflow of new foreign investment with a consequent net drain on the country's resources. (In the 1960s, gross direct investment outflows amounted to $2,500 million; as a result, the net outflow for the decade was $900 million.) The drain on the country's resources is further heightened by other costs of foreign investment that are paid by the country but cannot readily be identified in national accounts; overinvoicing (overpricing) and other forms of transfer pricing are used to move funds from one country to another without paying profit taxes or submitting to other governmental controls.[2] The World Bank warned that even the present unhappy situation might deteriorate further; they cautioned that the present high level of private investment

> would obtain . . . so long as foreign firms continue to reinvest as in the past. However, in the event of a change in attitudes on the part of foreign investors, outflows can be expected to continue at their historical rates, while inflows could drop. This would have very serious balance of payments effects. . . . Moreover, a sizable share of Mexico's capital stock is already owned by non-residents, particularly in manufacturing industry. If past behaviour on the part of foreign investors continues, the share of foreign-owned capital would rise further in the future. Clearly, a limit on the proportion of industrial capacity owned by nonresidents that is acceptable to the Mexican authorities may be reached eventually, thus reducing

TABLE 4.6
Private Capital Flows (US$ millions)

	1960	1965	1970
Direct foreign investment	−38	214	295
new investment	62	120	145
reinvestment	−100	94	150
Investment income outflow	142	236	444
reinvestment	−100	94	150
effective outflow	242	142	294
Net balance of payment effect	−180	−22	−149

SOURCE: Estimates based on IBRD data.

the scope for further expansion in this form of capital inflows, and strengthening the need for other sources of finance [IBRD, 1970: 45].

In other words, the Mexicans are being warned that: (1) foreigners have been given control of a large segment of Mexican industry as a way of paying for continuing trade deficits; (2) there is a limit to such expansion, even in Mexico; and (3) future balance of payments deficits will have to be financed from other sources, which will not be easy.

Rapidly rising foreign indebtedness is yet another source of concern. Used as a way of financing the current account deficit, the public foreign debt with a maturity of greater than one year grew from $842 million in 1960 to $3,511 million in 1969. Of this total, more than half (54 percent) was contracted with private concerns, of which North American financial institutions were most important; more than one-half of the remaining debt was with various U.S. government agencies. Payments for interest and amortization on the debt rose during the same period from $216 million to $618 million and are expected to continue rising in coming years. In 1969, 23 percent of all exports were needed to pay for the servicing of the debt; the World Bank (1970: 38) warned that "in the absence of remedial action, [the debt-service ratio] may reach the lower 30 percent range between 1973 and 1980." Although some corrective actions have been taken, especially in renegotiating outstanding payment schedules, still more than one-quarter of export earnings are now mortgaged to pay for past obligations. These obligations were undertaken deliberately by regimes anxious to establish "a close financial and credit relationship [with the U.S.]. . . . This link could have meant absorption. This, however, has not been the case, —thanks to Mexico's positive nationalism [*sic*]."

In sum, the Mexican development strategy has occasioned (1) heavy inflows of foreign investment that have permitted nonresidents to own a large part of the Mexican manufacturing sector and (2) a dependence on public funds from international banking—private and public—which has mortgaged a substantial part of Mexico's foreign exchange earnings for decades to come. Import needs continue to rise as a condition of maintaining the present style and pattern of economic growth with an extreme concentration of income and export prospects are not bright. The country seems to have given its economy to foreigners in return for a highly concentrated income distribution and social problems that are coming home to roost.

SECONDARY CAPITALIST DEVELOPMENT:
THE MEXICAN MODEL

Mexico's external economic problems are an integral part of its "imminent social crisis." A concentrated income distribution, a chronic balance of payments deficit, growing foreign control of the economy, social unrest, and urban chaos are only symptoms of a pattern of capitalist development that the Mexican bourgeoisie has warmly embraced.

The imperatives of domestic growth with a concentrated distribution of income made import substituting industrialization (ISI) a natural consequence of the closing of foreign sources of supply in the early 1940s. Such hothouse industrialization would have been threatened—because of small markets and inefficiency—by the United States had protective tariffs not been imposed. Protection was combined with industrial promotion to cater to the needs of a small elite who controlled the productive apparatus and were well served by the rising bureaucracy.

ISI almost always has the effect of reinforcing the existing structure of class and economic status. Starting from the supposition that the pattern of imported goods used by the country proves the existence of effective demand, producers merely substitute local production for foreign; although it need not be inefficient, in practice such development has generally resulted in inefficiency due to the high tariff protection afforded "infant" industries. At no time does this approach question the very desirability of the product mix available in the economy or the ability to satisfy the basic demands of the population as a whole.

In Mexico, ISI was complemented by agricultural development schemes that assured increasing exports and some minimum increase in basic food supplies for most of the population. Agricultural production, too, reinforced and heightened the prevailing pattern of income concentration by relying on existing market signals to indicate profitable areas for investment. These signals themselves reflect the relative demands and incomes not only of the Mexican population but of the whole capitalist world; as a result, the predominant influence of the United States on world commodity prices inevitably had its impact on the crops and other products Mexico would "choose" to produce.

ISI did not, however, close the door on foreign investors. Quite the contrary: few restrictions were imposed on foreign investment and free convertibility made the Mexican market—even with only 30 percent or so of the population actively participating—an attractive target. Even the imposition of joint venture and other regulations did not dissuade foreign investors from exporting substantial amounts of capital to build new plants with discarded equipment from other plants or even to construct brand new operations.

The U.S. government marveled at the ability of the Mexican system to continue this pattern of economic growth while systematically isolating substantial proportions of the population from its fruits without causing unmanageable social unrest. In return for such a model of political effectiveness, Mexico was rewarded with public largesse in the form of development loans to enable it to continue its work and import still more North American goods and equipment.

Progress continued to be measured in terms of the modernization of Mexico City, Acapulco, Monterrey, and several other centers of upper- and middle-class affluence. Even there, however, the facade was rough hewn and centers of urban misery contrasted with opulence. The income distribution continued to deteriorate as the relative isolation of agriculture and lack of resources in the subsistence sector induced many to migrate from rural areas to urban areas where job opportunities were limited. The all-encompassing tertiary sector continued to absorb those who were being expelled from agriculture but could not be absorbed by industry, for open unemployment is an unbearable luxury for most; high rates of demographic growth further swelled the ranks of the unemployed and the underemployed.

The choice of technology is often blamed for the inability of the industrial sector to absorb sufficient workers. This choice, however, is highly conditioned by the choice of products to be produced. There is an inherent contradiction between the production of goods for domestic elites and the satisfaction of basic demands for the masses. The masses are without incomes and an effectively repressive political system has been able to avoid substantial transfers to the poor. Consumption patterns for the upper 30 percent of the population are determined by people in the neighboring colossus with similar income; the disparity in average income levels in the two countries, however, implies that items that are popular, almost mass, consumption items in the United States become treasured items of social differentiation in Mexico. They imply a lifestyle and pattern of social relations that facilitate the encroachment of North American society into a small but crucial sector of Mexican society.[3]

The lifestyle is only a reflection of the pattern of development that Mexico successfully adapted from the North. Most people could not participate in this "progress," but the very existence of a large reserve of unemployed people permitted the affluent in Mexico to live more comfortably—in material terms—than their North American counterparts. The "marginal" populations in the urban areas and the rural peasants—essential in this process of rapid economic growth—were effectively cowed by the mechanisms of political control and police repression; the Mexican government has learned its lesson well from the few instances when the indiscriminate use of force caused it great embarrassment. The wide gaps between classes are expanding even more as a result of state policies that facilitate capitalistic concentration and denationalization.

Most Mexicans cannot participate in this imported lifestyle. They are still concerned with the basic essentials of a minimum subsistence diet, medical attention, and literacy. Buffeted about by the vicissitudes of economic cycles and subsistence production, Mexico's poor (more than one-half the population) are the object of scorn and exhortation. Although not able to participate in the country's "prosperity," they provide the labor-power needed for its continuance and are grist for the scholarly mills of myriad academics who describe but refuse to identify the root causes of poverty in Mexico.

The plight of the poor Mexican cannot be understood without reference to the United States. The "good-neighbor" supplies two-thirds of the country's imports while it repeatedly asks Mexico to restrain its exports; it advertises a lifestyle that only a few can achieve and exports the machinery to ensure that not many will be needed to work in the factories. It provides aid and investment to pay for its exports to Mexico but in return obtains control over industry and a mortgage on the country's exports. It cooperates with an affluent local bourgeoisie, coopts an occasionally recalcitrant politician, and subsidizes the loyal opposition—both academic and political—to promote its ideal of democracy and free enterprise.

Mexican leaders bemoan their dependence; some seem powerless to end it, but most capitalists see no benefit to changing the present pattern. Instead, politicians desperately try to defuse the latent discontent and to manage the crisis in the foreign sector, both symptoms of the deeper problem. The present government taxes the masses to subsidize exports; it exhorts foreign investors to be more responsible, and excludes them from certain particularly sensitive areas. It tries to maintain the overall rate of economic growth. At the same time, reforms are being implemented in virtually every area of social welfare in an effort to calm the rising ranks of poor people who are increasingly aware of the growing gap between themselves and their rulers. Regional decentralization is seen as the answer to the urban crisis and tourism a way to attract dollars and create jobs; education is said to be the panacea for unemployment and low labor productivity; political participation the route to democratic openness.

The contradictions persist. The American way of life is still the only alternative for the economic and political elite. The "free" market is the only allocating mechanism that guarantees its hegemony without abandoning the appearance of openness. ("The government of President Echeverría strives to achieve development in freedom" [Zapata, 1972: 7].) And yet, that lifestyle and market are part and parcel of the structure that has created the progressive immiserization of the Mexican masses. It is not only U.S. domination of the Mexican economy that is responsible for these contradictions, but the capitalist organization of production itself that makes concentration inevitable; in present-day Mexico the two are inextricably bound.

NOTES

1. The best-known work on income distribution in Mexico is by I. de Navarrete (1970), who provides a summary of available evidence. The 1969 data are based on a family income survey with data adjusted for underreporting of subsistence and capital incomes. Although there are serious debates about the quality of these data, there appears to be no doubt about the basic deterioration in the income distribution and the high concentration of income in Mexico. Another recent survey confirmed this trend (Banco de Mexico, 1973).

2. Constantine V. Vaitsos (1970) points out that much new investment is not actually a net gain as it involves the import of capital equipment and intermediate goods, but all repatriations generate their full negative impact on the balance of payments. Reinvestment does not, of course, generate foreign exchange earnings and may occasion expenditures for new plant and equipment.

3. For a general discussion of the problem of the relationship among consumption patterns, productive structures, income distribution, and development strategies, see Barkin (1973).

REFERENCES

Apprendini, Kirsten and Daniel Murayama
   1972 "Desarrollo desigual en Mexico," pp. 1-40 in David Barkin (ed.) *Los beneficiarios del desarrollo regional.* México: Sep-Setentas.
Banco de México, S.A.
   1973 *La distribución del ingreso en México.* Mexico: Fondo de Cultura Económica.
Barkin, David
   1971 "La educación: ¿una barrera al desarrollo?" *Trimestre Económico* 38 (October): 951-954.
   1973 **"Automobiles and the Chilean road to socialism," pp. 513-525 in Dale Johnson** (ed.) *The Chilean Road to Socialism.* Garden City, NY: Doubleday.
   1974 "La persistencia de la pobreza en México," pp. 186-207 in Miguel Wionczek (ed.) *La Sociedad Mexicana: presente y futuro.* Mexico: Fondo de Cultura Económica.
   1975 "Schooling and social distance in Mexico." *Politics and Society* 5.
Business Trends
   1971 *The Mexican Economy in 1970.* Mexico: Publicaciones Ejecutivas.
Ceceña, José Luis
   1970 *México en la orbita imperial.* Mexico: Ediciones El Caballito.
Centro de Investigaciones Agrarias
   1973 *Estructura agraria y desarrollo agrícola en México.* Mexico: Fondo de Cultura Económica.
Cinta, Ricardo
   1970 "Clases sociales y desarrollo en México." *Revista Latinoamericana de Ciencia Política* 1 (December).
   1972 "Burguesía nacional y desarrollo," pp. 165-199 in *El Perfil de México en 1980,* Vol. 3. Mexico: Siglo XXI.
Cockcroft, James
   1974 **"Misdeveloped Mexico," in Ronald Chilcote and Joel Edelstein (eds.)** *Latin America: The Struggle with Dependency and Beyond.* Cambridge, MA: Schenkman.
Echeverría, Luis
   1971 *State of the Union message* (September 1). Mexico: Secretaría de la Presidencia.
   1972 *State of the Union message* (September 1). Mexico: Secretaría de la Presidencia.
Eckstein, Salomon
   1968 *El marco macroeconómico del problema agrario mexicano.* Mexico: Centro de Investigaciones Agrarias. (Republished as part of Centro de Investigaciones Agrarias publication cited above.)
International Bank for Reconstruction and Development (IBRD)
   1970 "Current economic position and prospects for Mexico." Washington, DC. (mimeo)
Margain, Hugo
   1972 "Speech to the Bankers' Association." *Mexican Newsletter* 14 (April 31).
México, Secretaría de la Presidencia
   1964 *México: Inversión pública federal 1925-1963.* Mexico: Secretaría de la Presidencia.
   1970 *México: Inversión publica federal 1965-1970.* Mexico: Secretaría de la Presidencia.
Nacional Financiera, S. A. and Comisión Económica para América Latina
   1971 *La política industrial en el desarrollo económico de México.* Mexico: Nacional Financiera.
Navarrete, Ifigenia M. de
   1970 "La distribución del ingreso en México," pp. 15-87 in *El Perfil de México en 1980,* Vol. 1. Mexico: Siglo XXI.

Navarrete, Jorge
    1974 "Desequilibrio y dependencia: las relaciones económicas internacionales de México en los años sesenta," pp. 98-134 in Miguel Wionczek (ed.) *La sociedad mexicana: presente y futuro*. Mexico: Fondo de Cultura Económica.
Ortiz Mena, Antonio
    1969 "Stabilizing development: a decade of development strategy in Mexico." *El Mercado de Valores* (Supplement) 44 (November 3).
Stavenhagen, Rodolfo, Fernando Paz Sánchez, Cuauhtémoc Cárdenas, and Arturo Bonilla
    1968 *Neolatifundismo y explotación de Emiliano Zapata a Anderson Clayton y Cía.* Mexico: Nuestro Tiempo.
Vaitsos, Constantine V.
    1970 "Transfer of resources and preservation of monopoly rents." Harvard University Development Advisory Service. (mimeo)
Vaupel, James and Joan Curhan
    1969 *The Making of a Multinational Enterprise*. Boston: Harvard University Graduate School of Business Administration.
Vernon, Raymond
    1963 *The Dilemma of Mexico's Development*. Cambridge, MA: Harvard University Press.
Wionczek, Miguel
    1974 "La inversión extranjera privada: problemas y perspectivas," pp. 135-157 in Miguel Wionczek (ed.) *La sociedad mexicana: presente y futuro*. Mexico: Fondo de Cultura Económica.
Zapata, Fausto
    1972 *Development in Freedom: The Policy of Change in Mexico*. Mexico: Secretaría de la Presidencia.

5

Social Conflict and Inflation in Mexico

by
David Barkin and Gustavo Esteva*

Social conflict takes many forms. Violent confrontations, strikes, civil disobedience, and public demonstrations are some of the more obvious ways in which people can display their discomfort with existing social conditions. In most societies, government and established social groups will go to great lengths to prevent this discontent from overflowing the normal channels of social conciliation.

Mexican society has been particularly successful among Latin American republics in keeping social conflict within bounds. Although social conflict is a permanent feature of life in Mexico, as in most societies, there have only been a few occasions during the past half century when events have obliged and permitted social groups to resort to unusual tactics to attempt to redress grievous injustices. For the most part, the prevailing model of economic development has apparently been able to fulfill expectations sufficiently well to avoid serious outbreaks of violence that might threaten the existence of the social structure. It seems remarkable that there have been so few occasions on which conflict has been transformed into near chaos; by examining those occasions it may be possible to gain a better understanding of the underlying processes of social negotiation that promote stability.

We argue that inflation is a particularly important and revealing manifestation of social conflict. Inflation is actually part of the process of social conflict: it is its monetary expression. When examined as an expression of social processes instead of as a simple monetary manifestation of economic problems, the study of inflation may give us insight into the way in which government, itself an expression of a political balance of social forces, can develop institutional arrangements to resolve potential conflicts and defuse explosive situations. We can also derive some lessons about the kind of social process, linked to inflation, that cannot be readily controlled, thereby paving the way for authoritarianism.

---

*David Barkin and Gustavo Esteva are members of the economics faculties of the Universidad Autónoma Metropolitana and the Universidad Nacional Autónoma de Mexico, respectively. This chapter is adapted from their book *Inflacion y Democracia: El Caso de Mexico* (Siglo XXI, 1979), which was awarded the National Prize in Political Economy.

For most people, including economists specializing in the subject, inflation is synonymous with rises in the cost of living: "a continuous increase in the price level" of goods in the marketplace is the way one leading economist puts it (Frisch, 1977: 1289). This is understandable, because prices are the most apparent expression of a persisting problem. Prices, however, are only the final result of a social process that is far more complex, one whose roots penetrate deeply into the social and political fabric of society. An analysis that limits itself to the superficial phenomenon of rising prices cannot provide any analytical or political insight into that social process. We argue that *inflation is a reflection and expression of the ongoing struggle among the diverse forces that constitute society.* The inflationary process is a manifestation of the interaction among the diverse social classes whose continuous social struggle shapes the national productive apparatus and establishes the rules for commercial and political activity throughout the world. Rising prices also are used as a weapon in the service of a particular class in the struggle.

Conventional explanations of inflation reject this approach (Laidler and Parkin, 1975). Analysts explain it as a monetary phenomenon that arises exclusively in the sphere of the circulation of money and commodities and therefore influences production only indirectly, by affecting the rate of profit (thus determining the profitability of new investments) and the real incomes of the population (thus influencing the consumption options available to the different social groups). There is a wide divergence of opinion among the theoreticians of this analytical current, and the search for solutions depends on the analyst's interpretation of the cause of the problem. An excessive quantity of money in circulation might call for measures to reduce the excess, for example, by ending deficit spending; structural bottlenecks in the productive apparatus might call for solutions with respect to the supply of goods, for example, increasing imports, curbing exports, or adopting other measures to increase domestic production of the essential commodities; price rigidities occasioned by monopolies in production or distribution might be attacked with antitrust actions, jawboning, or even the creation of government enterprises to enter into direct competition with private firms.

In spite of the internal contradictions and differences among theoreticians, the several explanations for inflation all enjoy intellectual support (Bronfenbrenner and Holzman, 1963). An impressive analytical literature has grown up around the problem, and the conventional literature is becoming increasingly sophisticated. The elaborate theoretical models not only incorporate the traditional variables (money, aggregate and sectional demand, unemployment, capacity utilization rates, and so forth) with greater precision, but also include new variables that are difficult to define, such as expectations and the international transmission of prices through world trade. Among the varieties of explanation in the conventional current of thought, a wide range of policy instruments are identified as appropriate for manipulating prices. Generally, however, the proposals center on fiscal, monetary, and international trade policies as the most effective (Gordon, 1976).

A growing dissatisfaction with the technical advances in this area has accompanied the realization that inflation is becoming an increasingly serious problem. On the one hand, this has contributed to the deepening crisis of neoclassical economic theory, "which was not only incapable of offering practical and effective measures to avoid or mitigate the economic crisis, but also was theoretically incapable of contributing an analytical foundation to explain the causes of the new inflationary crisis" (Itoh, 1978: 2). On the other hand, one of its most traditional defenders has been moved to comment that the idea that "inflation is a monetary infirmity" is not helpful "in moving ahead our analysis of the forces underlying the excessive injections of money into the economic system" (Brittan, 1978: 161).

In recent decades, other analysts have suggested that price rises do not respond to purely monetary measures because there are more fundamental pressures that affect the social forces and influence the inflationary process. Marxists have attempted to explain inflation as an element of crisis theory: "It is a means to postpone or avoid [booms or busts], since it retards the arrival of the true crisis" (Bullock and Yaffe, 1975: 11). Within this school of thought, the emphasis has been on the rate of profit, because it determines the rhythm of accumulation. The historical tendency for profits to fall has occasioned increasing state intervention in the economy to maintain monetary stability, the profitability of private investment, and the rate of growth. Government now finds itself in a troublesome new dilemma: either it can slow down economic activity by reducing its own income and raise profit rates (that is, encourage accumulation), or it can increase economic activity by direct programs to reduce unemployment and preserve social peace and stability (but threaten accumulation). This clearly presents the new contradiction of the modern capitalist world: accumulation or prosperity, high profit rates or improved well-being for the masses.

In our view, monetary phenomena are insufficient to explain inflation. They do not *determine* inflation; rather, they *accompany* it. A more complete explanation must also account for social conflict among contending groups. Marx (1968: 71) pointed this out more than a century ago: "When a depreciation of money occurs, the capitalists are on the alert to seize this opportunity for defrauding the workman." In somewhat different language, Antonio Ortiz Mena, president of the Interamerican Development Bank and former secretary of the treasury of Mexico, pointed out (1966: 11) that "in inflationary conditions, corporations and the owners of businesses benefit from the forced savings extracted from the rest of society in the form of high profits." But high profits are not only extracted from workers by powerful business interests within the country; weak countries also find themselves "forced to save" by transnational corporations that enjoy high profit rates. These profits contribute to a higher standard of living for a small group of people in advanced capitalist countries when they are reinvested there.

The social component of inflation has long been recognized. Even the exponents of the conventional wisdom recognize that inflation has a profound social impact that is different for each group. These economists are also aware that their solutions are not neutral in their impact on different social classes, but their technocratic models mask this reality. The acceptability of the solutions derived from them to policymakers in capitalist countries is as alarming as the respect they command in international financial institutions. In our view, it seems appropriate to recall the insight and admonition of such eminent economists as Michal Kalecki and John Maynard Keynes that "inflation is essentially a political phenomenon" (Robinson, 1977: 1329).[1]

PRICE STABILITY AND
SOCIAL CONFLICT IN MEXICO

Keeping in mind these considerations about inflation, we now turn to the case of Mexico, where the distribution of national income between workers and those who control the wealth has become increasingly unequal in recent decades.[2] Since the onset of industrialization in 1940, a progressive increase in the concentration of personal income has been apparent. This reflects the growing difference between the portion of social production that remains in the hands of the workers and the share the capitalists have been able to claim (Banco de México, 1973).

For many years, these facts and trends seemed to be of concern only to academics. The demands of a particularly important part of the group that was experiencing a relative decline in its share of the national income were assuaged by the steady *absolute* improvement in its standard of living made possible by rapid growth in agricultural production and in the economy as a whole. The fact that the improvement in standard of living was not as rapid as the overall growth of the economy (occasioning the increased inequality in the distribution of income) was not readily perceived. To those who spoke for the working class, the relative shares of the national income of the different social groups did not seem to be as great a concern as the absolute improvement in real income. From the perspective of those who were enjoying the lion's share of the benefits of growth, an apparently ideal situation was emerging: the growing concentration of personal income paralleled the increase of capital's share of the national product without provoking discomfort in the well-organized portion of the population whose share was diminishing. For years, this continued without causing demonstrations of social malaise that might have endangered the whole system. The underlying class conflicts were clearly being controlled.

A generalized image of internal peace and low rates of increase in prices were characteristic of this period (1935-1968). These are two aspects of a single process: a process in which the violent social struggles of the postrevolutionary era appeared to be on the decline, direct confrontations being rare and easily managed with existing institutional controls. The principal participants in the prevailing social "understanding" were all beneficiaries, although the division of the benefits was increasingly unequal. In other words, although there was inequality in the *overall* distribution, the less privileged groups of organized workers and peasants appeared willing to support the status quo as long as their expectations of continuing modest improvements in their own situation were realized.

Popular and mass demands for improvements were not limited to a rise in monetary income. Throughout the period peasants were seeking more land, infrastructure, technical assistance, and credit for production, and workers were calling for a shorter workweek, more effective social security (medical) coverage, and more responsive union leadership. Many of these demands were met, especially those from the better-organized and more articulate working-class and peasant groups, those able to express their discontent most forcefully. These groups formed the nuclei of various peasant and worker organizations that the government was obliged to accord some measure of recognition as the (relatively low) price of some semblance of peace in a society in which inequalities were increasing. For a long time this strategy seemed to offer valuable benefits—high rates of profit accompanied by rapidly modernizing productive structures that facilitated Mexico's complete involvement in the world capitalist economy. This self-reinforcing process drew additional social groups into the network of capitalist social relations, making artisan production and self-sufficient agriculture no longer viable alternatives for large numbers of people who had been only marginally incorporated into the market economy. In this context a promising future seemed probable; strong discontent and pressures for change were dissipated by the optimism generated by economic growth, increasing employment, and rising living standards.

The events that altered this optimism can be understood only through closer examination of this social process of managed social conflict. First, the price stability referred to was not uniform and lineal. From 1935 to 1957, economic expansion was accompanied by far-reaching price changes. During the 1940s the rate of increase in wholesale prices was three times that of the previous decade. In the 1950s the cumulative annual rate of increase in prices was about 11 percent. The upward pressures continued until the 1960s, the decade of "stabilizing development," in which prices increased at a rate of less than 3 percent per year. Toward the end of the period, however, the upward pressures on prices were renewed, reaching their apogee in the last part of 1976, when the rate of increase reached 4 percent *a month*.

IMPORTED INFLATION?

In the conventional interpretations of these events it is customary to identify external forces as the culprits during the first part of the period (up to 1957). During the Second World War the demand for Mexican products increased dramatically, and international reserves held by the government rose at the same time that the supply of capital goods and intermediate products was restricted. This pattern was reversed during the first postwar years, a fact that is generally used to explain the inflation of that period. The high level of inflation in the next few years is associated with the many effects of the Korean War. The two devaluations of the peso are easily explained by the interplay of these "foreign" elements.

In our explanation, the international dimension also plays a fundamental role. In the midst of "hot" and "cold" wars, when disruption if not chaos defines the character of world trade, Mexico, an integral part of this international maelstrom, is seriously affected by the course of events in the advanced countries, particularly the United States. It is important to bear in mind that the productive expansion of the Mexican economy, with the simultaneous growth of the supply of wage goods and that of luxury items, was possible because of the availability of large volumes of idle productive resources, especially land and labor. It is also important to remember that foreign investors were enthusiastic about expanding their participation in the economy, financing in this way the increasing import of goods into Mexico that was a cornerstone of the economic policy of the period.

The change in Mexico's economic structure was possible because of the presence of strategically placed interest groups that committed themselves to support the new development strategy. This strategy accelerated the country's full participation in a new pattern of international specialization. Thus Mexico not only supplied raw materials and primary products, but also represented an important market for manufactured consumer goods and a source of some of these products for the advanced industrial countries. Perhaps an excellent early example of the nascent support that pushed the country in this direction was the "disinterested" offer by the Rockefeller Foundation in 1943 of financial and technical assistance for agricultural research and extension. This "aid" facilitated, some years later, the creation of modern commercial agricultural enclaves in irrigation districts that produced goods for export to the United States. This was part of a long-term agricultural development strategy that is now known as the *green revolution*; it generated increasing inequality within Mexico (and other countries), reoriented agriculture toward commercial and export production, and, paradoxically, left the country increasingly less able to supply the basic food products needed for its own population.[3] By 1980, the country was forced to import nearly half of all its basic grain needs.

The change in the agricultural sector was paralleled by similar transformations in the productive structure throughout the economy. These were stimulated by policies designed to make the nation's producers more efficient by exposing them to the forces of international competition. Official efforts to stimulate nontraditional exports were relatively unsuccessful, and the disastrous effects of the unbalanced economic structure on the nation's balance of payments could only be corrected by massive foreign borrowing until the relative price of petroleum on world markets was altered. With the rise in petroleum prices, it was possible to exploit the vast reserves that had long been known to exist.

Many nationalist groups warned, however, of the danger of using the petroleum, which would only provoke further distortions in the productive structure and social inequality. By exporting massive volumes of the "black gold," they argued, the country would expose itself to additional inflationary pressures from an economic structure increasingly incapable of responding to the basic material needs of the majority of the people. Furthermore, it would lead to even more problems of unemployment and dependency on the advanced capitalist countries, because Mexico would have to contract foreign debt to pay for the imports needed to develop the petroleum industry and the latter would be incapable of generating a significant volume of new productive employment.

In spite of its international dimension, therefore, inflation must be viewed as a product of internal struggles over the appropriate development strategy. Nationalistic, mass-oriented policies were advocated by progressive political and working-class organizations. Large capital, both international and national, committed to the world market and anxious to increase its global profit rates, advocated a policy of heavy industrialization based on petroleum and Mexico's full involvement in the world capitalist economy. The unequal balance of power between these factions and the state's commitment to the latter group have been forceful in shaping Mexico's recent development.

REPRESSION: AN ADEQUATE RESPONSE?

To understand inflation, however, historical analysis of recent social conflict in Mexico is needed. Social struggle increased dramatically during the 1930s, reaching a high point toward the end of the decade; the best-known manifestations of this process were the expropriation of the petroleum companies in 1938, the dramatic acceleration of land distribution, and the penetration of the school system into peasant and indigenous areas, bringing with it social services that promised important changes in lifestyle for all those affected by the program.

However, with the outbreak of the Second World War, the inauguration of a new president in 1940, and the ascendency of the bourgeoisie, the process was abruptly halted and many of its advances reversed. Many workers' organizations that had taken leadership positions in the conflicts of the previous period were subjected to control and then systematically broken up. Peasant organizations were particularly hard hit by the new administration: they were gradually displaced from the significant leadership position they had been able to achieve during the thirty years of revolutionary struggle. As a result, they were unable to oppose the new pattern of agricultural development that was wiping out many of their previous gains. Because of subsidies to modern commercial and export-oriented production, traditional agriculture was displaced, and millions of peasants were pushed into the urban areas or the agricultural wage-labor force. Workers were also forced to retrench; their living standards were threatened by rising prices and unemployment, and in an attempt to defend themselves they regrouped into a few large unions and labor federations that had a long tradition of struggle. The class character of the state was once again clearly defined in terms of its support for the national bourgeoisie, which was gradually allying itself with international capital. In this context, neither peasants nor workers could exert the kind of political leadership that had permitted them to advance collective demands for structural changes in the society in the 1930s.

These developments could hardly be expected to reduce social tensions. Even though violent outbreaks occurred only sporadically, the underlying conflicts began to reveal themselves in many other ways. During this period (up to 1958), price increases, which are an efficient mechanism for controlling or even reducing the real income gains of the workers and peasants, never really got out of control. This was partly because of the high rate of expansion of productive activities, which permitted constant, if modest, increases in real income for strategically placed groups in the working class that had been able to maintain and consolidate their unions during a difficult period.

Years later, Antonio Ortiz Mena, commenting on the period prior to 1958, said: "One should not forget that during the cycle of inflation-devaluation [as that period had come to be known], profits increased excessively" (1966: 11). His reference to "excessively increasing profits"—although not quite accurate, because under capitalism there are never "excessive" profits—is a good characterization of what was happening during the period. There was rapid and intense capital accumulation, the rhythm of which could not be maintained because of its high social cost. This cost was measured in heightened social tensions and the renewed strength of worker organizations.[4] The process exploded in 1958—the year in which the rate of increase in prices was at its zenith—when the social conflict could no longer be controlled within the normal channels of institutional negotiation and bargaining. The challenges to the system were so profound that they constituted a threat to the very existence of the Mexican state.[5]

The dramatic use of military force to quell the turmoil has been amply documented (e.g., Alonso, 1975). It helps explain the relative calm that prevailed during the next decade. Severe repression, strict military control, and economic reprisals served to control much social unrest. Many workers and peasants were killed, and even more were imprisoned. Thousands found themselves without work. Worker organizations were in disarray: either their strength was destroyed or they were tightly controlled by the political apparatus.

STABILITY: AN END TO CONFLICT?

In this social and political context, the decade of stability (1958-1968) ushered in a period of prosperity. There was rapid economic growth, industrial diversification, and high profits along with price stability. During this period a series of new measures were adopted to protect the profit rate. This protection required the state to intervene more assertively in the economy in favor of private capital. The government collected more taxes (fundamentally from the workers) and increased the foreign debt. The new resources were used primarily to stimulate private investment (with infrastructure, tax exemptions, subsidies, and so forth) and to provide some fundamental social services, such as education and health care, to support the rural and urban workers needed by the prospering private sector. The increase in real wages for certain privileged and/or potentially troublesome groups of workers was far more rapid than the increase in labor productivity in this period. Instead of reacting with horror, however, Ortiz Mena, who was secretary of the treasury at the time, cautioned that these wage increases "should not be considered as an increase in costs adversely affecting earnings, since they really were part of the process of adjusting profits to the new conditions of stabilizing development" (1966: 21). Because the small group of favored workers did not use its position to advocate improvements for all, the cost of these concessions was relatively low. He further noted that "the business community benefitted from a decline in the relative price of intermediate goods required for industry resulting from the great flexibility in the supply of agricultural commodities and the willingness to import raw materials and intermediate products." These policies clearly helped to accelerate the rate of accumulation. The proportion of the national income devoted to new investment rose from 12.7 percent in 1950 to 16.5 percent in 1958 to 20.9 percent in 1967.

Although not openly violent, social conflict in the decade of stability was profound. There was no way for it to be expressed clearly, no institutional mechanisms for communication or negotiation. By the second half of the 1960s its existence could no longer be ignored. Although different in form from that which had led to the organized struggle of 1958, it was clearly at least as intense. The crisis, which began to emerge as an economic problem as early as 1965, grew rapidly. It was accompanied by a series of uncoordinated responses to a succession of apparently unrelated problems that were springing up at all points in the social fabric. These were the years of guerrilla struggle, peasant revolts, and clandestine urban groups. These were the years that led to the violence of 1968.

A NEW WAVE OF CONFLICT

The very roots of the system were changing. To maintain the growth of basic production, especially in the agricultural sector, the government had to provide constantly increasing injections of new funds for current expenditures (subsidies for inputs, price stability, technical assistance, etc.). Public expenditures for social services (health care, education, etc.), essential for improving the living standards of the least favored groups in Mexican society, could not easily be reduced. In fact, huge new expenditures were required, for they were virtually the only counterbalance to the persistent deterioration in the value of the money incomes of broad groups of workers and peasants. In spite of their limitations, these government programs were effective in maintaining expectations of a real improvement in living standards, expectations destined to be shattered by an economic system that could not promise sustained dynamism.

Domestic and foreign investors were also clamoring for more support. They argued that, in order to maintain the pattern of economic progress achieved during the 1960s, they required not only subsidies for production costs, but also tax concessions, exemptions, subsidized credit, and official investment in supporting infrastructure. These supports had been an integral part of the policy package initially offered to the industrialists. The optimists had envisioned their gradual disappearance with the coming of age of Mexican industry. Quite the opposite turned out to be the case. The supports became so much a part of the structure of production that they became increasingly important for maintaining profitability in many parts of Mexican industry.

Although the state was subjected to constant pressure from all social groups and sectors, not all received equal hearing. The demands on the state for expenditures, investments, and concessions increased even more rapidly than the rising revenues it was able to obtain as a result of economic growth. The class character of the state was constantly manifested as productive expenditures in basic production (especially in agriculture) and social welfare programs foundered in the face of the more effective pressures for continued economic support from national and foreign capitalists. Without the stimulus of government programs, the production of basic consumer goods and services lost its dynamism.

The results of this pressure on the state were not long in coming. Although the increase of production permitted a small but continuing rise in living standards for a small part of the working class (those organized in strong unions), those of most unorganized workers and peasants suffered serious deterioration. Among the capitalists, many domestic entrepreneurs found themselves with an insufficient rate of return and were forced to sell or to join the transnational competition attracted by the myriad opportunities offered in existing and new ventures. This led to mergers and greater centralization of control of capital.

It is not difficult to foresee a more intense level of social conflict emerging as a result of these tendencies. Unsurprisingly, beginning in about 1965, when tensions began to rise again, higher rates of inflation also began to reappear. The consequences of the inequitable distribution of income were heightened by the appearance of two phenomena of strategic importance: the relative withdrawal of public-sector support for the production of basic consumer goods (especially evident in the reduction of government support for agriculture) and the accelerating centralization of control over industrial production of goods aimed at the upper-income groups (a tendency that allowed the affluent economic groups to find new resources to make up for the relative decline in official subsidies and supports). Ironically, emergency measures such as the massive import of basic food products (corn and wheat) aggravated the underlying problems instead of alleviating them because of the huge volume of government resources they required. The emergency measures were clearly inadequate responses to the ever deepening economic problems of the time: unemployment, massive migration to the urban areas, and stagnation or deterioration in material standards of living within the working class. The collective frustration that these problems occasioned began to find expression in popular demands and movements among broad segments of the population. Throughout the country there were chaotic and random outbursts of social discontent. At the same time there was a more systematic consolidation of worker and peasant organizations, unrest within a large cross section of the student population, and even armed insurgence by local groups. The government was confronted by a wide variety of insurgent movements, rarely united among themselves. The initial responses of negotiation and concession to the most effective groups quickly changed to open and sometimes violent repression. The absence of an articulated alternative program and competitive political organizations facilitated official attempts to undermine worker and peasant organization.

Although ostensibly stifled, this insurgency obliged the state to implement important changes in the distribution of the social product during the next few years. On the national level, public expenditures increased dramatically. In the private sector, labor conflicts led to some improvement for those groups of workers that were relatively well organized. At the same time, public subsidies to industry were restricted and new limitations were placed on the operations of private enterprise. These measures were taken in an attempt to stem an even further deterioration in the living standards of the working class. As might be expected, they provoked a retrenchment in domestic private investment—the equivalent of a strike by capitalists against the system, especially against the change in the correlation of forces within the government.

The government, concerned about the dangers of a slowdown in the rate of growth of economic activity, responded to the private sector's actions by further increasing public expenditures, but investment was not the only area in which official action was demanded. Domestic capitalists and the international financial community were pushing for a devaluation of the peso during the first half of the 1970s; large expenditures were made in an attempt to defend the peso and maintain stability while the monied classes exported their hoards. This policy eventually became unsustainable, and the peso was devalued in 1976, requiring further increases in public spending as additional capital left the country because of the uncertainty of the period. (It is probably significant that the process of "dollarization," as it was called, actually turned into a mechanism that converted the speculative gains of wealthy Mexicans who bet against the peso into public debt that would have to be amortized later with tax revenues from workers.) Thus the capitalists' strike ultimately had the desired effect of forcing the government once again to cut back on workers' and peasants' incomes with policies that directly favored the profit rate.

GOVERNMENT EXPENDITURES FOR ALL?

The conventional analyses of the very high rates of inflation of 1973-1976 place the blame on the money supply. There was a significant increase in the supply of money in circulation because the government had no other way to obtain the resources needed to increase public investment and to defend the peso. Examined from a broader perspective, however, the phenomenon of rising prices acquires a new dimension.

The relation between additional money in circulation and the fact that available commodities can be sold at higher prices is tautological. The process we have described could have occurred *only* if there had been a monetary expansion (that is, an increase in the quantity of money available through the printing of money and/or a credit expansion). On the surface, this increase might appear to be the initiator of the process: it is obvious that, when more money is circulating without a parallel growth in the volume of available goods, prices will increase. Given this, the corrective mechanism appears obvious: a reduction in the quantity of credit or money in circulation and/or an increase in the available quantity of goods and services will cause prices to fall.

To reveal the fallacy of this reasoning, it is essential to determine whether the monetary expansion (essentially the product of increased public expenditures) was the *stimulus* for the inflationary process or a *response* to existing social conditions. Given that we explain inflation as a response to ongoing social processes, we predict that a program that simply restricted the amount of money in circulation would not be successful in reducing the rate of increase of prices. A change in the manifestation of a response cannot erase the stimulus. The simple curtailing of monetary expansion will not eradicate the social unrest that in reality is the cause of inflation. It will probably also be ineffective in reducing inflation if the basis for social conflict remains unaffected. Given that the inflationary process is a response, we might ask if it is necessarily the only response to the existing social conditions. Would other options have been possible, or is inflation the inevitable consequence of social struggle? (Obviously, these questions require complex answers.)

Deficit financing of the public sector's expenditures program increased substantially in the 1970s only after direct confrontations among social groups had failed to produce any acceptable solution. These confrontations took many different forms and involved formal and informal organizations that engaged in political struggle to defend their own pecuniary interests. As the pressures from each social group mounted, there was an increasing danger that the established channels for negotiation and conciliation might be abandoned. When the confrontations threatened to become violent or to violate some of the fundamental rules of political and economic behavior, the government was bound to step into the fray. The official response was to attempt to reduce tensions and provide some immediate relief for the most pressing (that is, most strident) demands. The government's principal option was to increase expenditures to benefit the most vociferous worker and peasant groups—to create employment, offer social services, subsidize basic consumer goods, authorize the massive importation of goods that were in short supply, and so forth. From the other end of the social spectrum, the government faced increasing demands from capitalists and other wealthy social groups to continue its program of public investment and tax concessions to support private investment activity. Equally strong was the pressure that prevented the government from obtaining the needed additional tax revenues from the ranks of the rich by carrying forward a program of fiscal reform or forced lending.

The magnitude of these pressures was enormous, and they came from all sides. Investors made themselves felt through political channels and economic measures, including the "strikes by capital" described earlier. Other sectors of the population expressed their social discontent more directly, although not always as effectively, either through spontaneous political action or through systematic pressure by organized groups. This intensified process of political struggle was an explicit attempt by the majority to modify the prevailing distribution of the social product. The model of "stabilizing development," in which the workers had been able to enjoy real improvement in their standards of living even while they were experiencing a relative deterioration in the distribution of income, was no longer operative. Past experience and better political organization of workers and peasants made it clear that to maintain their current standard of living or to attempt to improve it would require a change in the social processes for distributing the national product. For the capitalists, the inoperability of the model meant the increasing unavailability of government subsidies and support upon which they had come to depend for their well-being; such support was essential to their obtaining the large proportion of the national income to which they had become accustomed. To defend this privileged participation of capital in the social product or to try to increase it would require new actions that could be successful only at the expense of the workers and the national treasury; that is, it depended on employers' success at the bargaining table or in increasing prices in the marketplace. Most important, however, it depended on their ability to win back their dominant position in the government.

In these circumstances, governmental intervention in the continuing confrontations seemed to be directed toward reconciling opposing positions. New institutions and instruments were created embodying the enormous energy and imagination involved in the attempt to resolve the growing problems. Tripartite commissions reminiscent of the worker-management-government forums in some parts of Western Europe were created for negotiation. All of these efforts were relatively unproductive, partly because the options available to the contending groups were limited by the underlying commitment to the laws of private capital accumulation.

The continuing pressures in the early 1970s appeared to be pushing the government inexorably toward authoritarian solutions, responses it was loath to adopt because of their high political cost. It could consider either *social repression*, if it chose to contain the demands of the masses for substantial economic improvement, or *repression of the private sector,* if it opted to harm the interests of domestic and international capitalists. Explicitly rejecting the first option (at least as a general strategy) after reflecting on the costs of the social repression of 1968, the government also saw the second option as impossible. In the face of international conditions and internal problems, repression of the private sector would create insurmountable obstacles to economic recovery or, worse, might even exacerbate the existing economic downturn. This would, in effect, further aggravate the very problems such a solution would be designed to resolve.[6] In any case, there was insufficient political support for either of these options.

Because of its inability to impose a structural solution to the social conflicts through institutional channels, the state deliberately elected to reduce tensions indirectly by increasing public expenditures. Higher governmental expenditures would reduce tensions by addressing the most immediate or most bothersome demands of the contending groups. The resulting acceleration of price increases, although an undesirable product of the governmental program, was considered tolerable. The alternative was an increase in the contradictory social pressures (that is, conflicting demands) that would inevitably lead to chaos.

As is now obvious, the deficit financing of the new public programs should not be viewed as the cause of inflation. It was, instead, an intermediate step in the official attempt to reduce the social tensions generated at various levels of society. The "natural" evolution of the social pressures the government was trying to dissipate would have led to confrontations endangering the very existence of the social order. By electing the route of increased government expenditures, politicians were trying to avoid one of several forms of social disruption. One of these, uncontrollable inflation, would not only have further intensified the confrontation, but also could have further concentrated the control of the social product because of the correlation of political and social power on the side of the well-organized capitalists. The ability of the monied sector to coordinate its activities for decision making was in sharp contrast to the ineffectualness of workers in organizing and imposing their demands.

To reiterate an important point here, deficit financing as a way of reducing social tensions gave the government the opportunity to regain control of the process of social struggle and to prevent the more violent and destructive forms of confrontation. The systematic increase in public spending can now be understood as a premeditated response to potentially dangerous political and social conditions. From this point of view, public policy, instead of being a cause of inflation, is a moderating force. The alternative to this policy would have been an even more severe problem of uncontrollable inflation and other forms of social disorder, which surely would have been more damaging than the administrative disorder the new spending programs created.

This history of the early 1970s in Mexico points up an unusual and contradictory characteristic of the state. Political leaders, remembering the outbursts of violence in the late 1960s and committed to improving the lot of the working class, attempted to change the class character of the state. They systematically imposed unacceptable restrictions on capital, the consequence of which was a strike and a transfer of resources abroad. For a while, the government attempted to counter this reaction with deficit financing and massive imports of official capital, which the international banking community felt obliged to supply in light of recent events in Chile. The government was, however, ultimately unwilling or unable to carry through consistently on this policy. Further, the working classes were not sufficiently well organized and lacked the appropriate leadership to take advantage of the power vacuum that existed within the government.

DEVALUATION FOR THE FEW?

When the terms of confrontation change, the various social groups react differently. Not all are equally well prepared to defend their own interest in a new social environment. Inevitably, certain groups have more power to alter conditions and thereby modify the distribution of income and wealth in their favor. Powerful financial groups, especially foreign ones, were in a particularly favorable position in Mexico in 1973-1976 to force a devaluation of the peso. The growing deficits in trade balances, product of the pattern of public spending and redistributive policies of a regime trying to deny the class character of the state, pushed the country toward greater foreign indebtedness. This exposed the country to a flight of capital that made the government more vulnerable to demands from capital for subsidies and other incentives. The blind defense of the peso's parity with respect to the dollar by the monetary authorities heightened speculative pressures even more, and the pressures from the international financial community and national capitalists forced the government to devalue the peso without even the most minimal preparations for the productive and social dislocations that would inevitably follow.

The devaluation heightened social struggle in several ways. To obtain the loans it needed as part of the devaluation process from the International Monetary Fund, the country was obliged to adopt an "austerity" program that halted the increase of public spending and economic activity for more than a year. By cheapening national resources on the international markets, it encouraged an influx of foreign investment. It became very advantageous for foreign capital to buy up prosperous domestic enterprises and expand their investments in Mexico; exports would be even more profitable because labor had become even less expensive. The powerful national economic groups also took advantage of the situation, centralizing their control of strategic industries, reinforcing their links to transnational corporations, and expanding both operations and their prospects for producing profits. The new situation again caused a change in the distribution scheme, channeling an even larger proportion of the national income toward domestic and international capital.

The devaluation clearly changed the orientation of official policy, imposing new priorities and reestablishing the traditional balance of power in capitalist countries. The working class and peasants immediately began to suffer a deterioration in living standards. Although the pressures for price controls grew, in practice the institutional mechanisms to restrict the workers' demands for wage increases were far more effective. Government could not increase public expenditures to compensate for the decline in economic activity in the private sector because its activities were tightly controlled by international committees whose task it was to oversee and restrict the rate of growth of the Mexican economy. This further contributed to reducing the real income of the workers, especially by increasing unemployment and decreasing the availability of social services and subsidies for basic consumer goods. The decline in economic activity therefore had a cumulative impact on the working class.[7]

In spite of the general recession, the capitalists continued to find ways of increasing their incomes at the expense of the well-being of an important part of the working class. Price increases and profitable speculative activity created an environment of uncertainty and fear and caused great hardship for the masses. The rise in profits, which made investments more attractive, might have been expected to create the preconditions for a new expansion of productive activity that would contribute to establishing a new equilibrium among economic groups. However, with the recent sizable decline in the real incomes of the working class, the demand for domestic consumer goods stagnated. Increasing profits were not reinvested in productive activities because of uncertainty about the new economic policy and the low level of demand. Traditional economic doctrine, however, does not offer any noninflationary means to increase demand that might practically be applied in the Mexican case. In this setting, the new government opted for continued restrictions on the growth of the wage bill, which is still falling as a proportion of national income. The regime is also stimulating investment in heavy industry that is complementary to the needs of the powerful domestic and international economic groups that are restructuring the productive apparatus of the Mexican economy.

This new wave of economic repression is an invitation to outbursts of social conflict. With workers experiencing a deterioration in their relative share of the national income and even in their real incomes, discontent may be expressed more violently in the coming years. The liaison between government and business cemented at the opening of the 1980s is a denial of the negotiation processes of previous regimes. The government's inability to achieve price stability in this environment is not surprising. Mexico had been successful in attracting substantial new investment by powerful national groups and transnational corporations interested in participating in the domestic market and in using the abundant supplies of relatively inexpensive energy. This success has contributed to reducing social conflict by generating jobs and economic growth, but it will merely postpone rather than eliminate the danger of new explosions of violence. The form that future confrontations will take is likely to be of great concern as high rates of price rises are increasingly built into the Mexican productive structure and workers are systematically denied the opportunity to defend their past material gains.

NOTES

1. Recently other analyses of inflation have also concentrated on conflict as a precipitating cause; see, for example, Pimenta (1978), Rowthorn (1977), and Rosenberg and Weisskopf (1981).

2. The details of Mexico's economic and political development on which this account is based can be found in basic texts on the Mexican economy; see, for example, Hansen (1971) and, for the more recent period, Tello (1979).

3. This phenomenon is quite common throughout the underdeveloped world; for more details about this process, see Lappé and Collins (1979).

4. Ortiz Mena (1966: 7) commented: "The high cost of the recurrent cycle of inflation and devaluation was unacceptable for the fixed income groups; it was never possible to compensate for the deterioration in the participation of wages and salaries in national income."

5. Recent studies (e.g., Alonso, 1975) stress the political nature of the workers' and union movements of the period. The participants foresaw the need for direct confrontation with the state in spite of their lack of a structure, their awareness of the problems of pursuing such a radical path, and their inability to see the confrontation through to its conclusion.

6. Throughout this period, "rhetorical repression" of private business interests provoked a reduction in new investment and prevented any "real repression" but did not achieve the objectives of limiting the scope of action or the profitability of private capital.

7. Of course, this depends on how one looks at things. After noting the lack of increase in sales of food because of, among other things, price increases, the bulletin of one of the most influential banking groups noted: "The inflationary process is provoking a constant modification in consumers' preferences." At times it appears that consumers prefer not eating; unfortunately, some die in the attempt to express these preferences.

REFERENCES

Alonso, Antonio
    1975 El movimiento ferrocarrilero en México, 1958-59. Mexico City: Era.
Banco de México, S.A.
    1973 La distribución del ingreso en México. Mexico City: Fondo de Cultura Económica.
Barkin, David and Gustavo Esteva
    1979 Inflación y democracia: el caso de México. Mexico City: Siglo XXI.
Brittan, Samuel
    1978 "Inflation and democracy," in Fred Hirsch and John Goldthorpe (eds.) The Political Economy of Inflation. Cambridge, MA: Harvard University Press.

Bronfenbrenner, Martin and Franklyn Holzman
   1963 "A survey of inflation theory." *American Economic Review* 53 (September):
   593-661.
Bullock, Paul and David Yaffe
   1975 "Inflation, the crisis and the post-war boom." *Revolutionary Communist* 2, 1:
   1-23.
Frisch, Helmut
   1977 "Inflation theory, 1963-1975: a second-generation survey." *Journal of Economic
   Literature* 15 (December): 1289-1317.
Gordon, Robert J.
   1976 "Recent developments in the theory of inflation and unemployment." *Journal of
   Monetary Economics* 2 (April): 185-219.
Hansen, Roger
   1971 *The Politics of Mexican Development.* Baltimore: Johns Hopkins University
   Press.
Itoh, Makoto
   1978 "The inflational crisis of world capitalism." *Capital and Class* 4 (Spring): 1-16.
Laidler, David and Michael Parkin
   1975 "Inflation: a survey." *Economic Journal* 85 (December): 741-809.
Lappé, Francis Moore and Joseph Collins
   1979 *Food First: Beyond the Myth of Scarcity.* New York: Ballantine.
Marx, Karl
   1968 *Salario, precio y ganancia.* Madrid: Ricardo Aguilera.
Ortiz Mena, Antonio
   1966 "Stabilizing development." Presented at the annual meeting of the International
   Bank for Reconstruction and Development and the International Monetary Fund,
   Washington, DC, September.
Pimenta, Carlos
   1978 "Para uma análise marxista da inflação." *Economia EC* 13, 1: 31-63.
Robinson, Joan
   1977 "What are the questions?" *Journal of Economic Literature* 15 (December):
   1318-1339.
Rosenberg, Sam and Thomas E. Weisskopf
   1981 "A conflict theory approach to inflation in the postwar U.S. economy." *American
   Economic Review* 71 (May): 42-47.
Rowthorn, Robert E.
   1977 "Conflict, inflation and money." *Cambridge Journal of Economics* 1 (September): 215-239.
Tello, Carlos
   1979 *La política económica en México: 1970-1976.* Mexico City: Siglo XXI.

6

State-Class Alliances and Conflicts
Issues and Actors in
the Mexican Economic Crisis

by
Nora Hamilton*

The world economic recession that began in the late 1970s has had devastating effects on the economies of most Third World countries. The drop in prices of primary commodities exported by Third World states, the decline in purchasing power of advanced industrial states, and in some cases protectionist measures enacted by the latter led to sharp declines in export earnings. The burden of Third World debt repayment for loans granted and in fact promoted by international banks during a period of excess liquidity was exacerbated by the subsequent contraction of financial resources and a 300 percent increase in interest rates in U.S. and London markets between 1977 and 1981. The external crisis has further debilitated weak internal economic structures, in many cases leading to cutbacks in production, unemployment, and the closing down of firms. Several countries have been forced to resort to loans from the International Monetary Fund (IMF) to maintain their credit standing, which has required the implementation of a series of austerity measures resulting in further economic contraction and general misery for the population of these countries.

The crisis inevitably raises questions regarding the models of economic development pursued by peripheral states, which, on the one hand, may be seen as causes of the crisis (particularly in the states' vulnerability to external influences) and, on the other, may be jeopardized by it (for example, through enforced contraction of the role of the state, often a primary actor in peripheral economies). This raises the possibility of structural realignments, both in terms of international relations—particularly between peripheral states and those of advanced industrial countries—and among class forces within the Third World countries

---

*Nora Hamilton is Associate Professor of Political Science at the University of Southern California. This chapter is a revision of a paper presented at the annual meetings of the American Political Science Association, Chicago, September 1-4, 1983. The author would like to thank Edna Bonacich, Barry Carr, James Dietz, Tim Harding, Michael Kearney, and Van Whiting for comments on earlier drafts.

themselves. At least in some measure such restructuring will depend upon the relative capacity of groups, classes, and the state itself to mobilize forces in support of the existing model of development, its modification, or even its replacement.

In the case of Mexico, the question is to what extent the current economic crisis and the measures taken to respond to it will lead to structural changes—specifically in relations between the state and private capital and in terms of development policy. The effects of the crisis in Mexico will be analyzed through a chronology of events, focusing on two issues that may be considered central to the question of state autonomy and the restructuring of class-state relations: the nationalization of the private banking sector on September 1, 1982, and negotiations over Mexico's foreign debt.

The hypothesis is that although situations of crisis may facilitate relative state autonomy with respect to domestic and even foreign capital, the fact that the state is embedded in a given class and international structure limits its propensity for decisive action toward change of existing structures. At the same time, the state is not a closed or monolithic entity, although membership or tenure in certain state institutions involves a process of socialization that may inculcate interests and values unique to those institutions. In general, the agencies, institutions, and personnel of the state reflect, represent, or reproduce, to a greater or lesser degree, social forces external to it: class and group interests, alliances, and conflicts. These social forces, functioning within the state or outside of it, constitute the decisive actors in the process of change.

THE MEXICAN CLASS STRUCTURE AND DEVELOPMENT MODEL

The economic policies pursued by the Mexican government have been characterized by its efforts to reconcile two conflicting models of development: one is nationalist and geared to the expansion of the internal market, the protection of national industries, the promotion of employment, and the restriction of foreign economic penetration; the other is internationalist and based on the assumption that efficient economic development requires that Mexican firms become competitive in the international market and therefore have access to foreign capital and technology.[1] The nationalist model emerged through the Mexican revolution of 1910-1917, which established the principle of state intervention in the economy. It was reinforced during the 1930s when the depression and consequent decline in export earnings led to efforts by several Latin

American governments to lessen their dependence on external markets through industrialization on the basis of import substitution and aggressive state intervention in the economy. This process, which benefited from a partial and temporary decline in foreign economic and political intervention, was pushed by a "populist" coalition of the state, private industrialists, and an emerging working class that challenged the hegemony previously exercised by the landowning and export interests.

The process was most advanced in Mexico, where the revolution had brought the peasantry and rural workers—the majority of the active population—irreversibly into political life. During the 1930s peasants and rural and urban workers were mobilized in support of a structural transformation of Mexican society. An agrarian reform gave land to individual peasants and peasant communities (often in the form of *ejidos*, a type of communal ownership), broke the economic and political power of the traditional landowners, and in the process removed impediments to agricultural modernization. The nationalization of the British and U.S. petroleum companies to some extent restructured Mexico's relations with foreign capital and at the same time reinforced the economic role of the state, which took control of petroleum production. The incorporation of major peasant and labor confederations into sectors of the corporate government party (now the Partido Revolucionario Institucional, or PRI) in effect established state control over the urban and rural working population, which has been a key factor in preventing mobilization threatening to the political system.

Since the 1940s the development model followed by Mexico has been predominantly (although not exclusively) oriented to the internationalization of the production process, as both agriculture and industry have become increasingly dependent on foreign capital, technology, and/or markets. In industry, large-scale, capital-intensive plants—partially foreign owned, dependent on foreign loans, often linking state, foreign capital, and private domestic capital in joint ventures and producing for high-income groups and for export—coexist with labor-intensive small and medium-size firms, often inefficient, that produce for the local market. In agriculture, small producers and ejidal communities oriented to the domestic market have been increasingly squeezed out by large-scale farms dependent on foreign finance and technology and producing for export.

Through its development banks (particularly Nacional Financiera, or NAFIN), the financial control exercised by the central bank (Banco de México) and its own enterprises, which include railroads, electric energy, steel complexes, and sugar processing firms, the government has promoted the internationalized sector of the economy. This sector has been structurally characterized in terms of a triple alliance among the state (or specific groups and agencies within the state), foreign capital, and dominant groups within the private sector, particularly economic groups, which comprise from 10-20 to 150-200 industrial, commercial, financial, real estate, and other categories of firms linked by common ownership (Evans and Gereffi, 1982: 117, 155-156).

One example of the linkages between the state (or certain agencies within the state) and the private sector is the historically close relation between official and private banking sectors, particularly those linked to the economic groups. Since the 1920s there have been interlocking directorates between the private and government banks, and it was not uncommon for members of the official financial sector to become officers, directors, and shareholders in private banks upon retirement from government. By the 1970s, officials of the Banco de México were graduates of the same U.S. universities (e.g., Chicago, Yale) as the private bankers, and, according to one observer, their economic and financial analysis bore a striking resemblance to those of major Mexican banking institutions such as Banamex and Bancomer, the International Monetary Fund, and the World Bank (Ramírez, 1982b: 10-11; 1982c: 17-18). It would presumably not be an exaggeration to note that by this time the values, interests, and operating principles of the private bankers had been completely internalized by their counterparts in the state financial sector.

Individuals and agencies associated with the state financial sector (particularly the Ministry of Finance, the Banco de México, and government development banks, notably NAFIN) have been among the major proponents of the internationalist model of development. This model reflects the interests linked with the more powerful private economic groups, which benefit from direct access to foreign capital (in the form of loans or equity) and technology as well as relations with the state financial sector and (until recently) the resources of their own financial institutions. The distinction between these interests and those of small and medium firms controlled by national capital, including manufacturing firms represented in CANACINTRA (National Chamber of Manufacturing Industry) constitutes a major division within the Mexican private sector.

This division is complicated by a second division between groups ideologically opposed to state intervention (centered in the northern industrial city of Monterrey), whose interests are represented in COPAR-MEX (Confederación Patronal de la República Mexicana) and the right-wing Partido de Accíon Nacional (PAN), and private interests that are linked to and/or dependent upon the state. The latter include manufacturing firms that developed under state protection and are represented in CANACINTRA, but also some of the more powerful economic groups, which, in fact, often have their origins in the state. Those sectors linked to the state are more likely to vote for PRI candidates.

The interests of the small and medium firms associated with CANA-CINTRA have traditionally been represented by nationalist elements within the state, which include sectors of the Mexican left. Policies oriented to national industry, increased employment, and state economic intervention, including nationalization of key industries, are also promoted by elements of the working class and particularly the major labor confederation, the Confederación de Trabajadores de Mexico (CTM), which is linked to the state through corporate membership in the government party. Proponents of the nationalist model have succeeded to some extent in checking the internationalist model, but the latter is clearly dominant, as is evident in the presence of foreign corporations in key sectors of the economy, an industrial structure that has become oriented to the capital-intensive production of consumer durables for high-income groups, a growing dependence on foreign loans and imports of foreign technology, and the concentration of domestic wealth by a relatively small segment of the private sector.

One effect of this model is that the presence of foreign capital (and particularly U.S. capital) in all its ramifications (investments, loans, technology transfers, and so forth) tends to have an overriding role in shaping the economic options and constraints within which economic actors (including the Mexican state, different groups of the Mexican private sector, and even, in some cases, certain sectors of foreign capital) may operate. The internationalist model has been a factor in the vulnerability of Mexico's industrial structure, which is heavily dependent upon the import of machinery, tools, and industrialized inputs (Arturo Cantú in Tello et al., 1983: 18). The internationalist model is also blamed for high levels of unemployment and underemployment in both rural and urban areas due to the capital-intensive nature of industry in the internationalized industrial sector, the reconcentration of land and agricultural modernization, and the growing orientation of production toward exports and, in the case of industry, toward high-income domestic consumers.

At the same time, critics of the nationalist model complain that government protection of national industries has encouraged inefficiency, waste, and high costs, which are translated into higher prices for consumers. This criticism affects many of the smaller labor-intensive industries, but affects larger industrial interests as well, as is evident in the recent collapse of the electronics division of the powerful ALFA economic group of Monterrey when tariff barriers to electronic imports were reduced. All industries have benefited from government subsidies in the form of low prices (in some cases far below cost) for goods and services, such as gas and electricity, provided by nationalized industries. The nationalist model has also come into question because of its heavy dependence on the state as an engine of progressive nationalist development and source of social justice, which has led to the assumption that strengthening the alliance of the working class and peasantry with the state is desirable (Bartra, 1982: 25). In effect, it assumes state autonomy with respect to business groups and foreign interests; critics argue that in fact these groups have often generated the policies articulated by the state (Roger Bartra, in Tello et al., 1983: 31).

Through limited pursuit of nationalist policies, the government has attempted to minimize the effects of the internationalist model—for example, through subsidies to relatively inefficient, labor-intensive national firms in order to maintain employment and thus partly offset the unemployment effects of capital-intensive firms or mechanized agriculture. The possibility of organized resistance on the part of groups negatively affected by economic policies has also been limited through such factors as divisions between urban and rural workers (in part resulting from their deliberate separation within the PRI structure) and within each sector—among workers with secure jobs, temporary workers, and the unemployed, or among peasants with land, landless rural workers, and a semiproletariat. The political repercussions of this model have been further limited by effective cooptive and social control mechanisms of the state and the corporate party structure, which have constituted a major factor in Mexico's long-term political stability.

THE "PETROLIZATION" OF THE DEVELOPMENT MODEL: 1977 TO AUGUST 1982

The discovery and development of Mexico's extensive petroleum reserves during the second half of the 1970s appeared to offer a solution to problems that had begun to appear in Mexico's development model by the end of the 1960s. Agricultural modernization and the expansion of large-scale agricultural holdings at the expense of small farms and ejidos had increased production for export at the expense of production for subsistence and for the local market. Basic food items formerly produced locally had to be imported, limiting the resources available for imports of capital goods and other inputs for industry, which grew as manufacturing became more capital intensive. During the administration of Luis Echeverría (1970-1976) private investment stagnated and was compensated by heavy government spending on the basis of foreign loans and the expansion of the parastatal sector. By the mid-1970s inflation had become a problem; the peso was increasingly overvalued in relation to the dollar, which discouraged exports and engendered capital flight. In 1976 the peso was devalued for the first time in 22 years, from 12.5 to 25 to the dollar.

The subsequent government of José López Portillo (1976-1982) benefited from the exploration and development of Mexico's substantial petroleum reserves. Arguing that the surplus generated by the petroleum could replace dependence on external resources as a basis for economic growth, López Portillo promoted the rapid development of petroleum resources for export and industrialization as the foundation for a new development model that would combine rapid growth with increasing equality.

Indeed, the next four years were a period of spectacular growth—manifested in an annual growth rate of 8 percent between 1977 and 1981—particularly in petroleum exploration, petrochemicals, construction, and to a lesser extent manufacturing, as well as agriculture and fishing. Government spending financed much of this growth; private sector savings were geared chiefly to investment in private residential construction, but there was also private investment in manufacturing (Aguilar M., 1982: 20-21; *Bolsa*, February 1983; *Wall Street Journal*, September 7, 1982). Economic expansion resulted in the creation of an estimated four million jobs—well above the growth of the labor force during this period—and thus reduced unemployment and underemployment.

But the new model did not succeed in reducing economic dependence or inequality, both of which in fact increased. Mexico's extensive petroleum reserves made it a favorite market for loans by U.S. and European bankers; both the public sector and private firms became dependent on foreign loans to finance their expansion, resulting in a foreign debt of $40 billion by 1980 and $80 billion by 1982, the second highest (after Brazil) in the world. U.S. direct investment more than doubled between 1977 and 1981, from $3.2 billion to $7 billion, undoubtedly an important factor in the growth of those years but also increasing dependence on foreign capital and technology.

The orientation of manufacturing to import substitution of durable consumer goods (rather than machinery and industrialized inputs) meant that production continued to be increasingly dependent on the import of capital goods. Furthermore, the rapid development of Mexico's petroleum resources itself generated a dependence on foreign technology for petroleum exploration and exploitation. Thus although petroleum exports generated a spectacular increase in export earnings from $6 billion to $19 billion between 1977 and 1981 (approximately 75 percent of that from petroleum) imports increased even more radically—from $6 billion to $23 billion—in the same period. In effect, the development model proposed by López Portillo was not a new model but the "petrolization" of the existing model. The negative trade balance, added to interest payments on Mexico's escalating foreign debt and the loss of foreign exchange through profit repatriation, aggravated the deficit in Mexico's balance of payments, particularly with the tripling of interest rates on the U.S. and London markets between 1977 and 1981, which raised the interest on Mexico's debt from 6 percent to 18-19 percent, and the contractions in foreign loans and investments in the early 1980s.

Despite the increase in employment, economic growth resulted in an increase rather than reduction in economic inequality. According to one source, the proportion of gross domestic product going to labor declined from 45 percent to 36.8 percent between 1976 and 1980 (Rodríguez, 1983: 39).

Although economic expansion benefited the private sector as a whole, the banking sector made the most spectacular gains. It was during this period that Finance Secretary David Ibarra Muñoz undertook the modernization of Mexican banking, creating multibanks through the fusion of different types of banks—commercial, investment, and mortgage—and the combination of smaller banks into larger ones, reducing the number of banks from 243 in 1976 to 63 in 1981. He also encouraged the internationalization of banking through which the largest banks (Bancomer, Banamex, Serfin) joined leading U.S., European, and Japanese banks in international banking groups that facilitated their access to foreign funds. The rapid expansion of financial resources led to a concentration of resources in the banks and particularly the larger banks; by 1982, 65 percent of banking assets and 75 percent of profits were concentrated in the three largest banks (Guadarrama Sistos, 1983: 31-33; Zuñiga, 1982a: 14-15).

The problems in the "new" model became evident with the growth in inflation, which reached 30 percent in 1980 and 1981 (cutting into the real wages of workers), and the sudden drop in oil prices. The high level of inflation combined with high U.S. interest rates led to a flight of resources to the United States in the form of consumer purchases, tourism, and investment and financial speculation. The net outflow of foreign exchange was aggravated by the drop in oil prices in the middle of 1981, which undercut a key element of Mexico's growth strategy and aggravated the balance of payments deficit.

Between January and March 1982, $1 billion left the country in the form of repatriated profits and an additional $7 billion in capital flight, Mexican tourism abroad, and frontier transactions (Ramírez, 1982d:

11). The decline in Banco de México reserves led the bank to withdraw from the exchange market on February 17, resulting in a devaluation of the peso from 25 to 47.25 to the dollar. But the devaluation created new problems—such as the doubling of the price of imports of inputs needed for industry—while failing to resolve the problem of speculation against the dollar. Throughout the next few months López Portillo repeatedly called upon bankers and other business groups to refrain from speculation, and the latter repeatedly assured him of their patriotism, their confidence in the peso, and their concern for the value of Mexico's currency. During this period relations between the bankers and the government remained cordial; bankers continued to benefit from the high interest rates as well as the growing differential between interest rates on assets and liabilities and their control of financial resources. Industrialists, however, fared less well, especially those who were not members of economic groups and therefore did not have privileged access to financial capital. With the devaluation and consequent increase in the price of the dollar, several firms were concerned about their ability to repay foreign debts and to import needed inputs; also, high interest rates continued to be an impediment to new investment. By mid-1982, industrialists as well as bankers were calling for the freeing of prices through the elimination of government controls on prices that provided a cushion for low-income groups in a period of escalating inflation.

One indication of the loss of confidence in the government was the outcome of the presidential and congressional elections in early July, the first presidential election since the electoral reform of 1979 opened up the process for opposition parties. The election of the government party candidate, Miguel de la Madrid, was a foregone conclusion, but at 70 percent of the total the PRI vote was lower than in previous elections. The Partido Socialista Unificado de México (PSUM), recently formed by a coalition of left-wing political groups including the Mexican Communist party, obtained only 3.65 percent of the vote, but the right-wing opposition party Acción Nacional (PAN) was the major beneficiary of the democratization process with 16.4 percent of the total. Founded in 1939, PAN has consistently represented the interests and the ideology of the right-wing private sector, particularly industrialists from Monterrey. During the presidential campaign it skillfully combined its traditional economic liberalism and opposition to state intervention with an appeal to democracy and to widespread resentment of government corruption.

During August the government took desperate measures to control the financial situation, many of which would have been politically difficult prior to the elections. On August 1, it decreed price increases on basic goods, including a 100 percent increase on bread and tortillas and 50 percent on gasoline, with predictable implications for the poorer sectors of the population. These increases led to panic buying of dollars, which again threatened to dry up the reserves of the Banco de México and cause Mexico to default on its foreign debt. On August 5, the government announced a dual exchange system for the dollar: (1) a preferential rate for payment of interest (but not principal) on foreign debt and for the import of essential industrial inputs and foodstuffs, and (2) a free rate, which became in effect a second devaluation.

A week later the Mexican government suspended exchange trading and froze dollar accounts in Mexican banks, amounting to $12 billion, which could now be drawn out only in pesos at 69.5 to the dollar. This move apparently limited opportunities for speculation by the banks, but the situation at the U.S. border was volatile with the peso fluctuating between 100 and 150 to the dollar. On August 22, a functionary of a Texas bank reported that Mexicans—chiefly businesspersons and industrialists—were depositing $1.5 million daily in the principal banks of El Paso (Islas, 1982: 1185).

In the meantime, the sudden realization that Mexico might be unable to pay interest on its $80 billion foreign debt profoundly shook the international banking community and mobilized Mexico's leading creditors, including the Bank of America, Citibank, Chase Manhattan, and Chemical Bank, as well as central banks in the United States, Europe, and Japan, to put together a "rescue package." Central to this operation was Mexico's agreement to negotiate a loan with the IMF involving agreement to a series of austerity measures that would further depress Mexico's already troubled economy. Finance Secretary Jesús Silva Herzog was also told that unless the Mexican government promised support to its private banks they would be cut off from all future credit (Bennett, 1982). Mexico undertook negotiations for a $4 billion IMF loan; in the meantime the Reagan administration provided a $1 billion agricultural credit, $1 billion in prepayment for Mexican oil (with interest charges of 25 percent), and a $700 million drawdown of Mexican foreign currency swap at the U.S. federal reserve. The central banks of the United States, Canada, Japan, West Germany, France, Italy, Spain, and Switzerland put together a $1.85 billion loan; negotiations were begun with private banks in these countries for $5 billion (*Banker*, 1982: 81-82; Kraft, 1983). The Mexican crisis initiated the system of "crisis cofinancing," involving the collaboration of commercial bankers, governments, and multilateral lending institutions to rescue "troubled country debtors and indeed the whole credit system from financial collapse" (Sanders, 1983: 53).

In Mexico, Finance Secretary Silva Herzog confirmed that negotiations were under way and grimly predicted up to three more years of austerity with additional firms closing down and more unemployment (*Latin American Weekly Reports*, August 27, 1983).

Throughout the month of August, labor confederations, left-wing political parties, and individual unions demanded the nationalization of the banks, effective exchange controls, and lower interest rates (Ramírez, 1982d: 12). At the end of August, nine leftist parties and organizations and 31 unions formed the Comité Nacional de Defensa de la Economía Popular (CNDEP), which called for total exchange controls. On August 31, President López Portillo addressed the 97th Ordinary General Assembly of the CTM, Mexico's largest labor confederation, pledging to devote his last three months in office to "recovering the national dignity" and proposing "to reconstitute this country . . . with the help of workers and peasants."

THE NATIONALIST INTERLUDE:
SEPTEMBER 1 TO DECEMBER 1, 1982

On September 1, in his last state of the union address, President López Portillo announced the nationalization of Mexico's private banks. This move, which eliminated a major bastion of the most powerful economic groups in the country, took the nation by surprise—none more so than the bankers themselves. Until that point they had enjoyed unrestricted presidential favor and had been among the few who continued to benefit when the economic boom of the late 1970s was transformed into an unprecedented crisis. The president also announced exchange controls that, with the bank nationalization, would give the government control over the buying and selling of dollars and, it was hoped, provide some protection for Mexican currency.

The cabinet and President-Elect Miguel de la Madrid had been informed of the decision to nationalize only a few hours prior to the president's speech, at which time he asked for the resignation of those who opposed the move. The director of the Banco de México, Miguel Mancera, resigned, as did Adrian Lajous, head of the Banco Nacional Comercio Exterior. Finance Secretary Silva Herzog offered his resignation but López Portillo refused to accept it, fearing the effect on Mexico's ongoing debt negotiations with the international banking community.

Allegedly the events leading to the expropriation began on August 5, when the president had been enraged to learn that the Banco Hipoticario Crédito had sent $300 million out of the country in a single day; he began an investigation into Mexican bank accounts and real estate in the United States and commissioned a secret emergency study on the probable effects of bank nationalization. This study was undertaken without the knowledge of Banco de Mexico director Miguel Mancera, who had published a booklet the previous April arguing against exchange controls and had been marginalized from government decisions when the dual exchange control was established in August. The investigation revealed the startling dimensions of capital outflow: $14 billion in over 1 million Mexican bank accounts in the United States and $30 billion in real estate owned by Mexicans in the United States, as well as $12 billion in dollar accounts in Mexican banks (Chávez, 1982: 8). Mexican citizens had 30,000 to 40,000 properties in southern U.S. cities; and there was an estimated $800 million annually in capital flight from expenses related to these properties such as taxes, water services, and electricity (Reveles, 1982: 16). López Portillo pointed an accusing finger at the bankers as *"sacadolares,"* stated that the lack of financial resources was stifling production, and ominously threatened to publish the names of those responsible if they did not return funds to Mexico within one month.

The bankers of course denied that they had acted unpatriotically or illegally and pointed out that the government had created the conditions that permitted their actions. Given the level of inflation in Mexico, the high interest rates in the United States, the fear of another devaluation, and the lack of exchange controls, the massive transfer of funds to the United States was logical from the perspective of capital, however undesirable for the national economy. In the end the government did not publish the names of sacadolares—apparently because the names of high-level officials of the López Portillo government would have figured prominently among them (Vazquez, 1982).

The euphoria and manifestations of support with which organized groups of the population—unions, peasant organizations, students—greeted the nationalization probably had as much to do with the long-term reputation of the banking establishment as a powerful monopoly dominating the economy in the interests of a small minority of families as it did with the responsibility of the banks for the capital outflow over the previous months. Bank loans had been concentrated among the more powerful economic groups—particularly those groups of which the banks were part, which often received low-interest or interest-free loans. Among the effects of this concentration had been the relative neglect of agriculture and the limited availability of credit for firms lacking their own banks, particularly small and medium industrial firms (*Punto*, 1983: 3-4).

The enormous profits of the banks during the previous five years had apparently been diverted to acquisitions rather than new investment. According to a colleague of Agustín Legorreta, director of Banamex,

Figure 6.1   Two Views of the Popular Demonstration on September 2, 1982, the Day after the Announcement of the Bank Nationalization Decree by Outgoing President López Portillo.

"When Agustin's father was alive, the bank tried to create at least one major business concern every year. But for the last five years it did not create one job. It bought up shares in existing companies. It created wealth for the bankers. The profit margins were as wide as that street out there" (Robinson, 1982: 50).

Although the government-controlled labor confederation, the CTM, had been calling for nationalization of the banks for some time, and the leftist PSUM had made this part of its platform in the 1982 presidential elections, few would argue that López Portillo's decision to nationalize the banks was a direct response to popular demand. At the same time, the fact that López Portillo recognized that he could count on popular support for the nationalization was undoubtedly a factor in his decision. It was also a means of outflanking the left and an effort to appease politically, with symbolic gestures, a population whose material conditions were being severely eroded and would face even greater austerity under the soon-to-be-implemented IMF plan. In both respects the nationalization appears to have succeeded, at least in buying time; the Left, lacking a strong popular base, appears more fragmented than ever, and the working class (for reasons that will be discussed below) has not yet succeeded in mounting an effective campaign against the austerity measures.

The nationalization decision seems rather to have been influenced by the nationalist sector within the government, particularly Carlos Tello Macías, who had briefly held the post of secretary of programming and the budget in the López Portillo administration until a dispute over economic policy led to his resignation in 1977. An advocate of strong intervention by the state to activate the economy, he had approved the policy of the previous Echeverría administration of state investment in heavy industry, wage support, and limited agrarian reform, and blamed its failure on the failure to restructure the financial, monetary, and credit system. In the late 1970s Tello coauthored with Rolando Cordera (now head of the parliamentary contingent of PSUM) an influential book, *La Disputa por la Nación*, which called for government stimulus of industry through protectionism; nationalization of key industries; greater control of the private sector, especially banks; low interest rates; strong exchange controls; and heavy direct investment (Robinson, 1982: 47-48; *Latin American Weekly Reports*, September 17, 1982).

Following the nationalization and resignation of Mancera, Tello was designated director of the Banco de México, which in turn was transformed into a decentralized agency controlling the newly nationalized banks. As one analyst noted, "Tello would command the biggest of all state agencies. He was being given the heart of the private sector on a plate" (Robinson, 1982: 48). But Tello assumed, correctly, as it turned out, that his mandate would be limited to the 90 days remaining to the López Portillo administration. President-Elect Miguel de la Madrid had been at best a lukewarm supporter of the nationalization of the banks; a strong believer in dependence on market forces, he would undoubtedly dismantle any "populist" measures Tello put into effect. As it turned out, Tello's financial control was strictly limited even during his three-month tenure as director of the Mexican banking system.

The bankers proved incapable of mounting an effective resistance. Along with the rest of the private sector they had been stunned by the nationalization, which represented a total departure from López Portillo's previous policies (Barta, 1982: 15). At stake were not only their banking assets and their control over the financial sector, but their shares in other firms. Still to be decided were amount and manner of compensation and the disposition of companies held by the banks (Ramírez, 1982a). Although the bankers contested the legality of the nationalization (without success), the fact that they still had much to lose was probably a factor in their limited reaction.

The Mexican bankers received little support from the international banking community, which had become quite nervous about the ability of private sector interests in Mexico to pay back their foreign debts— approximately 25 percent of Mexico's total debt of $80 billion. They were further concerned that the Mexican government, confronting its own massive debt, would not be in a position to guarantee private debt. The nationalization of the banks resolved that problem. As stated by a Bank of America spokesperson, "This is a positive step in that it puts the Mexican government clearly behind the banking system" (Bennett, 1982). Confronted with a contradiction between "their philosophical commitment to private ownership" and their interest in a sound banking system, the international bankers chose interest over ideology.

In the end, the Mexican bankers decided to wait for the Miguel de la Madrid government, which would presumably be more sympathetic to their needs—an assessment that ultimately has proved quite accurate. In the meantime, they still had a powerful ally in the López Portillo government in the person of Finance Secretary Jesús Silva Herzog.

Although his resignation had been rejected at the time of the bank nationalization, Silva Herzog apparently agreed to stay on only if he could have a say in the naming of the directors of the newly nationalized banks. He vetoed such leftist candidates as Muñoz Ledo (secretary of labor under Echeverría) and Flores de la Peña (Mexican ambassador to France, who was called from Paris to head the Foreign Trade Bank but allegedly would have been given one of the four main nationalized banks but for Silva Herzog's insistence). The final selection was one pleasing to the private bankers: two former finance ministers—David Ibarra Muñoz and Alfonso Carrillo—became directors of Banamex and Bancomer; most of the other 57 directors had been trained in the Banco de México and Nacional Financia, the government development bank (Robinson, 1982: 50). As stated by one banker, "The leftists seemed to have won the conceptual battle, but the conservatives have won the operational battle for now" (Rout, 1982).

In fact, the naming of Tello as central bank director did not so much turn the state financial sector over to Tello as create two separate and opposed financial centers. The populist conception of Tello and other nationalist and left-wing advocates—that banking should become an instrument of social and economic reform—confronted the orthodox financial philosophy of Silva Herzog and others, such as former Finance Secretary Mario Ramón Betata (at this point head of the previously nationalized banking and industrial complex Somex), who believed that profitability should continue to be a major criterion of banking operations.

One of Tello's most controversial measures was the reduction of the differential between interest rates by increasing those for savers while lowering those for borrowers. Previously this differential had been a major source of profit for the bankers. Interest on ordinary savings deposits was raised from 4.5 percent to 20 percent. At the same time, mortgage rates for lower-income housing were cut from 34 percent to 11 percent; other mortgage rates were cut by 10 percent. But these measures had little time to take effect, particularly given inflation, low levels of liquidity, the depressed market, and other conditions resulting from the economic crisis that discouraged both savings and investment.

Other proposals by left-wing and nationalist sectors for reform met with little response. Although the nationalization of the banks was institutionalized through an amendment to the constitution, the hopes that it would be followed by nationalizations in other sectors—particularly those in which foreign capital was important—were unrealized. In fact, on October 11, the government established special regulations facilitating foreign ownership in national firms by enabling foreign creditors to receive payment from debtor firms in the form of shares rather than funds. The PSUM condemned the measure as leading to the denationalization of some of the major branches of industry (Zuñiga, 1982b).

Contradictions within the state limited the scope of the "nationalist interlude"; international constraints became painfully clear with the negotiations between Mexico and the IMF for a $3.9 billion loan, which began in September. On the Mexican side there were three teams, one headed by Jesús Silva Herzog, a second by Carlos Tello, and a third by

Carlos Salinas de Gortari, head of Miguel de la Madrid's transition team and subsequently secretary of the budget and planning in the new administration. Undoubtedly there were differences among them regarding points of negotiation, and the final agreement, concluded in November, constituted a final blow to many of the nationalist programs instituted or proposed by Tello and others. The exchange controls, opposed by banking interests as leading to a black market in dollars (and thus ineffective in blocking the dollar outflow) and detrimental to the entry of new funds into Mexico, were to be dismantled by May 1983. But the major issue of the debate was the size of the government's 1983 budget deficit. The 1982 deficit was estimated at $25 to $30 billion, or 17 percent of gross national product. While government officials argued for a 14-15 percent deficit, IMF pushed for 6 percent, which would eliminate many of the subsidies to food producers and consumers. The agreement, concluded in November, settled on a budget deficit of 8.5 percent of gross national product in 1983: this would be further reduced to 5.5 percent in 1984 and 3.5 percent in 1985 (*Latin American Weekly Reports*, November 19, 1982)— clearly a defeat for the Mexican negotiators. An immediate consequence was the government decision to close 106 state companies and government agencies in an effort to streamline state operations and reduce the budget deficit (Chislett, 1982a).

In the meantime efforts by organized labor to raise wages to the level of cost of living increases met with frustration in a pattern that was to repeat itself in the coming months. Fidel Velázquez, the 83-year-old head of the leading official labor confederation CTM, threatened to bring out the CTM unions in a strike if agreement were not reached on a 50 percent wage increase. However, bargaining took place on a plant basis, which undermined the workers' position; many workers received no increase, others received 10 percent, some up to 30 percent. The strikes were postponed and in the end only about 100 of the projected 40,000 took place.

During 1982 an estimated 1 million workers lost their jobs, including 500,000 in construction alone. Thousands of small and medium firms closed down or fired workers; the closing of over 100 government agencies aggravated this situation. By the end of 1982, poor peasants and urban workers stated openly on radio and television that they were forced to resort to robbery in order to eat (Castillo, 1982: 35-36).

The last three months of the López Portillo administration demonstrated the contradictions in efforts of state officials to come to grips with Mexico's economic crisis. On the one hand, the nationalization of the banks, the establishment of exchange controls, and the appointment of Carlos Tello as the director of the Banco de México represented a late, desperate, and ultimately doomed effort to reverse a crisis, already far advanced, through the establishment of nationalist controls and reforms. The nationalization of the banks also raised the question of potential state autonomy versus actual autonomy. Nationalization had placed the state firmly in control of the banking sector, where technically it could be used to promote national development and social welfare. In his brief tenure as director of the Banco de México, Tello tried to implement nationalist policies, such as the reduction of interest rates to attract medium and small investors, but the effectiveness of these policies was limited by the brevity of his tenure and the constraints resulting from the economic crisis that made productive investment extremely risky as well as by the opposition of officials within the state financial sector who favored a more conservative economic policy closely resembling that of private banks. It is not clear whether Tello's program would have worked even in more favorable circumstances, but it is evident that it was not adequately tested in the circumstances existing in Mexico.

On the other hand, the IMF agreements portended the rationalization of the internationalist development model at the expense of the nationalist aspirations aroused by the government takeover of the banks and, in concrete terms, presaged continued economic contraction, additional bankruptcies, greater unemployment and underemployment, and further depressions of real wages. If the nationalization of the banks posed the question of the extent and limits of state autonomy in relation to the private sector in Mexico, the IMF agreements demonstrated the weaknesses of the Mexican state in its relation to international capital. The full implications of both measures would be realized in the subsequent administration of Miguel de la Madrid.

THE NEW ADMINISTRATION: RATIONALIZATION OF THE INTERNATIONALIST MODEL?

Miguel de la Madrid's presidential term began appropriately, with the most austere inaugural ceremonies in recent Mexican history. To administer Mexican society in a period of unprecedented crisis, the new president assembled a team of technocrats who closely resembled him in education and career experience: most were trained in economics and had advanced degrees from foreign universities and professional careers in government ministries related to finance. Miguel de la Madrid himself had a degree in public administration and had held several financial and economic posts in the Mexican government prior to his selection to succeed López Portillo, among them deputy finance secretary and secretary of planning and the budget.

In the first policy statement by the new president, the dominant theme appeared to be the rationalization of Mexico's internationalist development model through monetarist measures of fiscal austerity. Specific policy goals included cuts in public spending, the elimination of "irrational" subsidies, fiscal reforms to increase government revenues, measures clarifying the role of the state in the mixed economy, strict import controls, and increased investment in priority and productive activities and cutbacks in others. During his first month in office, which coincided with the last month of the legislative session, de la Madrid flooded Congress with legislative initiatives to implement his program.

The new president's choice of cabinet ministers as well as his rejection of "financial populism" and the monetarist policies he immediately put into effect endeared him to the Mexican private sector and to foreign bankers. The international banking community was particularly pleased by the retention of Jesús Silva Herzog as finance secretary and the return of Mancera as director of the Banco de México, replacing the controversial Carlos Tello (*Bolsa*, February 1983; Chislett, 1982b; Riding, 1982).

At the same time, the new policies quickly alienated nationalist and leftist sectors. Oscar Hinojosa, writing in the weekly *Proceso* compared the de la Madrid team with the *científicos* of the Porfiriato, a reference to the plutocracy of the prerevolutionary dictatorship of Porfirio Díaz, whose policies had led to the rapid modernization of Mexico on the basis of a massive influx of foreign capital as well as foreign models, and heavy repression. The de la Madrid team had launched the country "on a monetarist counterrevolution which attempts to solve the crisis without attending to the high social costs" (Hinojosa, 1982).

The return to the internationalist model evident in the early policies of de la Madrid implied the establishment of priorities by foreign rather than national capital, justified on the grounds of the crisis and Mexico's desperate need for dollars. At a meeting of representatives of over 90 major transnationals in January 1983, Commerce Secretary Hernández announced several incentives to encourage foreign investment in Mexican industry and trade. The government also encouraged foreign investment in border industries, in shares by foreign creditors in local firms for debt repayment, and in joint ventures for oil development and refining (Mantrop, 1983; Chislett, 1983).

In the meantime, those groups among the domestic private sector most affected by the bank nationalization have found their confidence in de la Madrid justified. At the end of December 1982, Miguel de la Madrid sent to Congress a bill authorizing the government to sell 34 percent of the assets of the nationalized banks to federal, state, and municipal agencies, bank workers, and bank clients, with no individual allowed to own more than 1 percent. However both supporters and opponents of the measure saw it as a means for private bankers to reassert their influence and control. It was suggested by a leader of the bank workers' union that bankers would in fact join forces to control the entire 34 percent, giving them substantial if not controlling interest. A Bank of America spokesperson praised the measure as enabling Mexico to take advantage of the skill and experience of its bankers (Orme, 1983). The left and nationalist sectors condemned the measure as a reprivatization of the banks—a major step backward.

In August 1983 Miguel de la Madrid announced the terms for compensation of 11 banks, which accounted for 73 percent of the paid-up capital of the 57 banks that had been nationalized. Shareholders were to receive government bonds with interest based on the average rate paid by banks on 90-day certificates (*New York Times*, August 23, 1983). Although there were complaints among business groups that the amount of compensation was not enough and among leftists that it was too much, the compensation seems to have been sufficient to restore good relations between the state and the private sector.

And in the spring of 1984, the government offered the shares of many of the nationalized banks' holdings in Mexican companies and foreign subsidiaries for sale, with preference given to former bank shareholders. The government plans to retain its holdings of a few formerly bank-owned companies in such areas as mining, steel, fishing, and paper, which are regarded as essential to the economy. Because the stocks are being offered in large, indivisible portfolios, only the wealthiest Mexican owners will be able to purchase them (Meislin, 1984).

Although these and other initiatives have undoubtedly benefited foreign interests and certain sectors of national capital, the government has retained control over finance and has taken other measures to rationalize and strengthen the state sector. Prices have risen on oil and other goods and services that the parastatal firms had previously provided to the private sector at subsidized prices, sometimes below cost. A reorganization of the parastatal firms called for the fusion of some and the liquidation of others. Several measures have been introduced to reform the tax structure, including an increase in the value added tax, a measure opposed by the private sector as another step toward "statization" of the economy and by labor leaders due to the regressive nature of the tax. Perhaps the most important measure for rationalizing the fiscal structure was the elimination of bearer shares, a device that had permitted anonymity in shareholding and thus constituted a mechanism for tax evasion. The elimination of bearer shares, like the nationalization of the banks and the introduction of exchange controls, had long been a demand of leftist and nationalist groups. Cutbacks in state services for the poor have been accompanied by the dismantling of those sectors of the bureaucracy linked to these services.

The de la Madrid administration succeeded in reducing the public sector deficit to 8.3 percent of Gross Domestic Product in 1983—even lower than the 8.5 percent projected by the IMF—and the balance of payments deficit (of $12,544,000 in 1981) was turned into a $3 million surplus in 1983 largely due to a surplus in the trade balance. These achievements have won de la Madrid the admiration of the International Monetary Fund and the international financial community but have had high domestic costs. The balance of trade surplus resulted not from an increase in exports but a drastic decline in imports, including industrial inputs needed for production. This in turn reflects the decline in investment by both the private sector and the government; the lower level of government investment is one factor in the lower public sector deficit. Industrial production declined by 9 percent between January and August 1983, and during the first six months of 1983 commercial sales dropped by 28 percent (Ramírez de la O., 1984: 5-6).

In the meantime, the full implementation of the IMF austerity program has fallen most heavily upon the organized and unorganized sectors of the working class. As noted above, during 1982 at least 1 million workers lost their jobs; cutbacks in public works programs as well as bankruptcies resulting from the increase in interest rates and the lack of liquidity led to fresh dismissals of workers in 1983. An ambitious $2.3 billion government program to provide temporary construction work for 700,000 workers on highways, railroads, irrigation, and housing projects would not begin to compensate for jobs lost in 1982 and 1983, let alone the growth of the labor force by 700,000 annually (*Business Latin America*, February 16, 1983).

Wage negotiations and strikes have failed to raise wages more than a fraction of the percentage increase in inflation and are often followed by drastic increases in the prices of basic necessities. In June 1983, following labor negotiations, hundreds of thousands of workers went on strike for a 50 percent wage increase. But the minimum wage increase was set at 15.6 percent, and the settlement was followed by increases in basic food prices (including a 41 percent increase in the price of tortillas). Thus a pattern seems to have been instituted whereby wage increases become an excuse for a new escalation of prices rather than a necessary adjustment of wages to rises in the cost of living.

The ability of the official labor leadership to respond at least in part to worker demands and yet remain within the guidelines imposed by the government has been a major element in the legendary stability of Mexico's political system. Today this flexibility of the official labor leadership is being eroded, not only by the nature of the crisis and the austerity regimen of the Mexican government that makes it impossible even to retain previous gains of organized labor but also, surprisingly, by a deliberate distancing of the government from the labor leadership, manifested in the reduction of the number of labor deputies in the PRI congressional contingent, the absence of labor appointees in certain government positions traditionally held by labor, and the rejection of "populist" rhetoric (Carr, 1983: 15-16).

Although independent unions and left-wing political organizations have formed coalitions and carried out effective mobilizations, especially the demonstrations and strikes of May and June 1983, the government strategy to fragment and divide organized labor—for example, through differential treatment of labor conflicts—has apparently been successful. Organized resistance is also weakened by differences among left-wing political organizations and parties and independent labor unions and coalitions on the most appropriate strategy to follow. Some groups favor a positive response to invitations by the official union bureaucracy to form alliances for combatting the austerity program; others reject such alliances as manipulative and as threats to the strength and direction of the more militant independent unions (*Punto Crítico*, 1984: 20-29).

The policies of the de la Madrid government have been most burdensome for workers and the unemployed who have experienced loss of jobs or of job security, cutbacks in real wages, and drastic increases in the prices of basic goods. But tax reforms and other measures have also alienated groups in the private sector already suspicious of the government after the nationalization of the banks. Allegedly, some former PRI supporters among the business sector are shifting their support to PAN, which continues to grow in popularity, claiming victory in 12 of the municipal elections that took place in five states at the end of June, 1983—a claim that was disputed by PRI (José Carreno in Tello et al., 1983: 35-36). Given the electoral success of PAN, a transfer of allegiance by the private sector would represent an effort to develop its own political resources rather than continue to rely on its traditional alliance with the state.

CONCLUSION

The complexity and fluidness of the Mexican situation precludes a definitive conclusion on the issue of structural realignment and changes in the Mexican model of development. On the basis of the above discussion of events leading to and immediately following the bank nationalizations and IMF agreements, however, certain trends can be identified—in some cases contradictory trends. Here an effort will be made to differentiate between dominant trends and weaker countervailing tendencies where these exist.

First, both government policy and private sector demands point to an even tighter integration of the Mexican state and private domestic capital with foreign capital. At one level this is an almost inevitable result of the process of debt renegotiation, IMF agreements, and new loans from private banks that could reinforce Mexico's international financial dependence for years—probably decades—to come. Other factors reinforcing this tendency include the encouragement by both government and domestic private capital of foreign creditors to take shares in debtor companies as repayment of foreign debt; government efforts (through tax incentives and other measures) to lure foreign investment, particularly in industries oriented to import substitution and export; the promotion of joint ventures with foreign capital in oil production and refining; and the loosening of controls on foreign investment to permit total foreign control in certain industries. At the same time, government measures to rationalize the state sector suggest that the state will continue to have a strong economic role in contrast to the neoliberal model that the de la Madrid administration seems to be pursuing in other respects.

Second, and clearly related, the dominant trend in terms of Mexico's development model is the reinforcement and rationalization of the current internationalist model involving the integration of the state, domestic private capital, and foreign capital, noted above; a further concentration of economic resources due to the loss of viability of small and medium firms unable to compete; and the further marginalization of Mexico's unemployed and underemployed population. Measures of the austerity program such as high interest rates, cutbacks in government subsidies, and the elimination of other forms of government protection will "rationalize" this model by eliminating weaker, less competitive firms. Unemployment, underemployment, and cutbacks in real wages lead to further contradictions in the domestic market and in firms producing for this market.

A countervailing element is the restriction on imports, which means that firms less dependent on imported goods will have certain advantages—a factor that would lessen dependence on foreign technology and would tend to favor less capital-intensive industries. Measures to promote industries producing industrial inputs could have a similar effect provided these industries are primarily domestic; in any event they might check to some extent the trend to greater unemployment. Some observers, however, have suggested that given the weakness of Mexican industry, the process of rationalization, carried to its logical extreme, would be tantamount to a policy of deindustrialization or industrial denationalization (see, for example, Jaime Ros in Tello et al., 1983: 22). It is doubtful that the process will go this far, but clearly the influence of proponents of the nationalist model, which had provided limited controls on the internationalist model, has been decidedly reduced.

Third, the economic crisis and especially the nationalization of the banks has clearly resulted in the realignment of relations between the state and the private sector, yet the implications of this realignment are still not clear. On the one hand, the nationalization of the banks dramatically demonstrates the autonomy of the state in terms of its ability to act against the interests of a powerful segment of the dominant class. It is evident that the bankers and their associates were surprised and chagrined by this move and, furthermore, that they were unable to do anything about it. It deprived them of a very lucrative source of income and, more significant, of a dominant position in the control and direction of financial resources that in turn had given them substantial power over investment decisions. Because of the central position of the banks in some of the major economic groups, it has undoubtedly weakened these groups by depriving them of a dependable source of finance. This financial control passed to the state, which is now in a position to direct credit policy to respond effectively to the social and development needs of the country.

On the other hand, even during the "nationalist" interlude, and particularly after the inauguration of Miguel de la Madrid, it was evident that the bankers had not lost as much as they feared and that the now nationalized banks would not undertake a radical renovation of credit policy. During the last three months of the López Portillo presidency, the influence of Tello as director of the central bank was offset by that of Finance Secretary Silva Herzog, who controlled the appointment of directors of the new nationalized banks and promoted the use of technical private bank criteria in providing loans. With the return of Mancera as director of the Banco de México, the allies of the bankers were in full control of the state financial sector. The decision of Miguel de la Madrid to reduce the state's share of the nationalized banks from total to majority control by selling 34 percent of the shares raised the possibility that the bankers would regain at least part of their holdings as well as positions in the administration of the banks; the agreement regarding compensation means that financial losses will be minimal; and many of them will be able to buy back shares in nonfinancial companies formerly controlled by the banks. In the long run, the most important effects of the nationalization could be felt in the political sphere due to the breakdown of trust between the private sector and the state as a result of the nationalization and the consequent distancing of the private sector from the state, manifested in a tendency for some PRI supporters in the business sector to transfer allegiance to PAN.

A final question, not adequately examined here, concerns the realignment of classes within Mexican society as a whole. Although the austerity measures forced upon the working class and the growing ranks of the unemployed and underemployed were expected to pose a major challenge to the stability of the political system, which could no longer provide economic concessions to organized labor or peasant organizations, this challenge has not yet materialized. The control exercised by labor confederations linked to the state over union leadership as well as the tendency of the labor leadership—and even sectors of the left—to regard working-class links with the state as desirable are undoubtedly elements in the government's ability to maintain political stability in the context of growing economic repression.

At the same time there are countertrends that must be taken into account, including the formation of new groups and coalitions composed of labor and peasant organizations and left-wing groups that have taken a strong position against IMF austerity measures. Whether the urban and rural workers, the unemployed and underemployed, and those individuals and groups who represent their interests can effectively mobilize around an alternative program for dealing with the current crisis and an alternative model for development is still unclear. But such mobilization is undoubtedly necessary if alternatives to the existing internationalist model are to be seriously considered, developed, and implemented.

NOTE

1. The distinction between the internationalist and nationalist models discussed here is developed in a somewhat different form in Cordera and Tello (1981), who distinguish between a neoliberal and nationalist option, both within the existing socioeconomic framework. The concepts "nationalist" and "internationalist" clearly do not exhaust all possible models of development in Mexico. In fact the dominant economic groups and even multinational firms have benefited from subsidies, tax relief, and protectionist measures of the "nationalist" model. In normal circumstances the Mexican government has to some extent pursued both models simultaneously. In the present economic crisis, however, it has been forced to choose between them.

REFERENCES

Aguilar M., Alonso et al.
    1982 *La nacionalización de la banca*. Mexico City: Editorial Nuestro Tiempo.
Banker
    (publication of Financial Times Business Publishing LTD. London).
Bartra, Roger
    1982 *El reto de la izquierda*. Mexico City: Grijalbo.
Bennett, Robert A.
    1982 "Takeover pleases U.S. banks." *New York Times* (September 2).
Bolsa
    (Bank of London and South America).
Carr, Barry
    1983 "The Mexican economic debacle and the labor movement: a new era or more of
    the same?" Presented at the Executive Workshop on Mexico's Economic Stabilization:
    Challenges and Opportunities, Center for U.S. Mexican Studies, University of Cali-
    fornia, June 2-4.
Castillo, Heberto
    1982 "Cambio?" *Proceso* 317 (November 29).
Chávez, Elias
    1982 "Exultación en la Tribuna, frente a la indignación empresarial y duda de Priis-
    tas." *Proceso* 305 (September 6): 6-8.
Chislett, William
    1982a "Mexico to shut state concerns." *Financial Times* (November 17).
    1982b "Mancera returns as Mexican bank head." *Financial Times* (December 3).
    1983 "Mexico allows full foreign control of Grupo Alfa Units." *Financial Times* (Feb-
    ruary 19).
Cordera, Rolando and Carlos Tello
    1981 *La disputa por la nación: perspectivas y opciones del desarrollo*. Mexico City:
    Siglo XXI.
Evans, Peter and Gary Gereffi
    1982 "Foreign investment and dependent development: comparing Brazil and
    Mexico," in Sylvia Ann Hewlett and Richard S. Weinert (eds.) *Brazil and Mexico:
    Patterns in Late Development*. Philadelphia: Institute for the Study of Human Issues.
Guadarrama Sistos, Roberto
    1983 "Estado, banca y política económica." *Estudios Políticos* Nueva época 2, 1
    (January/ March): 30-37.
Hinojosa, Oscar
    1982 "Culmina en este sexenio el desplazamiento de los políticos." *Proceso* 321 (De-
    cember 27): 6-10.
Islas, Hector
    1982 "1982: un año tempestuoso." *Comercio Exterior* 32, 11 (November): 1180-
    1187.
Kraft, Joseph
    1983 "World's banks are leaning too heavily on Mexico." *Los Angeles Times* (Septem-
    ber 12).
Mantrop, Stanley
    1983 "Mexicans say investors show greater interest." *Journal of Commerce* (Jan-
    uary 21).

Meislin, Richard J.
1984 "Mexico selling stock held by seized banks." *New York Times* (May 22).

Orme, William A., Jr.
1983 "Mexico is juggling peso dollar issue." *Miami Herald* (February 12).

Punto
1983 "El controvertido pago de la indemnización a los banqueros." (August 29).

Punto Crítico
1984 "Movimiento Obrero: enorme descontento, derrotas y dispersión." 13, 198 (February).

Ramírez, Carlos
1982a "Los barones del dinero perdieron el centro de su poder." *Proceso* 305 (September 6): 20-23.
1982b "Hasta el dia primero el Banco de México habia sido arrebatado al gobierno." *Proceso* 306 (September 13): 10-12.
1982c "El monstruo ahora destruido lo empezo a crear el mismo gobierno, desde 1973." *Proceso* 305 (September 6): 16-18.
1982d "La nacionalización de la banca, respuesta a la demanda popular." *Proceso* 305 (September 6): 6-14.

Ramírez de la O., Rogelio
1984 "El ajuste económico: Un balance." *Nexos* (Mexico), 73 (January).

Reveles, José
1982 "800 millones de dolares al año se iban para impuestos y servicios." *Proceso* 310 (October 11): 16-17.

Riding, Alan
1982 "Bankers cheer Mexico's austerity plan." *New York Times* (December 3).

Robinson, Alan
1982 "Portillo pockets the banks." *Euromoney* (London) 10, 82 (October): 47-53.

Rodríguez, Erwin
1983 "La transcendencia económica y politica de la expropiación de la banca privada en México." *Estudios Politicos*, Nueva época 2, 1 (January/March): 39-42.

Rout, Lawrence
1982 "Mexico's newly nationalized banks open amid doubts about controls on currency." *Wall Street Journal* (September 7).

Sanders, Linda
1983 "Can crisis cofinancing save the world?" *Institutional Investor* (February): 53-57.

Tello, Carlos Macías et al.
1983 "La crisis de México." *Nexos* 67 (July): 16-38.

Vazquez, Juan M.
1982 "Mexicans wonder who's on 'list.'" *Los Angeles Times* (October 5).

Zuñiga, Juan Antonio
1982a "La banca, accionista en todas las ramas de la economia." *Proceso* 306 (September 13): 14-15.
1982b "Para pagar la deuda privada se entregan las empresas a extranjeros." *Proceso* 311 (October 18): 26-27.
1983 "Los banqueros vuelven a casa y la banca recobra su meta utilitarista." *Proceso* 322 (January 3): 8-9.

PART III

THE WORKING CLASS AND POPULAR MOBILIZATION

7

The Mexican Labor Movement
1917-1975

by
Raúl Trejo Delarbre*
Translated by Anibal Yanez

The new attention given to the study of the history of the Mexican labor movement has not been accidental. Forgotten for several decades by political scientists and historians, this topic has taken on a new urgency. This has been partly because recent research in Mexican history has stumbled upon reservoirs of information in the course of attempting to answer the question: what has been the participation of the workers in the recent evolution of the Mexican state? It has also been due to the growing impact of independent trade unionism on national politics, and to the labor movement's need to find in its past the historical consciousness that official versions of labor history have attempted to obscure.

The history of Mexican trade unionism has oscillated between two extremes: the submission of the trade unions to the state, and the repression of the independent movements that have tried to extricate themselves from that situation. One of the characteristic features of the Mexican state since its formation has been its close relationship with the trade unions, which have served in turn as bases of support and as instruments for diluting the autonomous self-organization of the workers. Even the characteristics of trade union organizations, their programs and their political participation, have depended—with a few notable exceptions—on the needs of the state. This has been the case throughout the twentieth century, but it has been especially clear during the crucial moments in the evolution of the Mexican state, particularly during the regimes of Obregón, Cárdenas, and, most recently, Echeverría.

Some of the factors that have determined the subjection of the labor movement to the state include a nationalist ideology that even the independent trade unions have accepted without question, the close relationship between union leaders and the government, and the lack of

---

*Raúl Trejo Delarbre is a Professor in the Facultad de Economía, Universidad Nacional Autónoma de México (Mexico City) and the author of numerous studies on the Mexican labor movement.

appropriate and effective tactics among leftist groups. The state, in turn, intent on maintaining a strategy of industrial development at all costs, has concentrated on its relations with the trade union bureaucracy and has achieved the demobilization of the workers through a combination of concessions and repression, using the former in small doses to weaken discontent and the latter when this discontent could no longer be contained. In Mexico, the state has rendered workers powerless by organizing them and incorporating the unions into official politics. This has happened with the two most important labor federations: the Confederación Regional Obrera Mexicana (CROM) and the Confederación de Trabajadores de México (CTM), which have supported the actions of whoever has been president, have carried out electoral campaigns, and in general have controlled all outbursts of union independence. The state-party-union formula, characteristic of populist systems, has been the fundamental structure of the Mexican system. This essay outlines the development of the Mexican trade union organizations and their ties to the state.

From its birth in 1912 the Casa del Obrero Mundial was dominated by anarchist currents. Starting as a center for philosophical discussions, this institution became the embryo of a trade union. One of its creators would later note that in the Casa, "reformist trade unionism of a Marxist-socialist hue was left aside and attention was centered on . . . anarcho-syndicalism, without an ounce of bourgeois or proletarian politics" (Salazar, 1972a: 11). In their supposedly apolitical stance the leaders of the Casa attempted to remove themselves from the struggles between the groups that were fighting for power, but they also removed the workers from the political struggles.

After the victory of the constitutionalist (Carrancista) forces in 1914, the idea of establishing an alliance with the victors won out in the Casa. At first Carranza rejected the pact with the Casa, both because he considered that it "reneged on the Fatherland" and because he felt he did not need its support. However, when Carranza's forces were pushed out of Mexico City by Zapata and Villa, Carranza's lieutenants (especially Alvaro Obregón) with better political vision sealed the pact with the Casa del Obrero Mundial. Thus in February 1915 the leaders of the Casa promised to "suspend trade union and syndicalist organizing and enter into a different phase of activity in view of the urgent need to propel and intensify the revolution" (Salazar, 1972b: 79). The Casa appointed a "revolutionary committee" that cemented the alliance with Carranza, who in turn agreed to issue laws that would benefit the workers. The collaboration of the Casa with Carranza marked the alliance of the labor movement with the bourgeois wing of the "revolution" in exchange for a few concessions. The Casa organized its members into the Batallones Rojos (Red Batallions), which were six military units made up of almost 10,000 men, to defend the constitutionalist government. Thus "the urban workers, led by a handful of opportunist leaders, experienced a period of complete confusion. Unable to form an independent proletariat and to put forward a program for society based on their own class interests, they were overcome and strangled by the forces imposed upon them externally; thus they were driven to join those whom they considered the strongest, that is, the Constitutionalists" (Córdova, 1973: 16). Grouped into the Batallones Rojos, the workers from the Casa demonstrated that they had a great capacity for organization, but they used their strength to combat their class brothers, the peasants headed by Villa and Zapata in revolt against Carranza.

Not all sections of the labor movement agreed to the pact with the government. Some anarcho-syndicalist groups refused to join. Rank-and-file workers were divided, as many did not want to enlist in the Carrancista ranks. For Jean Meyer (1971: 12), the collaboration of the Casa del Obrero Mundial with the government was "a fatal step which would place the Mexican labor movement under the tutelage of the government, a tutelage which has persisted until today." Later, when the Casa began to be a nuisance, the Carranza regime brought about its disappearance.

Between 1915 and 1916 a wave of strikes engulfed the whole country. The elementary school teachers, the trolley car operators, the electricians, and in the state of Mexico, the miners all went on strike, some of them led by the Casa del Obrero Mundial. The government did not intervene at that point, but when workers demanded that their wages be paid in metallic coin and not in paper during the monetary crisis of 1916, Carranza severely repressed the trade unions and the leaders who supported this demand. This repression brought about the demise of the Casa.

In 1917, while the most outstanding labor leaders were still in prison, the convention in charge of drafting a new constitution included in the document some labor demands, concretely in Articles 27 and 123. Although Carranza was not in agreement with these articles, he was forced to accept them in order to avoid the resurgence of an organized opposition. However, although he signed the Constitution, Carranza did not make any concessions that hurt the interests he represented. He accomplished the consolidation of the Mexican bourgeoisie as the class in power.

For a long time, labor leaders had expressed the need for creating a central union federation that would include all the various isolated labor groups. In 1916, the Federación de Sindicatos Obreros del Distrito Federal (FSODF) called a labor congress. The Confederación del Trabajo de la Región Mexicana was the result of that congress and Louis N. Morones, who represented the FSODF, was elected the leader of the new organization.

Meanwhile, Carranza was concerned about staying in at least partial control of organized labor. Through the governor of Coahuila, Gustavo Espinoza Mireles, he issued a manifesto-invitation to a labor congress that took place in Saltillo, Coahuila, on May 1. Some organizations did not attend as they did not approve of the Carrancista maneuver to control the labor movement. After long discussions, the delegates from eighteen states agreed to form the Confederación Regional Obrera Mexicana (CROM).

From its origins, the CROM revealed itself to be closely tied to the state. As for its principles, "it formally accepted the class struggle, but it limited itself to the economic sphere; tactically it adopted the anarchist direct action strategy" (limited, of course, to the economic struggle and excluding all use of violence). It left the door open to political participation. Given that hard work had been done to discredit revolutionary principles in the working class, this political action had a bourgeois content. The CROM political action was aimed at gaining concessions, not building a proletarian revolution or struggling "for the organization and politization of the working class" (Iglesias, 1970: 43-44).

The CROM's policy was guided by several young leaders who made up the Grupo Acción, headed by Morones. The centralization of power was thus formalized within the labor organization. In 1919 the Grupo Acción created a Labor party to support Alvaro Obregón's candidacy for president. When Carranza was murdered and Adolfo de la Huerta became provisional president, the CROM and the Labor party accepted large sums of money from Obregón and Calles in return for CROM backing.

Obregón's election as president in 1920 allowed the CROM leaders to achieve two of their objectives: official support and posts within the government apparatus. Celestino Gasca and Luis N. Morones were named governor of the Distrito Federal and director of factory supplies and military provisions, respectively. In 1921 and 1923 a series of strikes exploded that were neutralized thanks to secret agreements between Obregón and the CROM leaders. However, in 1921 the Confederación General de Trabajadores (CGT) was founded, headed by the anarchosyndicalists Rosendo Salazar, Rafael Quintero, and José G. Escobar. The CGT supported the railroad and trolley car operators' strikes and confronted the CROM, thus initiating a stage of ideological division of the labor movement.

When Obregón smashed several strikes promoted by the CGT, especially the trolley car operators' strike in 1923, the CGT decided to oppose the government openly. On that occasion, the authorities opened the jails so that convicts backed by the army could act as scabs in the trolley operators' strike; this resulted in the death of several workers. The CGT got the support of Adolfo de la Huerta, who was also opposed to Obregón, although for different reasons. For his part, Obregón backed the CROM for some time—until various acts of his regime, among them the assassination of Felipe Carrillo Puerto, Governor of Yucatán, brought about a cooling off of relations between the CROM and the president. By then, the leaders of the CROM had acquired the administrative posts that they would keep during the succeeding regimes.

Having set the foundations for its own development, the constitutionalist regime turned its attention to securing the "conciliation of classes." By that time, the CROM had lost its combativeness. In May 1924 CROM leader Reinaldo Cervantes declared that his federation had changed its tactics: "No longer will destructive demonstrations proclaim the rights of workers . . . today all features of the confederation are true to the broadest justice . . . it is not a matter of destroying capital, it is a matter of consolidating labor and capital" (Salazar, 1938: 138). Not long before that Calles, who was already a candidate for president, had declared that "the trade unions today are in charge of limiting capitalism's absolute power, serving at times to protect it from possible attacks which might destroy it" (Iglesias, 1970: 98). The future president announced his policy: to control the trade unions through the CROM, to ensure order and a social base for the development of production.

When he was sworn in as president, Plutarco Elías Calles appointed Morones as minister of industry, commerce, and labor. In the same 1924 elections, twelve deputies and three senators belonging to the CROM won seats. Morones, in his double role as labor leader and government official, systematically favored the CROM-sponsored unions and persecuted those not belonging to this federation. If strikes earlier had served to consolidate the CROM, now Morones considered them to be damaging. A few weeks after being appointed minister, he referred to a railroad strike, declaring that "the government will not put up with these procedures." Meanwhile, the CROM experienced its period of greatest growth: between 1920 and 1924 its membership grew from 100,000 to 1 million.

The union would play the role of maintaining a truce between labor and capital, so that the regime could develop a policy of attracting investments. The declarations in August 1925 by the secretary of the FSODF, who was a member of the CROM, were very explicit: "Workers must not become systematic enemies of capitalism, but rather should only demand with full moderation and equanimity, as they have done up until now, that their rights be respected—rights which they recognize are intimately tied to reciprocal obligations. . . . foreign capital will always be welcomed by organized labor represented by the CROM, which will provide it with all kinds of facilities for better investment, thus furthering the policy of the national government presided by Citizen General Plutarco Elías Calles" (Salazar, 1938: 200).

In order to justify his arbitrary resolutions constantly in favor of the CROM's interests (which were the state's interests), Morones created the Juntas de Conciliación y Arbitraje (Arbitration Boards). In 1928 Obregón again ran for president and won, but he was assassinated in July of that year. The rivalry between Obregón and Morones was well known, and so the latter was blamed for the assassination, although nothing was ever proved against him. Nevertheless, the CROM was definitely weakened by its direct confrontation with Obregonism and interim President Emilio Portes Gil. Various trade union groups split from the CROM when they sensed Morones's political decline, and at the end of Calles's term Morones had to resign his ministerial post.

Having lost prestige and having been undermined by Morones's excessive authoritarianism, the CROM began to prove unable to provide the regime with the support it needed. Corruption within the confederation and the clear connivance between the latter and the federal government resulted in the CROM's gradual loss of its militants; some unions even decided to disown it publicly. On the other hand, Calles's policy, based on a mixture of despotism and paternalism, was somewhat unique. Years later he would define his view of the labor struggles in the following manner:

> Workers need the lessons of experience. They need to clash among themselves. If before this there should be an attempt to unify them, it would be useless. Simple convincing is sometimes seen by them as resistance and not guidance, because a sense of reality is only acquired through one's own experience. Therefore, I consider it necessary that the workers prove through hard practice what is feasible and what is utopian and inconvenient. It is useful for the workers to clash among themselves. From that will result, in a short time, a fertile lesson: that nothing is possible without the unification of the masses [Córdova, 1974: 23].

The world crisis of 1929 wreaked havoc on the Mexican economy. Silver was depreciated and exports to the United States declined. The government established the National Chamber of Labor to deal with the strikes that began to appear along with the economic recession. Because the "constructive epoch" of the revolution required the solid organization of all its forces, Calles in that same year created the Partido Nacional Revolucionario (PNR); its birth accelerated the disappearance of the Labor party, which had been an appendage of the CROM.

Since the time of Morones, the employers and the union groups had felt the need to establish legal norms for the institutional resolution of labor conflicts. In November 1928 a Convención Obrero-Patronal organized by the CROM had come out in favor of a labor code. On August 28, 1931, President Pascual Ortiz Rubio issued the Ley Federal del Trabajo (Federal Labor Law, hereafter referred to as "the law"), which regulated Article 123 of the Constitution. There was nothing "especially new" about this law; as Clark (1934: 215) notes, "Its chief merit lies in the fact it is federal. It is more conservative, on the whole, than many of the state labor laws and than many of the accepted practices in labor-employer relations."

The most important feature of the law was the requirement that companies sign contracts with their workers. Two weeks before the law's approval by Congress, the employers' organizations objected to this point, saying, "The employers' group maintains that neither jobs, nor the workers' opportunities to keep them, will be guaranteed by the fact that the law requires that contracts be perpetual; on the contrary, the effect produced will be unemployment" (cited by Salazar, 1970: 115). In fact, the contracts did not present this danger; on the contrary, they contributed to the stability of labor relations. In the motivation for the law it was pointed out that "in collective contracts resides the guarantee of order, of discipline, and of harmony in the relations between capital and labor . . . the trade unions make the relations between workers and employers more harmonious, just and orderly, permitting the elaboration of a permanent formula for class peace" (cited by Corona, 1971: 53).

Instead of being a guarantee of free union organization, the Ley Federal del Trabajo became one of the best instruments for the control of the labor movement in that it made the government the omnipotent judge of all strikes and demands. On top of this, the application and interpretation of the labor legislation was always left up to the authorities. Proof of this was the case of the trolley car workers in the federal district. As soon as the law was approved, they demanded extra wages for overtime because under an agreement signed in 1925 they had been forced to work a half-hour extra each workday without added pay. Although Article 123 of the Constitution as well as the newly created law guaranteed them the right to receive double pay for overtime, the Ministry of Industry, Commerce and Labor decided that the company did not have to comply. It argued that due to the country's difficult economic situation the workers should endure the sacrifice and not push for their demands. The situation persisted until 1940, when this unjust decision was revoked (Pedrueza, 1941: 353-354).

Not only was legal control over unions formalized, the state also perfected its institutional collaboration with the labor organizations. In June 1932 the Cámara del Trabajo de Distrito Federal (Federal District Chamber of Labor) was created. This was the first attempt at national unification in which both the Federación Sindicalista del Trabajo (FST), presided over by Fidel Velázquez, and the old CGT participated. With the Cámara del Trabajo the government wanted to achieve a labor movement sufficiently unified to be of value in the coming presidential election (Clark, 1934: 261). Nevertheless, the unification attempt was not successful, because the CROM and the Confederación Sindical Unitaria de México (CSUM) abstained from participation. The CSUM was created in 1929 thanks to the efforts of the Communist party and it failed on various occasions in its attempts to merge with the CGT.

By 1932 the reformist CROM was on the decline. The CGT's "revolutionary syndicalism," according to Iglesias (1970: 69), "did not amount to anything other than a bourgeois position, as it isolated the worker from the political struggle, preventing him from understanding his situation vis-à-vis the other classes and history, and therefore from acquiring a consciousness of his role as a vanguard." That is, although unlike the CROM, the CGT did not depend organically upon the state, its ideology coincided with that of the "Mexican Revolution." Years later the CGT even adopted an explicitly anti-communist posture and allied itself with Calles and the CROM to combat Lázaro Cárdenas's reformist program.

In September 1932 Morones accused Vicente Lombardo Toledano, secretary general of the FSODF, of propagating "exotic ideas" (that is, "alien ideology"). The next day Lombardo resigned from the CROM and in March 1933 he organized the "*purified*-CROM," as it was called by its members, made up of unions that had split from Morones's CROM. In its program, the purified-CROM declared trade union independence from the state. In October this organization and several others joined to form the Confederación General de Obreros y Campesinos Mexicanos (CGOCM), which during 1933 and 1934 promoted several strikes and even a national work stoppage in demand for better wages. However, later the CGOCM paid more attention to its alliance with President Cárdenas than to the needs of the working class.

By then the interim government of Abelardo Rodríguez was coming to an end (Ortiz Rubio had resigned in 1932). Rodríguez, who said he was on the side of the proletariat, summed up his pragmatic policy in one phrase—"The ideal formula, our slogan for struggle in economic matters, shall be: eight hours work, eight hours leisure, eight hours rest, and eight pesos minimum wage" (cited by Salazar, 1958: 337). When the members of the CGOCM challenged the policy of Abelardo Rodríguez, the latter launched a campaign of persecutions against the union.

The only noteworthy accomplishment in labor affairs by Rodríguez was the establishment of minimum wages, although he took pains to point out that the raises in wages would not hurt capital. In a letter to industrialists on August 29, 1933, he stated that they would, "on the contrary, . . . mean many benefits, as the wage raises will be compensated by higher productivity on the part of the workers, and in exchange the entrepreneurs will receive the great benefits of increased consumption within the country" (cited by Iglesias, 1970: 107).

The main points of support for the regime of the revolution had deteriorated. The labor movement, for its part, was divided after the split between the CROM and Lombardo's group. The mass politics posed by Cárdenas required a labor movement that was organized and independent but loyal to the government. After 1933 "the coincidence of interests produced collaboration, and collaboration produced the permanent unity between the state and the working masses: such was the process which led in short time to the institutionalization of the policy of the Mexican Revolution" (Córdova, 1974: 72).

Cárdenas sought to consolidate the state as the directing force of the national economy, subordinating to it all the productive forces. For this, he proposed to the workers that they organize themselves into unions. His populist policy was not designed to leave power in the hands of the working class. As Córdova (1974: 62) has pointed out, Cárdenas "wanted the workers to get power, on the condition that they organize and discipline themselves as a class; but he did not admit that this might signify the possibility of *taking* power itself. Cárdenas did not see any danger in the fact that workers would *enter* into power. He had come to the conclusion that revolutionary power could not be sustained for long if the workers were not *made the partners* of the state, if they were not also turned into a ruling force, together with the others which likewise should be partners in the task of exercising power." Thus Cárdenas expected the workers to share power with the employer class and in this manner his apparently emancipating policy revealed itself as conciliatory.[2]

Faced with the specter of foreign intervention in the economy, Cárdenas called for united support for the administration from all sectors. In his electoral campaign he warned that capitalism would always take advantage of the slightest division in labor. He said that peasants and workers should unite despite all obstacles. He called on the trade unions to support his "Six-Year Plan."

In contrast with the anti-union stance of Abelardo Rodríguez, Cárdenas exhorted the workers to strengthen their organizations. In the first year of his government, a movement for wage increases spread throughout the country. In 1934 there were 202 strikes, compared to 13 during 1933. By 1935 the strikes numbered 642. "The lightning of the workers' strike illuminates everything," wrote Rosendo Salazar (1958: 354). On June 11, 1935, former President Calles declared that many of the strikes were unjustified and that they constituted an ungrateful response to the government's policies.

The next day the CGOCM responded that Calles's declarations were a provocation, aimed at initiating an era of repression against workers. The main trade union organizations except for the CGT and the CROM (that is, the Cámara Nacional del Trabajo, the CGOCM, the CSUM, the FSODF, the graphic arts union, the miners, the telephone workers, the trolley car operators, and the railroad workers) issued a manifesto stating that the strike movements "are due to a collective malaise and to a state of social injustice" and warned that they could declare a general strike "as the only means of defense against the possible implantation of a fascist regime in Mexico." The union organizations met between July 12 and July 13 and agreed to form the Comité Nacional de Defensa Proletaria (CNDP), which issued a manifesto giving support to the Cárdenas government and calling on all trade union groups to participate in a Congreso Nacional de Unificación. On December 22, over 30,000 workers from the CNDP held a mass demonstration in support of Cárdenas. The CROM and the CGT formed an Alianza de Trabajadores Unificada to defend Calles and used anti-communist arguments against the "agitation" in the trade unions. (The CGT's anarchist doctrine had become anti-communist and a year later it collaborated with the employer's organizations in the struggle against the workers from the glass works plant Vidriera Monterrey; Iglesias, 1970: 68.)

Cárdenas got the support he needed to continue his policy of reforms, in spite of the opposition presented by the Calles group. He felt that the labor unrest could be resolved through institutional means and that this would result in the strengthening of the state and improved national productivity. He expressed this in responding to Calles on June 12, 1934, when he said that strikes were part of the process of accommodating workers and employers and that although they might cause trouble and even hurt the economy, their resolution could contribute to improving the economic situation. Presumably Cárdenas considered the improvement of wages as an increase in demand for goods as well as an improvement of the volatile social situation.

Between February 17 and February 20, 1936, the CGOCM held its second and last congress. It was dissolved to become the great central union created by the Unification Congress, which began the next day and lasted until the twenty-fourth of February. At that Congress was born the Confederación de Trabajadores de México (CTM), which immediately included more than a thousand unions. Into the CTM entered industrial unions (also called "vertical" unions) such as the miners, the railroad workers, and the like, as well as regional ("horizontal") organizations such as the state organizations from Jalisco, Michoacán, the Distrito Federal, and so forth. This mixed composition flowed from the new organization's purpose, which was to unify the majority of workers' organizations.

With the birth of the CTM, the CROM was definitely superseded. (The CGT continued to exist, but as a minority organization and grew increasingly weak.) Thus the Cárdenas government had accomplished one of its key objectives—now it could count on an organized mass movement that in no way constituted a threat to its own stability; quite the contrary, it consolidated the government. Since its founding, the CTM expressed its pro-government credo by declaring its unconditional support for the Cárdenas regime. One incident on the day of the appointment of the CTM executive committee anticipated the lack of democracy that would prevail later in the CTM. A Communist, Miguel Angel Velasco, who was proposed by the majority of organizations present to fill the position of organization secretary, had to cede that post to Fidel Velázquez, the CGOCM candidate. The latter group had threatened to withdraw if Velázquez's candidacy was rejected. Vicente Lombardo Toledano was elected secretary general; he too was a leader of the CGOCM and the main promoter of the CTM.

In March 1936 a group of entrepreneurs and bankers warned the president to beware of the dangers that agitation among the workers might bring for the country's stability. The masses, they said, "are natural elements which when unleashed respect no authority, government, laws, or institutions." Cárdenas replied that the strikes would be harmful only if they were to go beyond "the limits of the law and the economic capacity of the employers" (cited by Salazar, 1972a: 209). The president was sure that this would not happen, for, having a labor federation that supported the state's policy, the control of the workers was no problem.

On April 6 the mail train from Veracruz was dynamited and derailed; the responsibility for the sabotage was attributed by many to the Calles group. Four days later Plutárco E. Calles, Luis N. Morones, and his collaborators, Luis L. León and Melchor Ortega, were expelled from the country. On April 12, the CTM held a demonstration in Mexico City in support of Cárdenas, to which were taken the incinerated remains of the three railroad workers killed in the dynamiting incident. In that year there had been 674 strikes, and in 1937 there were 576. The strikes promoted by the pro-government unions, especially the CTM, did not go beyond the "limits of the law" as laid down by Cárdenas. Among the most important were the strikes against the San Rafael Paper Factory, which lasted six months, against the light company, and against Standard Fruit. All these strikes were decided in favor of the workers; the strikes by workers and peasants against the farms of La Laguna were brought to an end with the expropriation of the lands in the area and their conversion into *ejidos* (R. Salazar, 1972a: 247).

The strike against the Vidriera Monterrey in February 1936 was countered by the entrepreneurs of that city with an employers' lockout, but Cárdenas's personal intervention solved the conflict. On that occasion the president made known his *Catorce Puntos* (fourteen points), in which he reaffirmed that the state would regulate the national economy; he chided the employers for the lockout and suggested that "entrepreneurs who feel fatigued by the social struggle may hand over their industries to the workers or to the government. This, and not a strike, would be patriotic."

Although the victorious strikes strengthened the CTM, various tendencies within the confederation began to express their differences. In June 1937 the members of the CTM who belonged to the Communist party temporarily split from the confederation, arguing that there had been a violation of the statutes and that there was a lack of democracy. This move weakened Lombardo and left him practically alone against the Fidel Velázquez/Fernando Amilpa group. And, in fact, Lombardo had become isolated. Although his power had rested on the influence that he could develop from the rank and file, he could not consolidate his worker base. Anguiano explains that

> Lombardo really did not have his own social base with which to support himself at a given moment, since his ties with the masses were never consistent, because to relate to the workers he was dependent on the union leaders following his orders. These union leaders depended increasingly on the bureaucratic clique which had been developing within the CTM and whose interests and influence Lombardo had fostered. The power of the **Amilpa and Velázquez group was not based on fantastic speeches and** grandiose slogans or on impressive mass meetings; rather it had been developing through the day-to-day work of organization and bureaucratic imposition [Anguiano, 1974: 124].

"As the influence of the Communists was reduced, 'Fidelismo' [support for Fidel Velázquez] gained ground and became stronger . . . [while] the CP remained in its old sectarian and intransigent line, Lombardo lapsed into Fabian complacence in the face of the corrupt and class-collaborationist leaders. Lombardo, in spite of his privileged position as the head of the CTM, made no serious effort to create new workers cadres to replace the old ones who came from the CROM and other organizations already showing signs of decay" (Fuentes Díaz, 1959: 339). A few months later, at the end of 1937, the Partido Comunista Mexicano (PCM) changed tactics and decided that the international situation (especially the imminent Second World War) and the pressures exerted by the United States on the Mexican government made "unity at all costs" necessary; the PCM returned to the confederation, but the divisions within the CTM would not disappear.

Even with its internal disputes, the CTM continued to carry out effectively its role of supporting Cárdenas. The mass mobilization in March 1938 on occasion of the oil expropriation was proof of this. In May 1937 a strike had exploded against the U.S. oil monopolies. The Junta Federal de Conciliación (Federal Arbitration Board) ruled in favor of the Sindicato Petrolero and the companies sought an injunction, which the Supreme Court refused to grant them. The oil companies then refused to accept the court decision, leading the government to expropriate the foreign companies' property and nationalize the oil industry on March 18, 1938.

To command respect for its nationalist politics, Cárdenas's government had to counterpose a solid popular front to the foreign interests. In December 1937 the president proposed the restructuring of the PNR, the official party, which thereafter was named the Partido de la Revolución Mexicana (PRM). The mass organizations backed the presidential initiative and became an organic part of the reformed party, into which one could no longer enter individually but only through one of the sectors into which the party was divided. The PRM was not born as a complement to, nor in opposition to, the mass organizations that already existed (in particular the CTM), but as an organization that grouped all of them together. Through this party reform, Cárdenismo was able to impose and institutionalize its policy: the state, through the PRM, as the organizer of the masses. The participation of the CTM in the party was illegal, as labor legislation did not allow trade unions to act in politics. But the leaders of the labor confederation overcame this barrier by insisting on the need to consolidate a "popular front." Nevertheless, the members of the PRM did not have a chance to constitute a proletarian alliance that would allow them to control the party, for, according to the statutes, each sector (worker, popular, peasant, and military) was isolated from the rest and had contact only with the center.

In September 1938 trade union representatives from fourteen countries constituting the Congreso Obrero Latinoamericano met in Mexico City and agreed to create the Central de Trabajadores de América Latina (CTAL), which, according to its creator, Vicente Lombardo Toledano, "gradually became the most important force of opinion on the American continent" (Lombardo Toledano, 1964: 19). The CTAL organized various congresses in the decade of the 1950s and then disappeared in 1964.

Although it was able to control the workers, Cárdenismo—as one of the prerequisites that made that control possible— provided immediate benefits to the workers. Rivera Marín has pointed out that "between 1935 and 1940, the buying power of wages grew at a pace with the rises in the index of the workers' cost of living. There were even years like 1939, when the buying power of wages was higher than the cost of basic food and clothing" (Marín, 1961: 263). In contrast to these short-range improvements, the workers did not gain a political ideology or a program of their own in the course of their struggle for better wages. They continued to support and follow the leadership provided by the state. The last great demonstrations took place in 1938, during the epoch of the expropriations; at that time the process of consolidation of the CTM came to a stop. Thereafter it dedicated itself to its own perpetuation as the organic instrument of the state. With the bureaucratization of the trade unions, it was not the workers, as Cárdenas claimed, but the union leaders who became the government's partners. Cárdenas's policy toward the masses resulted in the corporatization of the Mexican state.

In February 1939 the CTM's Consejo Nacional Extraordinario declared its support of General Manuel Avila Camacho's candidacy for the next presidential term. Lombardo would later express the following opinion: "The CTM would make alliances, pacts, with other sectors of the people, with other institutions, even those alien to the proletariat (worker-employer pacts), with the goal of adding up the forces which could, at a given moment of the country's evolutionary process, easily lead to the triumph of Mexican society itself, which has been committed to the struggle for the betterment of the producing masses for a quarter of a century" (cited by Salazar, 1972a: 275). As is obvious, the founder of the CTM was not interested in the triumph of the proletariat but of "Mexican society." The CTM's participation in the 1939 elections was consistent with Lombardo's aim of defending the cohesion of the Mexican state, which was being threatened by Juan Andrew Almazán, the candidate of a rightist opposition. The CTM created the Frente Popular Electoral to support the PRM, while Lombardo and Fidel Velázquez toured the country organizing rallies in support of Avila Camacho. On July 7, 1940, 8 senators and 24 deputies belonging to the CTM were elected along with Avila Camacho.

On February 27, 1941, the Segundo Congreso General Ordinario of the CTM decided that Fidel Velázquez should be Lombardo's successor as secretary general. Speaking to trade union representatives, the country's new president demanded the unity of all in "one single united front," at a time when serious international conflicts were unfolding. In his inauguration speech, Fidel Velázquez promised to cooperate "loyally, sincerely, openly, and disinterestedly with the government of General Manuel Avila Camacho." Avila Camacho inherited a government with a controlled trade union movement and, desirous of eliminating any possible conflicts, his regime was characterized by repression of the workers.

In March 1941 Avila Camacho modified the Federal Labor Law so that workers could be fired for participating in "illegal" strikes; the new law made the procedure by which strikes could be formally legalized more complicated and subject to government control. All work stoppages were forbidden in companies of "great social importance." The Federación de Sindicatos de Trabajadores al Servicio del Estado (FSTSE) was stripped of the right to enter into union alliances, and workers employed by the state were deprived of the right to have sympathy strikes (Semionov, 1972: 119). As a result of these measures, the rank-and-file workers were, in effect, silenced. They no longer had channels through which to express their opinions. The CTM at that point docilely accepted the official policy and, far from analyzing or questioning the changes in federal law, applauded them without reservation.

Under Avila Camacho, the "crime of social dissolution" was defined and became, because of its ambiguous terms, the favorite legal instrument of the state in the persecution of political dissidents and union leaders for thirty years. The specter of anti-communism haunted the country. In September 1941 federal troops murdered eight workers from a union delegation that had sought a hearing from the president. According to Semionov (1972: 121), the funerals of these workers were "the most important political action of the Mexican proletariat during the years of the Second World War."

The Confederación Proletaria Nacional (CPN) and the Confederación de Obreros y Campesinos de México (COCM) were created in 1942. Meanwhile, the state used its participation in the Second World War to limit workers' actions. In May 1942 the CTM called its members to abstain from striking for the duration of the war and to leave the solution of labor disputes in the hands of the authorities. The following month, the main labor federations (CTM, CROM, COCM, CPN, and so forth) signed a "workers' solidarity pact" in which they agreed not to strike for the duration of the war and to collaborate with the government in supplying resources to satisfy military needs. These same organizations constituted the Consejo Nacional Obrero, an adjunct to the Ministry of Labor formed at Avila Camacho's suggestion to gather in one institution all labor groups. The attempt failed. The council lost prestige and eventually disappeared.

Labor unrest persisted because of the rising cost of living. Between 1941 and 1943 prices in the federal district rose by 60 percent and wages by only 20 percent. In 1943 the textile workers and the miners called strikes that won wage gains. There were also a series of railroad strikes and numerous popular demonstrations. On September 7 the Supreme Court handed down a decision to the effect that strikes constituted violations "of the work discipline."

At the end of the war on April 7, 1945, the Confederación de Cámaras Industriales (CONCAMIN) and the CTM announced that they had "agreed to unite at this decisive hour for the destinies of humanity and our fatherland to struggle together for complete national economic autonomy, for the country's economic development, and for the elevation of the material and cultural living conditions of the masses." They agreed to renew the wartime "patriotic alliance . . . for the defense of the nation's independence."

The labor representatives promised to suspend the protests against the rise in prices and to stop pushing for the gains that the workers had been demanding. A worker-employer commission was established with powers to suspend any strike for ten months. In Mexico City alone, this procedure was used in 164 disputes.

In 1947 the reelection of the executive committee of the CTM was once again a cause for conflict. The Communist party, which was back in the organization, tried to place Luis Gómez Z. in the secretary general's post, and Fidel Velázquez's group proposed Fernando Amilpa. Seeing themselves at a disadvantage, the Communist-led unions, including the railroad workers' union, headed by Valentín Campa and several other organizations that supported Gómez Z.'s candidacy, split from the CTM to create the Confederación Unitaria del Trabajo (CUT), which was not successful. Thereby the group of "the five" long-time CTM leaders (Velázquez, Amilpa, Alfonso Sánchez Madariaga, Jesús Yurén, and Luis Quintero) were left in absolute control of the CTM. Lombardo Toledano supported Amilpa, but the Communists' departure meant the loss of what little backing he had left. Soon after, the CTM split from the CTAL and broke with Lombardo Toledano altogether. It thus eliminated whatever might have remained of its populist strategy and even changed the motto on its seal: instead of the early concept "for a classless society," it became "for the emancipation of Mexico." Its leaders strengthened their commitments to the official party, which by then had undergone a new transformation. A few months earlier, the PRM modernized its structure: it decentralized some of its functions and widened its organizations in the states; it eliminated its military sector for tactical reasons and admitted a new "popular" (government employee) sector to become the present-day Partido Revolucionario Institucional (PRI).

In order to consolidate the country's industrialization, the government of Miguel Alemán (1946-1952) carried out a policy that favored entrepreneurs and hurt the working class more than ever before. This period was characterized by wage cuts, repression of the slightest outburst of discontent, and, above all, support of "*charrismo*" in the trade unions. The secretary general of the railroad workers' union, Jesús Díaz de León, alias "*El Charro*,"[3] developed a policy of collusion with government and repression within the union that has served as a model for the trade union bureaucracy ever since. Charrismo is a particular form of trade union control that is characterized by (a) the use of the repressive forces of the state to support a trade union leadership; (b) the systematic use of violence; (c) the permanent violation of workers' union rights; (d) misuse and theft of trade union funds; (e) dishonest dealing with the workers' interests; (f) connivance between union leaders and the government and capitalists; and (g) corruption in all its forms (Alonso, 1972: 98). The continuation of charrismo in Mexican trade unions is not only the result of the personal influence of labor bosses and the lack of opposition on the part of rank-and-file workers, but mainly the result of the close relation that exists between the state and the trade unions. Since 1940, the Mexican government has been able to depend on a disciplined trade union organization that is an integral part of the state and that allows the state to exercise control over unionized workers.

In 1949 Lombardo Toledano tried to unite the Sindicato Minero (miners' union) and other unions into the Unión General de Obreros y Campesinos de México (UGOCM); this organization met with little success. In 1948 a currency devaluation provoked an increase in the price of basic consumer goods and discontent spread. The main federations, headed by the CTM, reaffirmed their unconditional support for Alemán's government. In the railroad workers' Sindicato de Trabajadores Ferrocarrileros

(STF) there arose a movement to throw out Díaz de León and to prevent an army takeover of the union's locals in Mexico City. The assaults on trade union locals became customary, and in 1949 the trolley car workers and oil workers suffered similar acts of aggression. On January 20, 1951, 5,000 striking miners from Nueva Rosita, Coahuila, were repressed after they disavowed their charro leadership and walked from Coahuila to Mexico City to demand better economic conditions. This was the policy pursued by Miguel Alemán, who at the end of his term in 1952 was honored by the CTM with the title of "Mexico's Number One Worker."

Aleman's repressive policy was followed by the conciliatory style of Adolfo Ruíz Cortines, who in time resolved close to 40,000 labor disputes through "friendly agreements" (Díaz, 1959: 347). This policy, both paternalist and authoritarian, permitted the continuance of charrismo. In 1954, there was another attempt to unify labor union organizations, with the formation of the Bloque de Unidad Obrera (BUO), in which the CTM, the CGT, the CROM, the miners' and railroad workers' unions, and others took part. The state did not participate directly in this new attempted alliance; that is, there was no immediate interference, as this time the initiative for unification came not from the government but from the union groups. Nevertheless, the BUO was designed to function within the PRI, not independent of it. The currency devaluation in 1954 and the policy of "assignment of resources" to stimulate industrial development were severely cutting into workers' standard of living. Charro leadership was not capable of representing the workers' demands.

This critical situation came to a head in February 1958 when movements for trade union democracy sprung up among the telegraph workers, the teachers from section IX of the Sindicato Nacional de Trabajadores de la Educación (SNTE), sections 34 and 35 of the Petroleros (oilworkers), and the railroad workers in the STF. The contradictions of Ruiz Cortines's regime became apparent: at the same time that he made small concessions to the workers he also jailed the workers' independent leaders.

Within the PRI, the BUO proposed Adolfo López Mateos as candidate for president for the 1958-1964 term. López Mateos was then secretary of labor, so he was not a stranger to labor problems. He was well aware of the number of labor disputes he was inheriting from the Ruíz Cortines regime. In his campaign, López Mateos promised to respect the rights of workers, especially the right to strike. After his inauguration, it fell to him to resolve some of the conflicts that appeared in early 1958, and all but one of them were resolved through negotiations and institutional means, but not without recourse to repression to keep the oil workers' and teachers' unions under government control.

The railroad workers, who went so far as to pose the independence of the unions from the state in a direct confrontation, were another story. Having won some wage gains, the railroad workers proceeded to name democratically a new union executive committee headed by Demetrio Vallejo. In February 1959 the government refused to raise wages again, so on March 29 the railroad workers responded with a general strike. The López Mateos regime declared that the strike was "nonexistent" and federal troops proceeded to occupy the railroad installations and to arrest hundreds of workers, while the state imposed its own unrepresentative executive committee on the union. The railroad workers' movement shattered the relative stability the regime "of the Revolution" had maintained for so many years. When it found itself unable to channel the conflict within institutional limits, the government repressed it. The railroad strike movement is probably the most important challenge to the system of the PRI that took place after 1940. Although it posed the question of autonomy from the official unions, it did not reach political or ideological independence with respect to the principles that govern the Mexican state (Alonso, 1972: 178).

The repression of the railroad workers' movement weakened the labor movement as a whole in the years that followed. In 1960 the Movimiento Revolucionario del Magisterio (Revolutionary Teachers Movement— MRM), which grew out of the 1958 teachers' mobilization, defended the election of democratic leaders in section IX of the SNTE. In September of that year, the nationalization of the Mexican Light and Power Co. mobilized thousands of electrical workers in support of López Mateos's regime. López Mateos tried to revive the unity achieved during the nationalizations in the Cárdenas era. But there are substantial differences between the oil nationalization carried out by Cárdenas and the nationalization of electric energy undertaken by López Mateos.

On December 4, 1960, a new labor confederation independent of the CTM, the Central Nacional de Trabajadores (CNT), was formed. It claimed to have almost 400,000 members and was made up of the Sindicato Mexicano de Electricistas (SME), the Sindicato de Trabajadores Electricistas de la República Mexicana (STERM), the Confederación Revolucionaria de Obreros y Campesinos (CROC), the Federación de Obreros Textiles, the Federación Obrera Revolucionaria (FOR), the printers' Unión Linotipográfica, and the Sindicato de Telegrafistas. The CNT differed with some of the CTM's positions, but defended official nationalism and proposed "independence" only from the employers and from the state. President López Mateos was present at its formation.

In 1961, the police put down a telegraph workers' strike in Mexico City. At about the same time, the Cananea miners won a 50 percent wage hike. In midyear, the national bourgeoisie embarked upon a furious anti-communist campaign that the state took advantage of to persecute various union movements. On July 16 a caravan of (religious) pilgrims was incited by provocateurs to attack the site where a congress of the MRM was meeting with the pretext that the teachers gathered there were anti-clerical. In August, Fidel Velázquez announced that he would not seek reelection, but in April 1962 he was reappointed to head the CTM for another six years. In February 1962 Luis Gómez Z., now an ally of the CTM union bureaucracy, was installed as secretary general of the railworkers' union; he was repudiated by a majority of the union, but the workers feared repression and did little to show their discontent.

On November 21, 1962, Article 123 of the Constitution was amended to regulate profit sharing. This measure sought to turn the workers into consumers of the products of their own industries and the employers were thereby given a new weapon with which to buy off workers' militancy. This does not mean that the salary level of the workers increased with the application of the profit-sharing system, or that the law itself was always enforced. In reality, the sharing of profit was a demagogic pretext for not increasing the real salary of workers and for making them think that the well-being of the company where they worked would benefit them. The Employers' Confederation declared that if applied, the amendment would be "an objective element [that] will remove and help proscribe the class struggle" (Política, 1962). The reform also established that minimum wages would be set by federal councils instead of at the local level. Frequently the tactic of putting companies into "receivership" was used to stop strikes. Using this method, the government took charge of the company in question, arguing that because it was of public utility it could not be paralyzed by a strike. Then the government settled the strike by directly imposing a solution on the workers. Thus various protests were mediated, such as those of the airline pilots and stewardesses.

The beginning of Gustavo Díaz Ordaz's regime (1964-1970) was marked by a doctors' strike. The Alianza de Médicos Mexicanos demanded a general revision of wages and a halt to administrative repression against striking doctors. On September 1, 1965, in his yearly presidential address, Díaz Ordaz ordered the doctors back to work and threatened to prosecute them for "homicide by negligence," illegal association, job desertion, failure to render services, and intention to commit a crime if they did not end the strike. In the face of these warnings, and after several leaders were arrested and many doctors beaten, the doctors gave in.

In February 1965 the government organized the Asamblea Nacional Revolucionaria del Proletariado, which formalized the unity between the state and the charro leadership. This labor congress appeared as the organization responsible for this unity. Given the lack of a unified workers' federation (the BUO had disappeared) the labor congress carried out the task of unifying the different trade union groups with the state. On May 1 of that year, Díaz Ordaz commented that "the workers' unification is starting to be a promising reality—not in a federation per se, but in the ideals, the principles, the goals and the mutual help needed to reach them" (*Política*, 1966). What he did not say was that the ideology of the labor congress was not proletarian, but representative of the charro leadership. In November of that year, the CTM created the Sindicato Nacional de Empleados del Comercio (SNEC), to which 3 million workers would be affiliated.

In November 1967 the CTM's congress (called "Fidel's Olympics" in trade union circles because it was moved ahead a year due to the 1968 Olympic Games) reelected Fidel Velázquez for yet another term. During Díaz Ordaz's administration a "hard-line" policy was followed against all insurgent trade union movements. The federal district truck drivers and the oil workers, among others, suffered effects of this policy. The 1968 student mobilization moved beyond the framework of students' struggles to win popular support among some sections of the workers and created a crisis in the Mexican government unlike any since 1959; the result was the brutal repression of the movement in October 1968.

The process of industrialization that developed with particular speed in Mexico after 1940 caused a constant rate of inflation, which, in turn, drastically impoverished workers. The economic concessions gained by workers during Cárdenas's regime were gradually eroded. At the same time, the economic strategy of the Mexican state, which consisted of industrialization at all costs, entered into crisis in the final years of the decade of the 1960s. At that point, the government of the revolution required various changes to sustain itself. The man in charge of undertaking them would be Luis Echeverría, who in the course of his regime (begun in 1970) had to confront the conservative sectors of the bourgeoisie who had not accepted the need for such changes.

Echeverría's job was to save the Mexican capitalist system from the crisis that engulfed it and to revitalize the role of the state as the arbiter of social forces in conflict. One of his first measures was the establishment of the National Tripartite Commission in May 1971 as a consulting body to include union, employer, and government representatives. The Tripartite Commission was designed to study and propose solutions to the problems of productivity, unemployment, high prices, housing, and the like, and represented the most polished and functional example of the corporatist style that characterizes the Mexican state (by *corporatism* I mean the assimilation into the state of the different social sectors by areas of activity). The Tripartite Commission and other bodies of this type are designed to express the state's strategy of "class conciliation" for a higher ideal of "national unity," which seeks to harmonize the interests of the workers with those of the capitalist class. The Echeverría administration carried out a policy of concessions to the workers, seeking by these means to channel the outbursts of discontent in the trade union movement. The main achievements of this policy were the creation of INFONAVIT— an agency that builds workers' housing, fights for the 40-hour workweek for state workers, and struggles for wage increases that are also aimed at combating growing inflation and preventing the further loss of workers' buying capacity. Thus the state has become judge and jury, arbiter, and conciliator of the class struggle in Mexico.

On the other hand, the growth of industry and the consolidation in Mexico of state monopoly capitalism have posed other contradictions. Development has been possible only at the cost of rising inflation and unemployment, and although these are factors that the government has tried to attenuate, it cannot resolve them fully. That is, the concessions that the state has made to workers are not sufficient to improve the situation of the working class. The loss of purchasing power has made the workers seek noninstitutional means to resolve the situation. Thus the charro trade union leadership has entered into a crisis, and attempts have been made to organize workers outside of the official control mechanisms.

Between December 1971 and January 1972, the electrical workers' Sindicato de Trabajadores Electricistas de la República Mexicana (STERM) and student groups went on "marches for union democracy" in nearly fifty localities across the country. These events have marked the beginnings of a new worker insurgency. Alarmed by such developments that have threatened the stability of the trade union bureaucracy, in January 1971 Fidel Velázquez declared that "in the CTM and in the labor movement there shall always be an army prepared to carry out open struggle, be it constitutional or not." Velázquez was trying to stay ahead of the radicalization, and at the same time threatening any groups that got out of line. His unexpected declaration, suggesting that the CTM would not respect the legal framework should it find it adverse to its interests, was supported by the president of the PRI, Manuel Sánchez Vite, who was removed from that post soon thereafter.

Under Echeverría's regime, workers embarked on two types of struggles against trade-union charrismo: the first inside unions controlled by the spurious leadership, and the second working outside for the creation of independent unions free of official control.

The first type of struggle—to achieve union democracy—is illustrated by the electrical workers' efforts. Throughout the first half of 1972 the STERM workers fought a resolution by the Comisión Federal de Electricidad, which had signed an exclusive contract with a charro electrical workers' union headed by Francisco Pérez Ríos. The conflict was resolved by means of conciliation when Echeverría brought about the unification of the two unions (the STERM led by Rafael Galván and the charro SME union) into the Sindicato Unico de Trabajadores Electricistas de la República Mexicana (SUTERM). The electrical workers' experience proved that the spurious charro leaders are not about to tolerate reforms that will undermine their power, and that conciliation is a poor way to resolve union problems. The conflicts within the SUTERM did not take long to appear. The charro faction of the former SME and would-be charro bureaucrats of the former STERM systematically opposed the democratic resolution of labor conflicts; in the case of the General Electric strike, the charros defended the employers' arguments, while the democratic union leadership defended the workers. The ex-STERM tendency suffered all sorts of attacks, and in February 1975 Galván and other leaders were expelled from the SUTERM by a fake union congress controlled by the charros. This set loose once again the mobilizations of electrical workers struggling for a democratic union and of other sectors of the society that supported such a demand. Thus the electrical workers' fight became the most important struggle of the independent trade union movement. The electrical workers' struggle implied the possibility of winning to its independent banner the demands and the solidarity of other independent trade unions. However, this struggle ran the risk of being compromised by the reformist leadership of the democratic electrical workers who are grouped in the Movimiento Sindical Revolucionario (MSR). Using a nationalist-reformist ideology, the MSR was trying to organize an independent labor confederation. The MSR's position coincided to a large extent with Echeverría's modernizing and nationalist program.

The railroad workers, for their part, headed by the Movimiento Sindical Ferrocarrilero (MSF), tried to regain control of their union. The MSF is led by Demetrio Vallejo, who was freed from prison during the first months of the Echeverría regime. In 1972, the MSF took control of union locals in several cities, but was evicted by the Army in some places, such as Monterrey, with extreme violence. In 1973 the MSF won the elections for the executive committee of the railroad workers' union, but the charro leadership refused to recognize their victory and anti-democratically imposed one of their people. The government supported this action, and at the inauguration of charro Tomás Rangel Perales as union president, Secretary of Labor Porfírio Muñoz Ledo (a member of the reformist wing of the Echeverría regime) was present to back by his attendance the electoral fraud that had been committed against the railroad workers. Nevertheless, as in the case of the SUTERM, the campaign for union democracy was able to mobilize great sectors of workers who would continue to struggle for rank-and-file control of their organizations.

Along with the struggles for union democracy, there appeared movements that have sought the independence of workers' organizations. This happened with the bank employees whom the government did not allow to form a trade union as well as with the National University Workers' Union, which held a three-month-long strike in 1972; with the workers' movements at the Rivetex textile plants, and Ayotla, the Chrysler Subsidiary Automex workers, and so forth. Most recently, strikes led by independent groups of workers took place at the Saltillo steelworks and at the Nissan auto works, as well as in the unionization of instructors in various universities around the country.

Faced with this upsurge of independence within the labor movement, Echeverría's strategy showed strong contradictions. The reforms that he promoted needed a popular base he did not have. He could not undertake a mass policy in the style of Cárdenas, because in order to secure the support of the workers, Cárdenas first promoted a democratization of the trade unions, but Echeverría did not attack the charro leadership on this front. On the one hand, he tried to lessen the influence of the trade union bureaucracy by granting relative freedom to independent trade unions, by permitting the unification of the electrical workers, and by removing Sánchez Vite from the PRI after the latter came out in support of Fidel Velázquez's statement. But on the other hand, he maintained the power of the charros by naming one-time union leader Luis Gómez Z. general manager of the national railroads; by backing the electoral fraud in the railworkers' union; by repressing various independent strikes; by backing the weak wage demands promoted by the CTM; and by supporting the charro faction in the SUTERM. Echeverría did not want to, or could not afford to, lose the sympathy of the bureaucratic trade union leadership. When he addressed an assembly of the CTM in February 1971, he was long-winded in his praise of its boss Fidel Velázquez, saying: "How clear, how direct, how vigorous, how loyal to the interests of all workers

of Mexico are the achievements of Fidel Velázquez! It is the Fidel Velázquez of his youth! It can be understood that this is painful for the enemies
of the labor movement in Mexico. . . . As long as the Mexican Revolution has labor leaders, peasant leaders, and leaders of the popular sector,
or public officials, who have risen from the masses of these three great
sectors of our population, its future is assured" (cited in *Punto Crítico*,
1972: 22).

For their part, the charro leaders reaffirmed their role of collaborating
to promote industrial development and the employers' peace of mind,
even at the cost of the workers' interests. Fidel Velázquez was very precise when he noted in an interview in 1973 that "we do not aspire to workers' control, but to the participation of the workers in management
decisions. Management and workers participate in production and both
have a right to participate in these decisions, because [otherwise these
decisions] often hurt the workers and benefit only the bosses" (*Solidaridad*, 1973).

The trade union system is currently the weakest point in the Mexican
corporatist state. As the deterioration of the CTM continues, independent groups are organizing and winning gains for the workers. Workers
who struggle for trade-union independence run the risk that the reforms
they promote will serve only to strengthen the state, to renovate its structures, as long as they do not go beyond the policy of class collaboration.
However, proportionally as solidarity among workers spreads, the isolation of labor struggles will decrease and the simple reform struggles will
be superseded. As a worker at the Nissan auto factory said after the strike
in early 1974, "The mobilizations demonstrated the participation of all
workers in the strike, and they gave proof of the support of other independent workers' organizations and of other social strata, whose participation in the movement showed us that it is not impossible to win the support
of these other groups *outside* of the struggle, but that it is necessary to win
them over through the struggle" (Trejo and Meza, 1974).

NOTES

1. To study in detail the rise and decline of the CROM, see the second part of Basurto
(1975).

2. Translator's note: It should be clear that the Cárdenas program remained *capitalist*
despite the statements about labor participation.

3. Translator's note: The Mexican *charro* is a very *macho* expert horseman and dandy.

REFERENCES

Alonso, Antonio
1972 "El charrismo sindical y la insurgencia de los ferrovarois," in *El movimento fer-rocarrilero en México, 1958/1959*. Mexico: Editorial Era.

Anguiano, Arturo
1974 *El estado y la política obrera del cardenismo*. Mexico: Editorial Era.

Basurto, Jorge
1975 *El desarrollo del proletario industrial*. Mexico: Instituto de Investigaciones So-ciales, Universidad Nacional Autónoma de México.

Clark, Marjorie Ruth
1934 *Organized Labor in Mexico*. Chapel Hill: University of North Carolina Press.

Córdova, Andaldo
1973 *La ideología de la Revolución Mexicana*. Mexico: Editorial Era.
1974 *La política de masas del cardenismo*. Mexico: Editorial Era.

Corona, Armando Rendón
1971 "El movimiento sindical en México en la década 1930 a 1940." Thesis, Faculdad de Ciencias Política y Sociales, Universidad Nacional Autónoma de Mexico, citing Departamento Autónoma del Trabajo, "Proyecto de Ley Federal del Trabajo."

Fuentes Díaz, Vicente
1959 "Desarrollo y evolución del movimiento obrero." *Ciencias Políticas y Sociales* 17 (July/September).

Iglesias, Severo
1970 *Sindicalismo y socialismo en México*. Mexico: Grijalbo.

Lombardo Toledano, Vicente
1964 *La CTAL ha concluido su misión histórica*. Mexico: Popular Editories.

Marín, Guadalupe Rivera
1961 "El movimiento obrero," in *México, 50 años de revolución*, Vol. 2. Mexico: Fondo de Cultura Económica.

Meyer, Jean
1971 "Los obreros en la Revolución Mexicana: los Batallones Rojos." *Historia Mexicana* 81 (July/September).

Pedrueza, Rafael Ramos
1941 *La lucha de clases a través de la historia de México*. Mexico: Talleres Gráficos de la Nación.

Política
1962 64 (December 15).
1966 148 (June 15).

Punto Crítico
1972 1 (January).

Salazar, Marco Antonio
1970 "Communicación del Centro Patronal a la Cámara de Senadores del 11 de agosto de 1931," in *Las agrupaciones patronales en México*. Mexico: El Colegio de México.

Salazar, Rosendo
1938 *Historia de las luchas proletarias de México*. Mexico: Avante.
1958 *Del civilismo al militarismo en nuestra revolución*. Mexico: Libro Mex Editores.
1972a *La Casa del Obrero Mundial—La CTM*. Mexico: Partido Revolucionario Insti-tucional, Comisión Nacional Editorial.
1972b *Las pugnas de la gleba*. Mexico: Partido Revolucionario Institucional, Comisión Nacional Editorial.

Semionov, S. I.
   1972 "México durante el período de Avila Camacho," in *Ensayos de historia de México*. Mexico: Ediciones de Cultura Popular.
Solidaridad
   1973 Interview with Roberto A. Peña. 88 (March 16).
Trejo, Raúl and Julián Meza
   1974 "La solidaridad aumentada de los trabajadores." *Siempre* (May 29).

8

The Mexican Economic Debacle and the Labor Movement
A New Era or More of the Same?

by
Barry Carr*

No one who has followed Mexico's current economic crisis can doubt the seriousness of its impact on that country's 21 million workers. The most dramatic symptoms of the crisis by now are well known—hyperinflation (98 percent in 1982), a sharp decline in real wages, especially since the beginning of 1982 (the minimum daily wage in 1983, earned by 67 percent of the working population, is now 455 pesos [U.S. $3]), an increase in layoffs, and cuts in the "social wage." Another less dramatic but equally important development is the erosion (since December 1982) of organized labor's political base, signaled both by the victory of the technocrats in the de la Madrid cabinet and by the reduction in the presence of the labor sector in the Chamber of Deputies and in the management of key state organs.

The first half of this paper discusses characteristics of the contemporary Mexican labor movement that may influence the future course of labor-state relations. The second half analyzes how the economic crisis has affected, and will continue to affect, both relations between organized labor and the state and the stability of the Mexican model of development.

Among the mass organizations that give the Mexican state its peculiar strength, none is more important than the constellation of worker organizations centered on the Congress of Labor, an umbrella organization encompassing the major labor confederations (Córdova, 1979). Just over 5.3 million workers are members of labor unions, a figure that represented 26 percent of the economically active population (EAP) in 1982.

*Barry Carr is Senior Lecturer in History and Chairman of the Institute of Latin American Studies at La Trobe University, Melbourne, Australia. He is the author of a book on the history of the Mexican labor movement and is currently researching the development of Marxism and communism in Mexico. This chapter was first published in Donald L. Wyman (Ed.), *Mexico's Economic Crisis: Challenges and Opportunities.* La Jolla, CA: Center for U.S.-Mexican Studies (Monograph Series, No. 12). Reprinted by permission.

Because a large proportion of the EAP is made up of peasants and rural workers who are not entitled to join labor unions, the level of unionization in Mexico is exceptionally high and helps explain the overall importance of the labor sector in the political system.[1]

Thus far, this author has been struck by the limited and uneven response of both rank-and-file workers and the union leadership to the sudden and seriously damaging effects of the economic debacle. This should not come as a complete surprise; there is no mechanical correspondence between economic and political crisis. The impact on the labor movement of the economic disaster will be determined by a multitude of factors, including the reactions of a labor union leadership that is no longer homogeneous; the varying degrees of combativeness shown by a highly stratified work force, parts of which have suffered more severely than others from the economic downturn; the balance of forces within the de la Madrid regime; and whether state policy consolidates or erodes nonwage benefits.

LABOR STRUGGLES, 1971-1977: AN AMBIGUOUS LEGACY

Labor insurgency, a literal translation of the Spanish term *insurgencia obrera*, conjures up images of coordinated insurrection and extraconstitutional action. This would be a false characterization of the wave of union struggles that commenced in 1971 and that, over a period of just five years, succeeded in extending the boundaries of trade union democracy and autonomy in national industrial unions as well as in hundreds of plant unions throughout Mexico. Despite the inadequacy of the literal translation, for lack of a better choice this paper will use "labor insurgency" to refer to the *insurgencia obrera*. Many of the conquests of this labor insurgency will be difficult to revoke, but the history of these years is also a history of the enormous resilience of the "official" labor union leadership and an illustration of the difficulties facing independent unions in their attempt to translate their victories into a program that would threaten the existing pattern of relations between the state and the labor bureaucracy.

The labor insurgency began in 1971 with worker actions in a number of plants that manufacture automobile parts, including Spicer and Automex. This was followed by the reactivation of an oppositionist current in the railroad workers' union (STFRM) and, most importantly, by the surfacing of a democratic movement in the electrical workers' union. The Democratic Tendency, as this latter movement was called, was led by former PRI senator Rafael Galván, and over the next five years it became the major focal point of the independent workers' movement. The democratization of an important part of the mining and metal workers' union (SNTMMSRM), section 67, located at the Fundidora de Monterrey, occurred in 1972; and within a few years other sections of this powerful national union, in Monclova (section 147), Las Truchas (section 271), Real del Monte, Pachuca and so forth, established a considerable margin of autonomy and democracy within the framework of the national union.

The pattern established in these early years was maintained throughout the mid-1970s and affected unions of workers in automobile manufacturing, aviation, telecommunications, transport, metal working, and higher education. The characteristic feature of the insurgency, which distinguished it from earlier bouts of worker militancy, was that it transcended the purely economic (gremialista) concerns of the union movement by raising demands of a broad political nature. These included calls for an end to the corruption and violence of officially sanctioned, so-called charro union leadership, the assertion of rank-and-file rights in union elections, a push for greater employee control over the work process, and a struggle to increase individual unions' margin of maneuver vis-à-vis national organizations such as the Confederation of Mexican Workers (CTM), the Regional Confederation of Workers and Peasants (CROC), and the Regional Confederation of Mexican Workers (CROM).

Although the development of the insurgency did not follow a simple pattern, the movement toward labor union autonomy and democracy did exhibit some of the following general characteristics:

(1) The movement was often centered on strategically important national industrial unions employing workers with substantial skills and technical qualifications. This was true not only of sections of the mining and metal workers' union and that of the electrical workers (SUTERM), but also of the telephone workers' union (STRRRM), in which a corrupt leadership was replaced in a major battle in the spring and summer of 1976.[2] Struggles within national federations also affected key groups of state employees. For example, for three years the country's largest union, the National Educational Workers' Union (SNTE), with nearly 750,000 teacher members, has been the scene of a protracted and bitter struggle between its official leadership, a faction calling itself the Revolutionary Vanguard, and rank-and-file movements.

(2) Independent unionism has been able to exploit the official labor union sector's growing inability to organize new areas of the work force and those with a nil or irregular prior history of union activity. This is the case with the highly-skilled and well-paid nuclear industry workers of

SUTIN, with the rapidly growing network of unions of university teachers and employees, in particular at the National Autonomous University of Mexico (UNAM) and at state universities in the states of Puebla, Sinaloa, Guerrero, and Oaxaca, and with workers of the Mexico City Metro, bank workers, and so forth.

(3) The labor insurgency seems to have been a product of the incorporation in the work force of a newer, younger generation of wage earners, relatively free of the rural heritage that characterized a large part of the labor force of earlier decades.

To see the upsurge in independent unionism as a homogeneous phenomenon and to ignore the unevenness and contradictions would be a mistake. Unevenness and contradiction are inherent in the fragmented and differentiated Mexican working class itself and underlie the lack of a common perspective on larger political issues among the independents. At no stage has there been a united front of independent unions, some of which are grouped in loose federations (such as the Independent Labor Organization, or UOI, and the Authentic Labor Front, or FAT), others of which retain a staunch independence.

The Democratic Tendency faction of the electrical workers' union (SUTERM) acted for a while as an inspiration and umbrella group for many of the independents, but its ability to continue in this role was severely limited by the decisive defeat of its leadership within SUTERM during 1976.[3] Those sections of the national industrial unions that had managed to wrest a degree of autonomy from their national leaderships were, of course, committed to working within the existing framework of their unions, although at times they demonstrated solidarity with other foci of the insurgency. The UOI, by far the largest of the independent union groupings, explicitly rejected moves towards unification of the independent sector and all attempts at joint action with other unions. At its peak, the UOI claimed a membership of over 250,000 workers, including unions at Volkswagen, Nissan, Dina, Aeroméxico, Hoechst, Sidena, Euzkadi, and Singer Mexicana. It has maintained a virulently anticommunist rhetoric, combined with a denunciation of all forms of party political action and a rejection of the involvement of political parties in labor union activities.[4]

At the level of ideology, too, the insurgency incorporated a variety of often conflicting currents. Christian democratic ideas motivated the FAT; a militantly anti-political economism was preached by the UOI; the Democratic Tendency faction and those groups that sympathized with its aims identified themselves with the anti-imperialist and nationalist rhetoric of the Mexican Revolution in what was called the current of "Revolutionary Nationalism." As for the Marxist Left, it was clearly a minority current with scattered pockets of influence among metal workers, railway workers, and miners. Its only substantial presence was among opposition groups within the teachers' union and in the unions of university workers where the former Mexican Communist Party (PCM) and independent Marxist factions have disputed the leadership of the movement since the mid-1970s. Yet even in institutions of higher education, the influence of socialist currents has been under threat because of an increase in the taint of political corruption and opportunism that has surrounded the hegemony of the left at UNAM, UAP (Puebla), and the UAS (Sinaloa).[5]

Lastly, the most telling indication of the limits to the power of the independent labor activists is the failure of the much-touted political reform of 1976-1977 to tackle reform of the relationship between the state and mass organizations. Just as the official union movement had been successful in halting the timid efforts at reform of the union movement foreshadowed by Luis Echeverría in 1971, so it was able to ensure that the political reform limited itself strictly to electoral and party organization issues.[6]

This is not to suggest that the movement for labor union democracy and autonomy is fatally flawed. "Lack of unity" and "programmatic diversity" are inevitable consequences of the deep and broad roots that the labor insurgency has sunk within the organized labor movement. A movement that has been able with some success to tap the energies of a larger, more self-confident, but increasingly fragmented work force could hardly be expected to develop a unified package of strategic and ideological prescriptions.[7] The limited progress in coordinating the activities of the independents can also be explained by union fears of reviving the now largely discredited notion of a parallel organization of independent unions in direct competition with the CTM and other federations of the Congress of Labor.

THE DURABILITY OF
OFFICIALLY SANCTIONED UNIONISM

It would be a mistake to focus on only the weaknesses and ambiguities of the independents and their leaders as an explanation for the failure of the insurgency to smash the official movement. The enormous political and material resources of the official labor movement and the continuing high level of flexibility of its leadership must be the central focus of any examination of developments in the labor sector over the past decade, as well as of any attempt to look into the future of organized labor and state-labor relations. The following section of this paper is devoted to an examination of some of the characteristics of what Mexican social scientists increasingly prefer to call the *dirigencia sindical*, or official union leadership, in place of the colorful but misleading designation of *charrismo sindical*.

Until the early 1970s the literature on labor-state relations in Mexico was characterized by a crude interpretation that emphasized the role of violence, corruption, and manipulation. The official unions were viewed accordingly as a simple conveyor belt for the transmission of government directives to one of the key pillars of the regime. As a framework for comprehending the totality of labor-state relations and the surprising resilience of the official movement, this perspective is severely flawed. There is, of course, no shortage of evidence pointing to the systematic employment of violence and corruption in defusing challenges to labor orthodoxy. The struggles of Pascual industry workers in Mexico City during May-November 1982, to take just one recent example, demonstrate how important force and political coercion still are in labor relations. In this case, an attempt to change the leadership of the union at two plants owned by Pascual, a soft drink manufacturer, met with a reign of intimidation, bribery, beatings, and at least one fatal shooting.

But the widespread use of violence, intimidation, and manipulation in the labor sector serves to divert attention from an examination of the roots of the legitimacy enjoyed by the official union movement. Consent is as important as violence in explaining the durability of the official union leadership. Before passing on to a discussion of the sources of this legitimacy, one warning about over-generalization on this question is in order. No one schema explains how mechanisms of control work in the union movement. The successes and failures of the union bureaucracy can often be grasped only if we take as our unit of analysis the individual union, company, or enterprise (León, 1976; Woldenberg, 1980).

Let us begin first with the material basis of this legitimacy. After a sharp fall in real wages during the 1940s and early 1950s, the union bureaucracy was able to maintain a steady rhythm of real wage increases during the period from the mid-1950s until 1974. After this date, the upward momentum diminished and real wages have fallen quite sharply since 1976. Even bearing in mind that this extremely crude sketch understates major differences in the sectoral and regional experience of the organized working-class movement, it would seem reasonable to assume that the union leadership was able to consolidate its position during the period until the late 1970s partially on the basis of its supposed success in safeguarding at least one of the vital interests of its membership.[8] But an exclusive concern with the wage component of workers' remuneration is misleading.

What counts in Mexico is the social wage, that is, money wages plus the package of nonwage benefits (*prestaciones*). These include such state-originated services as subsidized or free health insurance; subsidized food, transport, clothing, and housing; and union- and employer-administered benefits in other areas. The proportion of the population covered by many benefits has increased dramatically over the past decade; the number of people covered by the social security organizations IMSS and ISSTE in 1982, to take one example, was 40 million, compared with 22.2 million in 1976 and 12.2 million in 1970. The state-run CONASUPO stores have expanded, and there are many unions that provide their members with some kind of subsidized retail facility.

Unions with a particularly strong bargaining base have often obliged employers to provide these facilities as part of labor contracts. Public transport tariffs, too, have been maintained at very modest levels, and in some cases, notably in the Federal District in 1981, this has involved government takeovers of privately owned bus networks. Not only the coverage but the range of benefits offered the work force has grown substantially since 1970. During the Echeverría administration, for example, a series of new nonwage benefits was introduced, including INFONAVIT, FONACOT, and the Banco Obrero.

Nonwage benefits are highly unevenly distributed among the work force and many of these benefits fail to rise above the status of feeble palliatives. But their increased number and coverage have provided an important supplement to the wage income of large sectors of the organized labor movement. More importantly, they are a continuing reminder that membership in the official union movement does bring tangible rewards beyond the framework of regular wage bargaining. Furthermore, the expanding network of benefits greatly enhances the official leadership's coercive resources, especially in those cases in which benefits are directly administered by the union movement.

The most notorious case of union manipulation of this kind is exhibited in union distribution of cheap housing under the INFONAVIT program. In certain extreme cases, the best known being the oil workers' union (SNTPRM), a veritable "parallel society," with its own economic and administrative resources in the hands of the union, serves as a powerful mechanism of control over both workers and management. The example of the PEMEX union is also a reminder of union control over the hiring of labor since, in this case as in others (the automobile industry is one), union leadership controls access to the permanent work force (*obreros con plaza*) by creating an artificially large pool of workers on temporary labor contracts (known as *eventuales* or *transitorios*) (Juárez, 1979: 241-243).

In addition to these relatively recent developments, the official union leadership also draws legitimacy from an earlier "golden age" of unionism in the 1930s. The negative imagery of corruption cannot completely efface the memory of the great labor battles waged during the classic period of revolutionary nationalism, the Cárdenas administration. The events of this period have continued to enhance the prestige of the aging leadership of the CTM and its sister confederations long after the heroic phase of union construction and unification has passed.

In one very important sense, then, the geriatric status of figures like Fidel Velázquez, who has headed the CTM as its secretary general since 1949, is a valuable asset for the official unions. It symbolizes the presence of a unique, unbroken line of revolutionary continuity and authenticity, forged in a battle against the over-mighty leaders of big business, and it contrasts with the ever-changing upstarts of what Mexicans call the "political class," who have only experienced the postwar era of "class peace." Unfortunately, the aura of authority gained in battle surrounds an ever-smaller group of union leaders. This partly explains the concern expressed by many leaders over the issue of succession to the secretaryship of the CTM.

Although the prestige and authority of the older figures in the labor union bureaucracy are factors of declining importance, the overall flexibility of the official union leadership and its negotiating ability had been increasing until the late 1970s. Indeed, some authorities would argue that the very existence of the labor insurgency paradoxically strengthened and revitalized elements of the official bureaucracy and forced the government to recognize its still considerable weight (Camacho, 1980: 70). Individual unions, union federations, and the Congress of Labor are not as homogeneous and monolithic as some of the more polemical literature would suggest. The relative autonomy enjoyed by local sections in certain national industrial unions has already been noted. But at the interfederation level, too, there is considerable diversity of leadership style and policy. This is one of the reasons why no unified national labor federation yet exists in Mexico, in spite of frequent calls for the creation of such a body.

The Congress of Labor (CT), established in 1966 as a forum for discussion with no executive powers, is frequently the scene of conflict among its affiliates. Disputes between union confederations like the CTM, CROM, and CROC are often centered on struggles over rights of exclusive control of labor contracts in particular enterprises. A recent example is the 1980 strike of automobile workers at General Motors, where the CROC's monopoly was challenged by the management's attempt to negotiate a plant contract with the CTM at a newly opened factory in Coahuila. An even more recent labor conflict, the already cited dispute at Pascual Industries, also centered around a contest for exclusive contract control between the CTM and the CROC.[9]

The smallest of the labor confederations in the Congress of Labor, the Revolutionary Labor Confederation (COR), also has the longest history of disputation with the giant CTM. In 1978 COR, along with the Mexican Electricians' Union (SME), argued that the independent unions should be invited to the National Proletarian Assembly organized by the CT for July of that year. The very existence of the SME, the oldest of the electrical workers' unions, demonstrates that the democratic and autonomous current within Mexican unionism long has been represented, if on a minority basis, within the Congress of Labor itself. There are a number of unions, including SUTIN (which joined in 1979) and the SME, which are independent of the large confederations.[10] In one important case, that of the telephone workers, a bitter and protracted struggle to throw off the tutelage of the CTM was resolved in the rebels' favor without the new leadership's breaking with the Congress of Labor. In the light of these developments, the Congress of Labor's decision in February 1983 to invite the independents to join its ranks is not so surprising.

The eagerness of certain independent unions to maintain close ties with the mainstream labor movement is partly a tactical decision. But their determination not to isolate themselves from the giant official sector is also strengthened by an awareness of the enormous weight of repression that the Mexican state can unleash against union dissidence beyond the limits of its tolerance. This combination of dissident "flexibility" and state violence assures that on occasion cooptation will limit the effectiveness of challenges to officially sanctioned union leadership. The nationwide rebellion of rank-and-file teachers against the leadership of the teachers' union (SNTE) is one notable example (Hernández, 1981). Although this bitter struggle between the state as employer and a strategically located segment of the work force is not yet over, the leadership of the dissidents in certain states has been demobilized by the offer of prestigious positions on state committees of the national union.

DESTABILIZING DEVELOPMENTS

Thus far, the emphasis of this paper has been on the strength and flexibility of the contemporary Mexican labor movement. Yet most observers agree that this flexibility and strength have been seriously eroded during the past five or so years. In the second half of this paper, therefore, the focus shifts to an examination of those factors that have subverted and destabilized the labor-state compact during this period. The background to the argument that follows is provided by the Mexican economic debacle of 1982 and the accompanying interruption, indeed reversal, of the cycle of economic growth and employment generation. A warning is in order at this point: information on the impact of the current economic crisis on wages, unemployment, prices, and so forth is still scanty and subject to substantial margins of error, and only the roughest kinds of trends can be sketched out.

DECLINE IN LIVING STANDARDS

The steady growth in real wages that was a feature of the mid-1950s, 1960s, and early 1970s stopped around 1974. Real and sharp falls have been registered only since the beginning of the López Portillo stabilization program of 1977-1978, with its accompanying package of price rises and limits on wage increases. Since the beginning of 1982, however, real wages have declined at an alarmingly rapid rate. Based on fluctuations in the minimum wage as a measure of the size of wage settlements (since changes in the minimum wage are the conventional benchmark for wage negotiations in general in Mexico), the situation for the Mexican working class during 1982 was disastrous (see Table 8.1).

Three wage adjustments occurred during 1982. The first, in January, was an across-the-board increase of 34 percent in the minimum wage. The second was an emergency adjustment in March that granted increases of between 10 percent and 30 percent, with higher-wage workers receiving the smaller proportion.[11] Finally, in October, a second round of emergency wage increases was granted to certain workers on a plant-bargaining basis; these ranged from 13 percent to 25 percent, averaging out at a monthly increase of 1,500 pesos.[12]

The most reliable estimate of inflation for the year 1982 is 98.8 percent, which means that only those workers who secured the highest bracket of the two emergency raises would have escaped a cut in real wages during the year. But not all workers received these two wage increases, although accurate documentation here is lacking. Many employers did not regard the first emergency increase as mandatory and refused to grant it to their employees; indeed, it was only in November that the minimum wage was formally adjusted to incorporate these March changes.[13] Similarly, the October increases were negotiated on a plant-by-plant basis, which undermined the position of the least strategically

TABLE 8.1
Purchasing Power of Minimum Wage

1976	100
1977	91.3
1978	88.1
1979	87.6
1980	80.7
1981	83

SOURCE: *Asi Es* (1982c: 5). The methodology employed is not explained in the source.

located segments of the work force. For many workers the October emergency wage raise was simply a catch-up award compensating them for their failure to secure an increase in March.[14] Furthermore, many workers in the state sector failed to win any increase at all at the end of 1982.

The annual minimum adjustment in January 1983 was of the order of 25 percent, making the minimum wage in most parts of the country 455 pesos a day, or a little over three U.S. dollars at the current rate of exchange (May 1983). Current estimates of the rate of inflation for 1983 range from 60 percent to 100 percent, so clearly another round of emergency adjustments is in order if working-class incomes are not to be devastated totally. However, given the direction of the de la Madrid stabilization program, it is most unlikely that wage earners will be compensated in full for the rise in inflation in 1983. At the time of writing (May 1983) it is likely that a round of emergency wage adjustments on the order of 20 percent to 25 percent will be completed by late June.[15]

UNEMPLOYMENT

Even in the best of times evidence on unemployment is notoriously difficult to gather and interpret. However, the hundreds of declarations by unions, employer groups, and government ministries point to substantial cuts in employment in both the state and private sectors. The cuts are caused by: (a) the foreign exchange crisis that has disrupted production by interfering with imports of raw materials and equipment; (b) cuts in public-sector expenditure beginning with the 8-percent cut announced by the López Portillo government in March 1982; and (c) a collapse in demand for certain consumer durables, notably automobiles.

The overall increase in unemployment resulting from the economic crisis is difficult to establish. The lowest figure for last year was provided in mid-October 1982 by Sergio Garcia Ramírez, minister of labor, who estimated the total number of dismissals at 400,000. But in just one sector, the construction industry, figures published by the Mexican Union of Heavy Equipment Operators estimated the number of dismissals by the third quarter of 1982 at 600,000, almost 70 percent of that sector's labor force (*Así Es*, 1982c: 8). Employer groups in the construction industry painted an even gloomier picture in January 1983; according to figures produced by the National Chamber of the Construction Industry, over 800,000 workers had lost their jobs in the industry over the previous year (Correa, 1983).

Unemployment has also hit highly unionized workers—25,000 unemployed in automobile manufacture, 21,000 in the metal industry, 25,000 in clothing and textiles. By the beginning of 1983, 40,000 workers on temporary contracts had lost their jobs at Pemex, and 30,000 government bureaucrats suffered the same fate. As the figures accumulate, the total number of dismissals by the beginning of 1983 approaches 1.2 million workers, with estimates by the National Confederation of Chambers of Commerce of another three-quarters of a million job losses during 1983 (Correa, 1983).

Clearly the scale and sectoral distribution of dismissals during 1983 will be dependent on such factors as the size of cuts in the public-sector deficit, the availability of foreign exchange for imports, and so on. But it is difficult to avoid the general conclusion that a sharp downward recomposition of the work force is occurring, with a weakening of job security for workers with permanent contracts and an inflation of the "casual" sector, with many temporary workers losing their jobs completely. Although many of the 800,000 or so construction workers who have lost their jobs may be able to retreat to the peasant economy from which they were recruited, alternative sources of employment will be much more difficult to find for the hundreds of thousands of workers dismissed from manufacturing, mining, and service industries. The end result will be a substantial erosion of the material welfare and self-confidence of organized labor, and perhaps the posing of severe challenges to the authority of the trade union bureaucracies.

DISPLACEMENT OF THE LABOR SECTOR

If major challenges from the rank and file do result, the union leadership's ability to resolve them without eroding its own authority will depend, in part, on its bargaining position within the new de la Madrid administration. Although the evidence here also is fragmentary, some trends are clearly visible. An examination of the first four months of the de la Madrid government shows a definite displacement of the labor sector within the new administration. This is indicated by a number of separate but interrelated developments. The influence of the PRI's labor sector and particularly its boss, Fidel Velázquez, during the negotiations to select the party's presidential candidate for 1982 was much more limited than at any other time in the past four decades. Although at a formal level Fidel Velázquez preserved the labor sector's traditional role of "unveiling" the candidate, on this occasion, as one source put it, "Don Fidel, the veteran kingmaker, suffered the indignity of finding out the candidate's identity only at the last minute" (*Latin American Weekly Report*, 1981: 10). This experience contrasts sharply with the crucial role played by the labor sector and Velázquez in the selection and unveiling of José López Portillo.

Following the launching of the de la Madrid government, a number of disquieting developments (for labor) have surfaced. The number of deputies from the labor sector is down significantly, compared to the exceptionally large number who sat in the Chamber of Deputies during the previous administration. At that time the labor deputies made up 25 percent of the Chamber's 400 members and one-third of all PRI deputies (Trejo, 1982: 37). In addition, a number of key management appointments within the network of state enterprises and institutions, most notably ISSTE and the National Railways, have ceased to be the patrimony of the labor sector.

Even more worrisome is the technocratic orientation of the de la Madrid government, about which many observers have commented. The eclipse of the "political class" must be seen as a storm signal by the official labor bureaucracy.[16] The latter's capacity for political bargaining depends on the presence of veteran political negotiators in positions of high authority.

Finally, the tone and content of government rhetoric registered in the first few months of the new administration is radically different from that which has been the norm. Of these changes the most troubling for the labor sector is the deemphasis of the populist tone of government pronouncements and the self-conscious promotion of "free market" criteria by a number of senior cabinet ministers. The frequent references to the need for more deregulation of aspects of the economy, that is, a scaling-down of price subsidies and the termination of what is ominously termed "the fictitious economy," pose a serious threat to the nonwage components of workers' incomes and hence to the long-term stability of the labor bureaucracy's position.

In the Mexican political system, the crucial skill required of the official union leadership always has been the ability to achieve a satisfactory balance in the performance of two roles that are often in conflict with each other. On the one hand, the official labor sector serves as a vital pillar of the regime and guarantor for the continuing reproduction of the model of capitalist development that Mexico has pursued since World War II. On the other hand, the official union leadership has to articulate and satisfy adequately the demands of the 26 percent of the economically active population that is active in the union movement. Since the mid-1970s, this double act has become more difficult to perform, and the crisis of 1982 has placed a whole new range of obstacles in the way of the leadership's future performance.

The union leadership has been showing growing signs of frustration over its diminishing margin of maneuver as a result. This mood is manifested in ever more frequent displays of verbal radicalism. For example, the CTM has adopted a number of demands that traditionally have been the property of the Mexican left and of the independent labor unions. These include demands for nationalization of the food processing and pharmaceutical industries, and a demand for the introduction of a system of wage adjustments based on price movements (*salario remunerador*). This latter demand shows considerable resemblance to the demand for wage indexing made by the former Mexican Communist Party and by the current United Socialist Party of Mexico and its union allies.

The first major moves in this direction were made at the National Assembly of the Congress of Labor in 1978, in the Manifest to the Nation launched by the labor deputies of the PRI in 1979, and at the Tenth Congress of the CTM in 1980. In these various pronouncements, the labor sector of the PRI developed a program of economic reform demands the broad outline of which resembles the position of some sectors of the Mexican left (Trejo, 1980: 85). It is true that these demands consist essentially of a package of slogans without any clear program of action, but their emergence is a measure of the pressure that a combination of economic stabilization measures and declining real wages is placing on the union leadership.

The labor union bureaucracy has also regularly employed threats to use its industrial muscle in order to influence the direction and content of the state's policies on wages and working conditions. A common tactic has been to foreshadow a wave of legally required notifications of intent to strike to force government decisions favorable to union interests. The most recent example was the specter of a general strike that the CTM raised on several occasions during October 1982. Typically, such threats form part of a traditional theater of maneuver and bargaining and, as happened in October 1982, result in strike movements that are far less serious than those anticipated in the original threat. But as wage levels become an even more sensitive issue because of the austerity program, the value of rhetoric in this contest may recede. The union leadership may then be obliged to play its trump card of union intransigency, even at the risk of unleashing energy from below that it might not be able to control.

Another potential threat to the authority of the official labor movement is posed by the recent emergence of new centers of dissidence (among "marginal" urban dwellers, the poor peasantry, and the like) in areas that traditionally have been peripheral to the organized labor movement. It is among these constituencies that PRI control is weakest.[17] This has left a gap for several loosely organized attempts to provide a permanent focus for the widespread, but poorly coordinated resistance to declining living standards. A number of these coordinating bodies, including the National Coordinating Committee of the Popular Urban Movement (CONAMUP) and the National "Plan de Ayala" Coordinating Committee, together with regional movements like COCEI (in the Isthmus of Tehuantepec) and independent unions, human rights organizations, and left-wing parties, have created a broad front of resistance to the austerity program and to increasing unemployment.

Although the movement of resistance to austerity is divided (there are two coalitions involved), the tentative links that it is sponsoring between the union movements and groups traditionally outside the corporatist umbrella have alarmed the union bureaucracy.[18] The reasons for this alarm are quite clear. Dissidence within the union movement is tolerated when it restricts itself to a mainly economic program (improvements in wages and conditions) and to the correction of intolerable abuses in the management of individual unions. It is seen as threatening, and therefore warranting firmer countermeasures, when the dissidence involves guidance, support, and especially direction from formal political organizations of the left.[19]

The fears of the official union leadership are certainly well founded, judging by developments over the past few years. The greater the degree of contact there is between isolated unions and the political parties of the left, the more likely it is that purely economic demands will expand to include demands for a restructuring of the national economy and of the relationship between the state and mass organizations. It is not surprising, then, that the growing convergence between independent unions and nuclei of highly skilled workers in unions like SUTIN and STUNAM in the past five years has contributed greatly to the much more pronounced political and national character of union demands in general.

It is, of course, easy for a simple listing of factors promoting rupture and destabilization to imply, in a misleading way, the existence of a uniform and inexorable movement toward destruction of the labor-state pact. Such a movement does not exist at present, although it is possible that it might develop momentum if the economic debacle of the past year and a half continues. So far, the depth and suddenness of the economic crisis have not brought about a correspondingly sharp and uniform response from the labor unions.

Some of the factors that help explain the durability of the labor-state pact, and that have been discussed earlier in this chapter, are clearly operating in the present conjuncture. But it is also true that long-term structural tendencies, by themselves, cannot provide a convincing explanation for the behavior of organized labor at particular points in time. Certain developments that are peculiar to the current crisis need comment. The most striking of these is the extent of the "demobilizing" effect of the bank nationalization decision in September 1982 on a population already shell-shocked by the sudden disappearance of so many features of the traditional order, such as free convertibility, the absence of hyperinflation, and the collapse of the oil *deus ex machina*.

López Portillo's assault on the citadel of finance capital helped restore a good deal of the legitimacy lost by the ruling party over the previous months. It also led to the consolidation of a massive, albeit temporary, bloc of forces in defense of the state's action, recalling, as was probably intended, aspects of the Cárdenas period. The expropriation of banking capital was widely seen as a vindication of the calls for a "strong state" and an illustration of the state's relative autonomy.

The enthusiastic response of both official unions and leftist parties and organizations was accompanied by a realization that the foreign debt position and the general economic crisis would lead inexorably to a tightening of the already severe austerity measures. And comparisons with the post-1976 stabilization program emphasized the much more serious implications of the present crisis. The most urgent task of the union movement, therefore, was seen as the defense of workers' living standards. With this end in sight, the independents intensified demands for further wage increases, for wage indexing, and for a deepening of union democracy.

However, beneath the rhetoric of calls for a popular solution to the crisis there was a distinct mood of uncertainty about the choice of appropriate strategies for achieving that objective. The vacillating, erratic response of the official union leadership came as no great surprise. After an initial lukewarm declaration by the Congress of Labor on October 4 of support for plant-by-plant negotiations for wage increases, the CTM instructed its unions to begin preparations for an all-out strike assault if its demand for a 50 percent wage increase retroactive to August 1 was not granted. Five days later, Fidel Velázquez called on unions to negotiate separately with each plant management and thus avoid the need for a general strike, a statement that was in clear conflict with the CTM's earlier stance. In the end only a small proportion of the 39,000 strike notifications threatened by the CTM resulted in strike action. Other unions and confederations within the Congress of Labor adopted a different position. The COR and CROC, for example, argued against generalized strike action and expressed fears for a collapse of weaker companies if wage increases on the order of 50 percent were granted (*Así Es*, 1982b: 3). The response of much of the political left showed a similar pattern of uncertainty about what to do in the face of the serious economic crisis and the sudden demonstration of the vast reserve powers enjoyed by the state.

LOOKING TOWARD THE FUTURE

The last part of this paper offers a brief examination of some of the key actors and issues in the current drama and a discussion of likely developments in each case.

UNEVENNESS OF WORKER RESPONSES TO THE CRISIS

The impact of the current economic debacle will be experienced unevenly by different sectors of the work force, and responses to the crisis by Mexican working people will not be uniform. This is, of course, a fairly obvious conclusion and is probably true of all previous crises as well. But it is worth emphasizing because the frequent use of terms such as *working class* suggests the existence of a homogeneous and undifferentiated mass of workers. The increase of wage labor in Mexican society (in both rural and urban areas) and the emergence of a larger and more clearly factory-oriented work force should not be confused with a trend toward the homogenization of urban labor. The latter is increasingly differentiated along lines of age, sex, skill, wage levels, plant size, location, degree of job permanency, and so forth. Most sources dealing with the evolution of the Mexican labor market have noted this point, emphasizing, for example, that wage differentials have steadily increased since the Second World War, averaging out at a 300 percent difference between skilled and unskilled workers.[20] The importance of the distinction between workers with permanent contracts and those with temporary ones has been noted earlier.

The economic crisis already is accentuating the differentiation and fragmentation of the labor force. The strongest sections of the labor movement and those located most strategically may be able to limit the impact of the crisis and to cushion some of the blows. Weaker sectors will be pushed downward in terms of both conditions and job permanency. The result may well be the strengthening of barriers to political and union cooperation in the workers' movement. At the same time, though, very few groups will escape the trend toward a downwards recomposition of the working class as a whole. Relatively privileged groups (automobile workers, metal workers) already are bearing the brunt of growing unemployment.[21]

NEW CENTERS OF TENSION AND OPPOSITION

The economic crisis will probably accentuate the displacement of the center of conflict away from the primary capital-labor relationship at the point of production (factory, mine, workshop) toward other areas. These involve struggles over housing, the deterioration in urban living conditions, transport problems and the maldistribution of food and other staple items. The growing unemployment and marginalization of the labor force, which are products of the current crisis, will increase the importance of issues generated at these other levels and inflate the size of the population not directly involved in production.

The political impact of these developments could be considerable. The extent of the impact will depend on a number of factors, including the degree of responsiveness to these new issues shown by existing organizations (in the union movement and in the "popular sector" of the PRI, for example) and the effect of austerity programs and unemployment on the urban population.

DEMOCRATIZATION OF THE OFFICIAL UNION MOVEMENT

The "conservative" shift in government policy will place an added burden on the official union leadership. The growing complexity of the labor-state pact places extraordinary importance on the need for labor to generate nuclei of politically and technically skilled leaders. Of the older generation of leaders, very few still survive, the most important being Blas Chumacero, Napoleón Gómez Sada, Luis Gómez, and Fidel Velázquez. There is a marked scarcity of experienced, informed, and flexible intermediate and senior union leaders able to judge the exact balance of concessions, bribery, and repression needed in every conflict. "Dainty-smelling and elegantly dressed men" are no substitute for old-timers like Jesús Yurén and Francisco Pérez Ríos.[22]

The succession to Fidel Velázquez, in particular, may promote considerable conflict within the official union movement. But it is also possible that concern over deficiencies of leadership might force the pace of democratization in the movement. Greater opportunities for discussion and debate within labor unions may well permit a new generation of skilled leaders to emerge who will be able to respond more sensitively to the requirements of their members.

The economic debacle itself will increase pressures for democratization within the official sector, if only because the union bureaucracies will be seen to be incapable of "delivering the goods" as before. An increase in the opportunities for discussion and a more representative union leadership at the local level might well be viewed as offering an opportunity to defuse tension and rapidly rising hostility toward the existing leadership apparatus. Whatever the intentions of the leadership, it is likely that an increasingly restive rank and file will demand, and perhaps impose from below, further democratization. We may, therefore, anticipate substantial modifications in traditional methods of bargaining and greater encouragement for and tolerance of worker militancy and mobilization. The sharpest break with tradition may occur in the normally sluggish FSTSE (Federation of Unions of State Workers) and in other state-sector unions whose members bear a larger-than-normal share of the burden of the austerity program.

It is only in the light of these developments that we can measure the significance of the decision of the Congress of Labor at the end of January 1983 to invite the independent labor unions to join the body (*Latin American Regional Report*, 1983: 5). Although the Congress of Labor has never been a monolithic forum, this development is a clear example of how the economic crisis has forced the previously unthinkable to be placed on the agenda. This line of argument should not be exaggerated, however. The economic crisis may also reinforce certain aspects of the traditional system of labor controls. For example, rapid inflation and falling wages may well make the proposed extension of labor union stores and other union-controlled benefits even more vital to the well-being of members of the official unions (*Excélsior*, 1983).[23]

The two issues raised above are a manifestation of the central dilemma facing the union leadership. On the one hand, the official leadership needs to incorporate demands of an economic and political nature and calls for democratization both from its members and from the independents. This is a reflection of the slow process of disintegration of the traditional mechanisms of control over labor and is a direct result of the economic downturn. On the other hand, the labor union bureaucracies are unable to do anything serious about implementing their newly acquired rhetoric without running the risk of detonating too rapid and uncontrolled a pace of democratization. They face the even greater risk of setting off challenges to the age-old identification of the official labor sector with the PRI. A sudden move here could end the cozy arrangement by which the state grants positions of influence to labor bosses, who in return limit the scope of worker demands.

This is a serious contradiction but not a static one. The pace of changes that affect labor, both inside the labor movement and external to it, has intensified dramatically over the past year and a half. This will in all probability increase the frequency of abrupt, unexpected developments and will make for more unpredictability in general in relations between labor and the state and between union leaders and the rank and file. The area where this development is likely to be manifested most sharply is at the level of particular plants and localities, where individual labor unions will have to respond much more quickly and accurately to pressures from their members.

When all this is said and done, the possibility of a grand rupture of the "labor-state pact" occurring in the near future is very remote. In part this has to do with the lack of any clear alternative focus capable of coordinating the thousands of isolated points of dissidence and opposition that are emerging within the labor and popular movements. The political left has not defined its positions clearly. The PSUM, which is the principal focus of the left's reorganization in the past three years, has still not created a unified front out of the parties that it superseded. Its performance in the 1982 elections and vacillating response to the crisis of late 1982 have also disappointed many elements within the independent union current. The party is at present engaged in an internal debate over the direction and value of its parliamentary work and over the correctness of seeking "points of convergence" between itself and disaffected sections of the official labor movement and the "political class."[24]

STATE-LABOR RELATIONS

Mention already has been made of the increasingly tense relationship between the official labor movement and the new de la Madrid government. The major reason is the government's failure to implement the Social Pact (*Pacto de Solidaridad*) announced in December 1982. The Pact consisted of promises to protect the prices of popular consumption items and pledged that government programs would increase employment. On January 7, 1983, Fidel Velázquez declared that the Pact had been broken by the government's decision to increase the value-added tax (IVA) and by increases in the prices of the so-called protected commodities (*Unomásuno*, 1983a). This was followed by labor demands for a price freeze, unemployment insurance, a forty-hour week, and veiled demands for the resignation of the new minister of commerce (*Unomásuno*, 1983b). Behind all these demands there is still a tendency to blame the crisis on everyone except the president and the PRI's inner circle. Still, the tone of the attacks, particularly against the commercial sector, is becoming more strident, as evidenced by the threat of Velázquez to mount a campaign against retailers, with the slogan "pots and pans and rolling pins, down with the businessmen."

The tenor of these demands is alarming groups within the private sector. A good example is the howl of protest that greeted the CTM's plans to establish a much-enlarged "parallel" network of union stores to provide goods and clothing free of IVA to its members. It is likely, then, that intersectoral conflicts, involving groups within and outside the PRI's corporate structure, will increase as the crisis deepens.

Within the Chamber of Deputies the reduced number of labor deputies may be expected to show increasing signs of independence along the lines of the walkout by several deputies on December 27, 1982. This action followed labor union criticisms of a new government law that would convert all government employees into "public servants" (*servidores públicos*), regardless of rank. It is likely, too, that areas of "convergence" between the official labor sector and the left parties in the Chamber will develop. Certain sectors of the PSUM, in particular the deputies associated with the former Popular Action Movement, are particularly anxious to encourage and build on such opportunities for extending the influence of the left; other sections of the party condemn such thinking as unrealistic and opportunist.

Whatever the attitude of the PSUM and its allies, points of convergence are bound to emerge with more frequency, albeit on an issue-by-issue basis, as long as the labor sector's disenchantment with the de la Madrid government endures. The PRI's labor deputies probably would not find the notion of convergence with the left very palatable, especially in view of the long history of anti-communism within the official labor sector. However, its more intelligent members might see in the search for convergence an opportunity to blunt the left's demands for a total overhaul of the labor-state compact.

PRI/STATE POLICIES TOWARD ORGANIZED LABOR

For the Mexican state one of the central issues over the next few years will be whether the government can continue to assert political control over economic considerations during a time of profound economic crisis. In other words, will the current crisis lead to the erosion or reaffirmation of the relative autonomy of the state (Purcell, 1981: 211-212)?

The greatest danger facing de la Madrid is the upsetting of the labor-state pact. This might happen if there were too rapid a shift away from the rhetoric and policies of populism and toward the positions of a more aggressive capitalist class. It is not clear how far the current government can go in its austerity program before it provokes not only food disturbances (such as occurred in Brazil), but also a fatal weakening of the understandings between itself and the official union leadership.

It is too early to determine how far the de la Madrid government will be able to cushion the urban working class from the worst effects of the economic crisis.[25] Early indications are that the new cabinet's drive to eliminate the "fictitious economy" will have serious repercussions for the popular classes and the "suffering" middle class. The most sensitive issue is the future of the elaborate network of subsidies on food and basic commodities. Within a month of assuming office, the de la Madrid government took controls off of four thousand prices, and thus far it has failed to regulate the three hundred items that make up the standard basket of consumer goods. The labor movement's anger so far has been directed at the private sector and the government's advisors. It seems the "king" himself is not yet guilty. One wonders how long this immunity will last.

But it is not the purely economic dimension of the crisis that most threatens the integrity of the labor-state pact. How far can the political distancing of the government from the labor sector go until the reduction in the political payoffs to the official labor movement threatens a key portion of the union leadership's reward for cooperation? It is, of course, possible that we are witnessing another attempt by the state, this time under the control of technocrats, to achieve a renewal (or *renovacíon*) of the leadership of the official labor movement. The economic crisis may permit the new government to achieve what Luis Echeverría failed to obtain in 1971 and 1972—the forcing of new blood and methods of bargaining into the labor bureaucracies in an attempt to reduce the sclerosis of the current labor leadership. If this is the case, then encouragement of closer cooperation between the Congress of Labor and the "independents" may well be a vital ingredient in the strategy. Its success will naturally depend on how far a bigger space for independent unionism can be exchanged for promises to limit contact with the political left and to curb strike actions in areas considered dangerous by the state. This is certainly the model underlying the "apolitical unionism" of the Independent Labor Organization of Ortega Arenas that has enjoyed the tolerance of the state. But will the severity of the economic debacle allow for such careful "fine tuning"?

CONCLUSION

This is not the first economic crisis to test the solidity of the labor-state compact. The 1954 and 1976 devaluations produced periods of austerity for workers, but in both these cases the official labor bureaucracy served the regime well. In fact, labor's acceptance of the policy of wage ceilings below the inflation rate during the stabilization program of 1977-1979 gave considerable plausibility, one authority has written, "to the claims of Mexico's old-guard labor leadership that it is they who [had] effectively rescued this regime" (Whitehead, 1980: 854).

So far (in the period to April 1983), the official labor sector has shown equally remarkable discipline in the wages area in spite of the rapidly widening gap between wage settlements and movements in the consumer price index. Although there is no longer an official wage ceiling, January's 25 percent increase in the minimum wage has become in practice an unofficial ceiling, with few of the annual labor contract negotiations exceeding this limit by more than 1 percent or 2 percent. In the few cases where larger increases have been awarded, as with the workers at the state-run DINA plants, unions have been forced to accept substantial cuts in the labor force.

Much will depend on the magnitude and duration of the current economic debacle. In previous crises, labor's acceptance of periods of austerity, especially at the beginning of a presidential term, was rewarded by a relaxation in controls later in the administration. The debacle of the past year, though, combines in a single conjuncture massive currency devaluations, hyperinflation, falling oil prices, acute foreign debt problems and a continuing crisis of agricultural production. A recent estimate by Abel Beltrán de Río, director of Wharton's Mexico Project, suggests that Mexico will lose 40 percent of the new jobs generated over the period from 1977 to 1981. In these circumstances, labor discipline cannot be sustained for very long without severe tensions emerging in the labor-state compact.

NOTES

1. There is considerable variation in the figures on the size of the unionized population. For a representative selection of sources, see Zapata (1979), Leal and Woldenberg (1976), Trejo (1979: 123), Camacho (1980: chap. 6), Bortz (1980).

2. The most detailed examination of the telephone workers' struggle is *Tres huelgas de telefonistas* (1980).

3. Following this defeat, the legacy of the Democratic Tendency was kept alive by the Movimiento Socialista Revolucionario (MSR). The Movement for Popular Action (MAP), which is now part of the New United Socialist Party, the PSUM, also draws heavily on the experience and ideology of the Democratic Tendency.

4. On the UOI, see Aguilar García (1982). In the past two years the UOI has lost a number of its most important affiliates in the automobile and aviation industries.

5. Symptomatic of these tensions are the serious splits in the PCM (now PSUM) leadership at the Universidad Autónoma de Puebla that occurred in 1981-1982 over the selection of a candidate for the directorship.

6. In spite of the limited scope of the political reform, the official labor leadership exhibited great anxiety over the potential destabilizing effects of the legislation, and in particular over the danger posed by closer links between the leftist parties and the labor union movement.

7. Independent unions frequently attempt to create forums for discussion and joint action. In January 1982, for example, representatives from more than sixty independent unions attended the First Gathering of Union Solidarity in Mexico City. From this meeting there emerged a new body, COSINA, which was to coordinate the work of the independent sector. See *Así Es* (1982a: 9).

8. This is not to suggest that this self-image is an accurate one, ignoring, as it does, the impact of the state's strategy and the policies of employers.

9. For data on the case of the Pascual workers, see *Insurgencia Popular* (1982) and *Semanario del P.M.T.* (1982a, 1982b, 1982c).

10. For a discussion of SUTIN's entry into the Congress of Labor, see the interview with Arturo Whaley, secretary-general of the union, in *Solidaridad* (1980: 6).

11. The percentages were as follows: under 20,000 pesos, 30 percent; between 20,000 and 30,000, 20 percent; more than 30,000 pesos, 10 percent.

12. In mid-April 1983, the Congress of Labor estimated that the increases restored only 60 percent of the purchasing power lost by workers' wages in 1982. Se *Unomásuno* (1983h).

13. The workers of Pascual Industries, to take one example, did not receive the March increase, and this was one of the several factors that brought the workers out on strike in May.

14. The Employers' Center of Nuevo León announced on November 9, 1983, that it had not granted any increases, but had merely confirmed the March emergency raise of 30 percent in those cases where it had not been granted. See *Punto Crítico* (1982: 6). The president of the Employers' Confederation of Mexico declared on November 12 that the employers were "very happy."

15. "In April and May, Fidel Velázquez demanded a general emergency wage increase of 50 percent to offset the effects of inflation. Just as in October 1982, a general strike was threatened and strike notices were readied. On this occasion, however, wage offers of 15 percent to 25 percent were not sufficient to force the lifting of several thousands of notifications and widespread strike action was expected in July" (*Unomásuno*, 1983f).

16. The minister of labor in the de la Madrid cabinet, Arsenio Farrell Cubilla, is a businessman and former director of the Employers' Center of Guadalajara.

17. For a good discussion of these developments, see López Montjardin (1979).

18. The two coalitions are the National Committee for Defense of the Popular Economy (CNDEP) and the National Front in Defense of Wages Against Austerity and Measures in the Cost of Living (FNDSCAC).

19. One of the militant opposition currents within the teachers' union, the National Coordinating Committee of Education Workers, was also connected with the anti-austerity

campaign. In the case of the Pascual workers' strike, the CTM's hostility toward its former members was strongly influenced by the guidance the strikers received from a lawyer of the Mexican Workers Party (PMT).

20. According to the Industrial Census of 1975, workers in large-scale enterprises received wages up to 360 percent higher than workers in small plants and workshops. It should be noted also that benefits in state enterprises and institutions are more than double those available in the private sector. See Movimiento de Acción Popular (1980: 38).

21. At the state-owned DINA plants, workers received wage raises in March in return for accepting the dismissal of 2,552 workers. See Unomásuno (1983d).

22. The quotation (which is a reference to Joaquín Gamboa Pasco, former head of the labor sector in the Chamber of Deputies) is from Jorge Fernández (1979: 18).

23. In March 1983 the CTM also reported that it was considering buying nearly a hundred enterprises from the Somex nationalized banking group; these were in the food, clothing, footwear, and household goods areas; see Unomásuno (1983c, 1983g). The CTM's secretary of political action, José Ramírez Garnero, admitted that the CTM's concern was to "prevent workers from 'taking over' the leadership."

24. For views on the "convergence" debate, see Hirales (1983: 6; 1982: 12-15).

25. Government spokespersons and official banking and economic sources are reluctant to discuss the impact of the economic crisis on real wages and living conditions. The 25-page report on the state of the Mexican economy published by the Bank of Mexico on March 22, 1983, for example, declined to comment on wage increments in 1982, noting only that the trend would be very uneven—possibly a rise in the first half and a fall in the second. Even taking into account the complexity of the problem, this is a strikingly evasive position. Unomásuno (1983e) published a brief summary of the report.

REFERENCES

Aguilar García, Javier
    1982 La política sindical en México: industria de automóvil. Mexico City: Ediciones Era.
Así Es
    1982a (February 12-19).
    1982b (October 15-21).
    1982c (October 22-28).
Bortz, Jeffrey
    1980 "Problemas de la medición de la afiliación sindical." A: Revista de la División de Ciencias Sociales y Humanidades de la Universidad Autónoma Metropolitana, Azcapotzalco (September/December): 29-66.
Camacho, Manuel
    1980 La clase obrera en la historia de México: el futuro inmediato. Mexico City: Siglo XXI.
Córdova, Arnaldo
    1979 La política de masas y el futuro de la izquierda en México. Mexico City: Ediciones Era.
Correa, Guillermo and Salvador Corro
    1983 "Se ataca el desempleo con medidas temporales y esto hace prever más subempleo y marginalización." Proceso 325 (January 24): 12-13.

Excelsior
   1983 (January 19).
Fernández, Jorge
   1979 "Qué tiempos aquellos, señor Don Fidel: el movimiento obrero mexicano."
   Nexos 2 (13).
Hernández, Luís (ed.)
   1981 *Las luchas magisteriales, 1979-1981* (2 vols.). Mexico City: Ediciones
   Macehual.
Hirales, Gustavo
   1982 "Debate en el Comite Central." *Así Es* 36 (October 8-14).
   1983 "Las convergencia." *Así Es* 47 (January 14-20).
Insurgencia Popular
   1982 78 (July).
Juárez, Antonio
   1979 *Las corporaciones transnacionales y los trabajadores mexicanos.* Mexico City:
   Siglo XXI.
Latin America Regional Report: Mexico and Central America
   1983 RM-83-02.
Latin America Weekly Report
   1981 "Enter the Mexican modernizer." WR-81-40 (October 9).
Leal, Juan Felipe and José Woldenberg
   1976 "El sindicalismo mexicano: aspectos organizativos." *Cuadernos Políticos*
   (January/March): 35-54.
León, Samuel
   1976 "La burocracia sindical mexicano." *Trimestre Político* 1 (4): 48-69.
López Montjardin, Adriana
   1979 "La lucha popular en los municipios." *Cuadernos Politícos* 20: 40-51.
Movimiento de Acción Popular
   1981 *Tesis y programa.* Mexico City.
Punto Crítico
   1982 "Las negociaciones salariales muestran la austeridad." 129 (November 16): 5-6.
Purcell, Susan Kaufman
   1981 "Business-government relations in Mexico: the case of the sugar industry." *Comparative Politics* 13 (2): 211-233.
Seminario de P.M.T.
   1982a (November 2-8).
   1982b (November 30-December 6).
   1982c (December 21-27).
Solidaridad
   1980 (December 6).
Trejo, Raúl
   1979 "El movimiento obrero: Situación y perspectivas," in Pablo González Casanova
   and Enrique Florescano (eds.) *México hoy.* Mexico City: Siglo XXI.
   1980 "Estructura y circunstancia en el Congreso del Trabajo." *A: Revista de la División de Ciencias Sociales y Humanidades de la Universidad Autónoma Metropolitana,
   Azcapotzalco* (September/December).
   1982 "Cultura política obrera: atrás de la raya, que estamos grillando." *Nexos* 52
   (April): 35-41.
Tres huelgas de telefonistas: hacia un sindicalismo democrático
   1980 Mexico City: Cuadernos de Unomásuno.

Unomásuno
    1983a (January 8): 113.
    1983b (January 22): 113.
    1983c (March 18).
    1983d (March 20): 110.
    1983e (March 23): 115.
    1983f (March 25): 103.
    1983g (March 29).
    1983h (April 10): 102.
Whitehead, Laurence
    1980 "Mexico from bust to boom: a political evaluation of the 1976-1979 stabilization programme." *World Development* 8.
Woldenberg, José
    1980 "Notas sobre la burocracia sindical en México." *A: Revista de la División de Ciencias Sociales y Humanidades de la Universidad Metropolitana, Azcapotzalco* 1: 16-28.
Zapata, Francisco
    1976 "Afiliación y organización sindical en México," pp. 81-148 in *Tres estudios sobre el movimiento obrero en México*. Mexico City: Colegio de México.

9

Immiseration, Not Marginalization
The Case of Mexico

*James D. Cockcroft**

This paper uses Marx's theory of immiseration and relative surplus population, together with examples from Mexico, to illustrate the direct relationship between immiseration and capitalist accumulation. As a reserve army of labor, the immiserated masses constitute a necessary condition for the development of industrial capitalism. More rapid increase of the laboring population than of the conditions under which capital can employ such increase, multiemployment and superexploitation of the immiserated, and use of a dual labor market (stable and temporary labor) all defray falling profit rates, hold industrial wages down, and provide for labor's reproduction at almost no cost to capital. Further examination reveals that Mexico's capitalist state regulates the immiserated, whose diversified economic activity is functional but whose political militancy is dysfunctional for capital accumulation. Also addressed is the question of the unevenly developed and mixed class consciousness of the immiserated and their potential proletarian class consciousness.

Though subject to much recent criticism (Bennholdt-Thomsen, 1981; Castells, 1975; Margulis, 1980; Moctezuma and Navarro, 1980; Perlman, 1977), the new scholarship on "marginalization" (e.g., Cardoso, 1971; González Casanova, 1965; Kowarick, 1975; Nun, 1969; Quijano Obregón, 1977; Touraine, 1977) is useful in its description of racism, sexism, oppression, and so-called internal colonialism asserted by stronger groups. It is undeniable that in Mexico exploitation occurs along racial and sexual lines (mestizos over Indians, men over women) and in geographically recognizable patterns (southern and central rural Mexico serving provincial capitals, regional submetropolises, and metropolitan centers such as Mexico City or major U.S. cities). Yet it is a mistake to reduce the immiseration of millions of people to a sociologi-

*James D. Cockcroft is currently Distinguished Visiting Professor at the University of Vermont. He is an editor of *Latin American Perspectives* and the author of a dozen books, including *Outlaws in the Promised Land: Mexican Immigrant Workers and America's Future* (Grove Press, 1985) and *Mexico* (Monthly Review Press, 1983).

cally marginal or geographically curious phenomenon of removal of people from the mainstream of capitalist "development/underdevelopment."

Far from being "marginal," these angry and overworked millions form a vast fraction of the working class that is the product of an ongoing process of immiseration, the other side of the coin of capital accumulation. The uprooting of people from the countryside, the separation of people from their means of production, and the crowding of tens of thousands of families into precarious living conditions in towns and cities constitute a fundamental dynamic of the capitalist mode of production in its historical evolution.

In the cities these human beings become enmeshed in relations of production, distribution, and servicing of commodities that are characterized by multiemployment, sometimes in wage labor and often in nonwage activity. The overwhelming majority come to form the immiserated fraction of the working class. They constitute a subproletariat in a double sense: first as a relative surplus population or part of the reserve army of labor and second as moving in and out of the agrarian, industrial, and service/commercial working class. Although there are exceptions, such as some thieves, prostitutes, or derelicts, these ill-housed, disease-prone millions are a historical result of the ongoing generation of a relative surplus population and its necessary role in capital accumulation.

MARX'S THEORY OF IMMISERATION AND RELATIVE SURPLUS POPULATION

In Chapter 25 of *Capital*, Marx laid bare the roots of immiseration in the process of capital accumulation itself. There he characterized reproduction of surplus value on an extended scale, that is, capitalist accumulation, as "more capitalists or larger capitalists at this pole, more wage-workers at that," in the course of which production becomes more capital-intensive, repelling workers even as it adds to the total number of the proletariat. According to Marx, "it is capitalistic accumulation itself that constantly produces, and produces in the direct ratio of its own energy and extent, a relatively redundant population of laborers, i.e., a population of greater extent than suffices for the average needs of the self-expansion of capital, and therefore a surplus population." Because of the revolutionizing effect capitalism has on production, expanding its scale and quantity immensely, there emerges the paradox of "greater attraction of laborers by capital" accompanied by "their greater repulsion" (Marx, 1967: 630-632).

Indeed, Marx defined the surplus population as "a condition of existence of the capitalist mode of production." The reserve army of labor power, always available for exploitation, can be swiftly mobilized for a sudden expansion of capitalist production and, thereby, of capital. This reserve army also reduces the likelihood of long strikes or rapidly rising wages that might reduce profits and thereby retard accumulation. Industrial capitalism, Marx pointed out, "depends on the constant formation, the greater or less absorption, and the re-formation of the industrial reserve army of surplus population, independently of the absolute growth of the population" (Marx, 1967: 633). In this sense, the roots of immiseration of the masses have little to do with population growth as such and everything to do with the nature of capitalist production and its penetration into the remotest rural areas.

Whether the relative surplus population takes the floating form (as in modern industrial centers, now employed, now laid off), the latent form (low-paid, subemployed agricultural labor, ready to migrate to town or city), or the pauper form (the unemployed, orphans, poor children, demoralized, mutilated, or sickly workers), this population, which functions as a reserve army of labor, grows in rough correspondence to the increase in social wealth, functioning capital, labor productivity, and the absolute mass of the proletariat. Immiseration is a necessary corollary to capitalist accumulation.

Marx (1967: 644-645) expressed this dialectical process as follows:

The same causes which develop the expansive power of capital, develop also the labor-power at its disposal. The relative mass of the industrial reserve army increases therefore with the potential energy of wealth. The greater this reserve army in proportion to the active labor-army, the greater is the mass of a consolidated surplus-population. . . . Along with the surplus population, pauperism forms a condition of capitalist production, and of the capitalist development of wealth. . . . The more extensive, finally, the lazarus-layers of the working-class, and the industrial reserve army, the greater is official pauperism. This is the absolute general law of capitalist accumulation. . . . The law by which a constantly increasing quantity of means of production, thanks to the advance in the productiveness of social labor, may be set in movement by a progressively diminishing expenditure of human power, this law, in a capitalist society . . . is expressed thus: the higher the productiveness of labor, the greater is the pressure of the laborers on the means of employment, the more precarious, therefore, becomes their condition of existence, viz., the sale of their own labor-power for the increasing of another's wealth, or for the self-expansion of capital.

It is not true that Marx called all these forms of surplus population the "dangerous classes," a colloquial term he applied only to vagabonds, criminals, and prostitutes, and then in quotation marks. Nor did Marx ever suggest that the most downtrodden, the so-called *lumpenproletariat*, could serve only reactionary causes. He saw in the suffering of the surplus population the same degradation of work that increasingly alienates all the proletariat as capitalism develops: "All means for the development of production transform themselves into means of domination over, and exploitation of, the producers; they mutilate the laborer into a fragment of a man, degrade him to the level of an appendage of a machine . . . estrange from him the intellectual potentialities of the labor-process in the same proportion as science is incorporated in it as an independent power." Marx described this antagonistic character of capitalist accumulation as "accumulation of wealth at one pole, accumulation of misery, agony of toil, slavery, ignorance, brutality, mental degradation, at the opposite pole, that is, on the side of the class that produces its own product in the form of capital" (Marx, 1967: 645).

THE ROLE OF IMMISERATION IN
MEXICAN CAPITALISM

Marx did not live long enough to witness the immiseration of masses of people on a world scale during the imperialist stage of capitalism. The antagonistic character of capitalist accumulation has, through its pauperization of millions of people, generated new contradictions that Marx did not discuss. Among these are the social problems generated by mass misery (disease, crime, drug addiction, gang war, and the like); the cost of maintaining a degree of stability or regularization of these immiserated masses, whether in public services, policing, food handouts, or checkpoints for migratory flows; and, most serious of all for capital accumulation, which is still served by such misery even as it generates it, the growing tendency of large numbers of the poor to organize, gain political consciousness, and resist or revolt.

The capitalist transformation of the forces of production in Mexico, accelerated by foreign capital's new technologies, has produced a situation in which the absorption of workers in industrial wage labor diminishes in relation to the total number of workers. Recently augmented investments by transnational corporations (new U.S. direct investments have been doubling every year since 1978, according to annual reports of the Banco de México) contribute to the abundance of Mexico's surplus population by elevating the level of capital needed for the creation of each new job. Furthermore, by taking out of Mexico in the form of dividends, interest, and other payments twice as much as they put in, foreign investors contribute to Mexico's relative decapitalization. Further aggravating Mexico's shortage of capital to create sufficient new jobs are its unfavorable terms of trade, growing foreign indebtedness (over $80 billion in late 1982), and periodic flights of capital.

Mexico's social productivity disadvantages vis-à-vis the more advanced industrialized countries, historically rooted in colonialism, foreign domination of the economy after Independence, and preference by Mexican investors for the utilization of low-wage labor to the detriment of a more complete technification and mechanization of production, are compounded by the relative decapitalization and growing indebtedness just mentioned. Given the lack of adequate capital to generate sufficient employment, the size of the relative surplus population has continued to increase. According to official statistics for 1980, less than half the labor force has regular employment, and many more are not counted as in the labor force in the first place.[1] In an imperialist-dominated economy with a relatively weak bourgeoisie such as Mexico's, the reserve army of labor grows to proportions Marx scarcely envisioned.

I have elsewhere noted (Cockcroft, 1983) how useful the reserve army, together with the *ejido* (village lands) and *minifundista* (small-parcel) land-tenure system alongside large productive estates and modern agribusiness farms, has proven to be for the capitalist transformation of agriculture and Mexico's post-1940 industrial development. Most peasants have become proletarianized but also in part "re-peasantized." Subsumed by a larger capitalist context that generates both their exploitation as low-paid farm workers for others and their recourse to "self-exploitation" of family labor in subsistence farming or domestic handicrafts for the purposes of survival, Mexico's rural labor force has been described by one sociologist as "proletarians disguised as peasants" (Paré, 1977). In terms of income, subsistence farming supplements wages, not, as is often stated, the other way around. In supplanting all other modes of production, capitalism in Mexico refunctionalizes some of their forms (for example, subsistence farming) principally to keep the labor force reproducing itself at no cost to capital.

Yet it is impossible for irregularly employed or nonwaged workers to revert to "precapitalist" production as such, since they buy some of their basic necessities and sell whatever surplus they can generate in a market which, however remote, is connected to a national and international process of capital accumulation. Whether impoverished farmers, artisans, or street peddlers, today's immiserated masses cannot survive outside of the commodity economy established by capitalism.

To maintain some semblance of social order among these desperate, hard-working millions, increasing amounts of capital and energy have to be channeled out of the accumulation process in order to provide state-run food stores (Mexico's CONASUPO), token welfare assistance, some minimal forms of housing, public services, and military or police control over ever larger slums, some of which become cities unto themselves. One such city is Netzahualcóyotl (Nahuatl for "fasting coyote"), commonly known as "Netza."

Founded in the mud flats and creeks of Texcoco Lake near Mexico City's international airport by 3,075 *comuneros* of the Santa María Chimnalhuacán ejido in the late 1940s, Netza had 60,000 residents in 1960 and some 600,000 in 1970. By 1982, it had mushroomed into an unmanageable urban jungle of between 2 and 3 million—the nation's third or fourth largest "city"—covering 150 square miles, mostly outside Mexico City. More than 20 percent of its new residents came from other "lost cities" of the Federal District. Although during Netza's growth infant mortality averaged 50 percent up to age 4, families averaged 5.4 persons.

Use of ejido land to house the urban poor became commonplace in the 1950s, when the number of ejidos declined by 80 percent in the Federal District. By 1970, *colonias proletarias*, as slums like Netza are called, accounted for nearly half of the Federal District's population, compared with 14 percent in 1952. Their annual growth is reported in 1981 to be proceeding up to 15 percent faster than that of the Federal District as a whole. (The metropolitan area of Mexico City, which receives 10,000 new residents every day, contains more than 18 million people, one-fourth of the nation's populace.) After authorizing land fractionalization for Netza in 1963, the state coopted a militant mass movement against rapacious land tycoons in 1972 and then established a regulatory agency that paid off the tycoons and billed the residents for "urban improvements." The original settlers protested this fraud, claiming legal title to the area on the basis of presidential decrees of 1862 and 1927, Article 27 of the Constitution, and the Law of Agrarian Reform. Of Netza's total land area, 95 percent is occupied by people who still lack state-recognized "legal title." In 1979, Netza's residents objected to the government's plan to spend $25 million to construct a "municipal palace," claiming it would be "a monument to misery when more than one and a half million persons here lack water, electricity, drainage, and other services" (*Uno Más Uno*, November 29, 1979).

Of those residents who were employed in 1970 (53 percent), some 80 percent worked outside Netza. Of those employed remaining in the slum,

51 percent worked in petty commerce, 20 percent in construction, 10 percent in small industry, and only 10 percent in services (Rosa, 1979; Iglesias, 1978-1982). By 1981, a report by organized labor's Labor Congress (Congreso de Trabajo—CT) showed only one-fourth of Netza's population as having even a remote chance of being employed, of whom 60 percent were receiving a stable wage and the rest were unemployed or subemployed.

There are many such slums with similar patterns of employment/ unemployment inside or on the outskirts of all Mexico's major cities. A study of one such slum found that 89 percent of heads of family were proletarians, 10 percent were in the petty bourgeoisie, and only 1 percent were "lumpenproletarian." Of the proletarians, 52 percent were receiving a stable wage and the rest were either unemployed or irregularly employed (Moctezuma and Navarro, 1980).

The state is under extreme pressure to provide these slums such services as transportation, sewage, electricity, gas, and medical assistance. Only 41 percent of Mexicans receive any kind of health-care assistance, provided through their labor contracts or by national social security. According to government statistics, the social-security program initiated in the 1970s for the so-called marginalized covers only 14.7 percent of the population. That leaves 42 percent of all Mexicans without any organized way of obtaining health care.

Although technically unemployed or underemployed, most of the immiserated are in fact "overemployed." Unable to obtain stable or adequate wage labor, the majority go from job to job. They often work more than one job per person and at least two jobs per adult couple per family. Children and the aged of immiserated families work when and where they can. The more than half of Mexico's labor force without regular employment is, in its urban portion, concentrated in "lost cities." There, subproletarians often live next door to more regularly employed proletarians. Many of the immiserated join the floating segment of the relative surplus population, which works for a time at a factory and then is laid off, only to repeat the process. In such ways as these, the immiserated take on a certain degree of proletarian consciousness and integration into a larger class (not "national") culture.

The slums offer a big market to a number of capitalists, including monopoly firms, for the sale of furniture, wood products, stationery, soft drinks, liquor, food, construction goods, and the like. Slum dwellers, unable to travel elsewhere to obtain commodities at reasonable prices, constitute a captive market paying exorbitant prices on everything from sugar to tortillas, from building materials to rent. Commodity sales are typically carried out by immiserated elements dependent upon wholesalers or retailers who possess semimonopolistic advantages in transport and capital.

Most of the immiserated function in production or distribution processes associated with accumulation for capitalists. They work for a pittance as street vendors, artisans, subcontracted seamstresses, carpenters, hawkers, carriers, small-scale workshop employees or owners, messengers, irregularly employed factory hands, and the like. Perhaps their most important item of production for capital is labor power, which they reproduce at substandard wages or without pay through far more hours of physical (and mental) exertion of labor per week than regularly employed proletarians.

Wages paid workers by capitalists supposedly cover the basic necessities for maintaining workers—the ongoing reproduction of labor power. Unpaid household tasks performed by women necessary for labor's reproduction are, in effect, being "purchased" by the capitalists when they pay workers wages. The part of the workday's total product equivalent to the wage is known as "necessary labor," and the part beyond that equivalent is known as "surplus labor" and is the surplus value appropriated by the capitalist. In a sense, then, women's domestic labor in the sustenance of workers and the upbringing of future laborers is part of "necessary labor." Yet capitalists pay only for the labor performed by the hired worker at the workplace, not for the labor performed at home. In the slums, women typically care for a few animals or a small garden plot, make clothes, take care of children, prepare meals, clean house, and generally oversee family consumption needs—all without pay.

In what Meillassoux (1977) has called "domestic economies," the immiserated's self-production of food, primitive shelter, clothing, furniture, and other necessities offers up to capital quantities of labor power for which capital never has to pay a living wage or offers pitiful wages to employ when convenient. Many factory workers augment their wages by weekly (unpaid-for) food supplies from relatives in rural areas. Thus factory owners exploit not only the labor of wage earners, but also that of their kin groups. In Mexico, the high levels of self-sustenance engaged in by the immiserated and the proletariat in general help fulfill functions which capitalism and its state avoid or barely address, particularly the function of social security.

The self-reproducing cycle of the Mexican bourgeoisie's accumulation of capital based on abundant cheap labor perpetuates not only the process of immiseration, but also harsh living conditions for the regularly employed proletariat. The abject poverty of urban subproletarians, as well as the extended length of their average work day (with or without pay), corresponds to the relative decline of real income for the employed working class as a whole experienced in recent years, a decline furthered by the presence of the poor. According to the National Commission of Minimum Wages, the average loss in purchasing power of legal minimum wages was 18.6 percent in 1977, 12.9 percent in 1978, 16.2 percent in 1979, and 24 percent through October 1980. As total wages fail to provide even the bare minimum necessary to meet the daily reproduction costs of labor power (socially necessary labor to reproduce the working class) and as the bourgeoisie and the state, alone or combined, refuse to assume the costs of reproduction of labor, these costs have to be met by the larger waged and nonwaged working class as a whole.

Reduction of wages below the value of labor power, as Marx pointed out, "transforms, within certain limits, the laborer's necessary consumption fund into a fund for the accumulation of capital" (Marx, 1967: 599). It constitutes a basis for the superexploitation not only of the immiserated, but also of large portions of the industrially employed proletariat, at least, in small and medium-sized industry, which in 1975 accounted for 60 percent of industrial employment but only 42 percent of industrial wage (Industrial census, 1975).

Most of those earning the legal minimum wage already experience superexploitation. In 1980, the legal minimum wage was less than half what a working-class family of five needed simply to maintain itself. The fundamental forms of superexploitation are increase in intensity of work, extension of the work day, and payment of labor power below its value (see Frank, 1978). Mexico experiences all three.

For example, the *ILO Yearbook* for 1975 shows Mexican nonagricultural and manufacturing labor working 45-46 hours a week, compared with 40-41 hours for corresponding U.S. workers and at one-fifth to one-sixth their hourly wage. Because working conditions are generally poorer and industrial diseases more frequent in Mexico than in the United States, the intensity of labor is also greater—for example, Mexican women perform electronic assembly operations with the naked eye while their U.S. counterparts use microscopes. All available studies indicate that the productivity per person-hour of labor of Mexican workers is roughly equal to and sometimes higher than that of comparable U.S. workers. Barraesen (1972) reports Mexican workers' productivity as 40 percent higher in metal products, 30 percent higher in sewing work, and 10 percent to 25 percent higher in assembly of electronic products.

Through the extended workday and the so-called independent labor they perform, the lower strata of the working class, rural and urban, are integrated into the overall dynamic of capitalist industrialization. Besides contributing to the capitalists' extraction of surplus value by helping to meet the costs of the reproduction of labor power, the immiserateds' multiple economic activities are integrated with the accumulation process directly through their production of surplus value or through their role in the circulation, distribution, and servicing of commodities.

THE IMMISERATED IN THE PRODUCTION, CIRCULATION, AND REALIZATION OF SURPLUS VALUE

A good example of the immiserateds' production of surplus value is the widespread use of sweatshops in the interior of Mexico. In the Federal District alone there are 300,000 *maquiladoras de ropa*, workshops that assemble clothing. Nationally, for the monopolistic shoe industry, there are many more such slum workshops, known as *picas*. These cobbling operations produce over half the nation's shoes, including exports worth $36 million in 1979. They often use modern imported machinery, as well as imported leather and synthetic materials. The surplus value produced goes to the tanners and shoe companies that dominate the industry. There are hundreds of thousands of other workshops producing furniture, housing parts, leather goods, various automotive parts or supplies, and so forth, for the profit of capitalists. To illustrate the pattern and its petty-bourgeois disguising of a proletarian reality, the clothing workshops may be considered.

The individuals (sewing at home) or the workshops' owners (household industries with small numbers of hired laborers) own part of constant capital, often modern sewing or cutting machinery. However, they are dependent for raw materials (such as textiles) on the capitalists, who often, like the traditional "jobbers" of New York City's Lower East Side, subcontract out the work to the slum workshops. When the workshop owners attempt to purchase the raw materials outside the monopolized market, the prices are hiked beyond their capacity or the purchase is simply denied them, because the sellers do the bulk of their business with the capitalists.

Thus the poor owners of the sewing machinery, which have been purchased on credit or with their lives' savings, offer themselves up on the labor market with two items to sell: part of constant capital and labor power. In turn, the capitalists appropriate the surplus value produced by the workers of the sweatshops in two ways: first with the subcontracting of the workshop owners' collective labor power and second with the control over the market of raw materials and eventual sales of the finished products. Recent case studies (Alonso et al., 1980; Alonso, 1981; Padilla, 1978) have estimated the rate of surplus-value appropriation by capitalists employing this type of productive labor as more than double that of large-scale clothing factories employing proletarians in Mexico as a whole.

Because the number of Mexican slum workshops in various industries has risen dramatically in recent years, in part because of the working class's feverish attempts to compensate for its inadequate earnings or employment, it is unreasonable to argue that these are "precapitalist" modes of production destined to disappear. On the contrary, these workshops are a product and a tool of modern capitalist accumulation. The same case studies show that even a workshop owner who exploits the labor of poorer neighbors fails to appropriate a portion of the surplus value thereby produced. In fact, usually he or she makes more when not having to hire other laborers, given that the "wage" paid oneself in "self-exploitation" is normally half that paid the hired laborer (in turn, less than half the legal minimum wage). Moreover, the owners of the workshops are themselves recent rural migrants who have not, normally, engaged in this type of activity before and are easily victimized by capitalist "jobbers."

Viewed from the capitalist's vantage point, exploitation of these slum elements is profitable because the wages are substandard or nonexistent, because there is no problem of labor unions, strikes, or state-enforced labor benefits, and because part of the costs of constant capital are assumed by the workshop owners. Moreover, the rate of recuperation of constant-capital costs is rapid for the capitalist—he recuperates the cost of raw materials with the sale of the finished products—but slow for the workshop owner, whose overhead and machinery payments are spread out over a much longer period.

Also present in these urban slums are capitalist-owned factories operating with fewer than a hundred employees and thereby avoiding constitutional stipulations for housing and other benefits. Case studies reveal that factory owners prefer to hire recent migrants, often from the same rural region. (Transnational corporations operating assembly plants in the border area also tap selected rural regions—see Cornelius, 1975; Eckstein, 1977; Fernández, 1980; Gambrill et al., 1981.) Paternalism and superexploitation characterize the extraction of surplus value here as in so many other activities of the immiserated. Owners contribute funds to the rural churches and often become godparents to the workers' children.

Foreign capital is involved in many of these factories or soon steps in to buy out the more successful ones. Eckstein (1977) has described the two largest factories she researched, a canning operation and the nation's largest chocolate factory, before and after their sale to U.S.-owned transnational corporations in 1971. The foreign firms, while modernizing administration, retained the old hiring patterns and paternalism wherever possible. Machado da Silva (1978) has discovered similar patterns of extensive use of unskilled labor by big industry in Brazil's urban slums, as has Nun (1978) in the case of Argentina's automotive industry.

The growing proportion of Mexico's "economically active population" engaged in the services or tertiary sector (43 percent in 1979, according to the national Budget and Planning Secretariat) has led many observers to suppose that this is where most of the immiserated go when they gain employment. Yet this supposition is shaky at best, because many of the immiserated do not appear in these statistics on the "economically active population." The growth in services (financing, wholesaling, and the like) reflects real demand generated by industrialization. Case studies indicate that although many of the poor do become involved in services of various kinds—for example, one of every five employed women in Mexico City is a domestic servant, and there are over sixty thousand girls from 8 to 14 years of age engaged in low-paid household labor—a much larger percentage become involved either in productive activities such as sweatshop or factory labor or in ostensibly "independent" commercial activities for the purposes of capital accumulation (though not their own).

Once again, now as shopkeepers, stall "owners," or street vendors (there were three million street vendors in the Federal District in 1980), a petty-bourgeois appearance masks a proletarian reality. Reproduction of the labor force includes reproduction of categories of labor, a process directly related to the circulation of capital and the realization of surplus value (Singer, 1975). Many of the 1.25 million small commercial enterprises tabulated by the National Chamber of Small Commerce are marketplace operations engaged in by the urban poor. As Chamber president Juan Rodríguez Salazar is reported to have said, "He who is without work in this country immediately engages in petty commerce." The same report (Uno Más Uno, November 14, 1979) cites figures of the Budget and Planning Secretariat that show "traditional and atomized commerce" in 1978 as constituting 80 percent of commercial enterprises but accounting for only 9.6 percent of invested capital, 6 percent of total sales, and 7 percent of "value added," while employing 46.4 percent of the 2.5 million people working in the commercial sector. Atomized shopkeepers and stall "owners" selling just basic food items account for 60 percent of small commercial establishments.

That these commercial ventures are actually subproletarian ones serving the interests of monopoly capital is illustrated by the hundreds of thousands of misceláneas, one-room stores selling tobacco, soft drinks, cookies, oils, and so forth. One study of misceláneas (Alonso et al., 1980) found that about one-third of the products sold were of foreign origin; that their prices were universally the same throughout the Federal District (that is, monopoly pricing); that over two-thirds of the goods were delivered direct from the factory; and that the average local store "merchant" worked 15 hours a day earning 45 percent less than someone receiving the minimum wage.

Monopolies control the distribution and sale of most other commodities (furniture, fruits, vegetables, chewing gum, and so forth) by immiserated street vendors, shopkeepers, market-stall operators, and hawkers. The millions of such subproletarians disguised as a petty bourgeoisie are dependent for their "business opportunities" on the Coordinating Federation of Small Industrialists and Merchants, a part of the National Confederation of Popular Organizations (Confederación Nacional de Organizaciones Populares—CNOP). The CNOP is the supposedly "middle-class" segment of Mexico's governing party, the Partido Revolucionario Institucional (PRI).

Thus, whether in production, distribution, or consumption of commodities, the immiserated are scarcely "on the margin of," or removed from, a national and international system of capital accumulation. In the case of Mexico, practically all their labor goes, directly or indirectly, to serve big distributors and businesses, at least in the realm of drinks, tobacco, processed or packaged foods, stationery and school supplies, and domestic articles, all of which have significant portions of foreign investment and monopoly domination. If a movement were carried through to improve the diet of the poor and reduce their consumption of superfluous or harmful products (snack foods, soft drinks, and the like), then, as Jorge Alonso has pointed out, a large number of people would be thrown out of work, because the immiserated "are amalgamated with those same capitalist enterprises, carrying out for them the labor of surplus-value realization, at the lowest cost and in detriment to their own subsistence" (Alonso et al., 1980: 245).

Capital accumulation is furthered not just in these direct ways. It is furthered politically by the false consciousness generated among many slum workshop owners and other "self-employed" that they are not proletarians because they own part of their means of production. Similarly, the workers hired by sweatshop owners tend to view their immediate "*patrones*" (bosses) as "the enemy" instead of the actual appropriators of the surplus value they produce, the capitalists who reside elsewhere.

The absorption of millions of unemployed and subemployed persons into petty economic activities such as those of the misceláneas or "self-employment" in conducting sweatshop, artisan, or craft activities for the purposes of survival atomize the immiserated and retard their development of a collective proletarian consciousness or a more organized political or class response to oppression. Such petty economic activities serve as a shock absorber in the class war. They also help reinforce the cycle of capital accumulation that relies on and regenerates the relative surplus population: low wages, low social productivity, the noncompetitiveness of Mexican industry internationally, and imperialism's economic power in Mexico. In terms of their overall relations of production, these "self-employed" and "self-exploited" elements are disguised proletarians whose "ownership" of a humble workshop or of a miscelánea masks their proletarian incorporation into a larger capitalist structure that appropriates the fruits of their labor.

IMPLICATIONS FOR MODE-OF-PRODUCTION AND CRISIS THEORY

In a country such as Mexico, the capitalist mode of production supplants noncapitalist modes of production; it does not merely "preserve" or "combine" them. While supplanting these other modes, it restructures many of their forms of economic activity in both rural and urban areas, reconstituting them and incorporating them, whether as noncapitalist or capitalist forms of activity, for the purposes of capital accumulation on an extended scale. Although unequal exchange between countryside and city is furthered to provide surplus transfers for industrialization, wage labor and the consumption of capitalistically produced commodities are extended throughout the society. Yet nonwage labor is generated anew by the capitalist accumulation process, as in the multiple activities of the immiserated.

Looked at from below, the unpaid "self-exploitation" of peasant, housewife, and child laborer in the subsistence production of a "domestic economy" or in the development of sweatshop or petty-trade activity constitutes an ever more common survival strategy of the immiserated and segments of the regularly employed proletariat. Looked at from above, capitalists accumulate by obtaining higher profits based on cheap or even unpaid labor.

Capitalists increase their profits also by revolutionizing the forces of production through technological innovation and transformation. Yet, as the constant portion of capital increases, the relative portion of capital (applied labor power, the ultimate source of value and profit) decreases—leading to a decline in the rate of profit and an increase in the relative surplus population. Capital structures and augments its exploitation of these laborers, whose high level of productivity every case study confirms. Capital realizes or obtains surplus value from their unpaid or low-paid work, especially through the mechanisms of markets, credits, subcontracting, transnational corporation assembly plants, and state organization or regulation. The entire process is socially reproduced through repeated cycles of employment and unemployment and increased use by capital of a dual labor market.

Noncapitalist forms of production and distribution offer up to capital cheap labor, raw materials, certain necessities of life for labor's reproduction, and even finished products. Superexploitation of labor develops and creates anew these noncapitalist forms of production and distribution, thereby helping to combat the tendency of the rate of profit to decline and also absorbing some of the unemployed and inculcating in them what Sol Tax once called a "penny-capitalist" ideology (Tax, 1963). Proletarianization of some into a modern industrial work force is thus accompanied by the proletarianization and immiseration of many into a relative surplus population that ends up overworked and, for the most, integrated into the accumulation of capital nationally and internationally.

The large numbers and ongoing reproduction of the immiserated in Mexico limit proletarianization as an all-encompassing process destined to "eliminate" noncapitalist forms of production or behavior, which, on the contrary, after being vastly reduced, are created afresh under new circumstances of the dominance and transforming impact of the capitalist mode of production. Widespread immiseration denies the benefits of proletarian status (such as social security) to millions while limiting those benefits won in hard-fought battles by the industrial proletariat. National capital of all sizes seizes upon superexploitation of the immiserated as a means of competing with more technologically advanced foreign capital. Yet monopoly capital, domestic and foreign, also benefits from—and pursues—direct exploitation of the immiserated.

Although in the countryside a depeasantization process is disguised by peasant production for subsistence (and, when possible, for capitalist markets), thereby limiting the completion of proletarianization in the modern sense, in the cities a process of proletarianization, subproletarianization, and immiseration is often disguised by petty-bourgeois forms of economic activity that actually generate surplus value or realize it on behalf of nonresident capitalists. Economic realities, including the tendency for outsiders to dominate business enterprises and to act as absentee creditors, landlords, and land speculators, continuously block all but the most dogged or lucky of the immiserated from actually entering the ranks of the petty bourgeoisie. In the meantime, many of the petty bourgeoisie are being driven by economic hard times into the ranks of the immiserated.

Objectively, proletarianization of the petty bourgeoisie is more common than petty-bourgeoisification of the proletariat, even though "penny-capitalist" activities are so widespread. Interview data in the studies previously cited suggest that subjectively almost everyone engaged in petty commerce and many workshop owners saw their situations as determined by class, social, and political forces beyond their control and had consciousnesses that mixed profit-making goals with subproletarian ones of hand-to-mouth survival and resistance to oppression. The large number of apparently (but not really) petty-bourgeois elements among the poor, especially in petty commerce, objectively serves capital accumulation and both sharpens and renews the growing gap between workers and appropriators. These activities are not simply fragmentary forms of participation of the relative surplus population in the production and reproduction of the capitalist mode of production; nor are they mere vestiges of earlier noncapitalist modes of production, destined to disappear. They are activities generated—and multiplying rapidly since the 1950s—by the type of capitalist domination and development Mexico experiences. They are part of the transition of an entire people in a short time into capitalism, as is illustrated, for example, by the fact that the immiserated now buy their clothing in the internal market instead of making it at home. More often than not, when the poor produce clothing for themselves they save neither money nor time. Instead, they sweat, produce, distribute, and, without getting a cent of surplus value from their labor, end up buying what they produce at inflated prices.

As with the assembly plants of the transnational corporations, which normally hire young women for a few years and then lay them off (Fernández, 1980, calls this "feminization" of the work force), rotation of labor rather than stable employment is often preferred by capital and enforced by the labor-union bureaucracy or other state institutions— because temporary labor keeps wages down, and no great skills are needed. In general, as Braverman (1974) and others have pointed out, modern productive technology and organization of the workplace have generated conditions that make possible capital's increasing dequalification (deskilling), fragmentation, rotation, and degradation of labor. These techniques for dominating labor are quite evident in Mexico, where, as capitalist transformation of agriculture proceeds and as transnational corporations and monopoly capital continue to migrate in quest of cheap and docile labor, the surplus-population-generating character of Mexico's capitalist development is reproduced afresh.

The automotive industry, the nation's fastest-growing industrial branch (13 percent annually in the 1970s), is a good example of this process. First establishing themselves in central Mexico's industrial cities, major foreign automotive and tire firms, which account for the nation's highest industrial wages, have recently begun moving from the Federal District and its environs to the northern cities of San Luis Potosí, Saltillo, Ramos Arizpe, and Ciudad Juárez, where the starting wages are from one-fourth to one-fifth those in the Federal District (Quiroz Trejo, 1980). (General Motors used this "runaway plant" technique in 1980 to debilitate the 106-day strike of 3,200 GM workers in the Federal District.) Thus the vicious circle of momentary employment, urbanization, and immiseration of the masses is intensified. An ever greater proportion of the populace is driven into the ranks of the relative surplus population, from which capital in turn obtains new cheap labor to exploit for a period before discarding it again.

Immiseration may be viewed not merely as a cause and effect of capital accumulation, but as a particular crisis strategy of monopoly capital. For example, in 1976, the devaluation of the peso by nearly 100 percent increased the costs of imported constant capital to the detriment of non-monopoly firms and the advantage of transnational corporations. Half a million workers were laid off, and three thousand small companies went bankrupt in the Federal District alone. The state's implementation of recommendations by the International Monetary Fund, letting prices move ahead of wages (that is, inflation in the name of combating inflation), permitted renewed capital accumulation at the expense of fixed- or low-income groups. The wages of workers as a percentage of the gross product from manufacturing dropped to under 15 percent in 1979. In residential areas with the highest working-class concentration, such as Mexico City, Guadalajara, and Monterrey, the 1980 loss in purchasing power of the minimum wage reached 40 percent or more. These events reflected a conscious strategy by monopoly capital, domestic and foreign, for extricating itself from the crisis it had generated. A large part of this strategy was directed at creating and benefiting from the immiseration of millions of Mexicans. Increasing labor's productivity through intensification of work or the extension of the work day, increasing the reserve army of labor through massive layoffs, letting real wages fall, augmenting the use of a dual labor market, and incorporating superexploited temporary workers are typical components of capital's immiseration strategy for bringing itself out of crisis (see Castells, 1978; Vuskovic, 1979).

The immiseration process is thus intensified by economic crisis. Yet, as Marx theorized and history has shown, "normal" accumulation and

crisis are interrelated parts of a necessary historical pattern in the reproduction and accumulation of capital. Immiseration and crisis are part and
parcel of capital accumulation.

A notable part of monopoly capital's crisis strategy is a growing direct
relation between monopoly capital or its financial institutions and "domestic economies." This is reflected in the World Bank's recently implemented strategy of "investing in the poor" (Bennholdt-Thomsen, 1980;
Lorenzen, 1980; Payer, 1980). Besides extending loans to subsistence
farmers, outgoing World Bank president Robert McNamara stated on
September 26, 1977, that the Bank planned similar programs for urban
slums, to create and aid "independent" producers in the development of
small artisanal enterprises, domestic workshops, small stores, and the
like. Tying some of the urban poor to international credit institutions is
one further step toward integrating them with monopoly capital, which in
turn accumulates new dividends in its realization of surplus value through
marketing of artisan products and sales of its own goods in the new stores
established.

Thus if it is inaccurate to call the immiserated "marginal," it is equally
misleading to call their labor "independent." In fact, they are necessary
to the capitalist mode of production in a social formation dominated or
heavily influenced by metropolitan capitalist development, that is, imperialism (see Cockcroft, 1979).

It is also mistaken to conceive of the immiserated as a separate
"class," given that their class characteristics are complex and transitional
and in a larger sense they are part of the general working class, rural and
urban, migratory and stably residential. They constitute the lower strata
of the working class, in main part the relative surplus population that today is emerging as the new majority on a national and world scale.

THE ROLE OF THE STATE AND
THE QUESTION OF CLASS CONSCIOUSNESS

Mexico's capitalist state plays an important role in regulating the immiserated, channeling their economic activity, concentrating them in
certain slums, and organizing their political behavior. The state does not
enforce tax or labor laws upon the labor-absorbing sweatshops; nor does
it crack down on the capitalists who exploit them. It tolerates a high degree of graft, deception, brutality, and police complicity in migratory
flows to the cities—and especially to the United States, where the surplus
value produced by the temporary migrants is transferred to foreign capital

that has not had to bear the costs of the production/reproduction of the migrant work force (Bustamante and Cockcroft, 1982).

A personalistic and paternalistic network of low-level officials in state organizations such as the CNOP takes steps to obligate vendors or store operators to appear at PRI political rallies or to line its own pockets. Failure to cooperate can lead to a local official's taking over a store or a vendor's route or placing another poor person in front of the store or stall selling one of the products at a lower price. There are less tactful means of enforcement as well, involving scandalous levels of violence and corruption (Eckstein, 1977). The state charges miscelánea "owners" various taxes, including one to the Department of Health, which periodically "inspects" the stores. Bribes are routine, and a gangland network of fake inspectors parasitically feeds off the many small shops. Lest the merchant feel too subproletarian, he or she is obliged to belong and pay dues to the National Chamber of Small Commerce. In such ways as these, the state serves as a labor-force regulator in processes not very different from the labor-union bureaucracy's control of jobs and wages for persons seeking employment with the transnational corporations' assembly plants (Fernández, 1980; Gambrill et al., 1981).

The state encourages a mock "petty-bourgeoisification" of the poor by organizing them into petty-trade networks, regulating their markets, and introducing land-distribution schemes and a minimal degree of public services to confirm them as "homeowners." It also sponsors or assists in occasional squatters' self-help, training, or services programs, but even these are designed to benefit capital—in this case, state capital. For example, the state has established "training centers" for Indian women who migrate to Mexico City (the so-called Marías) in which their home-craft skills are exploited to produce rag dolls, clothes, kitchen accessories, and the like. A token wage is paid them, and if they ask for more they are reminded that they are "students" being "taught skills." Their lovely products are sold to the residents of luxury suburbs such as San Angel and Polanco.

Generalizations about the political and ideological formation of the immiserated are difficult. They are located at the bottom of the class structure and yet in proximity to more class-conscious or politically motivated proletarian or petty-bourgeois elements. Their political direction is historically specific, depending on the social movements and political character of other groups in society, particularly the employed proletariat and petty-bourgeois constituencies.[2] Their economic suffering and vulnerability make them subject to a range of political responses, from massive revolt against the system to easy recruitment into the armed forces, police squads, and terror groups used by the capitalist state or employers to repress strikes and progressive political movements. Of all social movements, those of the immiserated are the least stable, consistent, and predictable. They are susceptible to religious superstition and mystification, and yet they also respond readily to the ideas and practices of the theology of liberation—as Iran's 1979 revolution dialectically illustrated (Cockcroft, 1980).

Eckstein (1977), Bartra (1978), and others have noted how the Mexican state uses populism and paternalism to channel peasant and urban-poor movements for social change into a fixation on owning a parcel of land or a dwelling, to regulate them and keep them as dependent as possible on state favors and penny-capitalist or paternalistic values. This develops in the subproletariat a tendency to support the status quo and to tolerate or even support capitalist and reactionary values. Eight years of literacy, cooperative, and political work in Netza showed Jesuit-socialist Martín de la Rosa that "the values of bourgeois ideology have been profoundly incorporated into the consciousness of a large share of the popular classes" (1979: 71). The left has until recently made little effort to win over the poor and has encountered many difficulties (for example, suspicion of "communists"), yet rightist groups such as the Partido de Acción Nacional (National Action Party—PAN) and the Partido Democrático Mexicano (Mexican Democratic Party—PDM) readily penetrate the neighborhoods and villages of the immiserated.

That the immiserated masses are nonetheless central to the capitalist productive process and a critical force in the struggle to replace it with a revolutionary socialist one is well recognized by the imperialists, who pour hundreds of millions of dollars into research projects designed to control or win over "the marginalized" at the same time as they arm repressive state apparatuses with the most sophisticated military technology for "crowd control," "counterinsurgency" and the maintenance of "internal stability." The objective basis of this policy is the superexploitation of labor and increased reliance upon the immiserated for capital accumulation, combined with the social explosiveness of the growing (international) reserve army of labor. These post-Second World War developments in the national and international accumulation of capital have generated a corresponding need for state intervention in the form of increased repression, militarization of society, and the technocratic bureaucratization of the organization of social groups—all tendencies manifested to one degree or another in Mexico. For example, the Batallón de Radio Patrullas del Estado de México (Radio Patrols Battalion of the State of Mexico—BARAPEM) regularly attacks slums and drives out new "land invaders" in greater Mexico City. It is an elite paramilitary organization founded specifically for this purpose. Its vicious and corrupt practices have led to a campaign by the poor and by national left-dominated coalitions to have it dissolved. In late 1981, the newly elected state governor promised to disband BARAPEM, but other elite paramilitary units are being developed.

That the immiserated are mobilizable for political change has been amply demonstrated, from the Algerian war against French colonialism to the Iranians' overthrow of the Shah, from the liberation movements of Vietnam, Mozambique, Guinea-Bissau, Angola, Zimbabwe, Nicaragua, and El Salvador to the urban community-organizing drives of Chile's *campamentos*, Cuba's Committees for the Defense of the Revolution and people's courts, and Mexico's National Coordinator of Popular Colonies. This last-named organization was founded in 1979 and brought together fourteen regional organizations, including Mexico City's Union of Popular Colonies, Monterrey's Land and Liberty Popular Front (fifty neighborhoods), and Durango's Popular Front (twenty communities). Typical of the numbers of people involved in such organizing endeavors are the 300,000 slum dwellers of the Committee of Popular Defense, operating in Chihuahua and Ciudad Juárez. In the 1970s, slum militants began to join forces with the student movement, the "democratic tendency" rank-and-file labor movement, independent unionists, and the "land-for-the-tiller" peasant movement. For example, in Mexico's Northeast there emerged in 1978 the Coalition of Independent Organizations for the Defense of Popular Economy, in which slum dwellers, workers, peasants, students, and housewives participate. Acapulco's Colonia Anfiteatro has mobilized marches of tens of thousands on the state capital, linking its "no eviction" demands against an urban "beautification" scheme to benefit the tourist industry with the call by students and faculty to "unfreeze" funds at the state university.

As such alliances have spread, the state has increased its repression. For example, in 1981 the leader of the Popular Defense Committee of Chihuahua was killed, and a large number of committee militants were wounded or arrested in Ciudad Juárez. Yet the proletarian colonies have stepped up their organizing and protesting activities. In many cities spontaneous marches and street barricades have rolled back bus fare increases or won other gains. A noteworthy example is the municipalization of public transport in the Federal District in the fall of 1981, a long-standing demand of leftist and popular forces. While by no means the only cause, the immediate provocation of the decree was the takeover and/or burning of buses in Netza by thousands of residents protesting recent fare increases. An important current development is the participation of organized segments of the urban poor, peasant groups, and independent or rank-and-file union democrats in the National Front Against Repression, a leftist-dominated coalition influential in Mexican politics.

By mid-1981, two National Meetings of Popular Movements had been held, during which programmatic demands were formulated for the self-named Movimiento Urbano Popular (MUP). The MUP denounced the state's National Plan for Urban Development as limited to dealing with colonias proletarias without touching the interests of the bourgeoisie. The state plan is accused of being "speculative and corporate," directed by the private banking and real-estate interests largely responsible for the urban poor's housing problems in the first place. The alternative offered by MUP to this "privatization of the economy" is continued struggle for self-management by the poor and development of the nascent multiclass coalitions to resist state repression and bring about genuine social change.

These popular political initiatives have caused the state to create parallel organizations, engage in widespread cooptation, and increase violent repression. For example, in Monterrey, a state-supported organization known as "Fomerrey" incorporates the PRI, the CT, the CNOP, and similar state apparatuses to combat the independent Land and Liberty Popular Front. The state has often succeeded in coopting leadership elements in militant slum movements, such as principal leaders of Mexico City's 2 de Octubre colony and of the Tepito "thieves' market" area. Prior to cooptation of the leadership, both neighborhoods had been noted for their high degree of self-management, from productive cooperatives to a system of self-policing.

Living conditions have become so desperate in Mexico (nationally, a million families without a roof and 40 percent of dwellings with only one room in 1980) that the immiserated are especially prone to cooptation as long as there are minimal payoffs by the state. Referring to "the irony of organization," Susan Eckstein concludes that many of the immiserated have shown great will and ability to organize only to find that their various organizations, through cooptation or government regulations, end up serving to "legitimate a regime, extend a government's realm of administration, and reinforce existing social and economic inequities" (1977: 101, 107). When cooptation fails, repression is used: from the burning of squatters' cardboard hovels to the assassination of leaders, including priests (as in Torreón and Chihuahua in the 1970s).

Yet cooptation is a tricky business. The coopted 2 de Octubre leader Francisco de la Cruz claims he was arrested in March 1981 because the PRI (which he had joined years earlier) had asked him to become a congressional deputy "in exchange for selling out my people." Most progressives thought he had already sold out; the 2 de Octubre colony was rife with divisions. More ominous for the urban poor, however, was what happened on the night of de la Cruz's arrest. Thousands of heavily armed police and military troops, many on horseback, stormed the 2 de Octubre colony in the early dawn hours and razed it to the ground. Sleeping children, women, old folk—all its inhabitants were herded into temporary camps pending "resettlement" of some of them in state-provided housing in another neighborhood. The savagery of the dawn raid had a political purpose. Although no longer strong, 2 de Octubre was the oldest (created in 1969) and historically most militant of the proletarian colonies. Its destruction served as a clear warning to all other slum dwellers, particularly the more politicized ones, that they could be next.

Nuevo Leon's governor soon threatened Monterrey's Land and Liberty Popular Front with a "2 de Octubre-style" action. The raid itself was not new. Such attacks have been going on for years. Leaders refusing to be coopted have often been shot, beaten up, or have "disappeared." The increased sending of troops and elite units such as BARAPEM to militant slum neighborhoods to kill, wound, or intimidate reflects the intensity of the class war raging in the daily lives of many Mexicans.

Recognition of the potential for political consciousness among the immiserated masses does not negate the reality of the obstacles to politicization in a corporativist, controlled, and regimented social formation such as Mexico's, particularly those obstacles differentiating strata, groups, or individuals within classes. The kind of stratification of exploitation that is often seen in the rural population also occurs in the huge urban slums and working-class neighborhoods of Mexico. Most of the day-to-day organizational networks among the immiserated masses are not politically progressive: petty crime syndicates, youth gangs, extended-kinship systems dominated by *macho* males, religious or social institutions such as godparenthood, the draining off of scarce resources by the celebration of holy days, deference to *el patrón* and related informal patron-client systems, the corrupt presence of the PRI and other state apparatuses, and so forth. Almost all these forms of organization and relative social cohesion constitute blocks to the political organizing of people for progressive change. Nonetheless, the potential for politicization must be emphasized precisely because too many bourgeois scholars and writers have emphasized these "quaint" or "fascinating" mechanisms of social cohesion, which in fact are integral parts of the larger despotism of capital holding millions of people down.

There are other reasons for noting the political potential of the immiserated. Those authors who have overemphasized the role of "dependency" in the development of metropolitan centers of capitalism at the expense of excolonial countries have generally blurred or even ignored the internal class dynamics of social formations in acute tension and flux such as Mexico's. Because these internal class dynamics are ultimately the most important, and because the immiserated are also affected by links to imperialism, it seems particularly appropriate to analyze them in a way that does not reduce them to either "hopeless dependency" or "hopeless marginalization." The class dynamics are far more complex, more deeply rooted in the internal economic growth and despotism of domestic monopoly capital, and more pregnant with hope and change than any vulgar dependency or marginalization theory would suggest. Misguided theory, like erroneous theoretical premises in general, usually leads not only to faulty political strategy, but also to one form of "hopeless" conclusion or another—in a word, to defeatism.

There is a growing recognition that progressive political parties, movements, and individuals suffer a long, uneven history of now underestimating, now overestimating working people, of talking down to them when not romanticizing them, and of generally failing to grasp the changing dynamics of their lives as the changes are occurring. These deficiencies of the past can be overcome only through two simultaneous efforts, each dependent on the other. First, the left must work at creating and diffusing a more accurate class analysis, for only such an analysis can reveal the strategic alternatives most likely to succeed. Second, political activists must work with the proletariat from a position of respect for people, which respect will deepen and spread as the struggle progresses.

From the viewpoint of slum dwellers, whose social movements have often been limited to struggles for public services, jobs, election of a local official, and so forth, lack of complete proletarian consciousness has serious political consequences. Similarly, those leftist organizers who attempt to instigate or support the slum political movements on the basis of a theory of "marginalization" are unlikely to achieve more than transitional goals bordering on charity, self-help, and mutual aid.

Only when both the working poor and left-wing organizers recognize the role of the immiserated not merely as a reserve army of labor, but as an activated arm of capital accumulation productive of surplus value or its realization can the burgeoning mass movement of the immiserated be linked to the fundamental dynamic of class struggle: capitalist owners versus urban and rural proletarians. Both theoretical reconceptualization and recognition of the new reality—expansion of ostensibly noncapitalist forms of economic activity for the purposes of resolving economic crisis or defraying falling profit rates, of reproducing the labor force, and of capital accumulation—can help integrate the present social movements of the poor with the main class struggle that ultimately will determine the future of all proletarians.

NOTES

1. Figures for 1960 show about one-third of Mexico's population "economically active," but for 1970 and 1980 the proportion is about one-fourth. In fact, many women, children, and aged who are economically active are not counted. They work as family labor and as shepherds, seamstresses, market-stall operators, servants, shoeshiners, and the like. Because of this tendency to undercount the economically active, those earning less than the legal minimum wage constitute a much larger percentage than the 60 percent of the work force reported in 1980. The truth is that almost everyone who can works. For most people, their very survival is at stake, and even with the entire family working they often cannot make ends meet.

2. Comments John C. Taylor (1979: 240): "In one period, sections of the semiproletariat can be attracted to socialist-based movements emerging from the urban and rural proletariat; in another period they could equally well rally behind a populist movement based on indigenous industrial capital and rural smallholders; in other periods, they can even aspire to the political ideologies of the urban petite-bourgeoisie. The contradictoriness and ambivalence of political movement among this large and powerful section of the proletariat must, therefore, be situated primarily within the place it necessarily occupies 'on the periphery' of production."

REFERENCES

Alonso, Jorge et al.
    1980 *Lucha urbana y acumulación de capital.* Mexico City: La Casa Chata.
Alonso, José Antonio
    1981 *Las costureras domésticas de Netzahualcóyotl.* Puebla: Universidad Autónoma de Puebla.
Barraesen, D. W.
    1972 *The Border Industrialization Program of Mexico.* Lexington, MA: D.C. Heath.
Bartra, Armando
    1978 "Colectivización o proletarización: el caso del Plan Chontalpa." *Cuadernos Agrarios* 1 (4): 56-110.
Bennholdt-Thomsen, Veronika
    1980 "Investition in die Armen: Zur Entwicklungsstrategie der Weltbank." *Lateinamerika: Analysen und Berichte* (Berlin) 4.
    1981 "Marginalidad en América Latina: una crítica de la teoría." University of Bielefeld. (unpublished)
Braverman, Harry
    1974 *Labor and Monopoly Capital.* New York: Monthly Review Press.
Bustamante, Jorge A. and James D. Cockcroft
    1982 "Unequal exchange in the binational relationship: the case of immigrant labor,"

in Carlos Vásquez and Manuel García y Griego (eds.) *Mexican-U.S. Relations: Conflict or Convergence.* Los Angeles: UCLA Chicano Studies Research Center.

Cardoso, Fernando Henrique
1971 "Comentario sobre los conceptos de sobrepoblación relativa y marginalidad." *Revista Latinoamericana de Ciencias Sociales* 1 (2): 57-76.

Castells, Manuel
1975 *La cuestión urbana.* Mexico City: Siglo XXI.
1978 *La teoría marxista de las crisis económicas y las transformaciones del capitalismo.* Mexico City: Siglo XXI.

Cockcroft, James D.
1979 *El imperialismo, la lucha de clases y el estado en México.* Mexico City: Nuestro Tiempo.
1980 "On the ideological and class character of Iran's anti-imperialist revolution," in Georg Stauth (ed.) *Iran: Precapitalism, Capitalism, and Revolution.* Saarbrucken/Fort Lauderdale: Breitenbach (Reprinted in *Review of Iranian Political Economy and History* 4 [Fall 1980] and [Spring 1981]: 1-26).
1983 *Mexico: Class Formation, Capital Accumulation, and the State.* New York: Monthly Review Press.

Cornelius, Wayne
1975 *Politics and the Migrant Poor in Mexico City.* Stanford, CA: Stanford University Press.

Eckstein, Susan
1977 *The Poverty of Revolution: The State and the Urban Poor in Mexico.* Princeton, NJ: Princeton University Press.

Fernández, María Patricia
1980 "'Chavalas de Maquiladora': a study of the female labor force in Ciudad Juárez' offshore production plants." Ph.D. dissertation, Rutgers University.

Frank, André Gunder
1978 "Super-exploitation in the Third World." Prepared for the Conference on Underdevelopment and Subsistence Reproduction in Latin America, University of Bielefeld.

Gambrill, Mónica-Claire et al.
1981 *Maquiladoras.* Mexico City: Centro de Estudios Económicos y Sociales del Tercer Mundo.

González Casanova, Pablo
1965 *La democracia en México.* Mexico City: Siglo XXI.

Iglesias, Maximiliano
1978-1982 *Netzahualcóyotl: testimonios históricos* (3 vols.). Mexico City: Taller de Impresiones Populares.

Kowarick, Lucio
1975 *Capitalismo e marginalidade na America Latina.* Rio de Janeiro.

Lorenzen, Hannes
1980 "Investment in the poor: a World Bank project in Mexico." Rome Declaration Group. Zürich. (mimeo)

Machado da Silva, Luiz Antonio
1978 "Lower-class life strategies: a case study of family and work in Recife's metropolitan area." Ph.D. dissertation, Rutgers University.

Margulis, Mario
1980 "Reproducción social de la vida y reproducción del capital." *Nueva Antropología* 13-14 (May): 47-64.

Marx, Karl
    1967 *Capital*, Vol. 1. New York: International Publishers.
Meillassoux, Claude
    1977 *Mujeres, graneros y capitales*. Mexico City: Siglo XXI.
Moctezuma, Pedro and Bernardo Navarro
    1980 "Clase obrera, ejército industrial de reserva y movimientos sociales urbanos de las clases dominadas en México: 1970-1976." *Teoría y Política* 1 (October/December): 53-72.
Nun, José
    1969 "Superpoblación relativa, ejército industrial de reserva y masa marginal." *Revista Latinoamericana de Sociología* 5: 178-237.
    1978 "La industria automotriz argentina: estudio de un caso de superpoblación flotante." *Revista Mexicana de Sociología* 40 (1) 55-105.
Osorio Urbina, Jaime
    1975 "Superexplotación y clase obrera: el caso mexicano." *Cuadernos Políticos* 6: 5-23.
Padilla, Cristina
    1978 "Maquiladoras de Santa Cecilia: ¿marginadas o asalariadas?" Tesis de Licenciatura, Universidad Ibero-Americana.
Paré, Luisa
    1977 *El proletariado agrícola en México*. Mexico City: Siglo XXI.
Payer, Cheryl
    1980 "The World Bank and the small farmer." *Monthly Review* 32 (November): 30-46.
Perlman, Janice
    1977 *O mito da marginalidade*. Rio de Janeiro.
Quijano Obregón, Aníbal
    1977 *Dependencia, urbanización y cambio social en Latinoamérica*. Lima: Mosca Azul.
Quiroz Trejo, José Othón
    1980 "Proceso de trabajo en la industria automotriz." *Cuadernos Políticos* 26: 64-76.
Rosa, Martín del la
    1979 *Promoción popular y lucha de clases: análisis de un caso, Netzahualcóyotl*. México: Taller de Impresiones Populares.
Singer, Paul
    1975 *Economía política de la urbanización*. Mexico City: Siglo XXI.
Tax, Sol
    1963 *Penny Capitalism*. Chicago: University of Chicago Press.
Taylor, John G.
    1979 *From Modernization to Modes of Production: A Critique of the Sociologies of Development and Underdevelopment*. Atlantic Highlands, NJ: Humanities.
Touraine, Alain
    1977 "La marginalidad urbana." *Revista Mexicana de Sociología* 34 (4): 1105-1141.
Vuskovic, Pedro
    1979 "América Latina ante nuevos términos de la división internacional del trabajo." *Economía de América Latina* 2 (March): 15-28.

PART IV

RURAL SECTOR, AGRARIAN REFORM, AND PEASANTRY

10

Collective Agriculture and Capitalism in Mexico

A Way Out or a Dead End?

by
Rodolfo Stavenhagen*

Land reform has played an important political, social, and economic role in the history of Mexico over the past fifty years. During that period, over 70 million hectares have been transferred from the large estates to circa 3 million peasant beneficiaries. An important innovation in the land reform process has been the institution of the *ejido*, a land-holding unit that has become the basis of different kinds of cooperative farming, carried out under government auspices and control.

The ejido was created by law to satisfy the demands of landless peasants who had seen their communal village lands eaten away by the expansion of the large agricultural estates during the last part of the nineteenth and the beginning of the twentieth centuries, or who were attached to these estates as servile labor. Ejido lands have been given to rural communities whose members satisfy certain legal requirements. An ejido is a communal tenure to which members have usufruct rights, usually in the form of an individual plot of land. By 1970, there were over 23,000 ejidos in Mexico, possessing 50 percent of the total agricultural land surface of the country. The term *ejido* refers both to such communal lands and to the community of peasants who own them. The ejido as a social institution has its own structures: the general assembly, a three-member governing board, a vigilance committee, and, under certain circumstances, a collective credit society.

Ejido holdings are divided into agricultural land, which may be farmed individually, and nonagricultural land (pastures, woods, and other kinds), which may be exploited only communally. The largest number of ejidos in the country are indeed farmed individually. The ejido plot holder is in fact a small, individual farmer. In most cases, his plot of land

---

*Rodolfo Stavenhagen is an Investigador in the Centro de Estudios Sociológicos at the Colegio de México (Mexico City), President of the Academía Mexicana de los Derechos Humanos, and President of the Facultad Latinoamericano de Ciencias Sociales (FLACSO).

is too small for him to obtain from it sufficient income, or to find on it full employment. Many ejido farmers buy additional land, if they can afford it, or else work part time on larger privately owned holdings or emigrate temporarily to seek employment in the cities or as agricultural laborers in the United States. A recent study in Mexico showed that fully 84 percent of all ejido plots can be classified as infrasubsistence or subfamily farms, that is, they are too small to provide full employment and an adequate income for a peasant family. To be sure, among privately owned farms, 85 percent fall into the same categories.

The constitution of ejidos is a lengthy and complicated administrative process. It begins when a group of legally qualified cultivators formally asks for land, and ends, after a presidential decree establishing the ejido, with the topographic delimitation of each individually assigned agricultural plot, and the distribution of individual usufruct titles to each of the plot-holders. In fact, most of the land reform beneficiaries (*ejidatarios*) have never received such individual titles, and only half of the 2.5 million beneficiaries over the years possess a provisional agrarian-certificate accrediting their right in ejido land without specification as to a particular plot. The other half does not enjoy even these certificates. The reason for this anomaly is partly to be found in administrative delays, but also in the fact that individual ejido titles can only be handed out if the ejido plot actually is of the minimum size required by the law. In most cases, however, the ejido plots that have been distributed are smaller than the legal minimum as a result of peasant pressures on insufficient land. Thus the majority of ejido farmers do not enjoy security of tenure; many observers regard this as one of the main obstacles to the development of ejido agriculture.

A survey of the files in the Ministry of Land Reform showed that on the average the administrative process of land distribution from the initial request to the final distribution of individual titles (in the few cases in which this final stage has indeed been reached) took thirteen years. The process from initial request to provisional occupancy (that is, when the beneficiaries may begin to cultivate the land) took on the average over five years. Many ejidos have been struggling for many years with the agrarian bureaucracy, at enormous cost to themselves in time, energy, and money, for the legal settlement of their land tenure rights. I am personally acquainted with ejidos where the process is still not completed after over twenty years and in which the second generation of beneficiaries has to carry on after their fathers.

The ejido has had an agitated institutional history. The original framers of the agrarian reform did not have a clear idea of the nature and characteristics of the institutions they were creating, and the role and functions of the ejido have changed over the years. At first, the ejido was merely a response to the political pressures and the land hunger of the peasants. It was thought that small ejido plots for subsistence agriculture would complement the estate workers' meager salary. During the 1920s the ejido was considered a transitional tenure form that would help train uneducated peasants in the management of farms, before they could "graduate" as full-fledged free-holding owners. Ejido tenure was conceived as a protective device against the renewal of land concentration in the hands of the *hacendados*, as had occurred during the decades preceding the revolution of 1910. It was not until the 1930s that it was recognized that the ejido had come to stay, and that the first systematic efforts were made to develop ejido agriculture on its own. During the Cárdenas administration, the first prosperous commercial plantations were expropriated *in toto* and handed over to their workers. Before that time only marginal parts of haciendas had been redistributed to petitioning peasants, without fundamentally affecting the large estate economy.

Indeed, it was never the purpose of the land reform policy to abolish private landownership, or even estate agriculture as such, but rather to develop a small peasant economy, either on the basis of individual freehold or collective ownership, as an escape valve for political unrest and an economic safety cushion. To be sure, the ejido has been the object of passionate, and sometimes, violent, political struggle. Many estate-owners considered the ejido a communist attempt to subvert the free enterprise and private property system. At the same time, radical proponents of the land reform have always seen in the ejido the possibility for the socialist transformation of Mexican agriculture. Others have argued that the straitjacket of ejido tenure imposes a feudal-like restruction on the dynamic agriculturalist's prospects for individual progress, and subsidizes the lazy and inefficient cultivator.

The fortunes of the ejido have thus reflected the changing political winds and government policies over the past five decades. The minimum legal size of the individual ejido plot has been raised several times, from 4 hectares of seasonally watered land or its equivalent in other kinds of soils (Law of 1922) to 20 hectares (constitutional amendment to Article 27, of 1946). The result has been that the ejidos in different parts of the country possess very unequal resources. Less than one-fourth of the 45 million hectares of ejido lands consist of cultivable soil. Almost half is made up of pastures, less than one-fifth of wooded areas, and almost 15 percent is classified as totally unproductive.

In 1960, the average ejido plot had 6.5 hectares of cultivable soil. But almost half of all ejidatarios possessed on the average less than 4 hectares of arable land, whereas only 15 percent enjoyed plots of more than 10 hectares. Regional variations are great. The smallest plots are found in the densely populated central area of Mexico, whereas some of the larger ejido farms are to be found in the newly irrigated areas of the northwest.

Ejido plots may not be bought or sold, mortgaged, rented, or transferred under any other form, except in particular cases stipulated by law. These restrictions have been designed to prevent renewed concentration of landownership in a few hands and to protect the land reform beneficiary and the ejido community as a whole from loss of land. Unless he cultivates it himself, the ejidatario may lose his rights in his plot, and these may be attributed to someone else by the ejido authorities.

Despite the legal precautions with which the ejido plot has been surrounded, the real situation is far from ideal. The renting of ejido land to outsiders, the downright sale of such land in contravention of the Constitution, the concentration of a large number of ejido plots under the management of one individual farmer, be he an ejidatario or an outsider, all this has been occurring for years, and the agrarian authorities have been unable and/or unwilling to stop it.

The rental of ejido land (which is contrary to the agrarian legislation and the spirit of the agrarian reform) has only been possible because, except in some areas (to which we shall return below), the ejidatorios who received the land were not provided with the institutional supporting services that would have permitted the ejido to develop as a dynamic institution, and hold its own against private capitalist farming. The lack of government support in most cases either condemned the ejidos to subsistence farming or has permitted the internal corruption that, linked to outside interests, has weakened the ejido as an institution. Some of the complex issues involved in this question will be further discussed below.

Agricultural land in the ejidos may also be cultivated collectively, when circumstances so require. During the 1930s a number of so-called collective ejidos were created, most of which have since disappeared. In recent years, the collective farming of ejidos has again become an issue, and public policy is once more inclined to favor such enterprises in the ejido sector, under certain conditions. Collective farming is no doubt the most interesting experiment of the Mexican land reform, and we shall devote a more careful analysis to some of its aspects below.

The ejido community, as a land-holding unit, is a political and legal institution. The maximum authority in the ejido is the assembly of ejidatarios, who elect an ejido board of three members for three-year terms. The president of the board is the key political personality in the ejido land tenure; deals with public agencies; manages the ejido's collective resources and properties; resolves individual tenure problems and conflicts, and so forth. He is not only accountable to the assembly of ejidatarios, but also to the federal agrarian agencies that may demand his removal in case he does not comply with official directives. An ejido president can play an important role in the development of his community, but he can also use his position for personal advantage. Unfortunately, the latter has been more frequently the case than the former, and there are innumerable cases in which ejido leaders have remained in power for many years and have obtained profits for themselves and their friends, disregarding the community's collective needs. Often, they have been able to do so in agreement with outside economic interests and corrupt government officials. This situation has become so serious over the years that the new agrarian law of 1971 contains special provisos against the concentration of too much power in the hands of the ejido authorities.

Aside from technical, legal, and economic tasks, the ejido leadership also plays an important role in the country's political structure. They constitute the basic unit in the pyramidal hierarchical structure of the National Peasant Confederation (CNC), which was created by presidential decree in 1935 and which is one of the three main pillars of Mexico's ruling party (for over 40 years), the PRI. Through its dependence on various official agencies for a large number of necessary services and on the official party structure for political support and control, the ejido finds itself well integrated in a tight network of bureaucratic relationships and control, which has not been the most efficient way of furthering the ejido's social and economic development.

Aside from the fundamental problem of land tenure, the national government early recognized the need for institutional support to the ejido sector, particularly with regard to the organization of production and the key question of agricultural credit. A national agricultural credit bank was established in 1926, but it operated principally with medium-sized and large private owners. Therefore, in the same year, a number of regional ejido credit banks were created, but they also did not operate satisfactorily. Agricultural credit laws were passed in 1931 and again in 1934, and the latter was modified substantially several times. Finally, a new agricultural credit law, still in operation, was passed in 1955. This vigorous legislative activity in the field of agricultural credit reflects the complexity of the problems involved and the difficulties in setting up an adequate functioning system.

Now, a number of governmental credit institutions service the agricultural sector, and a National Ejido Credit Bank was specially designed to provide credit to the ejido sector. Ever since its inception, this bank has not only looked after the financial aspects of ejido credit, but in some areas it has participated actively in the organization, administration, and supervision of new productive units that the agrarian reform set up. Particularly in its early years, the Bank played an important organizational role as a complement to the land distribution process. In later years, however, changing government policies vis-à-vis the ejidos as an organization, forced the Bank to limit its activities to providing credit at the local ejido level.

Two other official credit banks have served nonejido agriculture. There has been much duplication and little coordination among these institutions. For this reason, the federal government decided to merge them into a single National Agricultural and Livestock Credit Bank late in 1974. The Bank's credit is not provided directly to the ejido as a whole, but rather to a local Credit Society composed of individual ejidatarios who are collectively responsible for the credit they receive. At the beginning, these societies were required to have at least 51 percent of an ejido's membership, with a minimum of 15 members. Later, local societies could be established with a minimum of 10 members, and several societies were allowed within a single ejido. So-called solidarity groups of fewer than 10 members were also entitled to official credit but they lacked the stability and the legal protection of the credit societies. In 1969, slightly over 7,000 ejido credit societies were in operation, with a total membership of approximately 250,000 ejidatarios, a figure well below the all-time high of almost 400,000 ejidatarios who received credit from the Bank in 1937 at the height of the land reform process. The quarter of a million ejidatarios who received official bank credit in 1969 represents only about one-tenth of the total number of land reform beneficiaries.

The bank's credit has served principally for short-term operating expenses, rather than to finance the ejido's capitalization. By banking standards, only a handful of ejidatarios are "credit risks," so the Bank has concentrated on those ejidos that are economically successful. Still, due to corruption, mismanagement and top-heavy administration, the Bank has suffered considerable losses over the years. Between 1936 and 1961, only 73 percent of all credit was recuperated, signifying a loss of over 2,500 million pesos. Early in 1973, Mexico's president decreed that all outstanding debts to the official agricultural banks were to be condoned. The great majority of ejidatarios, having been qualified as "poor credit risks," are completely marginal to the official banking system. Not having access to private bank credit either (because their land cannot be pledged as collateral), these marginal ejidatarios are victims of local usurers and moneylenders, or lack any kind of financing altogether.

The extreme polarization of agriculture in Mexico in recent decades and the increasing impoverishment of great masses of peasant population has forced the government to take a new, hard look at the rural scene. This has led to a reappraisal of the land reform process and to new impetus being given the ejido as a social and economic institution. It has become clear that the doling out of tiny plots of soil to landless peasants is no long-term solution. Small peasants cannot improve their standards of living without ample institutional support, modern inputs and a modicum of so-cial and economic organization, particularly when the mechanics of the capitalist system tend to push those who do not "make it" ever further down the income scale. The present administration in Mexico is empha-sizing land reform anew and is actively engaged in the economic organi-zation of the ejido sector. Many activities are now being carried out collectively or cooperatively, and within the past three years 5,000 ejidos have become organized along these lines in some way or another. Consid-erable resources are being chaneled into the effort of organization, par-ticularly through the Land Reform Ministry (formerly the Department of Agrarian Affairs).

But the problems that these new efforts must face are many; it is not easy to overcome the resistances that have been nurtured over the past 35 years, and the political and economic structure within which they are tak-ing place is complex. The experience of the collective ejidos that were created by Cárdenas during the 1930s contain many lessons for today's issues. An analysis of what occurred then is useful for an understanding of the problems that the ejido institution faces today. In the following pages we shall review briefly a few cases of collective ejido organization.

COLLECTIVE FARMING IN THE LAGUNA[1]

The Laguna area covers approximately 8,800 square miles in the northern states of Durango and Coahuila. It is a semiarid basin in which agriculture, due to low and irregular rainfall, depends wholly on artificial irrigation. Before the Mexican revolution, the area was covered by a small number of large haciendas devoted partly to livestock and partly to the cultivation of cotton and grain on irrigated land. By the fourth decade of this century, the Laguna was one of the principal commercial farming areas in the country. About 200,000 hectares were watered yearly, and 35,000 agricultural workers labored permanently or seasonally on the estates. Early in 1936, an acute labor conflict opposed the militant agri-cultural labor unions and the estate owners, who refused to comply with the labor provisions of the Constitution of 1917 and the Federal labor code of 1931. To avert a general strike that would have caused consider-able economic losses in the area, the federal government decided to apply the agrarian legislation and carry out a far-reaching land reform in the region. President Cárdenas and his cabinet moved into the Laguna area to supervise the land distribution themselves. Within a few weeks, two-thirds of the agricultural land of the area, almost 150,000 hectares, had been expropriated and handed over to 35,000 peasants in 300 new ejidos. Each ejidatario-operator received four hectares of "irrigable" land, about one-tenth of the average size of the private holdings that remained in the hands of about 1,700 private landowners. In fact, however, the ejidatarios have never been able to water the land fully due to limited and diminishing hydraulic resources, and, over the past twenty years, every ejidatario has only been able to irrigate one-fourth of his plot (one hectare), the rest being useless for agricultural purposes.

Given the particular characteristics of large-scale commercial cotton farming, and the problems involved in irrigation, the government, in agreement with the peasants, decided to organize production in the ejidos collectively. Most of the ejidatarios became members in collective credit societies that were financed by the Ejido Bank. At the beginning, the Bank played a very important organizational role in providing technical assistance, advice on organization and management of the credit society, vocational training, marketing, and so forth. The collective ejidos flourished. After a slight initial decline in total output, agricultural production rose sharply, and the peasants' personal income increased considerably when compared to the income of the hired laborer. An institutionalized "Social Fund" in every ejido provided collective services and part of the ejido's profits were regularly reinvested. The peasants pooled their agricultural plots and worked the land collectively, according to the technical criteria that the irrigation system required and under supervision of the Bank's specialized personnel. The ejido credit society became the nucleus of the community's organization.

A number of regional cooperatives (composed of groups of local credit societies) soon began operating cotton gins, power plants, agricultural machinery centers, and internal railroads. Later, a regionwide Central Union of all credit societies also took over purchases and marketing for its members. The idea was that the Central Union would eventually manage the ejido's interests and the Bank would recede into a secondary supportive role. Peasant participation in the Union was high, and their level of mobilization and social conscience promised further success and development.

Nevertheless, a number of serious initial problems were not solved immediately, and they created a situation that, in conjunction with outside factors, contributed to the eventual decline and disintegration of most of the collective ejidos. In the first place, the lack of water imposed serious limitations to agricultural development. No matter how efficiently farmed, an average of one irrigated hectare of cultivable land per ejidatario was simply insufficient to enable the land reform beneficiaries to raise their levels of living substantially by agriculture alone. Second, at the time of land distribution a large number of agricultural laborers were present in the area, many more than the permanent labor force that the haciendas required. Over and above the 15,000 resident workers, there were another 15,000 seasonal migrant workers and yet another 10,000 strike-breakers whom the estate workers had brought into the region. All in all about 35,000 workers received land, many more than could be productively incorporated into the new agricultural units. Very soon a problem that was to become much more serious over the years made its appearance: underemployment. The rational and efficient exploitation of the new land units hardly required that much labor, and the new agricultural economy that arose was not able to absorb this problem. Rural unemployment created internal strife within the ejidos and fed the growing corruption that spread through the new organizations. Furthermore, the mechanics of land distribution itself did not allow for the emergence of optimum agricultural units. The estate owners were allowed to retain 150 hectares each of their best land, at their own discretion; the legal provision that ejidos could only receive land from excess hacienda lands that lay within a radius of seven kilometers from the peasant community that requested the land-grant; the speed and lack of planning with which the whole process took place due to the political pressures that had forced the government to act quickly (not only in order to satisfy the demands of the workers, but also in order to prevent the estate-owners from organizing an effective opposition); all of this resulted in an irregular mosaic of bits and pieces of haciendas and ejidos that was not conducive to efficient administration and management.

More important in the long run, however, was the change in public policy after 1940, the year in which a new administration took over the federal government. The new government, and those that followed it, were ideologically opposed to collective ejidos. The Bank's role was severely curtailed; the peasant organizations were boycotted and attacked by officially sponsored rival organizations. The regional credit cooperatives were dismantled; the Central Union of credit societies was deprived of its economic functions and was attacked politically for being "communistic." Internal division in the collective ejidos arose and was fostered by the Bank and other official agencies. Ejido credit societies split up into a number of smaller "sectors" and "groups," some of which continued to operate collectively whereas others became simply credit cooperatives. Corruption, graft, and mismanagement became commonplace in the ejidos, many of whose leaders stood in collusion with dishonest bank officials. No official attempt to clean up the situation was made by the government for many years.

Economic problems came to aggravate the political and social situation. Due to diminishing water levels, the number of irrigated hectares fell from 170,000 in 1936, to an average of 120,000-140,000 in recent years. At the same time, the agricultural labor force doubled to almost 90,000 in 1960, which means that more than half are landless agricultural laborers among whom the rate of under- and unemployment is high.

Still, despite all of these problems, the collective ejidos of the Laguna area (or what remains of them) have demonstrated surprising economic success under the circumstances. A recent survey of credit societies shows that the cooperative ejidos performed better, on the average, than individual ejidatarios working on their own, on such items as total output per ejidatario and output per hectare. This is particularly valid for the ejidatarios who cultivated smaller irrigated plots (under two hectares). Furthermore, the ejidatarios' income was considerably higher than that of the agricultural laborers in the area, even when considering full employment (which is not the case for most of the workers).

In recent years, as an answer to the region's needs and to increasing peasant demands, the government has again supported the collective organizations, particularly in connection with plans for the diversification of economic activity, such as the introduction of livestock, and the establishment of vineyards and other cash crops. Likewise, in order to raise productivity, it has fostered a "rehabilitation plan" whereby new irrigation works are to be carried out and ejido plots as well as private holdings are to be consolidated into new compact areas to rationalize the use of irrigation water. Together with increased extension services, credit, and technological assistance, this plan will require the cooperative organization of the ejidatarios. Nevertheless, unless new jobs are found for the landless, and unless the basic resource package per land-holding ejidatario is substantially raised and the bank and agrarian bureaucracies as well as the peasant organizations are cleaned of corruption, it is not likely that the overall situation of the Laguna peasants will improve substantially. The onus of change rests on the government and its bureaucratic apparatus; the ejidatarios themselves have shown over the years that given adequate economic and political incentives, they can do well with the collective ejido organization. Various examples of this are the small number of solid, well organized and functioning collective credit societies that have been able to resist internal strife and external pressures and have been economically and socially successful over the years.

A good illustration is provided by two credit societies that exist side by side within a single ejido, called Ana, in the Laguna Area. In this ejido, the original collective credit society that had been established at the time of land distribution had 82 members. A few years after its establishment, the ejido began having losses because some of its corrupt leaders mismanaged ejido funds in collusion with dishonest bank officials and the regional leaders of the official peasant organization. The rank-and-file ejidatarios who protested were ignored or harassed. Lack of internal democracy in the ejido left the management of the credit society in the hands of a small group over which the majority was unable to exercise any kind of control. Many ejidatarios decided to resign from the credit society and to try their luck on their own. This was facilitated in later years by the Bank policy of recognizing various credit societies within a single ejido community. By 1967, only eighteen members remained in the original society, which had by then accumulated a large amount of debts and possessed an average of $500 in capital per ejidatario. Since 1956, the society has had seven different leaders ("representatives" who deal with the Bank in the society's name). Five of these were removed by the Bank because of dishonesty, one was jailed for murder, and the other was also removed because he got into a fight with a Bank agent while drunk.

In 1946, 23 of the dissatisfied members decided to establish their own credit society (called "Sector 1"). At first they had to find private credit, because the Bank refused to recognize them. By 1951 they were able to return to the Bank, under the new policy, and since then they have been receiving an increasing number of loans not only for operating expenses but also for the perforation of irrigation wells, electric pumps and, more recently (1966), for the establishment of a collective stable for livestock. They regularly reinvested their profits. In 22 years they have had only two representatives, both of whom are highly regarded by the members for their initiative, dynamism, and honesty. Sector 1 also disaffiliated from the official peasant organization when it separated from the original society and affiliated with the politically independent, leftist Central Union. Internal democracy in Sector 1 is the rule, and the members are regularly kept informed of their accounts.

The contrast between the two groups in economic performance is striking. The remaining 19 members of Sector 1 cultivated 104 hectares, in 1966, as against the Society's 57 hectares, giving an average per ejidatario of 5.5 hectares, for the Sector vs. 2.7 hectares, for the Society. Capital investment per ejidatario in the Sector is over three times that of the Society. Distributed profits per member were about $230 in Sector 1 as against nil for the Society. Socially, Sector 1's members are a homogeneous, satisfied group, who are proud of their achievements, whereas the members of the original Society are dissatisfied, suspicious and torn by internal strife [Gómez Tagle, 1974].

The comparison between these two collective groups within the same ejido shows that although external factors definitely played a role in the disintegration of the original institution, internal factors (leadership, participation, more fibre, and so forth) are an equally important element. When the internal factors are solid enough, the group, as Sector 1 has shown, is able to withstand the external pressures successfully.

THE "GREEN REVOLUTION" IN THE STATE OF SONORA[2]

The arid plains of the state of Sonora in the northwest had been sparsely settled by a small group of large landowners who concentrated almost all of the irrigated land of the area, when the Cárdenas administration redistributed most of this property to the original Yaqui Indian owners in the late 1930s. By 1940, the ejido sector controlled 40 percent of all farm land in the state. In the following decades, the construction by the government of several dams and the drilling of hundreds of deep wells greatly increased the total amount of cultivable land, but most of this was appropriated by private landowners who were either descendants of the original *hacendados* of prerevolutionary days, or members of political families associated with the "revolutionary" governments. By 1950, the amount of irrigated land in the ejido sector had fallen to 17 percent.

In 1937, about 2,000 former day laborers were granted 17,000 hectares of irrigated farmland and 36,000 hectares of desert. Like their fellow beneficiaries in the Laguna region, they organized themselves into cooperative farms. But just as in the Laguna, these cooperatives did not fully incorporate the preexisting estates but rather chunks and pieces of different haciendas. This made efficient organization difficult from the start. The government provided credit for machinery and infrastructure as well as for operating expenses, and the ejidos proceeded to cultivate rice and wheat. The first years were difficult, mainly because of drought and plant disease, and yields as well as incomes remained low. In the early 1940s, due to irrigation works, the average amount of irrigated land per ejido member rose to fifteen hectares, and the ejidos began to pay back their debts to the official bank. Collective organization of production has never been able to provide full employment to all of the ejido's members, and, particularly in bad agricultural years, many ejidatarios had to look for wage-work outside of the collective. At the same time, competition for work produced rivalry and corruption in the internal distribution of tasks and labor within the ejido (aside from the distribution of profits at the end of the year to all members, ejidatarios received a salary for each day worked on their own farms). Still, during the 1940s the collective ejidos were able to save and capitalize considerably, as their investments in machinery and the accumulation of a "social fund" increased.

During the same decade, however, the change in public policy toward the ejido sector, to which reference was made before, was also reflected in Sonora. A concentrated official campaign for the division of collective ejidos into individual plots was launched by the government, and the co-operative experiments were described as being "communistic." The new local landowning elite, allied to governmental circles, had the greatest interest in "proving" that the ejido farms could not work and in weakening their structures. Internal strife in the ejidos was fomented by the government and its agencies, and the peasants' organizations were divided and torn apart. As in the Laguna, the Ejido Bank's policy was also modified. Medium-term credit for machinery and capital investments was withdrawn from the ejidos. The accounts of the collective societies were charged with all kinds of expenses that individual ejidatarios were exempted from. The Bank's role in institutional development was curtailed severely. The result was that the cooperative ejidos were thrown back on their own resources, and without federal support, suffering attacks from all sides, many of them soon disintegrated. Credit, marketing, and consumer spending were soon concentrated in the hands of a new, dynamic, and enterprising local merchant class that was able to make quick profits at the expense of the ejidatarios. Corruption spread like wildfire. The collective properties of the ejidos (machinery, livestock) were distributed or raffled among individual members who quickly sold what they received for a few pesos cash; or they were simply lost or stolen.

The main problem for the ejidatarios was credit. Just as an adequate supply of operating credit could ensure a good crop, a good sale, and a respectable income for the individual farmer, so the lack of it—or an excess of red tape in the official ejido bank—could break the bent of ejido farmers. Some ejidatarios were able to overcome these barriers and made sizable profits during the 1950s, the years of the agricultural boom. Most of them, however, were swept under by the new situation and have never been able to rise again. An easy way out for many ejidatarios was to rent their land to outsiders, which is forbidden by law, but which was tacitly agreed to by unscrupulous public officials. By 1958, one-third of the ejido land in the Yaqui valley was rented, and 38 percent of the ejidatarios were alienating their land. By 1962, it was estimated that 63 percent of the ejido land was being rented.

In 1953, the Ejido Bank for the first time provided new high-yielding wheat seeds to the ejidatarios as part of a national program to rapidly increase wheat production in the country. From one agricultural cycle to the next, the area planted with wheat in the ejido sector of the Yaqui valley almost trebled, from eight thousand to twenty-two thousand hectares. The green revolution was under way. In the end, however, the benefits for the ejidatario have been meager. To show why, I quote at length from an authoritative report:

> *The fact is that the ejido credit system made its clients the captives of the banking bureaucracy; they could not determine freely the amount of any input they would receive nor from whom it would be bought, nor at what price. Therefore employees of the bank did not find it necessary to dialogue with ejidatarios or to ask their consent when changes in methods of cultivation were to be made. This situation ensured that the institution of a costly new kind of wheat technology would almost certainly be detrimental, and even catastrophic, for the majority of the clients of the bank, although highly lucrative for bank officials and businessmen.*

At first, the ejidatarios only received the new seeds from the bank, but not fertilizers or insecticides. Using their traditional technology, they nevertheless managed to increase wheat yields slightly.

> *But then the bank began to supply clients with tons of fertilizers and insecticides, at a cost which frightened them, once again without any serious campaign to explain the necessity for the new products, and furthermore without an adequate period of training in the way the new inputs should be used. Goods were simply delivered to the ejidatarios' fields, charges made on the books of the bank, and each client left to decide what use he would make of his purchases. The complete abandonment of the small farmer in this critical moment was reinforced by the absence of an effective extension service. . . . The ejido sector was terribly impoverished by these developments. Cost per hectare of wheat, translated into credit with the Ejido bank, rose from around 200 pesos in 1945 to 1,000 pesos ten years later.*

Although a part of this increase can be attributed to a general rise in production costs, some of it resulted specifically from the new technology associated with the "green revolution." The report continues:

> *Costs were augmented during these years by an exorbitant overapplication of new inputs, freely agreed to (and in fact insisted upon, according to some informants) by the Ejido Bank. . . . It is likely that this startling waste of resources was intimately related not only to a lack of adequate criteria within the Ejido Bank, but also to the importance which technical advice from representatives of private companies began to take on at this time. . . . The most obvious result of increasing capital-intensive methods of wheat cultivation in an atmosphere of corruption and disorganization was a rapid and spectacular rise in ejido debts and since ejidatarios could never repay that debt in its entirety, a secondary effect was a heavy charge against the public treasury, through losses within the Ejido Bank. One might also see the process as the transfer of wealth from the ejido and*

the public sector to the private sector, through the forced provision of costly
inputs to captive buyers.

As the whole process of production was managed by the Bank, which kept each individual ejidatario's accounts and usually took a long time to distribute whatever income the farmer might in the end receive, many ejidatarios began to sell a part of their inputs, as well as their produce, on the black market, even though this simply meant increasing their debts to the Bank.

The field report continues: "All of these factors—inadequate technical assistance, disorganization, increasing debts, the sale of inputs and of the products of harvests in the black market—worked inexorably to lessen the competitiveness of the ejido sector as a whole in relation to the private sector of Sonoran agriculture." Yields in the ejido sector became increasingly smaller in comparison with the private sector.

By the mid-1960s, an estimated 80 per cent of the ejidatarios of the Yaqui
valley had abandoned control of their land, and had reconciled themselves
to receiving weekly or monthly rent payments augmented at certain times of
the year by daily wages received for working their own land. The final step
in the transfer of the benefits of the new technology from the ejido in the
private sector had been taken. Ejidatarios not only provided large land-
owners with cheaper inputs, and businessmen with extraordinary profits,
but they now also transferred the yield of their land to those who had the
capital and the knowledge to take it.

An exception to the general trend of the ejido sector in the Yaqui Valley has been the Quechehueca collective society. Here, as in the Laguna, a small group of closely knit, determined farmers, led by a dynamic, honest, and conscientious leader, has been able to buck the tide of ejido disintegration. This credit society consists at present of 28 members who work their 1,100 hectares collectively. All of them participate actively in their society's affairs and are at every moment well informed about their individual accounts. Internal democracy and participation is the rule. The society has a large social fund and invests in public services for its members. All members participate in the official social security plan and retired farmers receive pensions. The leadership has successfully fought off a number of official attempts to remove them from office, basing themselves on their record and the support of all members. They are also affiliated with an independent regional peasant organization that has been harassed for many years by the government and the official peasant associations.

In economic performance, the Quechehueca society surpassed the rest of the ejido sector consistently between 1955 and 1970. It adopted the new high-yielding wheat varieties and associated technology enthusiastically, but was unable to escape the general tendency of over application of insecticides and fertilizers and the general rise in production costs. The Quechehueca farmers were constantly in contact with a regional agricultural extension service, of which very few other ejidatarios in the area really took advantage. In contrast with other ejidatarios, the members of the Quechehueca society have not rented their land to outsiders; they have, however, increasingly used hired labor on their fields. They have been able to maintain above-average incomes from their farm work over the past twenty years, and their real income has increased persistently. Yet this has not all been fruitfully absorbed by the farmers. The new agricultural wealth of the 1950s led to a rapid rise in conspicuous consumption, increased consumer spending and indebtedness, and little personal saving and investment. Family expenditures rose considerably, particularly food, drink, and medical expenses. The farmers do not tend to grow their own food or keep animals for family consumption. Nutrition and health levels have apparently suffered in the absence of adequate family and home economic education.

Rising consumer expectations plus the difficulties inherent in any cooperative enterprise (particularly within an environment of capitalist accumulation) have put great pressures on the Quechehueca society over the years, and in 1971 it divided once again. The report already quoted concludes:

> *Thus the Quechehueca cooperative, one of the most promising experiments in ejido organization in the nation, has been increasingly undermined by the same tendency toward unwise personal spending which has brought the owners of most large private farms to the verge of bankruptcy. The collective society has, as noted above, suffered from some difficult technical and administrative problems: it has invested too much in machinery without taking adequate care of the investment; its expenditures on administration and "general" categories like contributions to political organizations have been high; its integration of the new technology has been incomplete. The latter problem is intimately related to the truly democratic nature of the society, which restricts its leadership to the pace of the majority, and to their ideas about how their fields should be worked. In addition, over the years, the society has lost its tradition of the importance of members' working their own land and has become an enterprise based on wage labor. . . . When the society began to break apart in 1971, the reasons for the general feeling of malaise were neither strictly technical nor administrative; they were the products of unrealistic rising expectation*

and uncontrolled commercial credit. Despite the excellent financial reputation of the society (better than many private farms) and its remunerative agricultural operations, the commercial debts of its members, reaching three quarters of a million pesos in 1971, were frightening. The feeling began to spread that one could make more money outside the society, working individually, like the small group of millionaire ejidatarios who have come to dominate the town. And in late 1971, 14 of the 41 members of the society—decided to strike out on their own. It is probable that the cleverest among them will indeed make more money than in the past; but if their intention is really to become wealthy, they can do so only at the expense of their weakest neighbors, and that will mark the end of the cooperative ideal in Quechehueca.

CAPITALIST AGRICULTURE AND EJIDO DISINTEGRATION IN MICHOACÁN[3]

In the state of Michoacán, in west-central Mexico, a low, semiarid hot valley locally known as Tierra Caliente, or valley of Apatzingan, has been the scene of a particularly instructive case of ejido development, for it has become a microcosm of all the problems that beset the agrarian reform and the ejido sector.

In 1938, after a period of labor strife, a large prosperous hacienda, Nueva Italia, was expropriated by the government and transformed into five ejidos the 1380 members of which were granted a total of 32,000 hectares, of which 2,600 hectares were of first-class soil with artificial irrigation. The rest consisted of pastures and unirrigated agricultural land. The capital equipment, buildings, and other installations of the hacienda were bought by the government for the peasants, who began operations with a two million pesos debt to the National Ejido Credit Bank.

It was decided that production would be organized collectively on the irrigated part of the ejidos; individual cultivation could be undertaken on seasonal land; the ejidatarios were to receive a fixed daily wage for work done and a proportional part of yearly profits; profits from special activities (such as a large and productive lemon grove) would go to the ejido's social fund; finally, foreseeing the already apparent problem of underemployment, a diversification of economic activities was planned. In fact, however, the organization of production and the administration of the enterprise was not basically modified. The Ejido Bank, in consultation with the local ejido leadership, took charge of all operations. Not all of the ejidatarios were able to work (and thus receive a wage) all of the time. Simultaneously, a small class of privileged ejidatarios, who had permanent administrative, specialized or supervisory jobs, began to look after their own interests. Corruption and favoritism were not long in coming, much of it fostered by Ejido Bank officials whose lowly salaries made them particularly prone to seek personal advantage from the collective farm's operations.

Nevertheless, the first years were an economic success. Profits were distributed, the ejidatarios' debt to the Bank decreased, and individual consumption rose considerably. Indeed, just as in the Yaqui valley, a spree of consumer spending, unchecked by any kind of meaningful investment or social planning in the ejido as a whole, weakened the community's initial potential for self-sustaining economic and social development.

By the second year of operations, fraud and larceny on the part of the ejido leadership and the Bank's officialdom were on the rise, and no serious attempt was made at any level to stop them. Soon corruption reached alarming proportions; everybody wanted a cut of the pie, and money ran freely. The ejido's solvency suffered, and much of its income was syphoned off for personal gain by corrupt officials. Production and productivity were also affected, and after a few years lower production and higher costs forced the ejido again into debt to the Ejido Bank.

Beginning in 1944, the single collective ejido credit society broke up into ever smaller production and credit units, each one of which continued to work collectively with the Bank. Internal democracy suffered; more and more ejidatarios wanted access to the lucrative leadership positions in the credit societies.

During the 1950s, massive government investments in irrigation works completely changed the agriculture of the region. Over 22,000 hectares of irrigated land were added to the agricultural surface of the Tierra Caliente, of which 45 percent fell to the private sector. The ejido of Nueva Italia increased its irrigated area by over 450 percent, each member being entitled to approximately 10 hectares.

Between 1950 and 1965, the cultivated area of Tierra Caliente almost trebled, and agricultural production rose accordingly. At the same time, an influx of migrants from other parts of the country produced a population jump from 22,000 to 88,000 in the twenty years between 1950 and 1970. The structure of agricultural production changed almost overnight. In 1954, cotton farmers from the North who were looking for new areas in which to expand their operations seized upon the favorable conditions in the valley, particularly due to expanding irrigation, and for the first time introduced the cultivation of cotton. Ten years later, almost 40 percent of the cultivated area and 70 percent of the irrigated area was planted with cotton.

The ejidos of Nueva Italia were ill equipped to adopt the technological, financial, and organizational innovations related to the cotton "complex." This new crop, for which there existed much demand and a high price in the market, was not the result of planned change by the ejido bank or other government agency, but was brought in by financially well-backed investors who began to rent private land in the area for cotton planting. They were soon able to establish two cotton gins and naturally turned to the fertile ejido lands to expand the area under cultivation.

By 1956, the internal disorganization of the collective ejido societies, stimulated by the corruption and inefficiency of the official agencies, led to the final breakdown and the distribution of the land in individual plots to each ejidatario. For some years a number of economic activities were still carried on collectively, such as a rice mill, the lemon grove, and the rather prosperous livestock operations. With the changeover to cotton, the rice mill fell into disuse; the lemon grove was rented out to a private operator and became seriously deteriorated. The ejido's cattle, which had been one of the pillars of prosperity in hacienda times and during the early years of collective organization, were also distributed equally among all members in 1957. Even though the assembly of ejidatarios had decided that the cattle should not be sold, but rather kept individually as part of the family economy, in fact within a very short time most ejidatarios had sold or gambled away most of the five head of cattle to which each had been entitled.

The parceling of ejido lands was not only the result of internal factors. As we have mentioned before, the new immigrant cotton entrepreneurs had avidly eyed the ejido lands from the beginning of their operations. It was obviously easier for them to deal with individual ejidatarios than with the complex structure of a collective ejido. It appears that highly placed government officials saw eye to eye on this score with the cotton capitalists. Two years after parceling had taken place, only one-half of the ejidatarios were actually working their land, and only two-thirds of these were receiving official credit. More than one-third of all ejidatarios were illegally renting their ten-hectare plots of irrigated land to other ejido members or to outsiders. Due to lack of instruments, machinery, credit, and technical know-how, most ejidatarios had to supplement their incomes by working off their farms.

Only a few ejidatarios were able to take up cotton cultivation on their own; the Ejido Credit Bank was unable fully to finance or provide technical assistance and institutional support for this new crop. The private investors were exerting pressure on the ejido holdings, and the rental of ejido plots increased sharply within a few years. It soon became necessary to "legitimize" these arrangements, and, in 1960, the federal agrarian department authorized contracts between the investors and the ejidatarios that appeared as an extension of credit by the former to the latter for the improvement of their land and the cultivation of cotton, but that in fact simply turned out to be a cover for the rental of ejido lands. The contract was revised, but not essentially modified, in 1963, and continues in force. In 1966, over one-half of the ejidatarios were renting their land, and only one-third were working their plots directly (with or without official credit). Most of those who rented their plots also worked as day-laborers on their own land for the tenant. As for the tenants, given the high initial production costs for cotton and the relatively rapid depletion of soil resources under this crop, they generally operate with no less than five ejido plots (that is, fifty hectares of irrigated land), and there are those who avail themselves of more than 300 hectares of ejido land.

The result of this development has been the concentration of high incomes in a small group of "investors" who take their profits out of the area and leave behind depleted natural resources; the continuing low standard of living of most of the ejidatarios, who are nevertheless a privileged group in comparison with the thousands of migrant cotton pickers who have drifted into the region and whose conditions of life and work are particularly depressing; the stagnation and decay of the ejido as an institution and the social and economic involution of the area's population.

AGRICULTURAL COOPERATIVES AND REGIONAL DEVELOPMENT IN TABASCO

The problem and relative failure of cooperative farming in those areas where collective ejidos were established during the 1930s dissuaded the government from further support of this kind of cooperation for thirty years. In 1971, a New Federal Land Reform Law was passed, and Book III of this law contains a number of guidelines for the economic organization of the ejidos. The present government is convinced that the cooperative organization of the ejidos is necessary to overcome the backwardness and poverty of millions of peasants in the country.

A recent and interesting experiment is taking place in the Chontalpa area of the state of Tabasco, in the humid, tropical lowlands of southeastern Mexico. In this area, the federal government, through a regional water-basin development agency, and with the financial help and technical assistance of the Interamerican Development Bank (IDB), began a large-scale investment program in 1966. About $60 million have been invested over the years in drainage, leveling of land, irrigation canals, road construction, and resettlement of population.

So far, 90,000 hectares of cultivable land have been cleared, and 5,000 peasants have been resettled in 22 new ejido communities. From the start, the federal agency organized agricultural labor collectively, under the technical and financial supervision of its own experts. Before the organization of the project, most of the peasants in the region were scattered in isolated hamlets and lived from subsistence agriculture. At present, they grow sugar cane, cocoa, bananas, rice, and other cash crops. They also own around 25,000 head of cattle.

The project did not get off to an auspicious start. Lack of adequate planning and foresight generated millions of dollars in losses due to wasteful investments. Miles of paved roads lead nowhere, and only a fraction of the land that was cleared by modern machinery is currently under cultivation. Insufficient and badly managed operating credit set production back time and again. No adequate agricultural research for tropical areas nor extension services were provided. Worst of all, the peasants did not take part in the planning and the decision-making processes and became completely apathetic toward the project, if not downright hostile.

In 1971, a concentrated effort at organization was begun. Ejido-assemblies were organized, new ejido bylaws were written, and the ejidos were asked to take major responsibility themselves in the development effort. The peasants became progressively convinced of the objectives of the project and began to respond enthusiastically. At present they take part actively in agricultural planning and economic organization. Agricultural labor is carried out cooperatively; several of the ejidos have cooperative pig and dairy farms; fertilizers and other inputs are bought collectively; and coconuts and bananas are marketed by the ejido cooperatives.

Early in 1973, the 22 ejidos joined to form a union of collective ejidos, which began handling the acquisition of inputs and the marketing of crops. It also owns a local bus line with five units. It has plans for further expansion including the establishment of a cooperative tractor station. The union's leadership is young and dynamic and appears to be completely devoted to the cooperative ideal. Local, state, and federal authorities give the ejidos support. Agricultural credit, although still insufficient, will likely be increased over the coming years. Above all, the ejidatarios now feel that this is their project, that they are participating, and that ultimately the success or failure of the regional program will depend on them. But government support at all levels is still indispensable, and unless there is continuity in this support over the coming years, the Chontalpa experiment may go the way of its predecessors.

CONCLUSION

The ejido land tenure system, designed as an alternative to private land-ownership, can be said to have slowed down the process of disintegration of the peasantry that usually accompanies the development of capitalism in agriculture. Indeed, the ejido was an attempt to recreate a peasantry in Mexico, mainly for political and social reasons rather than economic ones. However, it never became a real alternative to capitalistic agricultural development. Differences in the size of landholdings and differential access to economic resources and inputs have consistently placed the ejido at a disadvantage vis-à-vis the large agricultural entrepreneurs. Government policies in recent decades have tended to favor this polarized development of Mexican agriculture. Land reform policy must thus be seen simply as a complementary (albeit a politically indispensable) aspect of an overall strategy for capitalist agricultural development.

Does this mean that Mexican agriculture is divided into two independent, and even opposing sectors: a traditional small peasantry made up of ejidatarios and private smallholders, and a modern, dynamic sector of agricultural entrepreneurs? At first glance it might seem so, and the hypothesis might be put forward that as the Mexican economy develops so will the small peasantry become modernized and turn into that much sought after "rural middle class" that so many land reform-mongers set up as their ideal. A second look, however, reveals that the situation is more complex.

Within the peasant structure of the Mexican economy neither the ejido sector nor that of the private smallholders have any chance whatsoever of developing into middle-size family farms unless there occurs a radical transformation in agrarian policies and development strategy at the national level. And, even then, a country where still fully one-half of the labor force is in agriculture cannot achieve widespread agricultural prosperity unless and until a large part of this population has been absorbed into nonagricultural occupations. The process of industrialization in Mexico is basically non-labor absorbing, and the economic growth of recent decades has produced a large mass of low-productivity, low-income marginal labor in the urban areas. Rural emigration—which is a continuous flow—has simply transferred poverty and underemployment from the countryside into the cities.

Under these circumstances, the small ejidal and landowning peasantry plays a supportive role to the main centers of agricultural development. On the one hand, the peasant economy provides a minimum subsistence income to its members, at little cost to the national economy, and it helps to keep the process of rural-to-urban migration in check. On the other hand, it is unable really to increase levels of living substantially with the poor resources at its disposal and thus necessarily forces peasants to seek complementary sources of income elsewhere. It constitutes, thus, a reserve of labor not only for the larger agricultural farms but also for industry, construction, services, and so forth (for example, many members of ejido or smallholding families regularly migrate back and forth between their agricultural tasks and occasional nonagricultural labor whereby they obtain monetary incomes). This peasantry also produces staple crops not only for its own subsistence (thus allowing the larger farmer to supply the commercial circuits of the national and international markets), but also supplies its surplus products to local and regional markets. In sum, the small peasantry does not constitute a self-contained, self-sufficient agricultural sector. On the contrary, by providing cheap subsistence products and, particularly, cheap labor to the other sectors of the economy, it is actually contributing to the development of the national capitalist economy. Putting it another way, the surplus value produced by the peasantry plays an important role in the country's economic development. As long as labor does not constitute a scarce or expensive element among the factors of production, it is in the interest of the system to maintain a numerous but unstable peasantry from which it can draw its inexpensive labor force for the process of capitalist accumulation.

Clearly, the ejido institution has only limited possibilities within this framework. To be sure, a number of supportive government policies may strengthen particular ejido economies at any one time. There are even "model" ejidos that can be visited by interested observers. But, as the first three case studies discussed above have demonstrated, the ejido as a cooperative enterprise will generally be unable to break the framework of individualism, corruption, private profit-seeking, and exploitation that characterizes the wider society. The ejido cannot become a sociological and economic "enclave" within the framework of a society that collectively rejects it—despite political rhetoric to the contrary. The collective ejido in Mexico was born with the sins of the capitalist society upon it. It can function as an institutional alternative only if it manages to cut the umbilical cord that links it to the society that generated it. But this is of course impossible unless that society itself becomes totally transformed.

I do not, however, wish to end this paper on a note of total pessimism. Societies do not become transformed by themselves or through the use of a magic wand. Ultimately, human beings make their own history, and they do so not individually but in groups: as social classes, ethnic groups, nationalities, corporate entities, religions, political parties, and so forth. The ejido institution in Mexico can become the basic structure (but it is no more than a possibility) from which a politically mobilized peasantry could conceivably organize itself to press demands for structural changes in agriculture. At one time, in the late 1930s, it already had this possibility, but later developments, as shown above, altered its course. Yet if we accept that in politics nothing is ever permanent, then we may posit that the ejido—given adequate circumstances—could eventually reawaken as an institution from its present lethargy. The most recent changes in Mexico's agrarian policies may signal such a reawakening.

NOTES

1. The data for this section are taken from Eckstein (1973) and Stavenhagen (1970).
2. The material for this section is taken from Hewitt de Alcantara (1974).
3. This section is based on material in Barbosa and Maturana (1972).

REFERENCES

Barbosa, A. R. and S. Maturana
    1972 *El arrendamiento de tierras ejidales*. Mexico: Centro de Investigaciones Agrarias.
Eckstein, Shlomo *et al.*
    1973 *La experiencia colective en la Laguna*. Mexico: Centro de Investigaciones Agrarias.
Gómez Tagle, Silvia
    1974 *Organización de las sociedades de crédito ejidal de la Laguna*. Mexico: Centro de Estudios Sociológicos (Cuadernos de CES 8), El Colegio de México.
Hewitt de Alcantara, Cynthia
    1974 "The social and economic implications of large-scale introduction of new varieties of food grains." UNRISD, Geneva. (mimeo)
Stavenhagen, Rodolfo
    1970 "Collective farming in Mexico." in Rodolfo Stavenhagen (ed.) *Agrarian Problems and Peasant-Movements in Latin America*. Garden City, NY: Doubleday.

11

Capitalism and the Peasantry in Mexico

by
*Roger Bartra**

THE FAILURE OF TECHNOCRATIC POPULISM

During the last years of Luis Echeverría's administration, a political strategy was developed to get Mexico out of its agrarian crisis. This strategy, which I have called *technocratic populism* and which emerged under the aegis of state capitalism, collapsed noisily in 1976. It is useful to analyze this situation in order to extract from it some lessons.

In the face of the despotic and corrupt power of the old *caciques* (local chieftains), supported by the most inefficient and parasitic sectors of the rural bourgeoisie, an incipient alliance was attempted between the interests of large monopoly capital, both agroindustrial and agrocommercial, and those of the middle agrarian bourgeoisie:

> *The interests of state capitalism found an ally in certain sectors of the middle agrarian bourgeoisie and challenged the old structure of mediation—the "old populism," the control exercised over peasant communities. During the last years (1970-1973), this tendency sought without success to build an alliance with the agrocommercial and agroindustrial factions of the rural bourgeoisie, an effort which gave birth to a kind of technocratic populism [Bartra, 1974: 169].*

For this alliance to be politically viable it was necessary for the political bureaucracy to mobilize a popular peasant base, and this required two important measures: the collectivization of the *ejidos* and land redistribution. This is where the incipient alliance began to founder, because the first measure directly affected the large tenants of ejido lands and was ideologically repugnant to a large part of the bourgeoisie and the second directly affected the large landowners among the agrarian bourgeoisie. These measures faced not a weak, archaic rural bourgeoisie, but a mod-

---

*Roger Bartra is currently a full-time researcher in the Instituto de Investigaciones Sociales of the National University of Mexico, Tinker Visiting Professor at the University of Wisconsin—Madison, and a Fellow of the Guggenheim Foundation. His works include *Estructura Agraria y Clases Sociales en México* (Era, 1974) and *Campesinado y Poder Político en México* (Era, 1982).

ern, powerful stratum of agricultural entrepreneurs that had developed as a result of the agrarian reform itself. In fact, the failure of the technocratic populist project was such that the new government of López Portillo has made sure that its two principal leaders, the two former secretaries of agrarian reform, cannot attempt any further political overtures: Augusto Gómez Villanueva lives in gilded exile in the Mexican embassy in Rome and Félix Barra is in jail for fraud.

We will now take a look at the political events that resulted in the elimination of the populist sector in agrarian politics. Toward the end of 1975, with a year to go before the end of Echeverría's term, it was clear to everyone that the government's collectivization of the ejidos had failed. In haste, the government turned to the redistribution of land in an attempt to recuperate its loss of popular support. In October 1975, peasants invaded private lands in the Yaqui Valley. In November, the government redistributed some land, but of very poor quality. At the end of November, the large agriculturists were dealt a heavy blow: the government announced the expropriation of a large *latifundio* (consisting of 2,507 hectares) whose owner was none other than Alicia Calles de Almada, daughter of ex-President Plutarco Elías Calles (a sort of founding father of the new "revolutionary" agrarian bourgeoisie of Mexico's northwest). A few days later, 4,387 hectares of good irrigated land were expropriated in the Yaqui Valley and distributed to 433 peasants from San Ignacio.

The northern agrarian bourgeoisie, the most modern and powerful in the country, reacted vigorously to these measures. On December 1 they called an agricultural strike, and even though this took place when the wheat harvest was practically over it had a significant political effect because it occurred at a point when agricultural production was declining, forcing Mexico for the first time to import large quantities of wheat and corn. At the same time, the northern farmers (principally in Sonora and Sinaloa) withdrew from the confederation of small property owners, Confederación Nacional de la Pequeña Propiedad (controlled by the government), and founded the Unión Agrícola Nacional.

However, things did not stop here. The populist group decided to play its last card a few weeks from the end of the president's term. On October 7, 1976, Secretary of Agrarian Reform Félix Barra announced, "Before the government of President Echeverría comes to an end, all the latifundios of Sonora and Sinaloa will be expropriated." Immediately there were land seizures fomented by the national peasants' confederation, Confederación Nacional Campesina (CNC; part of the PRI), and obviously with the approval of the government. The secretary said that in these two states there were 80,000 hectares of irrigated land and 50,000 hectares of pasture land that would be affected. The peasant claimants to this land, as a result, denounced the most important *latifundistas*. (These latter are, it should be noted in passing, one of the most typical products of the institutionalization of the Mexican Revolution. Many of them are descendents of revolutionary political and military leaders: families such as Calles, Obregón, Bórquez, Ramos, Bours, Esquer, Topete, Vargas, Parada, Zazueta Ruís, Clouthier, Creel, and so on.)

The first act of defense on the part of the capitalist agriculturists was to seek an *amparo* or injunction (in Sinaloa there were 550 requests for such an injunction and in Sonora over 600) to block the process of expropriation until after December 1, the date on which the Echeverría government came to an end. During the first week of November, there were negotiations between the agriculturists and the government. The former offered to give up 20,000 hectares, but the latter insisted on expropriating 80,000 hectares. The situation became very tense, as thousands of peasants began to surround and in some cases to seize the lands in question, and the police and army were mobilized to keep a close watch on the situation. It was a race against time. The property owners, for their part, had succeeded in postponing the expropriation of their lands by resorting to the constitutional guarantee of the injunction.

However, on November 18, 8,000 peasants in Sonora began to take possession of 37,000 hectares of irrigated land and 61,000 hectares of pasture land in the Yaqui and Mayo valleys. The furious capitalist agriculturists directly accused Félix Barra and Augusto Gómez Villanueva of violating the injunction. As a result of this situation, hurried negotiations were carried out in Sinaloa between the government and the state confederation of agriculturists, Confederación de Asociaciones de Agricultores del Estado de Sinaloa (CAADES), and the latter agreed to give up 10,000 hectares of irrigated and 3,000 hectares of pasture land in place of the 37,000 hectares originally demanded. In Sonora, the farmers, supported by the local merchants, maintained a protest strike until December 1, when the new president took office.

The new government openly declared that its principal objective was the *organization of production*. In December, the new president, José López Portillo, in a conciliatory meeting with the governor of Sinaloa and the secretary of agrarian reform, succeeded in getting the peasants to "agree" to abandon the seized properties and to "await legal proceedings." Meanwhile, a court battle ensued, with the expropriated agriculturists of Sonora formally accusing the ex-president of violating the injunction. In Sonora, the leader of the league of agrarian communities, Liga de Comunidades Agrarias (part of the PRI-controlled CNC), recognized that there had been undue haste in the expropriation of the lands. The official line had changed totally, and the political forces began to accommodate to it accordingly. For example, the governor of Veracruz, during the celebration of the anniversary of the 1915 agrarian reform law, censured the "Pharisees of agrarian policy." Four days later, the top leader of the CNC "resigned" his position to head the Fondo Nacional de Fomento Ejidal, a national development fund in the process of being liquidated. In February, the new leader of the CNC declared that demagoguery would be replaced by work. In May, President López Portillo held a working meeting in Ciudad Obregón with the "small" property owners affected by expropriation and stated that there were "doubts" about 17,600 of the 37,000 hectares expropriated. Negotiations immediately began between the farm owners of Sonora and the new secretary of agrarian reform over payment of an indemnification for the 17,600 hectares of irrigated land that had been expropriated.

PEASANT ECONOMY AND CAPITALISM

In order to understand the failure of the technocratic populist strategy, it is necessary to take a look at the specific forms that the peasant economy has adopted as a result of its insertion into the capitalist context. During the past fifteen years, a process I call the *permanent primitive accumulation of capital* has been manifested in a slight reduction in the polarization of the distribution of land accompanied by an increase in the inequality of income distribution.

During the 1960s, two parallel phenomena occurred with reference to the distribution of land: in the first place, the censuses of 1960 and 1970 show that during this ten-year period the area of ejidal lands increased from 44.5 to 70 million hectares; 4,000 new ejidos were created, and the population occupying ejidos increased by more than 1.5 million persons. In the second place, the number of small production units (less than five hectares) in private hands declined during the same period by more than 40 percent. The number of units larger than five hectares also declined, but only by 13 percent. The total population occupied in agriculture on their own land decreased by more than 1.5 million persons. The enormous decline in the number of units of private production is due in part to a change in census classifications, which in 1970 took as the production unit not the individual piece of property but all properties exploited by the same owner with the same resources. Nevertheless, the decrease (confirmed by the population census) in the number of persons occupied in private agricultural production shows that the number of small production units has indeed declined. These statistics clearly reveal the dialectical articulation between the ruin and proletarianization of the peasantry, on the one hand, and the extension of state protectionism that attempts to compensate for the disorder and conflicts inherent in this process. This situation calls for closer examination, however, for despite formal similarities it is very different from that which prevailed during the golden age of land distributions (during the 1930s under the presidency of Lázaro Cárdenas). During the Cárdenas period, small property-ownership increased in importance with the distribution of ejidal lands, but in the 1960s the opposite has occurred. Although during the 1930s the distribution of land ran parallel to the growth of agricultural production, three decades later we observe a critical decrease in agricultural production. Finally, under Cárdenas, the agrarian reform generated a peasant base of support that helped to legitimate the state apparatus, but the 1960s have seen sharp confrontations between the peasant movement and the government.

What has occurred within the ejidal sector is very complex. This sector is extraordinarily heterogeneous, and its unity comes essentially from its peculiar political and juridical position. On the one hand, the ejido shelters and conceals extremely backward, unproductive, pauperized, and/or proletarianized sectors of the peasantry. On the other hand, it has given rise to powerful tendencies toward the monopolistic concentration of capital (for example, in the production of tobacco, sugar cane, cotton, and coffee). Various indicators demonstrate the extension of capitalist forms of production into agriculture; the best of these indicators are the importance of salaried labor and chemical fertilizers in the costs of production (see Table 11.1).

Although ejidos have increased in importance in terms of the total value of agricultural production (see Table 11.2), the productivity of the labor involved has declined because of the increasing mass of *ejiditarios* (titleholders of ejidos) with very small and poor-quality plots, a product of land distributions that have not touched the good lands of the latifundios. Thus the average area under cultivation per producer (plus family members occupied in production) in ejidos declined from 3.6 hectares in 1960 to 3.4 hectares in 1970 even though the average total area increased. The statistics in Table 11.2 require some explanation and comment. The increase in the organic composition of capital (that is, increase in fixed capital, machinery, raw materials, and means of production in all forms relative to the capital laid out in wages or in the purchase of labor) in private agricultural production has provoked a decline in the population occupied on lands of five hectares or more. This same factor, combined with the creation of hundreds of thousands of new ejiditarios, has brought about an enormous increase in the importance of ejidal production without decreasing the population occupied in this sector of agriculture. The great importance of ejidal production in agriculture should not lead to an overestimation of its importance in the agrarian sector as a whole. If one adds the value of livestock production, animal products, and forest products, private farms with more than five hectares account for 51.2 percent of the total, private farms with less than five hectares for 11.8 percent, and ejidos for 37 percent. Finally, the economic crisis and the concentration of capital have brought about a decrease in production on private farms with less than five hectares and provoked an abrupt decline in the number of small property-owners.

POPULIST ROMANTICISM

Is it possible to interpret this process as a resurgence of the small peasant economy and an alternative to the crisis of the capitalist system? What is happening in the sector of small private farms, along with the political defeat of those elements within the state that promoted a populist alternative, appears to provide a negative answer to this question. However, the growth of the ejidal sector is part of a much more complicated process. In effect, today in Mexico there is no "peasant alternative," yet no other alternative is viable unless it includes the small peasant economy.

It is for this reason that today there is an intense polemic in Mexico about the characteristics of the country's agrarian structure. From any point of view, it is clear that at least over the past fifteen years agrarian Mexico has experienced a crisis that has gone beyond the boundaries of rural society to affect the nation as a whole. Today, all sectors recognize the obsolescence of the old forms of struggle and reform and are proposing new approaches. The government has proclaimed an end to the redistribution of land, the agrarian bourgeoisie is no longer willing to tolerate the whims of the state with regard to the peasantry, the guerrilla movement has accepted, at least implicitly, its defeat, and the independent movement of the masses has announced the end of the traditional populist features of its political line. The government is trying to impose forms of state monopolistic concentration and organization, the bourgeoisie is screaming for a policy that will favor the productivity of the capitalist sector of agriculture, and the forces of the left are seeking the independent organization of the pauperized masses of the countryside, particularly the rural workers.

From the point of view of the independent revolutionary organizations, it is of crucial importance to liquidate accounts with the agrarianist past. The Marxist interpretation of the agrarian problem in Mexico is of extraordinary relevance, because it means—at the level of the ideological

TABLE 11.1
Distribution of Cost of Agricultural Production
(percentage of total costs)

Type of Production Unit	Salaries		Chemical Fertilizers	
	1960	1970	1960	1970
Private, more than 5 hectares	28.9	34.2	6.1	8.8
Ejidos	18.0	37.6	5.5	12.6

SOURCE: Censo (1960, 1970).

struggle—distinguishing precisely between the theoretical-political space of the bourgeoisie and the petty bourgeoisie and that of the proletariat. In sum, the enormous weight of agrarian populism that is the legacy of the Mexican Revolution of 1910 and the Cardenist reforms has to be clearly distinguished from the positions of the proletariat, and the independent popular movement that is beginning to grow in Mexico has to be freed of this weight. What is lacking at present is a proletarian perspective not only on the characteristics of the bourgeois class and its forms of domination, but also on those of other classes and popular strata (principally the peasantry) that frequently constitute an especially solid base of legitimation for bourgeois power. This is what I attempted to initiate in polemical form in *Estructura agrária y clases sociales en México* (1974) and in later works. The polemic thus initiated has blossomed, and I would like to extend it here by taking advantage of the opportunity afforded me by the work of Robert Wasserstrom (1976).

Wasserstrom, in the name of a poorly understood and even worse digested populism, accuses me of nothing less than refusing to accept that "distinct social classes exist within peasant communities" and of denying the existence of class struggle in the countryside. His confusion is total: there is no basis at all for deriving either of these ideas from my assertion of the existence of a simple, classless mercantile mode of production. Nevertheless, he insists on arbitrarily labeling my interpretation of agrarian Mexico "dualistic," like the interpretations of Ricardo Pozas, Gonzalo Aguirre Beltrán, and Rodolfo Stavenhagen (whose positions in fact differ widely), because I have distinguished two modes of production in the countryside, the simple mercantile and the capitalist. Rather than merely attempt to demonstrate that his criticism is unfounded, I prefer to consider what has motivated such strong opposition to my definition of the peasantry in terms of its participation in the simple mercantile mode of production (an "ordinary type of petty-bourgeois economy," as Lenin called it). I venture to suppose that the principal reason for it is that this

TABLE 11.2
Value of Agricultural Production and Population
Occupied in Agriculture (percentage of total)

Type of Production Unit	Value of Agricultural Production		Population Occupied in Agriculture	
	1960	1970	1960	1970
Private, more than 5 hectares	53.5	44.7	28.2	19.6
Private, less than 5 hectares	5.7	4.0	26.8	15.2
Ejidos	40.8	51.3	45.1	65.2

SOURCE: Censo (1960, 1970).

conceptualization delimits the peasantry as *a social class distinct from the proletariat.* All the accusations of dualism, of not recognizing the revolutionary potential of the peasantry, of indicating the petty-bourgeois traits that limit the capacity of the peasantry as an independent force, and so forth, stem, in my judgment, from a rejection of a proletarian (that is, Marxist) interpretation *external* to the peasantry that reflects the interests of a different social class. In other words, this polemic has an eminently political character. I am accused of maintaining an interpretation that is *foreign, external* to the peasantry—which is *relatively* true; but what is this "internal" interpretation in whose name I am criticized? Wasserstrom (1976) tells us:

> To understand the peasant is neither to treat him as a reactionary nor to seek his proletarianization through the superior forces of capitalism. It is to live with him, speak his language, provide him with our theoretical reflections so that he can instruct and criticize us. Only in this way will we attain our principal goal: to radicalize the social sciences, decentralize scientific research, and—it has to be said—demystify the role of the researcher, guru of an insensitive and academic Marxism.

A typical expression of populist romanticism! What is my critic really complaining about? That Marxism necessarily offers a vision of the world different from that which emanates from the peasantry and that it is only by understanding this *difference* of class interests that separates the peasantry from the proletariat that it is possible to realize the *alliance of classes* that both Lenin and Mao Tse-tung not only proclaimed, but realized in practice.

The horror that the concept "simple mercantile mode of production" inspires in some critics illustrates my argument. To define the mode of production by which the peasantry lives implies defining its *specific, transitory historical* character (that is, examining its internal contradictions, mechanisms of exploitation, the forms in which class contradictions are expressed within it, and so forth). It is important to note that the interesting discussions among Marxists in recent years concerning the concept "mode of production" have, despite the richness of the polemic, resulted in a vicious circle. Defining a mode of production in a particular society might appear to imply setting up an insurmountable structural wall that abstractly separates different segments of the society. In fact, the influence of structuralism on Marxism has led many researchers to apply the concept of "mode of production" mechanically. In my view, the definition of a mode of production implies the *concrete historical determination* of the way the relations of production and productive forces are organized. It is not a descriptive-analytical, but an explicative-historical concept. In this form, the concrete comprehension of the small peasant economy contributes to an explication of its dual tendency to reproduce and to destroy itself.

What is the difference between those who, according to Wasserstrom, "defend the peasantry" and those who "treat it as reactionary"? On this, the North American researcher is very clear: in contrast to "the Mexican tradition of *grand theories*, another kind of research in the countryside has developed, research carried out primarily by foreigners." Who? Manning Nash, Frank Cancian, Eric Wolf. . . . In sum, Wasserstrom recommends that we worship the empiricism of North American anthropology, which supposedly offers an example of a revolutionary interpretation of the Mexican countryside. Should we also accept studies such as those carried out by the Harvard Chiapas Project—in which Wasserstrom came in contact with Mexican reality—as a guide for revolutionary action? It should be remembered that this project was denounced a few years ago as another imperialist "Project Camelot." The supposed "principal goal" of these researchers, as opposed to *grand theories* (read Marxism), is, according to Wasserstrom, "to radicalize the social sciences, decentralize scientific research, and demystify the role of the researcher." I doubt very much that these three endeavors can mobilize the peasant masses. I also doubt that they have arisen from the peasant communities in which the North American anthropologists have immersed themselves, not like "fish in water," in the Maoist way my critic recommends, but more like questionable foreign bodies.

In contrast, the principal goal of the so-called insensitive Marxists is the revolutionary transformation of capitalist society. Perhaps they sin by living in the world of grand theories, but it is these theories that illustrate great revolutionary processes. It is better to risk the sin of utopia than to fall into the petty bourgeois context of minor calls for a radicalization, decentralization, and demystification of research—empty words that can serve any cause.

Theses of a populist nature, with an authentic revolutionary character, have developed within currents of Marxist thought. The review *Cuadernos Agrários* most openly reflects the Marxist formulation of populist theses. In it an argument has been developed around my propositions concerning the peasant economy that attempts to demonstrate that there are no transfers of value within agriculture and that as a result no relations of exploitation (unequal exchange) exist between different social classes in agrarian Mexico. I refer here to the essay on land rent by Armando Bartra (1976a), whose whole critical argument on transfers within agriculture rests on a false assumption, namely, that the leveling out of the fixed share of profit refers only to the distribution of surplus value among the different branches of production and can in no way be applied to the distribution of profits among individual capitalists who operate in the same sphere of production. His error consists in thinking that a sphere of production is defined exclusively by the identity of use values that are produced, when in reality the determining factor, for the problem that concerns us, is the identity of the organic composition of capital, even if there is no identity in use values. Marx (1967, III: 157) was very explicit in this regard: "Only within the same sphere of production, that is, where the same organic composition of capital reigns, can masses of profit in direct relation to the mass of capital employed be found." Thus the whole argument that there are no transfers within agriculture remains in the air if one ceases to consider the agrarian sector of a relatively backward country as a homogeneous sphere of production from the point of view of the organic composition of capital. It is obvious that within a sphere of production with the same organic composition of capital there are no transfers between enterprises. This does not mean that no transfers exist within agriculture, given that—at least in Mexico—this sector cannot be identified as a homogeneous sphere of production in the sense that Marx uses the concept to explain the formation of the average rate of profit. Actually, the agriculture of the so-called underdeveloped countries is far from homogeneous; at the minimum there are diverse *forms* of production and even different *modes* of production. This situation negates the possibility of considering agriculture in these countries as a sphere or branch of production in the process of the leveling out of the average rate of profit.

The problem is complex, but Armando Bartra has sought to simplify his critique by arbitrarily attributing to me the idea that the superprofits of private agricultural enterprises are *provided directly* by the peasant sector, in which case it would be possible to infer that any struggle for land is a populist fiction. He even manages to mutilate a quote on unequal exchange, eliminating my reference to the industrial sector, in order to "prove" that my interpretation falls into the false schema that he has constructed. My analyses of the problem of transfers led me to a different conclusion than he assigns me, namely, that "therefore, it is the bourgeoisie *in its entirety* which benefits from the peasant's surplus labor" (Bartra, 1974: 82). I have never thought that such transfers are provided directly by the peasant sector. The peasantry's surplus labor is given over to society through the mechanisms of the market and distributed among the different branches of production, including agriculture, in accordance with a complex combination of factors that rests, in the last instance, on different organic compositions of capital.

It is evident that it is other aspects, not made explicit, that irritate my critic. When he is outraged by my assertion—which he takes out of context—that the peasants have inherited and fulfill some of the functions of landowners, it is evident that he dislikes the word "landowner," which recalls the petty bourgeois aspect of the peasant. Nowhere do I assert that the peasant fulfills the landowner function of obtaining a profit beyond that from the sale of his product. This is absurd. The peasantry, as property owner, monopolizes a portion of the land; this is its landowner (albeit a ragged landowner) function, because it forces the capitalist to generate a superprofit if he wants to invest in this land—a phenomenon very common in the irrigated districts of Mexico.

These misunderstandings lead me to put forward what appears to me to be the real problem: the populist interpretation refuses to accept the petty bourgeois character of peasant production that is obvious in the simple mercantile nature of their production and their property ties to the land. Those who hold this interpretation seem to want to close their eyes to these facts and instead emphasize the revolutionary character of the peasantry. The fundamental duality of the modern peasant eludes them.

A good example of this duality is provided by Armando Bartra himself in his study of the Chontalpa (1976b). It is clear that the peasant there oscillates between the interests of the Plan (a monopolistic state enterprise with peasant participation) in terms of profitability and efficacy and the necessity of an organized struggle as workers who are not compromised by the profitability of the enterprise. That is, even under the specific conditions of participation of the peasant as a (disguised) salaried worker within the framework of a falsely collective enterprise, the peasant's property ties to the land and the production unit provoke a conflict with the objective proletarianization to which he is subject. What kind of political conclusion can be drawn from this? Bartra maintains that the principal force that confronts state capitalism in this situation "is not the political potential of a new class in the making, but the old potential of peasant rebellion, deeply rooted and unwilling to disappear." With regard to the "new class," he states: "In the first instance, proletarianization manifests itself as political disintegration and ideological deterioration that brings about a phase of vacillation and passivity." On the other hand, the peasants "can be the point of departure for a definitive struggle to create a new social order in which the peasant condition will not be condemned to transformation into proletarian slavery." In sum, we have here the old populist thesis: in the face of the most refined and modern forms of capitalist exploitation (state monopolistic concentration), the alternative of a peasant struggle is presented. I do not doubt the great revolutionary potential of the peasantry; this is expressed, however, in precise and concrete historical conditions. Social classes are not in themselves carriers of a preestablished historical destiny. It is the specificity of the structures and mechanisms of exploitation, of the accumulation of experiences in struggle, that converts the peasants into a revolutionary potential. The concrete situation in Mexico shows that the peasantry—led in most cases by the dominant classes—has left deep traces of its revolutionary potential, so much so that its petty-bourgeois side has exhausted its revolutionary potential. Now it is the turn of its proletarian side. This facet of the peasantry, so long stifled and silenced, today finds itself in circumstances conducive to its political development. These circumstances are presented by the blind alley in which the peasant economy finds itself and by the development of modern forms of capitalism in agriculture.

THE DYNAMISM OF THE SYSTEM

David Goodman and Michael Redclift (1978) call attention to the difficulty of understanding that, although the development of capitalist agriculture tends to bring about the ruin of the peasantry, the capitalist sector cannot exist without a noncapitalist environment—that is, that Mexico's agrarian structure is enmeshed in a permanent contradiction.

We have various alternatives for interpreting this situation. Goodman and Redclift appear to suggest that the capitalist sector is not a dynamic force and even doubt that its character is exclusively capitalist. If, in contrast, we assume that the capitalist sector is dynamic, it is necessary to show why, in spite of everything, the peasant economy continues to reproduce itself. In my judgment, the discussion should center on determining the characteristics of the *articulation* of these two economies.

If the development of the large-scale commercial economy had as its base only mechanisms of superexploitation of salaried labor, and this superexploitation required a peasant economy that contributed to the regulation of the price of labor power (maintaining it at low levels, levels of "subsistence"), then the development of the capitalist economy would be blocked. However, in my opinion, the articulation of the peasant economy should be analyzed in relation to *the entirety* of the capitalist economy, not just the large agricultural enterprises. By so doing it is possible to locate two series of contradictions: those that arise from the expansion of capitalist relations of production, tend over time to ruin the peasantry, and generate a process of proletarianization and/or pauperization; and those that arise from the difficulty for the capitalist economy as a whole of productively absorbing, at the same rate that the peasantry is being destroyed, the mass in the process of proletarianization and/or pauperization and that generate a process of refunctionalization of the peasant economy. These two processes, in a feedback effect, provoke a peculiar dissociation of the agrarian sector of the capitalist economy. In effect, as Goodman and Redclift note, the mass of rural under- and unemployed peasants serves as an industrial reserve army and, once salaries of superexploitation have been established, permits a segment of the large enterprises to take forms that are not entrepreneurial (as rentiers, with a low organic composition of capital). At the same time, however, there is another segment of capitalist agriculture that operates with entrepreneurial criteria and constantly increases the organic composition of capital; this segment combines modern monopolistic agroindustrial and agrocommercial complexes.

Why, given ample facilities for superexploitation, do modern enterprises develop through mechanisms for the expanded reproduction of capital? Are we to suppose that, in reality, the capitalist road is blocked and the dynamism can only be channeled by the small peasant enterprise? The reality shows us that there are elements of dynamism (expansion, reproduction, growth) in the capitalist sector. The answer to this problem can be found in the inevitable crisis of the capitalist system: the rise and fall of agricultural prices affect the most backward enterprises especially harshly, forcing many of them to modernize or perish. This permits us to understand that the capitalist agrarian sector, if it develops in a modern entrepreneurial form, does not require a peasant environment, *but the capitalist economy as a whole does require a refunctionalization of small noncapitalist units*, because it is not in a condition to absorb the population expelled from agriculture. The dimensions of the rural pauperized mass greatly exceed its functions as an industrial reserve army. Here it is important to note that certain measures for the protection of the peasant economy (for example, guaranteed prices) reinforce the entire backward sector (whether peasants or latifundistas). We are dealing here with a vicious circle, but only relatively speaking. It can be characterized as a process of permanent primitive accumulation of capital that simultaneously contains primitive forms of capitalist exploitation, a destruction of the peasant economy, a modern expanded accumulation of capital, and a refunctionalization of the noncapitalist economy. This is not entirely a vicious circle (its "permanent" character is relative) because the forms of expanded accumulation of capital and refunctionalization of the peasant economy gradually rise to higher levels of organization, division of labor, productivity, and so forth, to produce forms of monopolistic capital concentration and cooperative or collective organizations (frequently connected to state development plans). These phenomena, which become part of the spiral of permanent primitive accumulation, do not succeed in breaking this spiral, but modify some if its tendencies.

REFERENCES

Bartra, Armando
    1976a "La renta capitalista de la tiera." *Cuadernos Agrarios* 2 (April/June): 2-38.
    1976b "Colectivización o proletarización: el caso del plan Chontalpa." *Cuadernos Agrarios* 4 (October/December): 56-110.
Bartra, Roger
    1974 *Estructura agraria y clases sociales en México.* Mexico City: Era.
Censo
    1960 *IV Censo agrícola, gandadero y ejidal.* Mexico City.
    1970 *V Censo agrícola, gandero y ejidal.* Mexico City.
Goodman, David and Michael Redclift
    1978 "The transformation process in Latin America." Presented at the Institute of Latin American Studies, London.
Marx, Karl
    1967 *El capital.* Mexico City: Fondo de Cultura Económica.
Wasserstrom, Robert
    1976 "La investigación regional en ciencias sociales: una perspectiva chiapaneca." *Historia y Sociedad* 9: 58-73.

12

The Class Basis
of Patron-Client Relations

by
Frances Rothstein*

This paper describes and analyzes patron-client relations in a rural community in Mexico. It shows that clientelism in that community is determined not by cultural lag or precapitalist conditions but by the nature of dependent capitalism in contemporary Mexico and its particular class structure. More specifically, it is argued that dependent capitalist development, by transferring abroad a large part of the domestically produced surplus, limits the internal distribution of industrial benefits and encourages such particularistic relations as clientelism.

Clientelism or patron-client relations is a form of politics in which ties between leaders and followers are personal. The patron grants favors in return for political support, material goods, and/or other services (Hall, 1977: 510). Because patron-client relations often occur between members of different classes and because individual rather than group interests appear to be paramount, bourgeois social scientists have often argued that class is irrelevant to an understanding of clientelism (see, for example, Landé, 1977: xxxv). Rather than recognizing the class basis of patron-client relations, most studies attribute clientelism to "traditional" political culture. Powell (1970: 425), for example, while acknowledging the existence of clientelism in "modern" political systems, suggests that such behavior is a survival from traditional politics.

In anthropology, tradition has also been invoked to explain clientelism (see, for example, Miller, 1973: 137), but most attention has been focused on very narrow situational analysis. Situational analysis of individual decisions and networks, however, is, as Strickon and Greenfield (1972) suggest, a descriptive process. Such studies have led to a number of empirical generalizations, for example, that factionalism and clientel-

* Frances Rothstein teaches in the Department of Sociology and Anthropology at Towson State University, Baltimore, Maryland. This chapter is a revision of a paper presented at the 1977 annual meetings of the American Anthropological Association. The author would like to thank M. Barbara Léons and the editors of *Latin American Perspectives* for their comments, as well as the Faculty Research Committee of Towson State University for financial assistance during the preparation of the manuscript.

ism are widespread in underdeveloped nations, but they are limited in their explanatory potential because they assume structure rather than investigate it. For example, in their introduction to *Structure and Process in Latin America*, Strickon and Greenfield (1972: 15) suggest that perhaps the most important variable in analysis of patron-client relationships is the resources available to the actor. Without an understanding of the structure, however, it is impossible to understand the distribution of resources.

Strickon and Greenfield recognize the limitations of the situational approach. They suggest that it is most useful in providing in-depth analyses of particular cultures (1972: 16) and is best viewed as a preliminary, and not an alternative, to structural analysis (1972: 14). But how does one go from the detailed, particularistic analysis of individuals to the study of structure?

Dependency theory[1] provides an analysis of structure at the national and international levels. Most studies using this approach, however, have focused on macro-analysis. As Long (1975: 263) suggests, the conditions under which different types and degrees of dependency and domination exist must be specified. Dependency theorists have done this at the national and international levels, but they tend not to study the local level.

We are thus faced with a general approach, dependency theory, at the macro level and a very particularist approach, the actor-oriented perspective, at the local level. This paper will show that not only are class and clientelism related, but class analysis provides the framework to link the goals and resources of actors at the local level to the broader national and international structure of capitalism in Latin America.

DEPENDENT DEVELOPMENT AND THE MEXICAN CLASS STRUCTURE

Before turning to a description of local-level, patron-client relations, it is necessary to consider briefly the national and international structure of Mexico's dependent capitalist development. It is this structure that, by transferring part of the domestically produced surplus to foreign capitalists, limits the extent to which the benefits of industrialization can be distributed to the Mexican producers. Among other things, patron-client relations are one of the ways used to pare down the number of potential recipients of industrial gains.

The First World War, the Depression, and the Second World War created the international and national conditions that gave rise to industrialization attempts in Mexico and other Latin American countries (Frank,

1972: 39). Mexico particularly has experienced what many observers call miraculous economic development. Most of the standard indicators of economic progress when applied to Mexico sweep upward, some at a dizzying rate (Anderson 1968: 178-179). There was a 3.6-fold increase in industrialization between 1940 and 1959 (Frank, 1969: 299). Since 1960 the annual growth of the industrial sector has been more than 8 percent (Gollás and García Rocha, 1976: 424). At the same time, however, Mexico's dependence, especially on the United States, has increased. This dependence is apparent in the nature and the recipients of exports, the extent of foreign investment, and the extent of foreign debt.

Despite rapid economic growth, Mexico, like other Latin American countries, still exports primarily raw materials and extractive commodities. There has been an increase in manufactured exports, but there is still a substantial and widening trade deficit (Hofstader, 1974: 24).

The sector of the economy that has been experiencing the most development—manufacturing—is also the sector in which U.S. investment has increased the most (Barkin, 1975). Significantly, between the years 1955 and 1965 foreign investors received almost U.S. $1,700 million from new direct investment, of which they reinvested less than 20 percent (Cockcroft, 1974: 227). The trade deficit and loss of profit through foreign control is balanced by heavy foreign borrowing. An increase in foreign borrowing, however, has led to amortization and interest payments on foreign loans equal to almost 50 percent of export earnings (Cockcroft, 1974: 303). The transfer of a large part of the domestically produced surplus (to repay foreign debts and as profit to foreign investors) has enormous consequences for the class structure of Mexico and the distribution of the benefits derived from Mexico's economic development of the past 35 years.

The process of development often eventually permits the incorporation of such newly generated underclasses as the hard-core unemployed into the working class and the right of citizenship (Johnson, 1972: 295). But in Mexico, where development is constrained by dependent capitalism, the extent to which industry can absorb the rapidly growing population is severely limited. Capital intensive and labor-displacing technology from the advanced capitalist countries has meant that the rate of labor productivity has risen faster than the rate at which labor is absorbed. At this point, 40 percent of the labor force is still in agriculture although agriculture accounts for only 16 percent of production (Cockcroft, 1974: 282). Unemployment estimates range as high as 40 percent (Cockcroft, 1974) and have been increasing in recent years (Hofstader, 1974: 160), with the government acknowledging that about half the labor force is without employment.

Mexican development has undoubtedly meant gains. The middle class has experienced considerable numerical growth (Cockcroft, 1974: 287). But capitalism by its very nature differentially distributes the gains of industrialization even in advanced capitalist countries. In dependent capitalist economies the disparities are greater and the gains for the majority of the population are more limited. Although the middle class has grown and the gross national product per capita doubled, the Mexican class system is almost as sharply skewed today as it was in 1910 (Cockcroft, 1974: 287).

Hansen suggests that income inequalities, in developing countries such as Mexico, are sometimes mitigated by government tax and expenditure policies. In Mexico, however, neither tax nor expenditure policies have been geared to a redistribution of the solid wealth generated by the country's rapid growth (Hansen, 1971: 83-84). The greatest proportion of public sector funds has been spent on infrastructure investments for agricultural and industrial expansion. Although some of the population have benefited from the shifting occupational structure, the main benefits have gone to entrepreneurs and the upper-middle sectors because wage increases have been slower than price and profit increases (Hansen, 1971: 71-77). In agriculture most of the public money invested has been spent on the construction of irrigation works that benefit large landholdings (Hansen, 1971: 44). The extent to which the standard of living of most of Mexico's population has been raised through public-sector investment in social welfare has also been extremely limited. In the late 1950s, for example, expenditure on education averaged only 1.4 percent of the gross national product (Hansen, 1971: 85-86), and despite an increase in social security coverage in the 1960s, three-quarters of the Mexican labor force was still not covered in 1970 (Mesa-Lago, 1976: 238).

In sum, as Frank (1969: 313) suggests:

> *Industrialization, rapid as it has been, education, capitalization of agriculture, public works, and other "modernization" measures have not so far been sufficient to absorb the population increase, let alone greatly raise the economic level of the peasant base.*

There are opportunities, but social mobility is limited (Frank, 1969: 314). It is this limited mobility, particularly characteristic of dependent capitalist development, that accounts for the patron-client relations to be described. As Schmidt (1977: xxiv) suggests, "Personal favors [i.e., those granted by patrons] are favors only when . . . the same benefits are not available to everyone." Although the same benefits are not available to everyone in any stratified society, favoritism is exaggerated in a dependent developing society because benefits are scarcer. On the one hand, development often requires the granting of some benefits for political and economic reasons. On the other hand, however, dependent capitalist development limits the extent to which the benefits of industrialization can be shared by the Mexican producers. As Waterbury (1977: 332) suggests, "patronage relations provide discriminatory access to desired goods." Patronage is a way of paring down the number of recipients of industrial gains.

LIMITED MOBILITY AND PATRON-CLIENT RELATIONS IN SAN COSME[2]

San Cosme, Mazatecochco, is a nucleated *municipio*[3] in central Mexico. Until the early 1940s San Cosme was a relatively homogeneous Indian peasant community. During the Second World War, as a consequence of the national textile boom, some men from San Cosme were able to make inroads into factory work. The proportion of the economically active population of San Cosme in the industrial sector grew from 12 percent in 1950 to 27 percent in 1970.

The men of San Cosme who work in factories (primarily textile factories in Mexico City, about sixty miles away, and Puebla, about fifteen miles away) demonstrate upward social mobility. Compared to their parents, the peasants of San Cosme, and the population of Mexico in general, they live well. The monthly income of San Cosme's industrial workers is higher than that of most peasants in the community and higher than much of the Mexican population.[4] Whereas 49 percent of the economically active population in Mexico earned less than 500 *pesos* per month in 1969, 69 percent of the factory workers in San Cosme earned more than that (see Table 12.1). Their income has allowed them to participate in a variety of innovative and relatively lucrative financial investments such as the purchase of taxies and trucks. They have also been able to take advantage of the educational, medical, material, and recreational opportunities of the nearby city of Puebla. With the help of contacts made through factory work, they were able to have San Cosme's political status changed from a section under another municipality to a free municipio. With federal assistance, San Cosme received electricity in the early 1960s, piped water in the late 1960s, and educational facilities. Electricity, water, schools, roads, buses, and municipal status were all obtained by playing the patron-client game. As Frank (1969: 313) suggests,

"There are economic, political, social paths, which afford opportunities or, maybe better, chances—for higher rank, to those who play according to the rules of the game." Not only have the workers of San Cosme always worked within the "official" political party, the Partido Revolucionario Institucional (PRI), but they have used personal ties to those with resources, union leaders (with jobs and contacts and state politicians with access to federal funds) to secure their goals.

The personal relationships used by San Cosmeros to achieve political and economic success fall into the type commonly called *patron-client relations* or *clientelism*. This relationship is characterized by an alliance between two persons of unequal status, power, or resources involving the exchange of favors (Landé, 1977: xx). Because of the difference in status, the favors exchanged are different. As is true of most patrons, those in this study have many clients and are clients themselves to higher-level patrons, that is, the patron-client networks are pyramided.

In San Cosme patron-client relations exist between local leaders and fellow San Cosmeros and between local leaders and regional and national leaders. Within the community, leaders or patrons offer jobs, bureaucratic knowledge, and political influence in return for political support and, to a lesser extent, financial contributions. Regional and national patrons similarly offer jobs, bureaucratic knowledge, and political influence to the local leaders in return also for political support and occasional financial contributions.

LOCAL LEADERS AND THEIR CLIENTS

Most of San Cosme's patrons are or have been union leaders. Using their position, they control jobs in the factories, and because their factory unions are federated within the labor sector of PRI,[5] they also control access to higher-level labor and party leaders. The local patrons use their control of jobs to get political support for themselves in local politics and to gather political support for their patrons outside San Cosme. While the greatest number of clients that a union leader has ever gotten by controlling jobs is only 125 men, the union leaders use their union positions and worker support to tap into derived (state) power,[6] that is, to get municipal posts that give them access to additional resources such as regular meetings with state officials, allocation of some municipal jobs, and some decision making in the municipality. With this additional power, they gain other clients.

The following case illustrates the use of both control of factory jobs and political resources by some of San Cosme's patrons. In 1967 the mu-

TABLE 12.1
Monthly Income of Economically Active Population in 1969

Pesos per Month	Factory Workers in San Cosme		Campesinos in San Cosme		Economically Active in Mexico	
	%	No.	%	No.	%	No.
Not declaring	1.7	5	10.3	77	10.3	1,334,588
0 to 199	9.0	26	37.5	281	16.4	2,126,367
200 to 499	20.8	60	49.6	372	23.7	3,072,729
500 to 999	49.5	143	1.6	12	24.2	3,134,300
1,000 to 1,499	16.6	48	.3	2	11.4	1,473,323
1,500 to 2,499	2.1	6	.3	2	7.3	951,003
Over 2,500	.4	1	.5	4	6.7	862,746

SOURCE: Dirrecion General de Estadisticas (1970).

nicipal authorities and the majority present at a municipal meeting voted to build a new school on the land of Juan Díaz. Initially Díaz agreed on a purchase price of 10,000 pesos. Shortly after, however, he decided he did not want to sell his land at that price. Díaz was a peasant and, until that time, had not been involved in community politics. He had neither patrons nor clients, nor did he have political contacts who might help him fight the sale of his land. By aligning himself with several local patrons, two union leaders, and a teacher, he managed to fight the sale for several years. Although he eventually lost, his patrons helped him by getting the new municipal president (whom they had put in office)[7] to delay the building of the school. Eventually, when the opposition brought the issue to the state courts, his local patrons, using their state federation and party contacts, helped him to secure a lawyer, gave advice as to bureaucratic procedures, and informally spoke to state officials. He in return provided financial resources for them in this and other political conflicts in which they were engaged, and he and his family supported them in local politics.

Political support through control of jobs was also important in this case. The dispute over Díaz's land eventually developed into a dispute over locating the new school in the second barrio (on Díaz's land) or in the fourth barrio. Several of the local leaders who lived in the fourth barrio wanted the school located there. This issue eventually divided most of the community. But whereas the leaders' choice of location was influenced by the barrio in which they lived, the nonleaders of the community made their choice, not according to where they lived, but where their union leaders lived. Many workers who lived in the second barrio supported locating the school in the fourth because their union leader was in favor of that location. Similarly, nonfactory workers who were clients of union leaders for political reasons[8] supported the location of the school according to where the patron lived. When the state court finally decided the issue in favor of locating the school in the second barrio, the leaders favoring the location in the fourth barrio proceeded to build their own school. In some cases a factory worker living close to his neighborhood school but must send his children to a more distant school because his union leader (that is, his patron) is supporting that school. Those people, mostly peasants, who are not clients of any leaders send their children to the nearest school.

LOCAL LEADERS AS CLIENTS

The position of the local union leaders is strongly influenced by decisions of federation officials who are in turn under the PRI and business interests.[9] For example, in 1972 a new factory was being opened in Tlaxcala. Officials of the Confederación de Trabajadores de México (CTM), one of the two main labor federations in Tlaxcala, told a San Cosme leader to collect names of men who wanted to work in the factory. Local leaders also get more individualized job favors. In another case, a retired union leader contacted his former federation leaders for help in obtaining a job for his daughter in a government office in Mexico City.

Most often, however, the local patrons exchange political support in return for help in community politics. Candidates for municipal positions are picked by state leaders for the state agrarian, popular, and labor sectors of the party. For a San Cosmero to be selected as a candidate[10] for a municipal post, he needs someone to speak for him at the state level. Similarly, since 1943 the state patrons have helped their San Cosme clients get municipal status, electricity, potable water, a kindergarten, two new primary schools, and a tele-secondary school.[11] They are currently in the process of soliciting a drainage system. The state patrons advise their clients where to go to request community development, speak to other state or national leaders on behalf of the San Cosmeros, and sometimes help with financial aid that they collect from clients elsewhere. Their clients from San Cosme in return provide disciplined workers, participants for marches, demonstrators for rallies, as well as financial contributions. The interaction of financial and political support is apparent in the request made by a state leader that the people of San Cosme make financial contributions (by buying raffle tickets) to the fire department of the city of Tlaxcala. He urged them to buy many tickets so that the next time he went to the governor on behalf of San Cosme he could remind the governor how generous the San Cosmeros had been.

That the people from San Cosme have been successful is apparent not only in their high rate of participation in the industrial sector, 27 percent compared to 17 percent for the nation as a whole, but also to the extent they have been able to get community services. As of 1974, of the eight municipios in San Cosme's district, three did not have electricity throughout the community and six did not have potable water throughout the community. In the nation as a whole 41 percent of all households still lacked electricity and 36 percent were without running water in 1970 (Niblo, 1975: 115).

Although San Cosme's proximity to Mexico City and Puebla has been beneficial, the fact that other communities in the same region have not shared in the gains to the same extent suggests that proximity alone cannot explain success. Proximity isn't enough, one has to know someone in a factory to obtain employment. To keep the job and to get additional benefits, requires political support both in the factory and the community.

PATRON-CLIENT RELATIONS IN SAN COSME AND THE CLASS STRUCTURE OF DEPENDENT CAPITALIST DEVELOPMENT

The dyadic nature of patron-client relations has often obscured its class basis. As Scott points out, most studies of clientelism treat class and patron-client relations as mutually exclusive forms (1977: 496). Superficially the patron-client relationship appears to be a series of dyadic alliances that link the lowest to the highest members of a society. Not surprisingly, bourgeois social scientists have focused on appearances, "the visible and spontaneous representations which members of a society devise from the nature of things, from their own activities or from the universe" (Godelier, 1977: 3) and have ignored the inner relationship between clientelism and class.

The patron-client relations of San Cosme are similar to those described for communities elsewhere in Mexico and the world. Patrons provide goods and services in return for political and sometimes financial support. By looking, however, not only at the dyadic relations of the actors but at the national and international class structure, these relations are revealed as a strategy determined by capitalism and used by capitalists and workers to adapt to the transfer of much of the surplus from the Mexican proletariat to an international bourgeoisie.

Patron-client relations are not confined to Mexico and capitalist development. Nor are they the only way that workers struggle against capitalism and capitalists struggle against workers. Clients in Mexico also strike and protest, and the state, which in other situations acts as patron, responds to workers' demands with repression as well as concessions.[12] Patron-client relations are neither unique to dependent capitalism nor the only method used in Mexico to limit the distribution of industrial gains. As many observers of patron-client relations have noted, however, some societies appear to be more "patronage-prone" than others (Waterbury, 1977: 336). Mexico appears to be such a "patronage-prone" society. Patron-client relations have been reported to all levels of Méxican society and in urban as well as rural areas.[13]

Any stratified society requires ways to distribute benefits selectively. In advanced capitalist societies, however, where much of the domestic surplus is not being transferred to another center, some benefits can be more widely distributed. In addition, in advanced capitalist societies supposedly nonparticularist criteria, such as education, are used to distribute benefits.[14] In Mexico, dependent capitalist development has meant that both industrial jobs and community services such as potable water, schools, and electricity can be distributed only to a very limited segment of the population. Personal ties, such as those that characterize patron-client relations, pare down the number of people who can get jobs and services. Men from San Cosme get jobs by knowing someone in the factory and giving the factory their labor and the union leader not only a day's work but political support and often kickbacks as well. Where government policy focuses on investment for the upper class and devotes very little to health, education, and welfare, requests for government funds must similarly be supplemented by political loyalty, financial contributions, and other personal favors.

In sum, patron-client relations are one of the means used to adapt to the limited mobility that characterizes dependent development. From the workers' perspective, clientelism yields access to some of the benefits of industrialization. From the capitalists' perspective, patronage is a way of paring down the number of beneficiaries of jobs and distributing token benefits while at the same time assuring political support and a disciplined labor force. Not unlike cooptation, however, which is also a widely used mechanism in Mexico to maintain the class structure, patron-client relations depend on "payoffs." Thus there is a built-in contradiction in patron-client relations. The function of patronage is to limit payoffs, but it can be maintained only by making payoffs.

NOTES

1. On dependency, see dos Santos (1968), Cardoso and Faletto (1970), Johnson (1972), Chilcote (1974), and Chilcote and Edelstein (1974).

2. This discussion is based on fifteen months of fieldwork in San Cosme from June 1971 to June 1972 and May 1974 to August 1974. Unless otherwise specified, the data are from my field notes.

3. A nucleated settlement pattern is one in which the population is concentrated in the center of the town and the fields are on the outskirts. This contrasts with a dispersed community, in which houses and fields are interspersed throughout the area.

4. For a more complete discussion of the differences between factory workers and peasants in San Cosme, see Rothstein (1975, 1979).

5. While not all factory unions are so federated, the unions that are important in San Cosme politics, and to most San Cosmeros who work in factories, are members of the state federations and the national confederations.

6. See Stuart (1972: 36) for a discussion of derived state power.

7. Because of the Mexican law against reelection, leaders hold the presidency only for one term of three years. They often, therefore, put clients in political posts and control municipal politics indirectly.

8. For example, those whom union leaders helped to obtain municipal positions (see, for example, Cockcroft, 1978).

9. It is beyond the scope of this study to examine the relations of higher-level federation leaders, the state, and monopoly capital. But the pattern described here for San Cosme is very similar to the pattern of arrangements between foreign capitalists and confederation labor leaders.

10. The party candidates have always won. Thus selection as a candidate assures an election victory.

11. The tele-secondary school in San Cosme has one teacher. Subjects out of his area of expertise are taught through television.

12. See Cockcroft (1972, 1978) and Stevens (1974) for discussions of coercion in Mexico.

13. See, for example, Fagen and Tuohy (1972), Miller (1973), Cornelius (1977), Eckstein (1977), and Grindle (1977).

14. Increasingly, education is being used in Mexico to limit employment. The unskilled jobs that San Cosmeros have held for thirty years without a sixth-grade education now require six years of primary school. For a related discussion of increased educational requirements as a screening device in the United States, see Braverman (1974: 438).

REFERENCES

Anderson, Charles W.
    1968 "Bankers as revolutionaries," pp. 103-196 in W. Glade and C. Anderson (eds.) *The Political Economy of Mexico*. Madison: University of Wisconsin Press.
Barkin, David
    1975 "Mexico's albatross: the United States economy." *Latin American Perspectives* 2 (Summer): 64-80.
Braverman, Harry
    1974 *Labor and Monopoly Capital*. New York: Monthly Review Press.

Cardoso, F. and E. Faletto
1970 *Dependencia y desarrollo en América Latina.* Mexico City: Siglo XXI.
Chilcote, Ronald
1974 "A critical synthesis of the dependency literature." *Latin American Perspectives* 1 (Spring): 4-29.
Chilcote, Ronald and Joel Edelstein (eds.)
1974 "Introduction," pp. 1-87 in *Latin America: The Struggle with Dependency and Beyond.* New York: John Wiley.
Cockcroft, James
1972 "Coercion and ideology in Mexican politics," pp. 245-268 in J. Cockcroft, A. G. Frank, and D. Johnson (eds.) *Dependence and Underdevelopment: Latin America's Political Economy.* Garden City, NY: Doubleday.
1974 "Mexico," pp. 222-303 in R. Chilcote and J. Edelstein (eds.) *Latin America: The Struggle with Dependency and Beyond.* New York: John Wiley.
1978 *Lucha de clases, imperialismo y estado en México.* Mexico City: Editorial Nuestro Tiempo.
Cornelius, Wayne
1977 "Leaders, followers, and official patrons in urban Mexico," pp. 337-353 in S. Schmidt et al. (eds.) *Friends, Followers, and Factions.* Berkeley: University of California Press.
Dirección General de Estadísticas
1970 *Censo General de Poblacion.*
Dos Santos, Theotonio
1970 "The structure of dependence." *American Economic Review* 60 (May): 231-236.
Eckstein, Susan
1977 *The Poverty of Revolution.* Princeton, NJ: Princeton University Press.
Fagen, R. and W. Tuohy
1972 *Politics and Privilege in a Mexican City.* Stanford, CA: Stanford University Press.
Frank, André Gunder
1969 *Latin America: Underdevelopment and Revolution.* New York: Monthly Review Press.
1972 "Economic dependence, class structure, and underdevelopment policy," pp. 19-46 in J. Cockcroft et al. (eds.) *Dependence and Underdevelopment: Latin America's Political Economy.* Garden City, NY: Doubleday.
Godelier, Maurice
1977 *Perspectives in Marxist Anthropology.* London: Cambridge University Press.
Gollás, M. and A. García Rocha
1976 "El desarrollo economico reciente de Mexico," pp. 405-440 in J. Wilkie, M. Meyer, and E. Monzon de Wilkie (eds.) *Contemporary Mexico.* Berkeley: University of California Press.
Grindle, Merilee S.
1977 "Patrons and clients in the bureaucracy." *Latin American Research Review* 12 (1): 37-66.
Hall, Anthony
1977 "Patron-client relations: concepts and terms," p. 510-512 in S. Schmidt et al. (eds.) *Friends, Followers, and Factions.* Berkeley: University of California Press.
Hansen, Roger
1971 *The Politics of Mexican Development,* Baltimore: Johns Hopkins University Press.
Hofstadter, Dan
1974 *Mexico 1946-1973.* New York: Facts on File.

Johnson, Dale
    1972 "On oppressed classes," pp. 269-301 in J. Cockcroft et al. (eds.) *Dependence and Underdevelopment: Latin America's Political Economy.* Garden City, NY: Doubleday.
Landé, Carl
    1977 "Introduction: the dyadic basis of clientelism," pp. xxiii-xxxvii in S. Schmidt et al. (eds.) *Friends, Followers, and Factions.* Berkeley: University of California Press.
Long, Norman
    1975 "Structural dependency, modes of production and economic brokerage in rural Peru," pp. 253-282 in I. Oxaal, T. Barnett, and D. Booth (eds.) *Beyond the Sociology of Development.* London: Routledge & Kegan Paul.
Mesa-Lago, Carmelo
    1976 "Social security stratification and inequality in Mexico," pp. 228-255 in J. Wilkie et al. (eds.) *Contemporary Mexico.* Berkeley: University of California Press.
Miller, Frank
    1973 *Old Villages and a New Town: Industrialization in Mexico.* Menlo Park, CA: Cummings.
Niblo, Stephen R.
    1975 "Progress and the standard of living in Mexico." *Latin American Perspectives* 2 (Summer): 109-124.
Powell, J.
    1970 "Peasant society and clientist politics." *American Political Science Review* 64 (June): 411-426.
Rothstein, Frances
    1975 "Differential integration: a comparison of the economic, political, and social relations of peasant and factory workers." *Ethnology* 14 (October): 395-404.
    1979 "Two different worlds: gender and industrialization in rural Mexico," pp. 234-266 in M. B. Léons and F. Rothstein (eds.) *New Directions in Political Economy: An Approach from Anthropology.* Westport, CT: Greenwood.
Sanders, Thomas
    1975 *Mexico in the 1970s.* Hanover, NH: American Universities Field Staff.
Schmidt, Steffen W.
    1977 "The transformation of clientelism in rural Colombia," pp. 305-323 in S. Schmidt et al. (eds.) *Friends, Followers, and Factions.* Berkeley: University of California Press.
Scott, James C.
    1977 "Political clientelism: a bibliographical essay," pp. 483-505 in S. Schmidt et al. (eds.) *Friends, Followers, and Factions.* Berkeley: University of California Press.
Stevens, Evelyn
    1974 *Protest and Response in Mexico.* Cambridge: MIT Press.
Strickon, Arnold and S. Greenfield (eds.)
    1972 *Structure and Process in Latin America: Patronage, Clientage, and Power Systems.* Albuquerque: University of New Mexico.
Stuart, William
    1972 "The explanation of patron-client systems," pp. 19-42 in A. Strickon and S. Greenfield (eds.) *Structure and Process in Latin America.* Albuquerque: University of New Mexico.
Waterbury, John
    1977 "An attempt to put patrons and clients in their place," pp. 330-339 in E. Gellner and J. Waterbury (eds.) *Patrons and Clients in Mediterranean Societies.* Hanover, NH: American Universities Field Staff.